World Heritage Regensburg

A Guide to Art and Cultural History in Regensburg's Old Town and Stadtamhof

Eugen Trapp

World Heritage Regensburg

A Guide to Art and Cultural History in Regensburg's Old Town and Stadtamhof

With a contribution by Lutz-Michael Dallmeier

SCHNELL + STEINER

Front cover: aerial view of Regensburg's Old Town
Photograph: Nürnberg Luftbild (Hajo Dietz)

Illustrations
p. 15 Stolz/Ferstl
p. 71, 190 Achim Bunz, Munich
p. 115 (published by permission of the State Building Office, Regensburg)
p. 144, 154 Roman von Götz, Regensburg
p. 159, 161 Prince of Thurn and Taxis Museums; photo Clemens Mayer
p. 178 Photo Studio Zink, Regensburg
p. 227 *Baualtersplan,* City of Regensburg VIII, Fig. 28
p. 229 acc. to KDB III, Fig. 100
p. 240 Prince of Thurn and Taxis Court Library
All other photographs Peter Ferstl, Regensburg
Maps, cover inner sides, and tour routes: City of Regensburg, Office of Urban Development, Department of Surveying and Cartography
Translation: Alison Thielecke, Regensburg

Bibliographical information in the German Library
The German Library has registered this publication in the German National Bibliography; detailed bibliographical data is obtainable in the Internet under <http://dnb.ddb.de>.

1st edition 2008

Cover design by grafica, Regensburg
Set by Vollnhals Fotosatz, Neustadt a.d. Donau
Printed by Erhardi Druck GmbH, Regensburg
ISBN 978-3-7954-2080-2

Further information about the publishers' programme may be obtained under:
www.schnell-und-steiner.de

Contents

Foreword by the Lord Mayor of Regensburg

UNESCO (United Nations Educational, Scientific and Cultural Organisation), a subsidiary of the United Nations, which was constituted in 1946 in order to secure world peace, is responsible for education, science and culture. One of its aims is to define mankind's common heritage, for which all the peoples of the world are responsible, and to ensure a commitment to preserving this heritage for future generations. This was the background against which UNESCO passed the 'International Convention concerning the Protection of the World Cultural and Natural Heritage' in 1972. This so-called World Heritage Convention has meantime been accepted by 184 nations. The UNESCO World Heritage Committee is the expert body responsible for the list of World Heritage Sites, which is internationally binding. On matters concerning the conservation of monuments, it is advised by ICOMOS (International Council of Monuments and Sites).

On the initiative of Klemens Unger, the city's Director of Cultural Affairs, the City Office for Archives and for the Conservation of Historic Monuments, under its head, Dr Heinrich Wanderwitz, prepared Regensburg's 1500-page official application. I extend my thanks to them and all their colleagues who worked untiringly to produce a scholarly account of Regensburg's historical, art-historical and historico-cultural dimensions.

The decision was made on July 13, 2006 in Vilnius: the Old Town of Regensburg and Stadtamhof would be added to UNESCO's World Heritage List. Regensburg's Old Town, with almost 1000 historic monuments, was able to claim its rightful place in the World Heritage field.

For the City of Regensburg, 'World Heritage' status entails the obligation to protect and maintain what has been preserved here. This is a great challenge for city building authorities, since the city is a living, constantly developing organism. The protection and conservation of the existing monuments has highest priority.

This publication represents the fulfilment of a promise made to UNESCO by Regensburg's delegation in Vilnius on July 13, 2006. I would particularly like to thank the author, Dr Eugen Trapp, who was also responsible for the most important sections of the application. Thanks are also due to Dr Lutz-Michael Dallmeier, the City Archaeologist, for his contribution, the tour of the remains of the Roman legionary camp. Particular thanks also go to Peter Ferstl, the official city photographer, for the pictures accompanying the text. For permission to reproduce original photographs thanks are due to the Thurn and Taxis Court Library, the Art Collections of the Diocese of Regensburg, the Chair of Architectural History, Historical Architectural Research and Conservation at the Technical University, Munich, the State Building Office in Regensburg, and the Museum of Regensburg History. Grateful mention must also be made of the commitment shown by the publishers, Schnell and Steiner.

Hans Schaidinger
Lord Mayor

Foreword by the author

Vital parts of the city's administration are still accommodated in Regensburg's Town Hall, which evolved gradually between the 13th and 18th centuries. This is symptomatic of Regensburg. Despite all sorts of structural changes, the Old Town has retained its unshakeable vitality. It was my intention that this theme of vitality should also have a place in this guide, as far as the limited space would allow it. Thus the aim was not just to portray the buildings and streets as they appear to an architect, but also to convey an idea of the role they played in mediaeval city life.

The Middle Ages form the principal point of orientation for this book. It was the epoch in which Regensburg acquired that intellectual, political, economic and architectural profile to which it owes its inclusion in the UNESCO World Heritage List. This status encompasses the whole of the mediaeval city on both sides of the River Danube, a large area which is characterised by the presence of an exceptionally large quantity of listed buildings. This copious number of historic monuments and the requirement for a book of manageable size forced me to be very selective. The essential criteria here were the accessibility of buildings and their suitability as examples.

The World Heritage area is explored in the context of eight tours, each one related to a particular aspect of city history. Each tour is prefaced by a historical introduction and a map. The mediaeval buildings form the unifying theme. Thus, it may seem surprising that the first tour, which Dr Lutz-Michel Dallmeier, Regensburg's City Archaeologist, has kindly described, concentrates on the built remains of the Roman legionary camp. However, the development of the mediaeval city was, in fact, based in many respects on what the Romans had left behind. Examples of post-mediaeval architecture and art are described only when required by the thematic context or by the route taken.

Buildings used wholly or partially as museums are marked in the text with [M]. Further details of the museums touched on during the tours are to be found in the appendix. This also contains a short list of more detailed works in German on Regensburg's history, architecture and art.

This book is not intended to be a brief city guide, but a compact companion for all those with a special interest in exploring art and art history in 'World Heritage Regensburg and Stadtamhof'.

Eugen Trapp

Regensburg's Historic Cityscape as Part of the UNESCO World Heritage

The United Nations (UN) was created in 1945 in the aftermath of two devastating world wars. The chief aim of the community of nations was to secure world peace. In 1972, UNESCO (United Nations Educational, Scientific and Cultural Organisation), a subsidiary of the UN, adopted the 'International Convention Concerning the Protection of the World Cultural and Natural Heritage'. This so-called World Heritage Convention has now been ratified by 184 states. The basic idea that underlies it is that the international community of nations should assume responsibility for cultural and natural monuments whose preservation is in the interest of all mankind. The names of such outstanding monuments of universal significance are contained in the World Heritage List, which has been compiled since 1978. At present it embraces 830 cultural and natural heritage sites in 138 states.

The first German cultural monument to be added to the World Heritage List was (in 1978) Aachen Cathedral with its Palatine Chapel – a key work of post-Roman Christian architecture and a symbol of the mediaeval renewal of the Roman Empire. However, entire historic cities are included in the list, insofar as these have been classified by the World Heritage Committee as unique and worthy of preservation in their entirety. In Germany, the listed cities are – in the order in which they were listed – Lübeck (1987), Goslar (1992), Bamberg (1993), Quedlinburg (1994), Stralsund and Wismar (2002). They were joined by Regensburg on July 13, 2006.

In what way is Regensburg's old town of exceptional universal significance? Since the end of the Second World War, which left the historic centres of Cologne, Nuremberg and many other cities in ruins, the city of Regensburg, alone, has continued to offer an authentic picture of a large mediaeval German city. As one of the chief centres in the Holy Roman Empire and as a great international trading city, Regensburg was of significance for the whole continent. The city, which then had about 15,000 inhabitants, was among the most densely populated centres in the German-speaking area around the middle of the 12th century. The wealth and the international connections of Regensburg's merchants found their expression, throughout all the phases of the Middle Ages, in unique architectural solutions.

- Regensburg has the greatest concentration of original romanesque and gothic architecture to be found north of the Alps.
- Regensburg was the most important centre of mediaeval building activity in Southern Germany.
- Regensburg's historical monuments bring together evidence of political and religious significance in a manner that is unique in Germany.

This quantity of original romanesque and gothic architecture has been unparalleled since 1945 because Regensburg's city centre remained almost completely unharmed during the war. The urban network of public buildings, burghers' mansions, merchants' palaces and craftsmen's properties, as well as important churches, monasteries and canonical foundations, is an authentic document of mediaeval urban culture that has either disappeared altogether or been preserved only in fragmentary form elsewhere in Germany. What is more, Regensburg has a particularly complex internal structure which equally reflects the history of the royal city, of the episcopal city and of the inland trading metropolis.

The numerous stone-built romanesque and gothic mansions with their towers are outstanding examples of a type of building which – influenced by Italy – is unique in this density and impressiveness north of the Alps. Apart from this magnificent collection of early stone buildings, Regensburg also probably possesses Germany's earliest completely preserved wooden house – No 2 Keplerstrasse has been dated to c. 1250.

The continuity of urban life from Antiquity to the early and then the high Middle Ages went hand in hand with Regensburg's growing political and economic significance. Between 917 and 920, Duke Arnulf of Bavaria commissioned the fortification of the entire western suburbs together with the extensive site of St Emmeram's Abbey. No other European city had a comparable wall built around it before 1000 A.D. This was the first post-Roman city extension north of the Alps and in parts it can still be traced in the city's present-day layout.

Regensburg was the setting for important events in European history: as a Roman legionary camp, as the early mediaeval centre of the East Frankish Empire, as a preferred meeting-place for imperial assemblies right up to early modern times, and, above all, as the seat of the Perpetual Imperial Diet from 1663–1806.

Throughout the ages, the desire to make a powerful impression in the political field has influenced building styles in Regensburg. That is why the Romans under the Emperor Marc Aurel in 179 A.D. chose this particular location, at the northernmost point of the Danube, to erect the legionary camp of Castra Regina, whose outline can still be traced today on a map of the city. After the Roman soldiers had withdrawn, Bavaria's first political centre developed, at the beginning of the 6th century, in the north-eastern section of the legionary camp. Until 788, Regensburg remained the principal seat of the Agilolfing dukes, then, together with Frankfurt, it became the chief palatinate in the East Frankish Empire, the 10th-century Bavarian dukes' capital, the preferred meeting-place for imperial assemblies until the Thirty Years' War, and the seat of the Perpetual Imperial Diet from 1663 until its dissolution in 1806.

All these phases in the city's history have left visible traces in the form of buildings: the mighty walls of the Roman fort with its north gate (Porta Praetoria), the Carolingian palaces in Alter Kornmarkt and near St Emmeram's, the 10th-century monasteries and the buildings where bishops and counts held court, the halls where the Perpetual Imperial Diet took place and the embassies that were connected with it.

Furthermore there are rare and fine examples of buildings that illustrate certain local, politically independent, bodies that existed within the boundaries of the free imperial city. From 739 on, Regensburg was the seat of a bishop. His power is illustrated by St Peter's Cathedral, the Cathedral Parish Church of St Ulrich, the Bishop's Palace and the residences of the cathedral canons. On the other hand, there were three monasteries that were answerable only to the king: St Emmeram's, the Niedermünster (Lower Minster) and the Obermünster (Upper Minster). St Emmeram's, formerly a Benedictine abbey, and the Niedermünster, once a convent for noble ladies, can still be seen today; only the Obermünster, also a former convent, has been a ruin since 1945.

In Regensburg, more than in any other German city, the urge to impress in the political field in all its varied forms and continuity throughout the ages is easily discernible in the city's present-day appearance. Even in the former imperial seats of Prague and Vienna, the architectural evidence of the urge to impress that has survived since the Middle Ages is of a much more recent date and has, moreover, undergone considerably more alterations.

Finally, Regensburg has one of the most important princely residences of the 19th century – the palace of the Princes of Thurn and Taxis, the well-preserved mediaeval core of which is made up of the secularised buildings of St Emmeram's Imperial Abbey.

Apart from the politicians' desire to impress, that of religious groups is also reflected in Regensburg's buildings. Regensburg lay further south-east than any other imperial city and thus, in the 16th century, it became the bridgehead for the spreading of the Lutheran faith to Austria, Hungary and the present-day states of Slovenia and Croatia. This vital function is illustrated by two striking ecclesiastical buildings: Neupfarrkirche (New Parish Church) and Dreieinigkeitskirche (Holy Trinity Church). Whereas the former was founded as a Roman Catholic pilgrimage church, the latter uses architectural language to distinguish itself very clearly

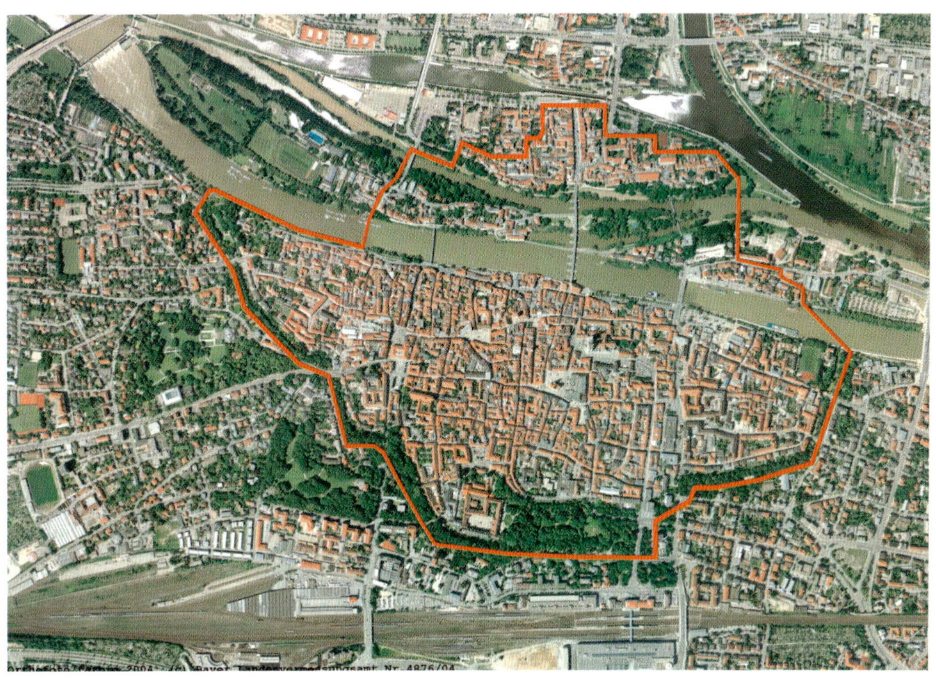

City of Regensburg from the air (2004). The World Heritage area is marked in red (core zone).

from the Catholic building styles of its age. Holy Trinity Church is a central example of Protestant architecture in southern Germany. From the late 16th century until 1732/33, thousands and thousands of Protestants from the Austrian territories sought refuge in their 'mother parish' after fleeing to avoid the process of re-Catholicisation.

Although the Protestant imperial city of Regensburg was very influential among Protestant Christians in the south-east of Central Europe, at home its image was determined by numerous possessions inherited from the Catholic church. The competitive co-existence of the two churches often influenced their buildings between the 16th and 18th centuries. This is still visible in many places in the city today. Similarly, the history of the city's Jewish inhabitants, who were expelled in 1519, can once again be experienced through their buildings, since an archaeological exhibition under Neupfarrplatz permits access to some of the cellars from the mediaeval ghetto.

The fact that all these historical developments can be illustrated in Regensburg owing to the survival of the original buildings is due primarily to the fact that the city was surrendered to the Americans on April 27, 1945 without any fighting, a step that was decided on at the last minute for reasons of military tactics. Just three days earlier, three men had been executed as saboteurs by the Nazis because they had tried to save Regensburg. They were Dr Johann Maier, a cathedral prelate, Josef Zirkl, a pensioner, and Michael Lottner, a retired police inspector.

Building policies during the years of Germany's economic miracle did cause some painful damage to the ancient building fabric and to the city's historical layout, yet this damage was slight compared to that in other German cities. The city's greatest architectural monuments, such as the Cathedral, the Old Town Hall, the Stone Bridge, the romanesque churches, as well as the gothic churches built by the mendicant orders, still stand in their familiar urban surroundings and do not stick out like isolated survivals in a cityscape consisting of post-war buildings that could be found almost anywhere.

Both the quantity and also the high quality of the historic buildings in Regensburg led to the entire historic city area on both banks of the Danube (Fig. p. 15) being included in the list of historic monuments in the Free State of Bavaria in 1976, after the Bavarian parliament had passed an act designed to protect historic monuments in 1973. In 1982, this 182.8-hectare area was defined as a cultural monument – in the sense of the Hague convention – that should be protected in case of armed conflict. UNESCO, too, and its International Council on Monuments and Sites (ICOMOS) have now determined that Regensburg's ensemble of historic monuments is worthy of protection in its *entirety*. This is because even the buildings on

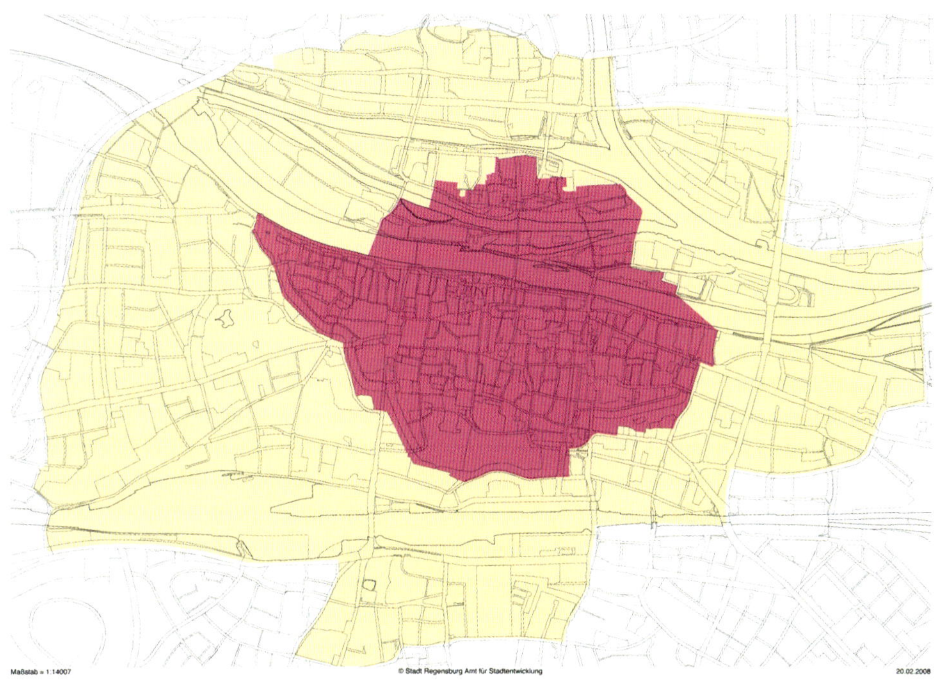

The core zone of the World Heritage area (bright red) is surrounded by a puffer zone (beige).

the fringes of the old town, where the ancient fabric may not seem particularly spectacular at first sight, contribute to a picture of Regensburg's mediaeval development that is, in itself, clearly differentiated: to the west lies a former craftsmen's quarter, to the east, an area which was once only sparsely populated and used for intensive horticulture; there are fishermen's and boatmen's settlements on the islands in the Danube, and, finally, – north of the Stone Bridge – St Katherine's Hospital and Stadtamhof. The latter still looks a bit like a Bavarian country town, having lain in 'foreign' Bavarian territory for five and a half centuries, during the period when Regensburg was a free imperial city. Nevertheless, Stadtamhof's mediaeval origins and its growth as an urban settlement are inseparably connected with its location at the northern end of the Stone Bridge and adjacent to St Katherine's Hospital, which belonged to the imperial city. This is the reason why, despite its separate political development, Stadtamhof is an integral part of Regensburg's historic ensemble.

UNESCO has also created a 'buffer zone' around the actual World Heritage Area (Fig. p. 17). This is several times larger in area than the 'Old Town Ensemble' and its function is to protect the central core. Within this buffer zone, for instance, the authorities have to prohibit the erection of buildings which could compromise the appearance of the World Heritage ensemble due to their height or sheer size.

Particularly in a living city organism which is constantly developing socially and economically, there is constant pressure to make changes to buildings. These changes must take place only in such a way that the World Heritage ensemble is not harmed. The protection and preservation of historic monuments must have first priority. Where new buildings are possible or even necessary in order to keep the old town in a state of good repair, it is essential to show respect for the historic layout of the city as well as for the proportions and stylistic features of the surrounding properties.

The arms of the City of Regensburg in the stained-glass window at the end of the choir in the New Parish Church

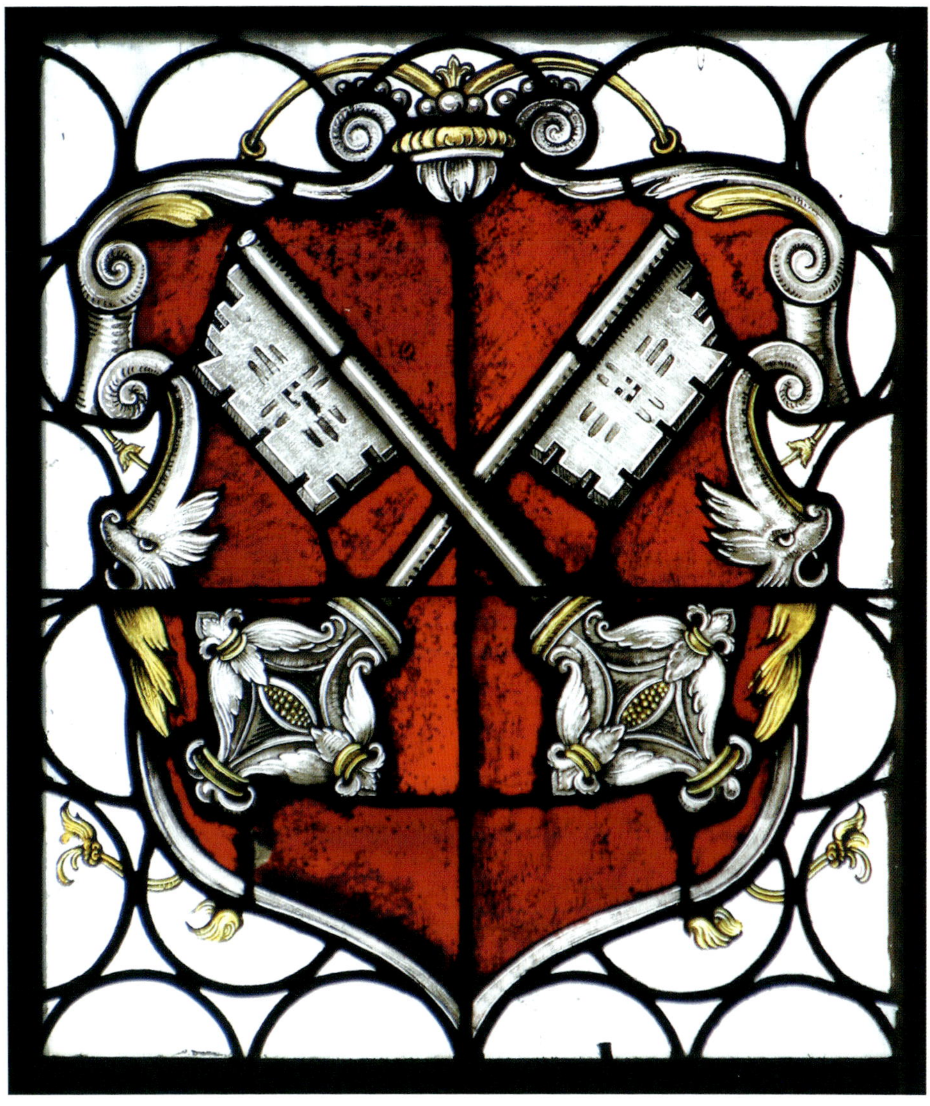

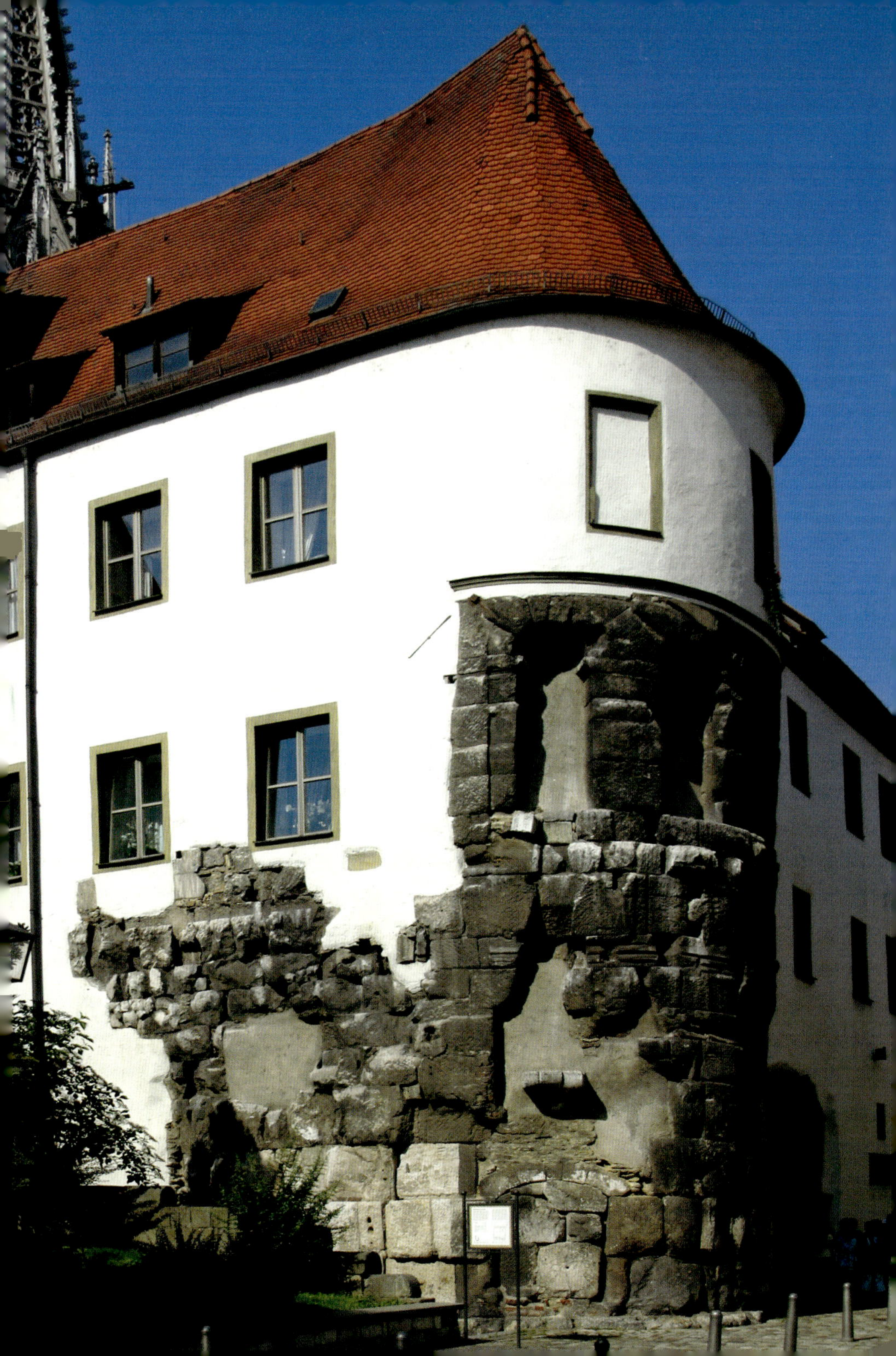

The Walls of the Roman Legionary Camp and the Porta Praetoria

In 179 A.D., Roman troops moved into a very large military camp which replaced the fort in Regenburg-Kumpfmühl that had been destroyed. The new camp was positioned right on the southern bank of the Danube. It provided accommodation for the 3rd Italic Legion, whose approximately 5000 soldiers played an important role in protecting the Danube frontier of the province of Raetia against Germania, a free country. Possible contemporary names for the camp were *Castra Regina, Reginum* or simply *Legio*.

The legionary camp with its four gates, the nucleus of the later city of Regensburg, was laid out in the form of a rectangle measuring 450 by 540 metres which had a surface area of about 25 hectares. In many places in the old city centre, it is still possible to find sections of the outer wall, which once had a ditch around it. This wall was about 8m high and up to 2.5m thick; it had 22 turrets and soil was piled up against it on the inside (forming an *'agger')*. Regensburg's legionary camp was the only fortified construction on the Rhine and Danube, and its walls consisted of two lines of gigantic stone-blocks with rubble between them. These fortifications in limestone and sandstone were erected from scratch; there were no earlier walls on the site.

Nearly everything that was constructed within the walls in Roman times – the two main streets that crossed each other in the centre, the 'Principia' (the commandant's office), the living quarters for the officers and legionaries, the military hospital, the baths, etc. – now lies buried under cultural strata several metres deep. The northern edge of the camp can still be detected from the course of the streets now called Unter den Schwibbögen and Goliathstrasse. The houses that stand today in Kohlenmarkt, on the corner of Goliathstrasse and Wahlenstrasse, have almost exactly the same curve as the former north-east corner of the Roman fort – even though the ancient wall has not survived here at all. The west side of the Roman camp follows the line of Wahlenstrasse, Augustinerplatz and Steckgasse, the east side runs along Adolf-Kolping-Strasse, crosses Schwanenplatz and continues southwards to the excavated area at the south-eastern corner of the camp beside Ernst-Reuter-Platz. The south side is reflected in Fuchsengang and its (imagined) continuation westwards, slightly to the north of St.-Peters-Weg.

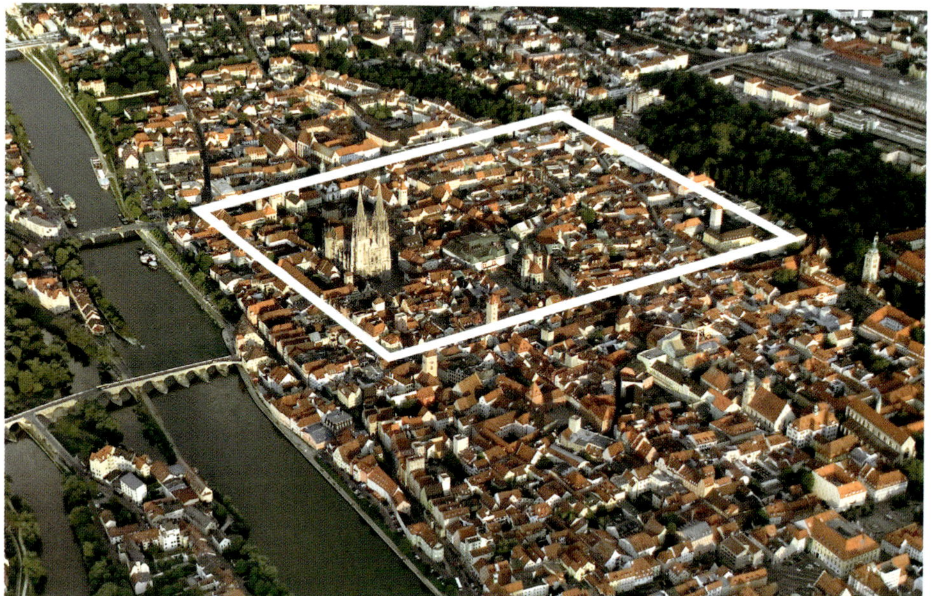

Outline of the Roman camp superimposed on the present-day city. Even today, the course of defensive walls is clearly visible in the position of Wahlenstrasse, of Obere/ Untere Bachgasse and of Goliathstrasse/Unter den Schwibbögen.

Beyond the walls, there were extensive civilian settlements in all directions, with the exception, naturally, of the northern, i.e. Danube, side, where the river formed the frontier, the *'Limes'*. These *canabae legionis* have been most extensively investigated in a westerly direction and have been found to reach as far as the present-day tree-lined avenue around the city. On the periphery of the settlements, and along the main roads out of Regensburg, there were several cemeteries with thousands of graves.

Even after the Romans withdrew at the beginning of the 5th century, their fortifications remained in use for many centuries. Almost completely unaltered in the early mediaeval period and in Carolingian times, the former Roman west wall was abandoned about 920 to permit the first city extension, and completely removed. Major sections of the ancient southern and eastern walls, on the other hand, fulfilled their original function for over 1600 years, until they were finally built over or pulled down in the course of the 19th century.

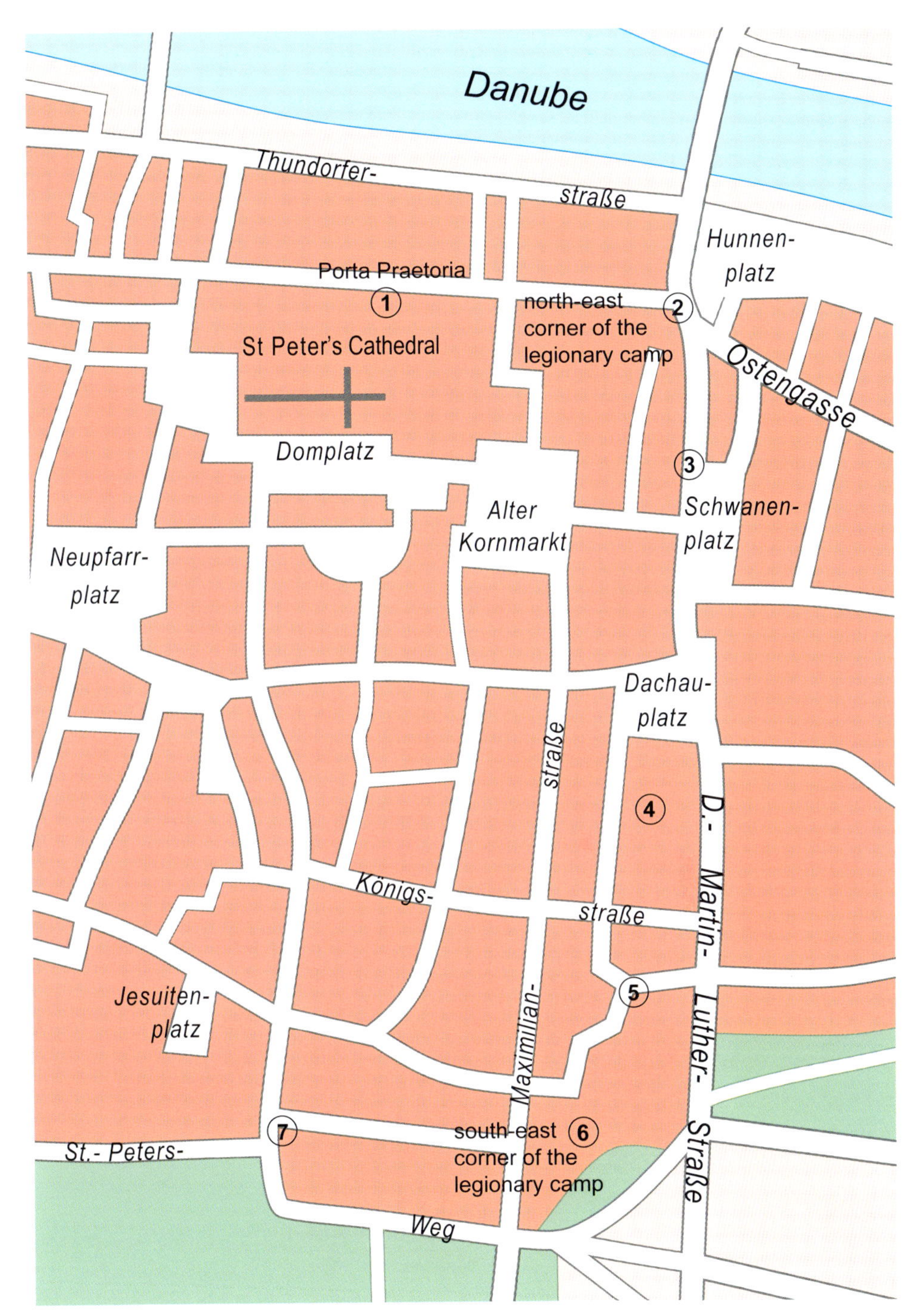
Danube
Thundorfer-
straße
Hunnen-
platz
Porta Praetoria
1
north-east
corner of the
legionary camp
2
St Peter's Cathedral
Ostengasse
Domplatz
3
Alter
Kornmarkt
Schwanen-
platz
Neupfarr-
platz
Dachau-
platz
straße
4
D.-
Martin-
Luther-
Straße
Königs-
straße
5
Jesuiten-
platz
Maximilian-
7
south-east
corner of the
legionary camp
6
St.- Peters-
Weg

Many sections of the Roman walls were not demolished, however, mainly because of their robustness; the quantity of surviving Roman masonry makes it justifiable to speak of this as the most significant antique site in Southern Germany. Due to the fact that the ground-level in the city has 'risen' by several metres since Roman days, one sometimes has the impression that sections of the former curtain wall of the legionary camp are well below ground-level. In some places, too, the wall actually survived in the cellars beneath later buildings, where, of course, it is not usually possible for casual visitors to inspect them.

According to the latest scientific findings, two phases may be distinguished in the construction of the 'Roman walls', as they are known in Regensburg. The first part consists of a base made of dry, undressed stone and a double layer of square stone blocks, on which there is another layer of stone which typically slopes outwards, forming the lowest free-standing line of stones. On top of this are placed – also without using mortar – the very large stone-blocks that form the shell for the walls. These exist, in most places, only in a single layer. In the second construction phase, workmen used rough-stone masonry consisting either of re-used ashlar or of dressed stone, both set in mortar.

Porta Praetoria

If one stands in front of the **Porta Praetoria (1)**, it is possible to get a very good idea of the former extent of the Roman legionary camp. To the west, one looks past the Bischofshof (once the bishop's palace), whose facade stands right on the wall of the camp, along to where Goliathstrasse enters Kohlenmarkt. This was the curved north-eastern corner of the camp in Roman days. Looking eastwards in the other direction, one can see that the street called Unter den Schwibbögen follows the ancient line of the wall until it opens into St.-Georgen-Platz, where the north-east corner of the camp can still be seen.

The Porta Praetoria is the largest surviving ancient monument dating from Roman times in Southern Germany, and one of Regensburg's landmarks; it is also regarded as the most important

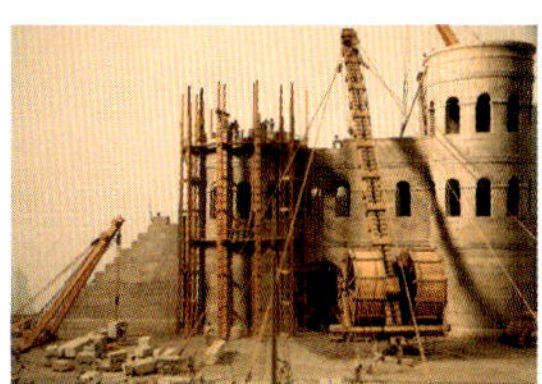
Model of the building site at the Roman Porta Praetoria. The elaborate construction of the stone defences from about 40,000 cubic metres of limestone and sandstone is vividly represented (Museum of Regensburg History).

Roman building anywhere along the Danube. Its only equal in Germany is Trier's Roman city gate, the Porta Nigra. The Porta Pretoria is the northern gate of the rectangular legionary camp, the gate facing what was then the hostile territory of Germania. Of the other three gates, only some foundations survive, far down in the ground.

The now visible parts of the Porta Praetoria were rediscovered in 1885, in the course of rebuilding operations involving the demolition of a brewery which stood on what is now the open ground east of the gate. Until then the gateway was surrounded by masonry, and thus unrecognisable, as a result of the *Via Praetoria,* the original main street through the Roman camp, being built over in in the high Middle Ages and of the construction of further buildings for the episcopal brewery in 1649 and later. As late as 932, the gate was known as the *porta aquarum* and was obviously still in use; it subsequently lost its function because of the re-structuring of the city fortifications – this happened at the latest when the Stone Bridge was erected in the mid-12th century or when the southern gate-tower was built (before 1307).

The masonry that is visible today consists of four main elements, which are all integrated into the north facade of the Bischofshof: the east tower (of which the ground floor and one upper floor survive); the western gateway; the wall built of re-used large stone-blocks in place of the eastern gateway; the remains of the ashlar wall immediately beside the west tower. The whole complex, especially the tower, shows traces, even damage, resulting from the long years of use, above all through the construction of post-Roman buildings. Holes for beams and openings for windows survive, together with the opening for another gate, on the eastern side, which was later closed up again with large blocks of stone. As a result, the Ancient Roman surfaces have been preserved in only few places.

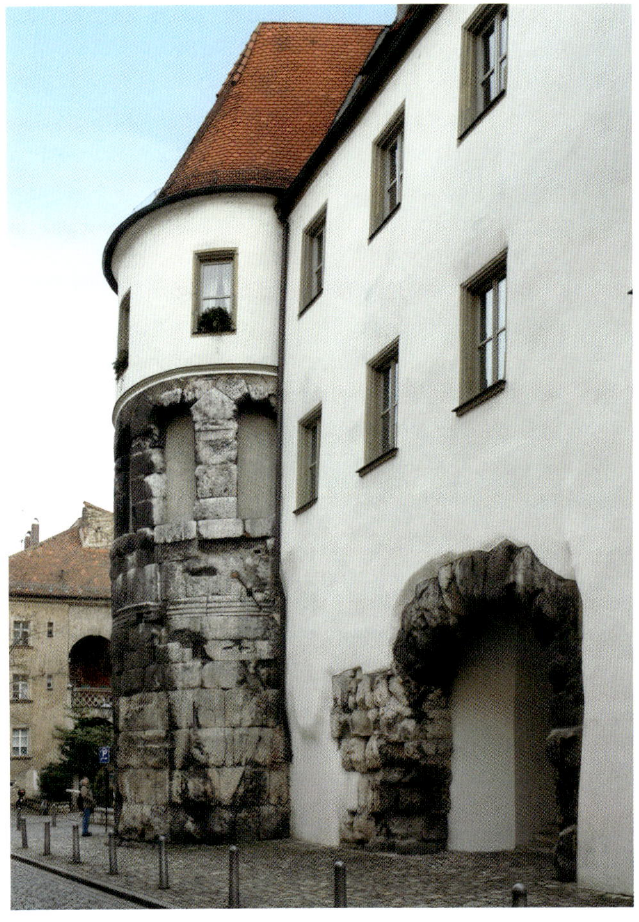

The Roman Porta Praetoria, revealed again from 1885. As the legionary camp's northern gate, it stood right on the Danube frontier and thus faced the enemy state of Germania.

What remains of the Porta Praetoria rises to a height of approx. 11 metres above present-day street-level; the entire base still reaches one metre down into the ground. If there were, as is assumed, three storeys, the overall height of the towers must once have been about 20 metres.

The east tower is constructed as a hemispherical flanking tower and consists – like the entire gateway complex, as we know it – of gigantic limestone blocks placed one upon the other without any mortar. About 5 metres up the tower, there is a relatively well-preserved cornice, which was once connected with an architrave. The latest results of research have only recently demonstrated that the Porta Praetoria was planned in the architectural language of the Corinthian Order. On closer examination, the remains of three pilasters can be made out on the east tower, most clearly the one on the west side of the tower. As has been proved, the decoration of the building was never finished, although the gateway as a whole was so far completed as to be fully functional.

The upper floor of the tower rests on a projecting layer of stone blocks and has five round-arched windows in it. The pillars between these windows still have relatively well-preserved profiles on their imposts. Above this, another cornice functioned as a link with a former second storey. The fabric now visible here, however, dates from post-Roman times and belongs to the hotel.

The gate-arch, which is 4 metres wide and was once 6 metres high, consists of 13 blocks of stone so shaped that they fit together, although not quite precisely, as segments of a circle. The block that forms the impost beneath the eastern base of the arch still has clearly visible traces of its profiles. The west base of the arch, in contrast, is so badly damaged as to be unrecognisable. Since several metres of cultural rubble have accumulated within the camp since Roman times, a steep flight of steps now leads up through the gateway into the courtyard of the Bischofshof. In Roman days, however, the *Via Praetoria* ran in a straight line – about one metre lower than today's level – to the *Principia* in the centre of the legionary camp.

The masonry consisting of irregular stone-blocks that can be seen between the tower and the arch is the fabric used to block up what was once a second gate arch, whose purpose and age have not yet been established. The suppositions which form the basis for the position of the no longer existing west tower, whose outline is shown in the pavement beside the Porta Praetoria, are the result of archaeological soundings. Only a few stones have survived from the walls of the camp, which were once directly attached to the tower. No further Roman masonry, by the way, remains hidden beneath the facade of the Bischofshof.

In order to trace the course of the walls of the camp eastwards, it is worth noting the following 'passing points': on the eastern side of the tower it is possible to locate the place where the wall used to be joined to it by determining where the two aforementioned cornices end. The projecting layer of stone-blocks in the upper storey also indicates where the wall was attached. Further, more masonry from the Roman walls lies concealed, yet accessible, on the ground floor of the Renaissance loggia of the house at No 2 Unter den Schwibbögen, about 25 metres east of the tower.

North-Eastern Corner of the Legionary Camp

The north-eastern corner of the walls of the legionary camp, a section rising to a height of about 3 metres, has survived in St.-Georgen-Platz **(2)**. Its discovery in 1905 came as the result of the demolition of some city offices, which had themselves been built on to the mediaeval Hallertor, pulled down in 1868. In the course of demolition, the wall of the mediaeval chapel of St George and St Afra with its romanesque windows was also revealed on the western side.

The irregular way in which the stone blocks have been placed here makes it impossible to distinguish any of the typical elements dating from the first phase of building work, e.g. a protruding base or the foundations of a corner tower. The outer sides of the blocks have not survived at all. Only the two or three lower layers of ashlar possibly date from the first phase of building. Further up, a number of stones from other sources have been built into the wall; in some cases, these blocks have been turned round, revealing holes made in them to hold lifting devices – these are easy to identify as re-used parts of stone build-

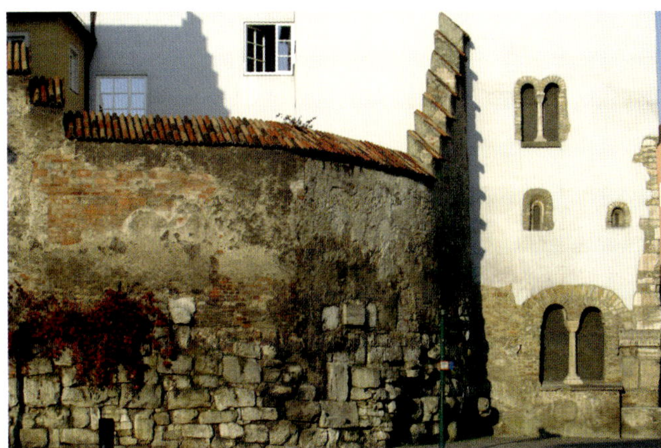

The rounded wall at the north-east corner of the legionary camp, rediscovered in 1905, was originally about 10 metres high. It may be assumed that there was a stone corner-tower here of the type recognisable at the south-east corner.

ings in the legionary camp. At the top of the arch, in particular, there are no traces of the corner-tower that would be expected here, so that it must be presumed that repairs or re-building took place in several phases.

Although the section of wall above the stone blocks dates from more recent times, at its greatest height it can give an idea of the former dimensions of the walls of the legionary camp. The gap in the walls with the steps leading up to Erhardigasse – note the level of the street within the legionary camp due to the accumulation of cultural rubble – also dates from post-Roman times.

The Walls on the Eastern Side of the Legionary Camp in Adolf-Kolping-Strasse

If one follows the curve of the corner of the camp into Adolf-Kolping-Strasse, one can now follow the line of the Roman fortifications for more than 500 metres; in some places the walls are still preserved **(3)**. At the beginning of Adolf-Kolping-Strasse, the wall is integrated into the facades of the houses for a good hundred metres. The section under the archway beside the Kolping building – which collapsed while the new building was being erected in the 1950s and had to be reconstructed – cannot be regarded as a

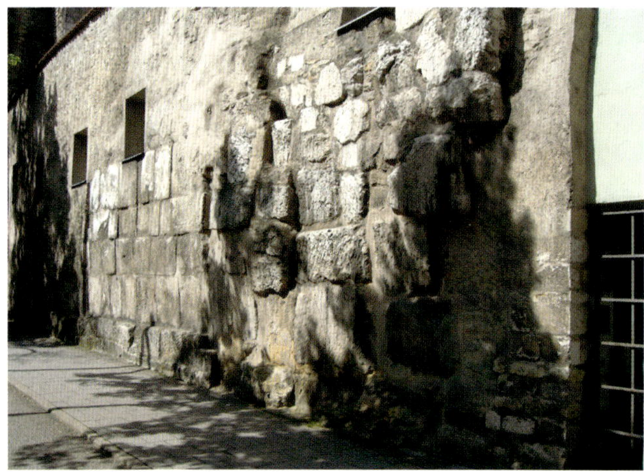

Part of the eastern flanking wall of the Roman legionary camp in Adolf-Kolping-Strasse. These are the best-preserved walls made of stone-blocks during the first phase of construction.

model example, nevertheless the projecting base can be clearly observed here. It reveals the lowest part of the formerly visible wall of the camp, thus indicating the level where the Romans walked. Further south, only a few sections of the base have survived, until – about 15 metres before the pedestrian passage that cuts through the choir of the de-consecrated Church of St Peter and St Paul – more sections of ashlar masonry can be seen. Here, for about 5 metres, there is a section of the walls consisting of four unaltered layers of stone-blocks; this may be regarded as the best surviving example of the early building phase.

As one continues in the same direction, the present-day road goes slightly uphill, so that the base of the wall gradually disappears below the level of the pavement. Up to three layers of stones from the ancient wall are visible until the road is interrupted by Pfluggasse; like the base, the stones here are in varying states of preservation.

The Eastern Walls of the Legionary Camp underneath Dachauplatz Multi-Storey Car Park

The next accessible section of the walls is about 150 metres further on. The road to Dachauplatz leads past the eastern side of the Carmelite Monastery (see p.63), which was built on top of the Roman walls. The adjoining junction with Drei-Kronen-Gasse corresponds, more or less, to the location of the Roman *porta principalis dextra*, the camp's eastern gate. When parts of its foundations were excavated in the 19th century, the stone inscription recording the foundation of the camp was also found, allowing the date of the completion of the legionary camp to be established as 179 A.D. The massive stone tablet is displayed in the Museum of City History, which is in the immediate vicinity, on the opposite side of the road.

When the multi-storey car park (No 2 D.-Martin-Luther-Strasse) was built in Dachauplatz in 1971, almost 50 metres of the legionary camp's walls had to be sacrificed. However, one section of the walls – 70 metres in length and up to five ashlar layers in height – was preserved, and can be viewed in the basement of the car park **(4)**. Apart from the camp's south-eastern corner, this is the longest surviving section of the Roman fortifications.
What is particularly impressive is the sloping base that runs the whole length of the walls here; together with the first horizontal layer of sandstone and limestone blocks, it is a survival of the first

Fragments of the enormous stone inscription from the Roman legionary camp, found near its east gate. This record of foundation makes it possible to place the date of the camp's completion in 179 A.D. under the Emperor Marcus Aurelius (Museum of Regensburg History).

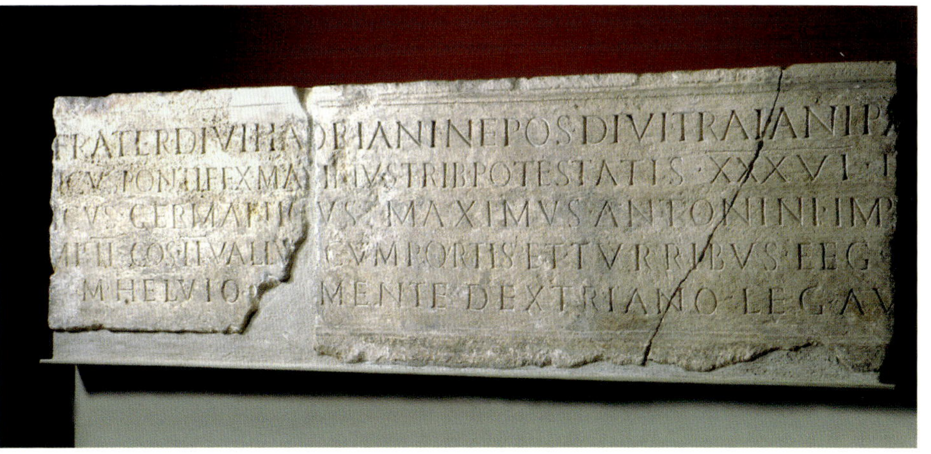

construction phase. The following layers of stones date for the most part from the rebuilding operations in the 3rd century, which were connected with the construction of a long building (*fabrica*) right behind the walls.

On leaving the car park, one should again note the difference in height between the level of the Roman pavement, which corresponds with the level of the base of the walls, and the present-day street-level.

The Section of the Roman and Mediaeval Fortifications in D.-Martin-Luther-Strasse (5)

Even if it is possible, from the north side of No 10 D.-Martin-Luther-Strasse, to get only a fairly distant glimpse of the sunken area at the back of it, it is well worth the effort. This is because the 20-metre stretch of wall preserved here shows that the Roman and mediaeval or early modern fortifications ran along the same course for a period of more than 1600 years **(5)**. Only up to this point do we know that the site of the walls was identical for such a long period because, just a few metres further north, the fortifications for the eastern extension of the city were constructed at a right angle to the existing walls in about 1300. Here, only two Roman stone-blocks form the base, on which – for the

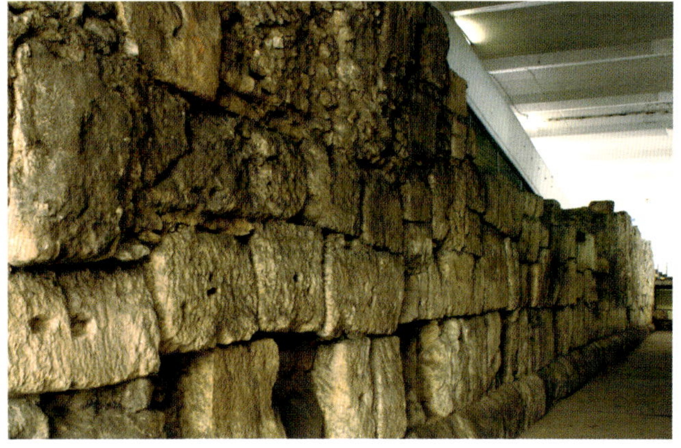

The eastern flanking wall of the Roman legionary camp underneath the multi-storey car park in Dachauplatz. 70 metres in length, this is the longest section of the walls to have survived.

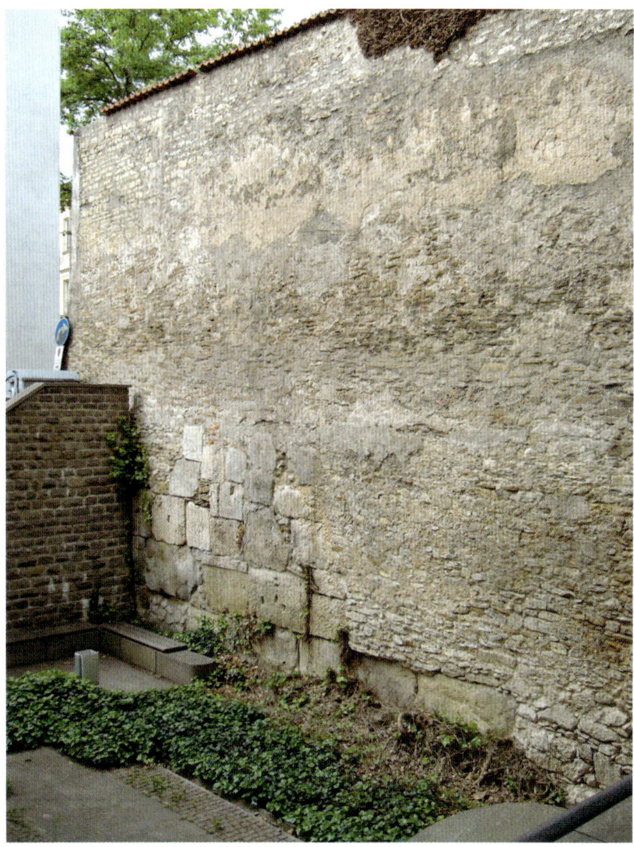

Section of the Roman and mediaeval defensive walls behind the building at No 10 D.-Martin-Luther-Strasse. This site offers proof that the defensive walls were functional for 1600 years without interruption.

most part – re-used blocks form a wall about 4 metres high. On top of it, mediaeval workmen built their town wall using small rough-hewn stones.

The South-Eastern Corner of the Legionary Camp and the Mediaeval City Walls

Continuing in a southerly direction, one passes a long complex, No 12 D.-Martin-Luther-Strasse; the construction of these buildings was, unfortunately, the reason for the demolition of more than 30 metres of Roman wall in the early 1950s.

At the junction with Ernst-Reuter-Platz, one can turn right and go down to an archaeological site. This was created in 1955 and 1961 after excavations had taken place here prior to the erection of the surrounding tower-blocks.

The curve of the south-eastern corner of the legionary camp **(6)** is an impressive sight and it has a considerably larger radius than the north-eastern corner. It is fairly easy to work out where the base of the wall was situated, although its typical sloping form is not so well preserved. Part of the foundations are also exposed here because the level of the site has been lowered quite considerably. The walls were built without mortar as far as the first layer of sandstone ashlar, which is a partial survival of the first phase of building. This is followed by masonry consisting of spoils, re-used stones, which were set in mortar in Roman times, as were various sections that were repaired at that time. Where the curve of the walls reaches its outermost point, there seem, especially near the foundations, to be traces of a tower which once leaned slightly outwards. It has not yet been established whether the extensive facing in rough-stone masonry was added in Roman times already.

Regarding the stretch of wall on the north side, it should be noted that only the base and the two lowest layers of stone blocks have survived in their original form since Roman times. The masonry above them was erected again, re-using Roman stone blocks, in the 1950s. At the northernmost point, there are the remains of the base of a tower belonging to the mediaeval city walls, which proves that at this point the Roman and mediaeval city fortifications followed an identical course. Further evidence of this is offered by the remains of the fortified gateway and its tower just outside the walls.

At the former *Porta Decumana*

After the south-eastern corner, tourists cannot visit any further sections of the south wall of the legionary camp, since the few stretches of wall that have been excavated in this area are all

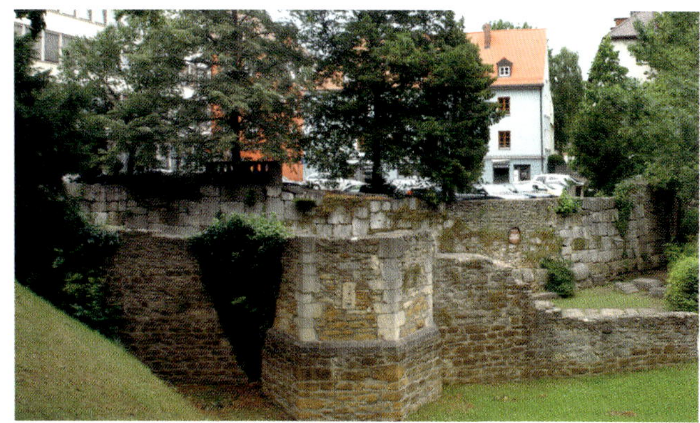

The south-east corner of the legionary camp and part of the mediaeval outer ward, excavated in the1950s, are visible at an archaeological site accessible to the public north of Ernst-Reuter-Platz.

hidden away on private property. By walking from Maximilian-strasse through Fuchsengang, where the facades of the houses on the south side stand exactly on the line of the Roman walls, one can at least get an idea of the size of the legionary camp. The junction of Fröhliche-Türken-Strasse with St.-Peters-Weg is situated where the former *Porta Decumana* used to stand. This gate, which one may imagine as being the counterpart of the Porta Praetoria, acted as the southern exit of the legionary camp and was in the middle of the approximately 450-metre-long south side of the walls. Its mediaeval successor was St Peter's Gate, of which nothing is now visible either, except for the remains of the bridge which led to it, and a section of the city moat.

A short section of the Roman ashlar wall and of the mediaeval city walls has been incorporated into the ground-floor of the café at **No 2 Fuchsengang (7)**. The blocks of stone in the wall on the other side of the road are misleading as they do not reveal the further course of the Roman walls. In the course of building work in the early 20th century, they were removed from the original Roman wall, which was, in fact, a bit further north, and placed here as a reminder of it.

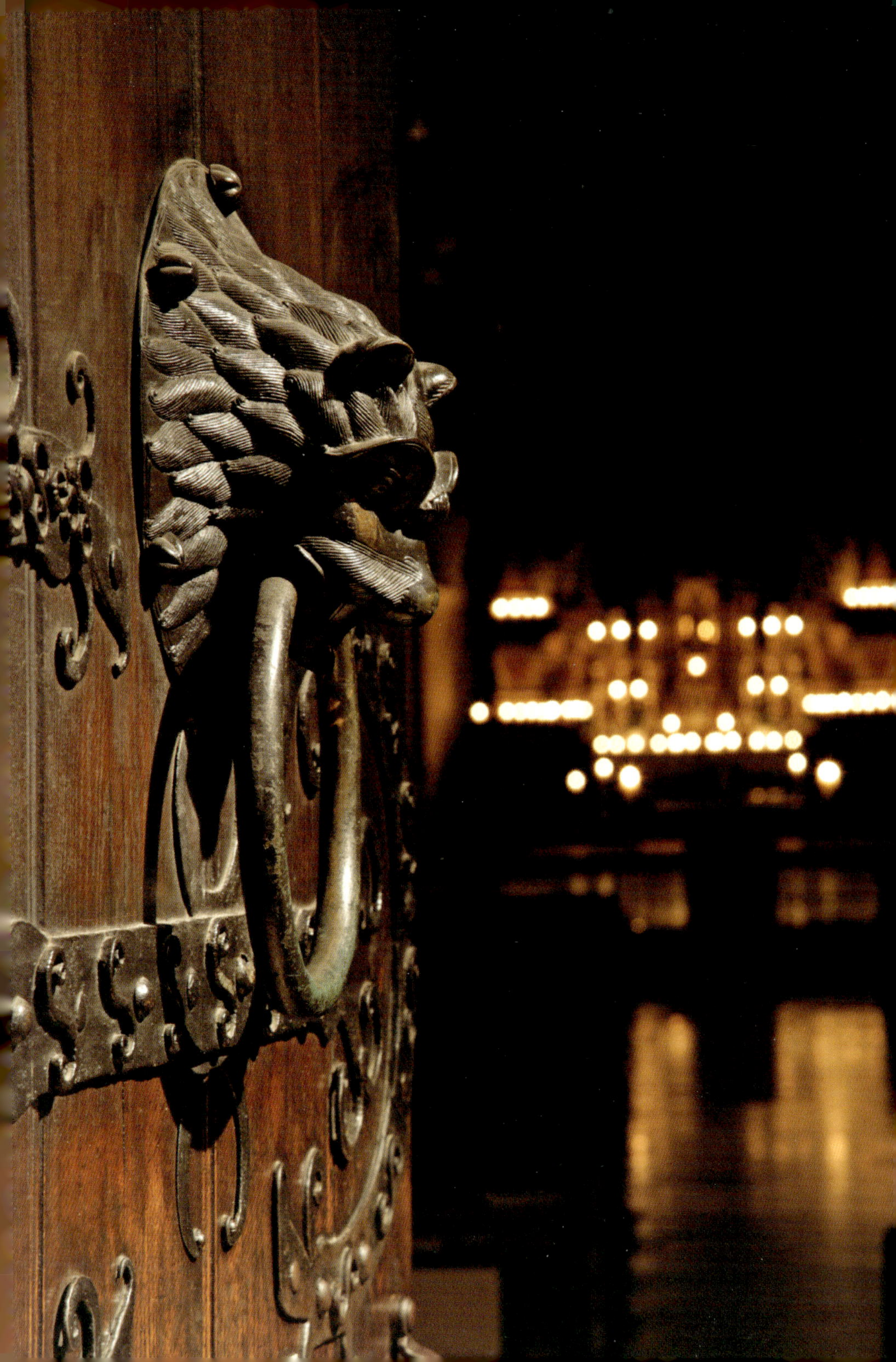

The City of Bishops, Dukes and Kings

This tour covers the north-eastern area of the former Roman legionary camp. After the withdrawal of the 3rd Italic Legion from the 4th century on, a late-Roman fortified town seems to have established itself here; it became in turn the core of the early mediaeval ducal city. Dukes from the House of Agilolfing resided here from the 6th century. They made Regensburg into the first capital of Bavaria, and encouraged the spread of Christianity by bringing bishops to their court. As far as the church was concerned, Regensburg was then under the supervision of the Patriarch of Aquileia. In 739, St Boniface created a canonical bishopric with its seat in Regensburg.

About 770, Arbeo, the Bishop of Freising, compiled the first description of the city. According to him, *Rataspona* was an impregnable fortress, built of great blocks of stone, equipped with tall towers and plentiful wells.

Charlemagne, the Frankish king, deposed Tassilo III, the Agilolfing duke, in 788 and took possession of Bavaria in Regensburg. Ludwig the German established his royal palace near present-day Kornmarkt. Thus, under the Carolingians, the north-eastern part of the former legionary camp became the centre of power of the East Frankish kings. This period also saw the start of Regensburg's significant role as the setting for imperial assemblies, a role it was to retain until the end of the Holy Roman Empire.

On the periphery of the political centre, visiting bishops, abbots and counts took up residence in what were known as 'courts'. Thus, by the year 1000, the basic structure of this part of town was complete, as far as its buildings were concerned. Its further, varied history, its shifts between ecclesiastical, ducal and – in some periods – imperial influences, is illustrated even today by the individual historical buildings.

St Peter's Cathedral

Lower Minster: west door with bronze door-knocker (early 13th cent.)

Together with the Stone Bridge, the **Cathedral (1)** is one of the instantly recognisable sights in Regensburg. A bishop's church dedicated to the Apostle Peter is first mentioned in 778, and even

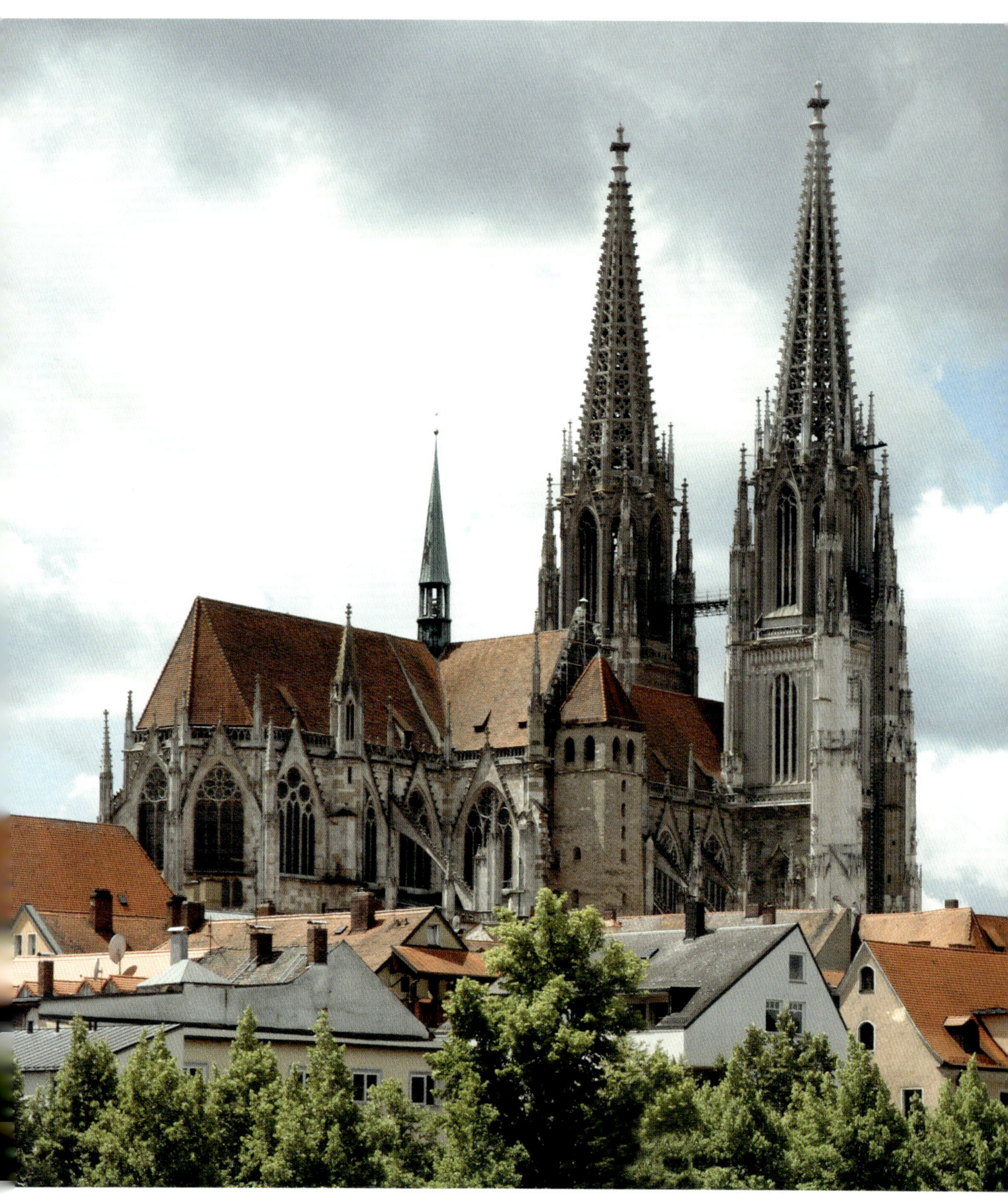

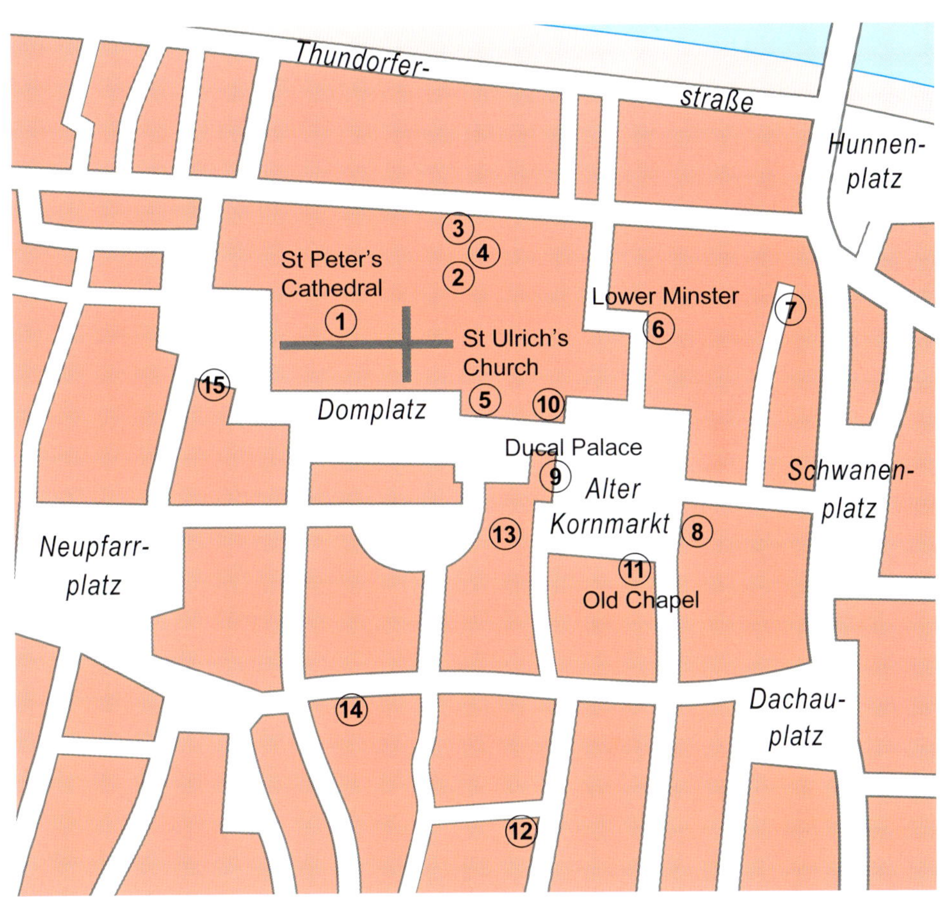

more specifically in 852. In the first half of the 11th century, the then existing basilica, consisting of a nave and two aisles, was extended westward, when a crypt, two towers and a courtyard were added. Of the two towers, the northern one still stands today (see p. 46).

After a fire in this complex, which had frequently been altered in the period up to the 13th century, the city's patrician leaders took the initiative and, in 1273, began building the present cathedral, which was more or less completed in the Middle Ages.

The north aspect of the cathedral, intended to be viewed from a distance. The 11th century north tower of the earlier cathedral still stands in front of the transept facade.

On a site of very limited area, the cathedral initially grew quickly from east to west, but then progress was held up for a time because the old collegiate church of St John (see p. 75ff.) and a chapel dedicated to St Nicholas that adjoined it both stood in the way. Only after the collegiate canons had given permission for these two sacred buildings to be pulled down in 1381, was the way clear for the construction of the parts of the west front that stood north of the south tower. Building work continued on the west front until the end of the Middle Ages. In the end, the towers could not be completed for financial reasons. Nor was the gothic tower over the crossing finished.

Regensburg Cathedral is the only cathedral east of the Rhine to have been built in the classical French style; it can, moreover, be justly described as the most significant and most fully documented gothic building in Southern Germany.

From 1415 on, we know who the cathedral architects were: Wenzel Roritzer (d. 1419) was followed by Andreas Engel (d. 1456), Konrad Roritzer (d. 1477), Matthaeus Roritzer (d. 1495), and Wolfgang Roritzer (who was beheaded in 1514 for leading a rebellion against the emperor). Erhard Heydenreich (d. 1524) and his brother Ulrich, who was active until about 1538, no longer had any great influence on the architecture of the cathedral.

As a result of the Romantic enthusiasm for the Middle Ages, King Ludwig I of Bavaria had the interior 'purified', i.e. had all its post-mediaeval decoration removed. The spires were added between 1859 and 1869, under the direction of the cathedral's master mason, Franz Joseph Denzinger, who had been urged by the king to do this for a long time. In 1870–72, the gable on the transept was completed.

Exterior

The dominant role played by the cathedral in the city's architecture is further increased by the fact that the huge building rises from a base, 3 metres high, that it is possible to walk all around. The oldest parts of the building are at the east end. The main

Placing the cathedral on a high plinth was an original idea.

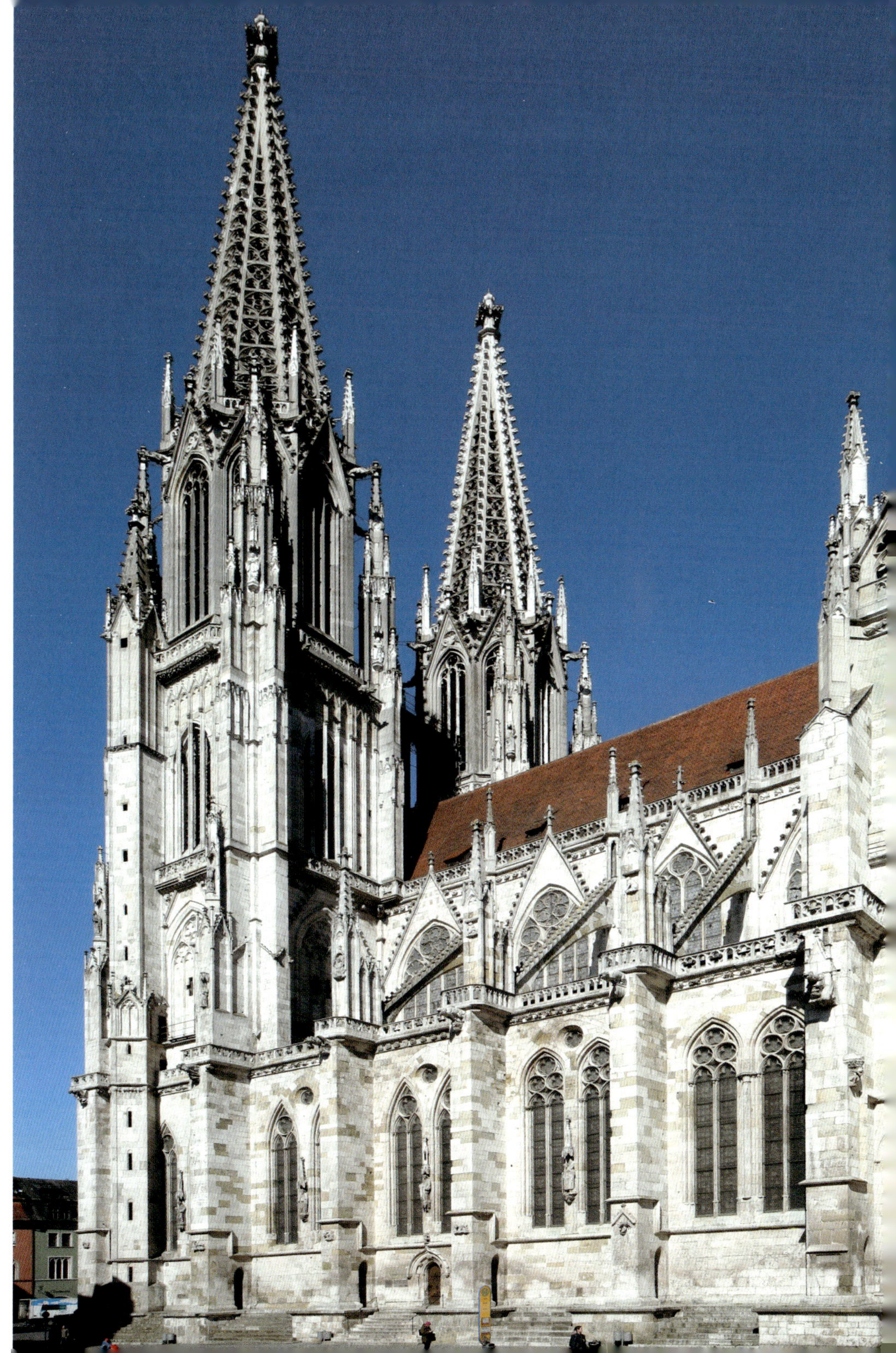

chancel, which rises steeply and is closed on three sides of the octagon, is impressive because of the lavish windows high up in the walls, whereas the massive plinth still betrays a more conservative architect. The design diverges from the classical French cathedral style in that there is no ambulatory with radiating chapels.

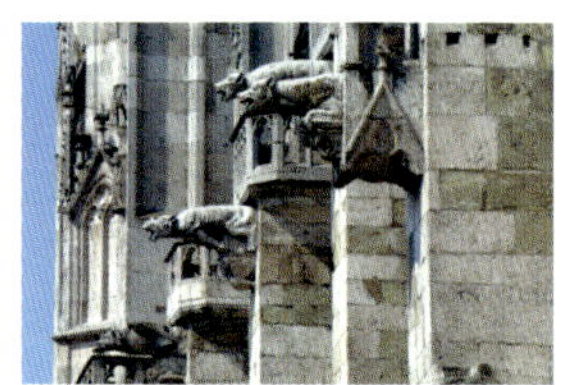

Gargoyle on the south facade of the cathedral nave. The grotesque creatures were supposed to ward off evil.

The choirs in the two aisles are flanked to the east by additional buildings, several storeys high, which were constructed later, so that their terminations and the sides of the chancel are partially obscured on the outside. The entrance to St Nicholas' Chapel is on the ground-floor of the southern annex. The depiction of the saint in the tympanum (c. 1280) still shows traces of the original paintwork.

Even better than the chancel, the facade of the south transept illustrates the contrast between the solid lower zone and the more transparent upper zone, thus reflecting the change of architect around 1300. From then on, Regensburg Cathedral was constructed in the modern style of high gothic French architecture. A very original feature are the mullions that were placed in front of the arches of the clerestory and are continued in the gable. The latter was not added until 1868–71 (by Denzinger) and was steeper than had been intended in the Middle Ages. The tympanum over the doorway, which is flanked by pinnacles, contains sculptures that were added later on: the Apostles Peter and Paul (c. 1370) and the Crucifixion (c. 1320). Contemporary with the building, in contrast, is the statue of St Peter between the two groups of windows in the triforium (c. 1310/15).

On the exterior of the nave, which – architecturally speaking – continues the pattern developed in the upper zones of the chancel and transept, the use of sculptures as decoration becomes more frequent. The figure of St Christopher (c. 1325/30) in the second bay from the east is remarkable for its determined expression. The four allegorical reliefs on the buttresses are also interesting because of the light they cast on the imagery current at that time; among them – to the right of the side entrance –

View of the cathedral from the town hall tower. The spires with their open work were added between 1859 and 1869.

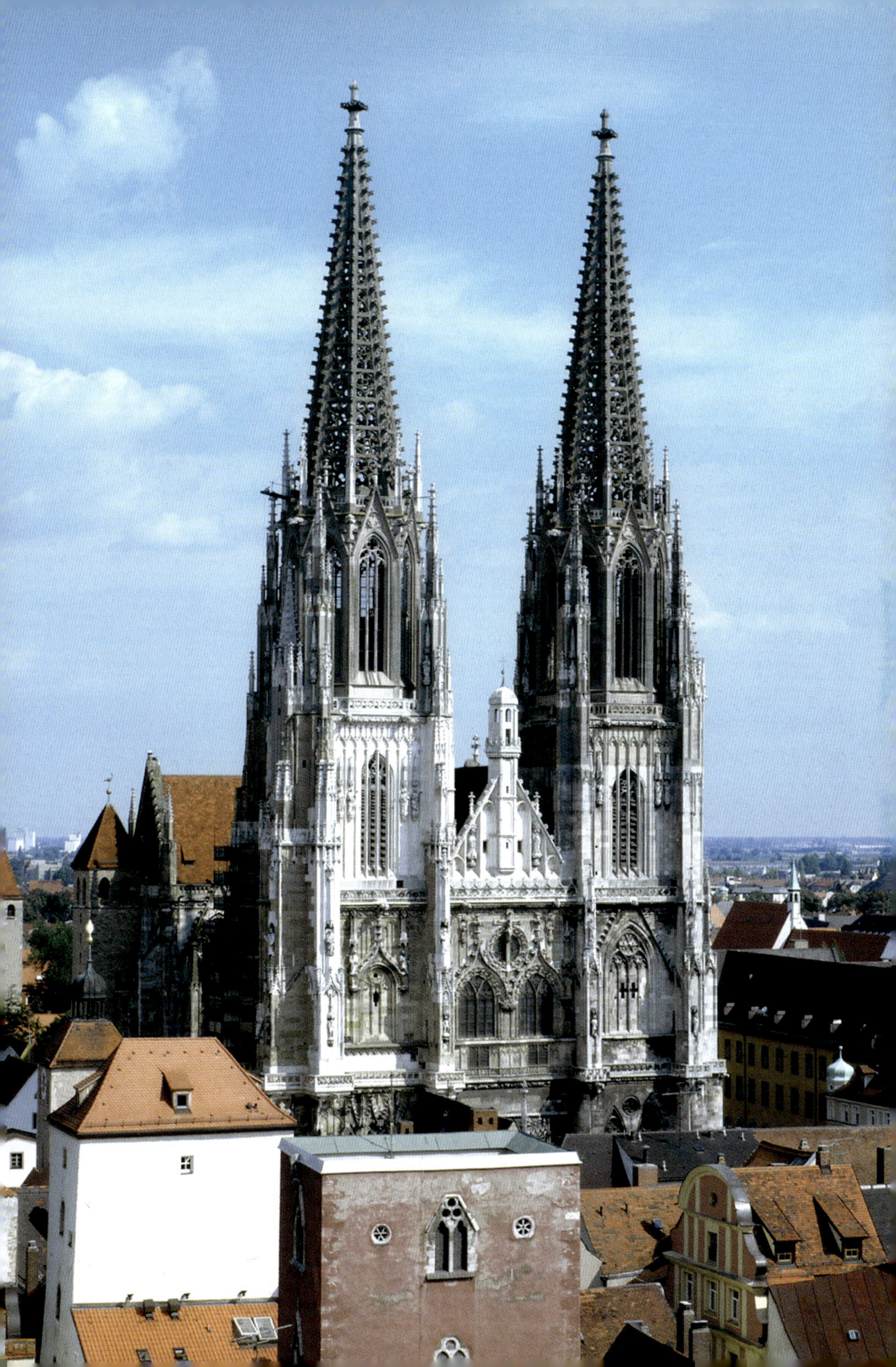

is a so-called 'Jews' sow' (c. 1330/40): the deadly sins of gluttony and lust are interpreted in anti-Semitic terms by showing Jews sucking at a sow's teats. On the next buttress to the west, one finds Samson, who is the complete antithesis to the 'Jews' sow', in that he represents the Christ-type in the Old Testament. In this way the traditional theme of the contrast between 'ecclesia' and 'synagogue' was extended anecdotally. To this same end, the two outer reliefs show, on the left, the Virgin Mary with the unicorn, a traditional allegorical reference to Mary and Christ, and, on the right, a dragon, a depiction of the Devil.

The massive West Front with its richly decorative sculptures grew fairly slowly, beginning from the lowest storey of the south tower, from the mid-14th century. Building work continued intermittently for about 180 years, until the north tower had been (temporarily) finished. From c. 1530 until well into the 19th century, the two towers ended above the belfry. The octagonal storeys and the spires, which consist only of tracery, were added from 1859–69.

The West Front possesses an amazing amount of architectural homogeneity despite the long period over which it was built and the various alterations in its planning. Compared with the ideal form of the gothic cathedral facade, it lacks the great central rose window. Instead, the central axis is emphasised by a porch which has a triangular base, thus creating a spatial dimension for the facade. The structure of the facade above the porch is also unusual. In the middle section, for instance, the rose window is replaced by two windows with an ogee arch above them. On top of them is a round window, with a crucifix placed in front of it, while beneath the crucifix is a sculpture of St Peter in a ship (the arms of Regensburg's cathedral chapter). The gable, which was completed before 1487, has so-called acorn turrets on top of it.

On the south tower, reflecting the progress of construction, the decorative principles of the south facade of the nave are carried on. The doorway is surprisingly small; the tympanum has an

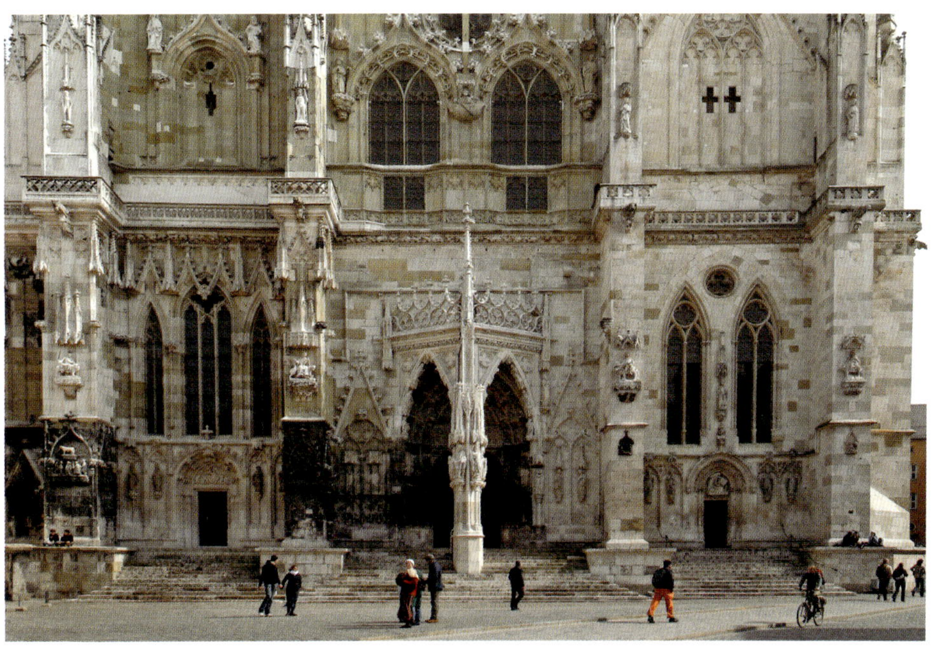

Cathedral, West Front. It was originally intended that the triangular porch outside the main doorway would have two storeys.

original depiction of St Peter being freed from prison (c.1345). There is another sculpture of the saint between the lancet windows above. As regards its doorway, the later north tower is very similar to the south one. The tympanum relief shows the handing over of the tablets with the Ten Commandments to Moses (c. 1410/20). Particularly remarkable from the iconographic point of view are – in comparison with the other sculptures here – the four kings on horseback, who are placed on the buttresses of the north and south towers: they embody the four empires according to the vision of the prophet Daniel. Looking from south to north, they are Nebuchadnezzar (Babylon), Julius Caesar (Rome), Alexander the Great (Greece) and Cyrus (Persia). The originals, which dated from 1350/60 (south tower) and 1410/20 (north tower) were replaced with copies in 1898/99.

The West Front reaches its artistic climax in the great doorway with its triangular porch. The latter – as is proved by the experts' findings and a sketch of the facade dating from 1390/1400 – was to have had an upper storey. Although all that was completed was a balcony that could be reached from the inner gallery, the balcony was probably intended, even in this restricted form, for the presentation of relics. If one compares this porch with others, what is most striking is the highly unusual triangular shape, for which the only parallel is found at the earlier north doorway of Erfurt Cathedral.

The decorative sculpture on the main doorway and in the porch, which dates from 1385–1410 and is of very high quality, constitutes the most comprehensive cycle of gothic figures in Regensburg. These portrayals underline stylistically the crucial supra-regional significance of the sculpture on Regensburg Cathedral for the eastward spread of French influence. The 22 reliefs in the archivolts of the west door show scenes from the life of the Virgin Mary and from Jesus' childhood. The reliefs in the tympanum complete the mariological programme with Mary's death, burial, ascension and enthronement. It is significant that it is not Mary who appears on the trumeau, but St Peter as Pope. The Bishop of Rome is flanked in the innermost jamb niches by the archdeacons and patron saints of the city of Rome, Stephen and Laurence. Moving outwards, there are two apostles on each side; the other eight are placed round the free-standing pillar of the porch. The embrasures of its arches have sculptures of the prophets on them. These, like the figures of the apostles on the porch, were replaced with copies in 1907/08.

The north facade is only partially accessible from the east via the Cathedral Garden and is primarily intended to impress people looking at it from a distance. This distant view is best obtained from the Stone Bridge. The 11th-century north tower of the earlier cathedral, the so-called Donkey Tower, still stands in front of the facade of the transept. The intention was, as various pieces of 13th-century masonry indicate, to encase the old tower and turn it into a more massive specimen.

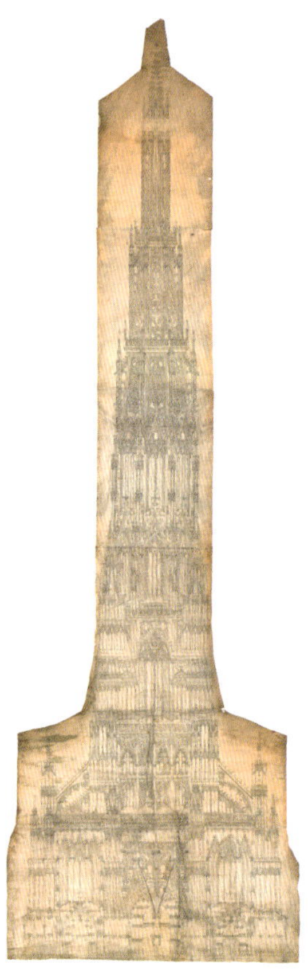

Detail from a sketch of the facade (c. 1390/1400, Cathedral Treasury Museum) showing a two-storey porch on a triangular base. This design also features only a single tower about 150 metres in height.

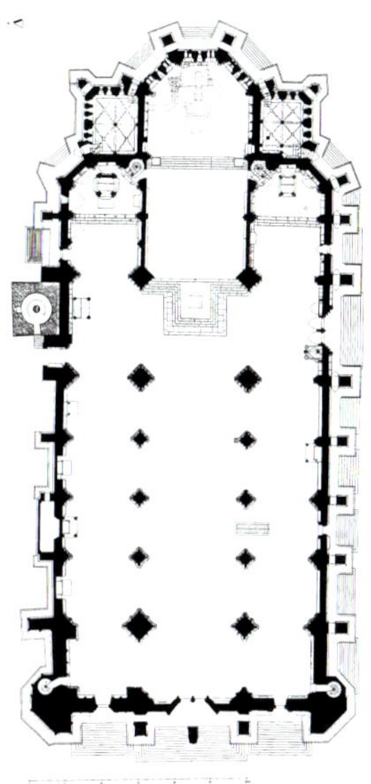

The Interior

The basilica-style interior with its nave and two aisles still appears, architecturally speaking, just as it presented itself when the final pieces of scaffolding were removed in 1442. All that is missing is the rood screen, which was demolished in 1644. The chancel is unusually high because of the inclusion of parts of the earlier cathedral. The base of the polygon in the choir is structured by means of arcades, as if there were an ambulatory behind it. In fact, these arcades contain aumbries which were used for storing relics. In the aisles, the two choirs are only dimly lit because of the buildings adjoining them and their walls are characterised by blind arches and a walkway running along above the base area that once led to the rood screen. In the south choir, the first part of the cathedral to be completed, two small pillars dating from about 1220 were placed in the blind arcades of the polygon; very probably, these pillars were taken from the old cathedral for reasons of tradition.

On the western pillars in the crossing are the cathedral's most famous sculptures, the Annunciation group created by the Erminold Master (c. 1280/85). These two brilliant statues once stood in the chancel. Their creator, named after the tomb he made for the Blessed Erminold in the former Benedictine abbey church at Prüfening, had, after a period of training in Paris (?) already worked on the minster in Basle before he became the greatest exponent of early gothic sculpture in Regensburg.

On the south wall of the transept, the walkway coming from the choir in the south aisle leads in a triangle over the double doorway and continues into the nave. The central pillar of the doorway has on it a figure of Petronella (c.1330), according to legend the daughter of St Peter, with well-preserved original colouring. The wall of the north transept has very few windows or openings in it because the Donkey Tower stands behind it.

The nave with its five bays and cross-ribbed vaulting is most obviously in the tradition of classical French cathedrals due to its clear three-storey structure: the unlighted, accessible triforium

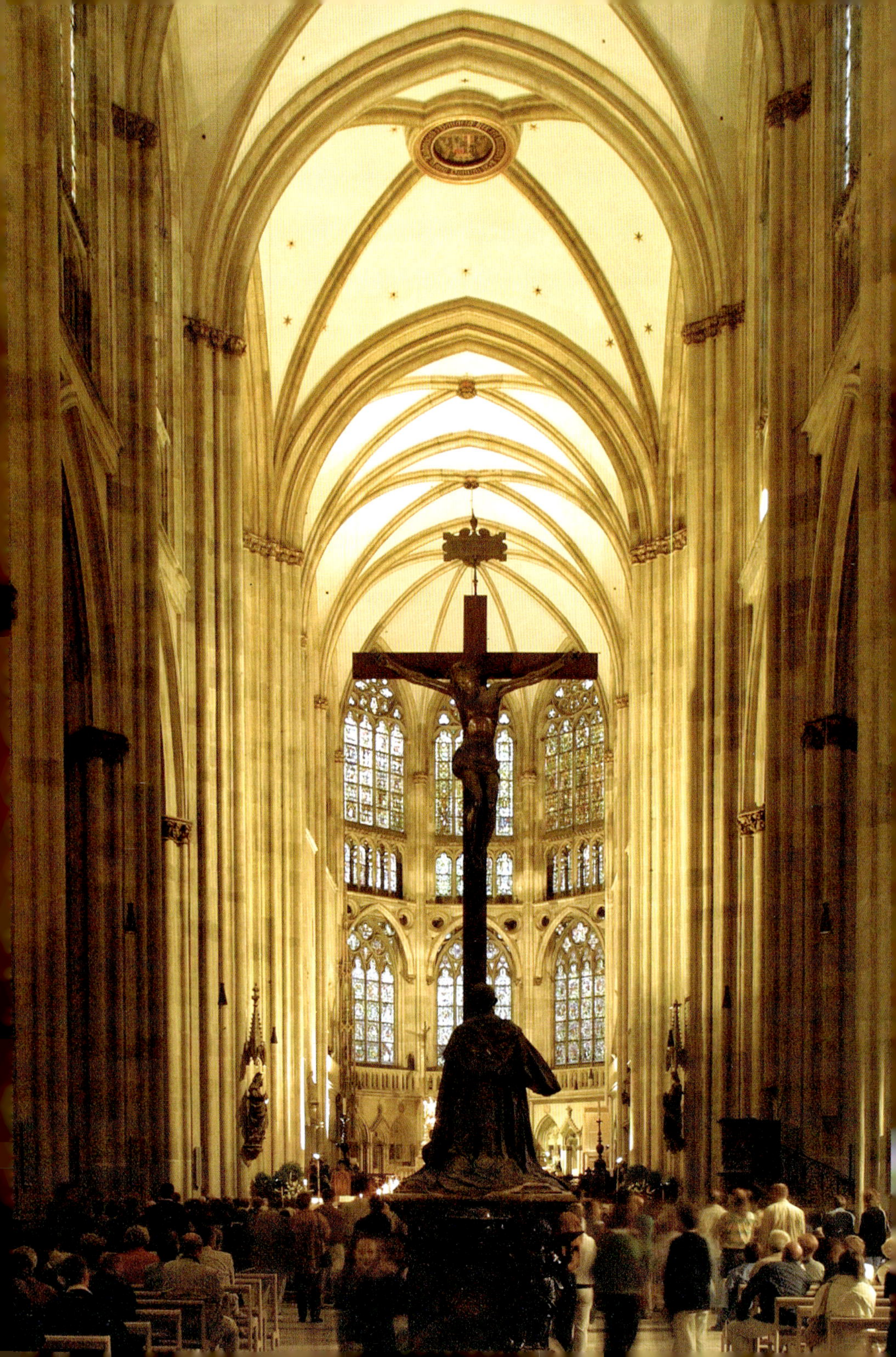

runs along above the arcades which are emphasised by groups of pillars. In the style of high gothic architecture, this leads, formally at least, up into the clerestory with its large windows. The inner west facade has corner turrets on each side (extended in 1838). Inside them a spiral staircase links the lower walkway with a balcony which forms a bridge over the west door and allows access to the balcony over the porch. In front of the shafts on the wall at each side, there are two figures on horseback, made by different sculptors, who face each other like sentries: on the left, St George in knight's apparel, on the right, St Martin clad as a nobleman. In the third bay is the entrance to the Bishops' Crypt, which was completed in 1987 and incorporates part of the romanesque atrium. The visible columns and wall pillars of this date from the last rebuilding phase (c. 1205/10).

The walls in the aisles are horizontally structured by the foot-way running along them above the base zone, but differ otherwise in appearance. In the south aisle, a frieze with pointed arches (the little console figures date mainly from the 19th century) marks the limit of the base area and the walls above are structured by means of pairs of lancet windows; in each of the three middle bays on the north side, in contrast, one arch in the base area led the way in to the former side chapels. The foot-way here runs along a straight cornice. The wall-space above is filled entirely by traceried windows, the lower halves of which are bricked up because the roofs of the chapels used to be behind them.

Furnishings

A characteristic feature of Regensburg Cathedral are its gothic canopied altars. The oldest one (c. 1320) stands in the third bay of the north aisle. The only one still in its original position is that in the second bay of the south aisle (c. 1330/35). The others are in the south choir (c. 1415/20), in the north choir (c. 1430) and in the north transept (1473). Since raising the height of altars by means of stone canopies is a sign of respect copied from the graves of early Christian martyrs, the high altar must certainly

The cathedral interior. The early baroque memorial to Cardinal Philipp Wilhelm, Duke of Bavaria, which was erected facing the high altar, survived the restoration of the cathedral in gothic style in the 19th century.

have been of this type, too, before it had to give way to the baroque silver altar. A stone canopy, made by Konrad Roritzer in 1500, is also to be seen over the well beside the doorway in the south transept.

Among the tombs, the most striking is the bronze memorial set up in 1611 for Cardinal Philipp Wilhelm, Duke of Bavaria, which is ascribed to Hans Krumper and which occupies a prominent position in the central aisle in the nave; it shows Philipp Wilhelm, who died at the age of nineteen, kneeling before a crucifix. A neo-classical marble memorial designed by Canova's pupil Luigi Zandomeneghi to commemorate Prince-Bishop Carl von Dalberg, the last Arch-Chancellor of the Holy Roman Empire, was relocated to an insignificant position in the passage leading from the north transept into the bishop's palace when the cathedral was re-gothicised. A rare example of Nazarene sculpture is offered by Konrad Eberhard's memorial for Bishop Johann Michael Sailer, which was placed in the south choir in 1837.

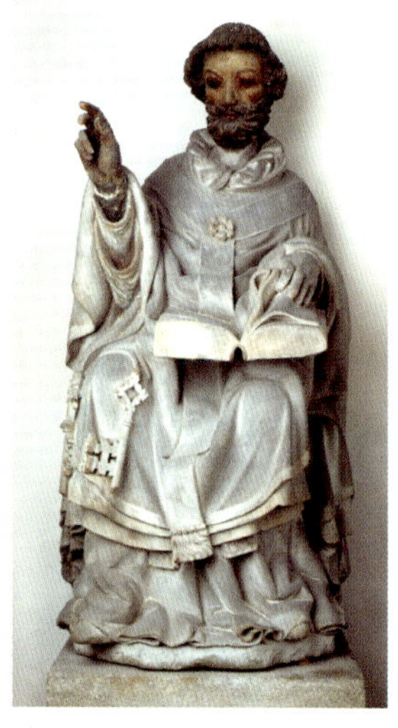

The enthroned figure of St Peter (c. 1290, Museum of Regensburg History) is the work of the Erminold Master. It once stood in the cathedral. The model for it was the only slightly earlier seated figure of the apostle in St Peter's in Rome.

The **stained glass** is of outstanding importance. Regensburg Cathedral is one of the few gothic cathedrals to have an entire complement of stained-glass windows, thus particularly reflecting gothic mysticism vis à vis light. The use of stained glass began in the south choir and was well-advanced by about 1370. The oldest of the approximately 1100 mediaeval panes were taken from a window illustrating Christ's family tree that had been placed in the earlier cathedral in about 1230, and built into the triforium of the south transept. The clerestory window on the south-east side of the chancel is of special iconographic significance: it shows what is probably the first large-scale representation of the 14 Holy Helpers. From 1827, at King Ludwig I's instigation, craftsmen began to put stained glass into the windows of the west front and other hitherto plain windows. This was one of the first instances of this type of work following the revival of the technique of making stained glass.

The Cathedral Precinct

Leaving the cathedral via the north choir, one comes to the chapter house, which was erected about 1320, making use of the walls of the north aisle of the Carolingian cathedral. Walking under the gothic buttress which joins the chapter house to the cathedral sacristy, one enters the cathedral garden. From the time the Carolingian cathedral was pulled down until the early 19th century, this was the cathedral graveyard. Evidence of this is provided, for instance, by the Eternal Light Pillar dating from 1341. Nowadays a large part of the cathedral garden is used by the Cathedral Workshop.

In Carolingian times already, Regensburg Cathedral had two adjoining sets of cloisters. From the 11th /12th century on, the centre wing was extended to act as a burial place (mortuarium).

Via the chapter house, one reaches the **cathedral cloisters (2, M)**, which were once attached to the north side of the Carolingian cathedral. The double set of cloisters was constructed in the early Middle Ages already. The central passage, which was used for burials, was extended to make a hall in the 12th century and restored in the 15th/16th centuries. From the start

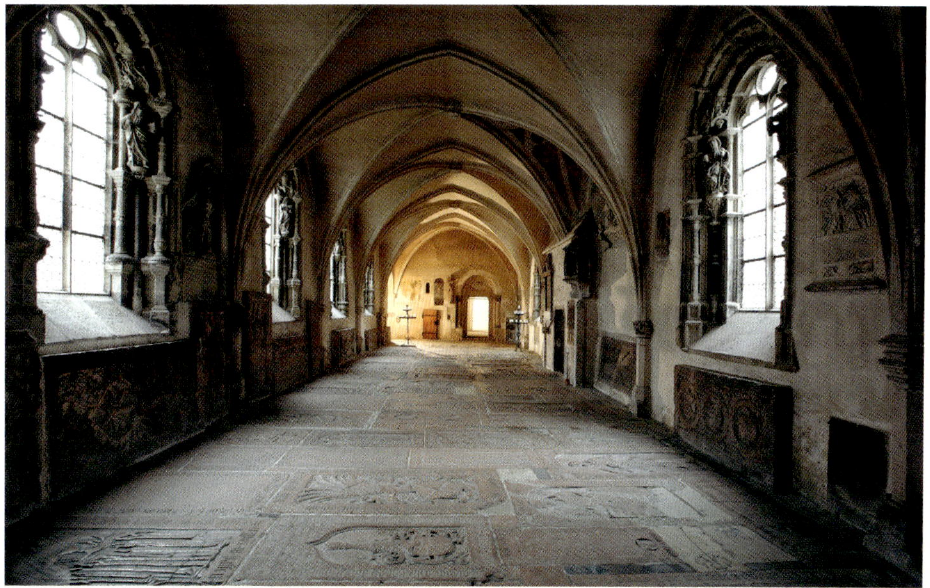

it connected the cathedral with **St Stephan's Chapel (3)**, which lay north of the cloisters. This chapel was built around 1070/80 on the site of a larger previous building dating from the 8th (?) century, which had a nave and two aisles. This was most probably the church for the bishop's court. The present building, a lofty hall with two bays, is characterised by hemispherical alcoves of a type which occurs several times in 11th-century architecture in Regensburg (see p. 145f., 149, 151). Ultimately, this is a feature that was handed down from Antiquity and used again in the Carolingian period, for instance in Aquileia at the beginning of the 9th century. The altar (10th/11th cent. or earlier), which stands in the apse, is a block of limestone with little blind windows and probably also stood in the earlier church.

Adjoining the east side of the central hall is **All Saints' Chapel (4)**. Bishop Hartwich II (d. 1164) had it built as his own mausoleum by craftsmen from Lombardy. The architecture of the absolutely harmonious central building does in fact show great similarity to the baptistries of Galliano di Cantù and Mariano Comense. In contrast to the finely detailed exterior, the interior

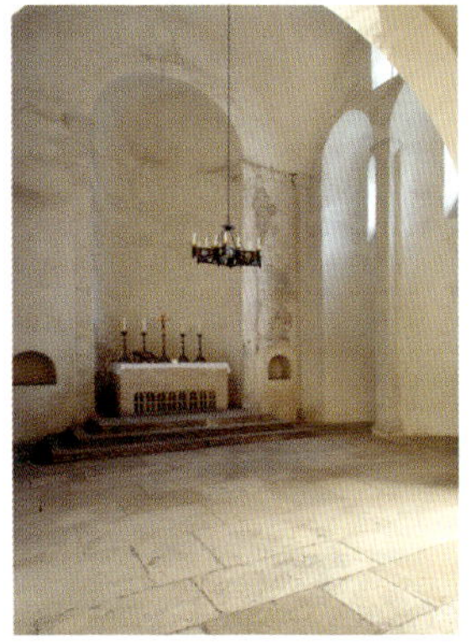

St Stephan's Chapel in the cathedral cloisters was erected c. 1070/80 on the site of an earlier building (8th century?) with a nave and two aisles.

St Stephan's Chapel: three sides of the altar block (10th /11th cent.) have small openings in them, indicating that a saint's relics were once kept under the altar.

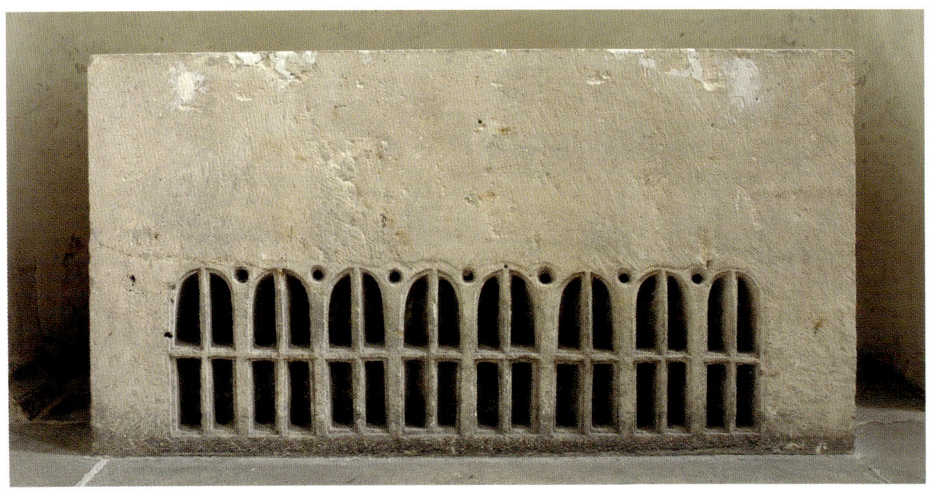

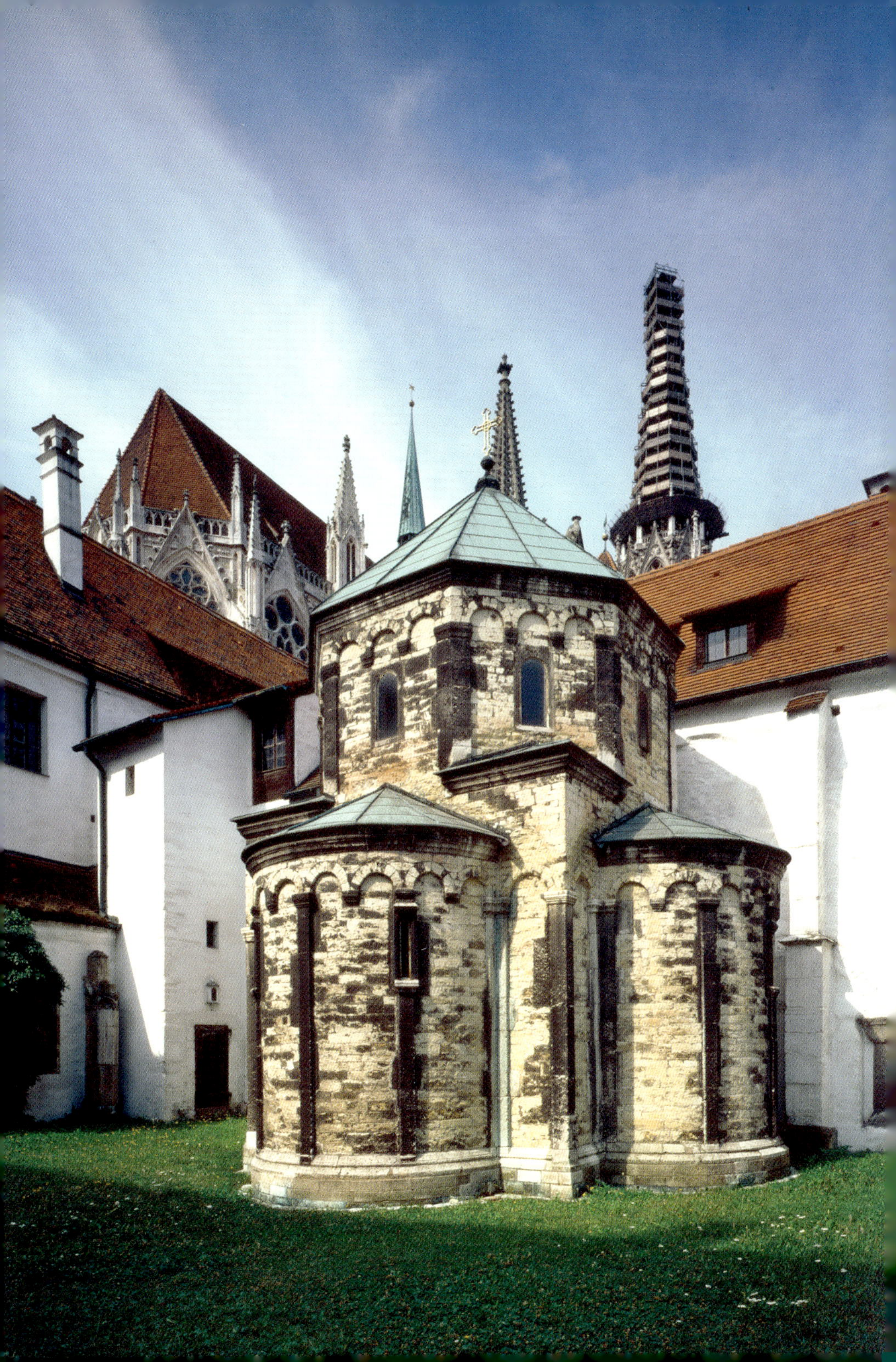

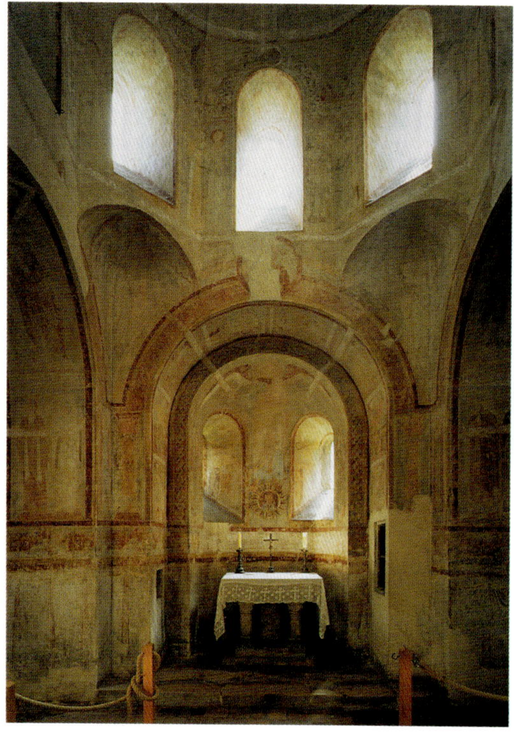

p. 53: All Saints' Chapel (c. 1160), a splendid example of the work of masons from Lombardy in 12th-century Regensburg.

Interior of All Saints' Chapel. It functioned as a mausoleum for Bishop Hartwig II (d. 1164), the first Bishop of Regensburg who did not wish to be buried in St Emmeram's.

walls have no obvious structure, since their purpose was to provide the base for the paintings which covered all the interior surfaces and had their own inner artistic structure. Of the frescoes that were painted when the chapel was built, only a distant echo survives following some 'restoration work' carried out in 1955. The paintings refer to the interpretation of the Feast of All Saints according to St John's Revelations, the emphasis being on the beginning of the Last Judgement with the salvation of the Elect. The table altar in the eastern apse, one of three apses, is also a survival from the time the chapel was constructed.

St Ulrich's Church

St Ulrich's Church (5, [M]) is adjacent to the cathedral garden, on its south side. Begun as a church for the duke's palace, it lies on what was once the border between ducal and episcopal territory. However, even while St Ulrich's was being built, the plan to make it a two-storey building, a typical feature of a palace chapel, was abandoned. Instead, the builders decided in favour of a gallery running around the interior. The reason for this was probably that the influence of the duke within the city was waning after 1230. The church obviously shifted into the bishop's sphere of power and was turned into the cathedral's parish church (with a tower at its south-west corner). It is first mentioned as such in 1263. Its parish-church function ended in 1821, when the cathedral parish was transferred to the Lower Minster. The church was de-consecrated during the period of Secularisation and only nar-

St Ulrich's (2nd quarter of the 13th cent.), the first gothic building in Regensburg. Behind it, the so-called Roman Tower.

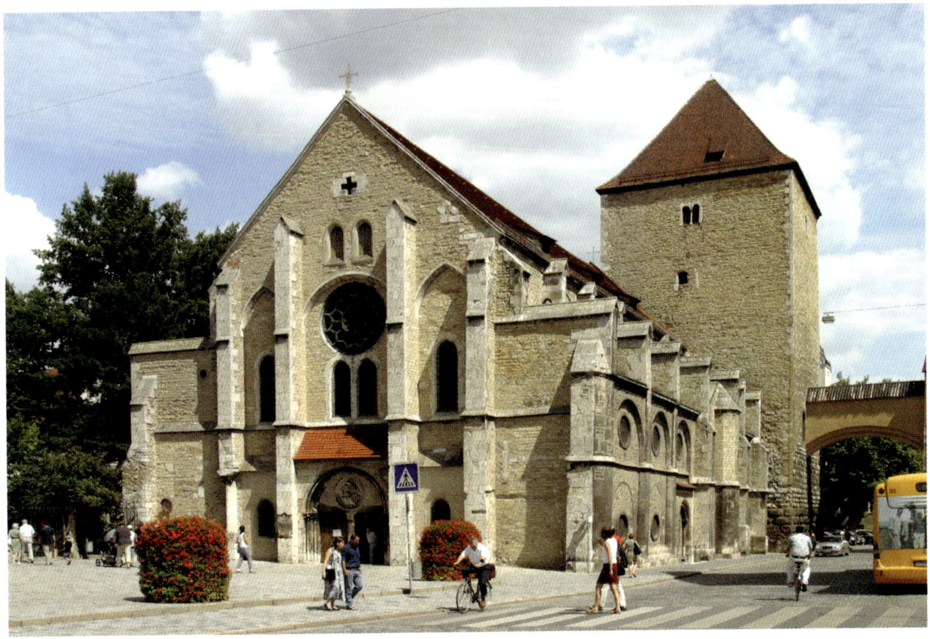

rowly escaped demolition. In 1859, the tower and the porch were removed. Since 1986, the Diocesan Museum has been housed in the church.

St Ulrich's long and varied history cannot conceal the fact that the church, despite its rather squat appearance, is one of the earliest gothic buildings in Southern Germany. Particularly striking in this connection is the rose window, which was constructed exactly according to the model of the rose windows in the chancel and at the west end of Laon Cathedral. This rose window is unique in Regensburg's gothic architecture.

Exterior

The basilica-type church rises from a rectangular ground-plan. The west, north and south facades are structured by means of buttresses, which reflect the division into bays on the longer sides of the building. The oval windows in the aisles date from 1688. The doorway on the south side has survived in its original state; the tympanum relief depicts Christ's Ascension. In contrast, the west door has been greatly altered and its tympanum has featured a relief of the Virgin Mary by Fidelis Schönlaub since 1859.

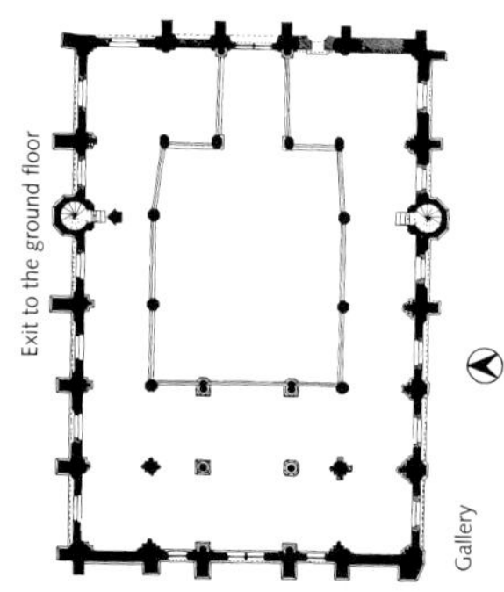

Interior

The unconventional appearance of the church, with its nave and four aisles, can be explained by the early decision to build a parish church rather than a two-storey court church. It was originally intended that the vaults which now support the gallery would be closed in the middle, too, thus creating a crypt-like space in the lower storey, while the upper floor would have had a high nave with lower aisles. In the end, however, no ceiling was built over the nave and two inner aisles between their third and fifth bays.

What can be seen in its original form, however, is the contrast between the two large groups of windows at the east and west ends of the upper storey. Whilst at the west end, as in the clerestory in Reims Cathedral, a rose window has been placed above two windows with pointed arches, in the east this combination of windows, on the model of the clerestory windows in Notre Dame in Paris, has been merged into a single large rose window. Thus the wall above the altar has the largest possible degree of transparency. Beside this window, there are remarkable wall paintings dating from the time when the church was built; the other wall-paintings date from 1571 and from the early 17th century.

Niedermünster (Lower Minster)

To the east of the cathedral garden, one comes to the **Lower Minster (6)**. The origins of what was formerly a convent for noble ladies are closely connected with the veneration for St Erhard. The saint was commissioned to organise the church in Bavaria by the Agilolfing dukes in the late 7th century. He appears to have combined the functions of a regional bishop and a court bishop. When Erhard died soon after 700, he was interred within the confines of the duke's palace, on the north inner wall of a 25-metre-long hall church that had been erected there, partly using Roman walls. This church was, as some of its memorials suggest, the Agilolfings' palace chapel. It was, however, the saint's grave and the adjoining north wall that determined the position of later buildings on this site. Both the Carolingian hall church (c. 800) and the Ottonian basilica incorporated the north wall of the Agilolfing church. Even before 833, the Carolingian building must have been the centre of a convent for noble ladies that had been established as a result of the veneration for St Erhard. Its Ottonian successor was begun by Henry I, Duke of Bavaria, brother of the Emperor Otto the Great, and completed by his widow Judith after Henry's death in 955. She entered the convent in 973 and became its abbess. Judith's grandson, the Emperor Henry II, granted the convent imperial status in 1002. Fifty years later, Pope Leo IX declared Erhard's grave sacred. When the present-day romanesque basilica was erected in the

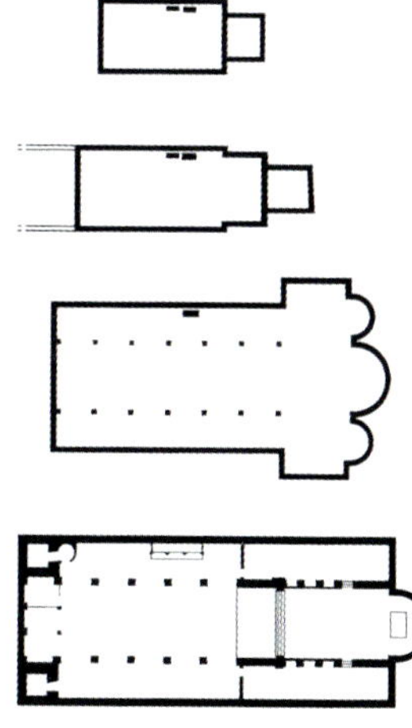

The four phases in the building of the Lower Minster: Agilolfing palace chapel (c. 700); Carolingian hall church (c. 800); Ottonian basilica (c. 955); romanesque basilica (after 1146)

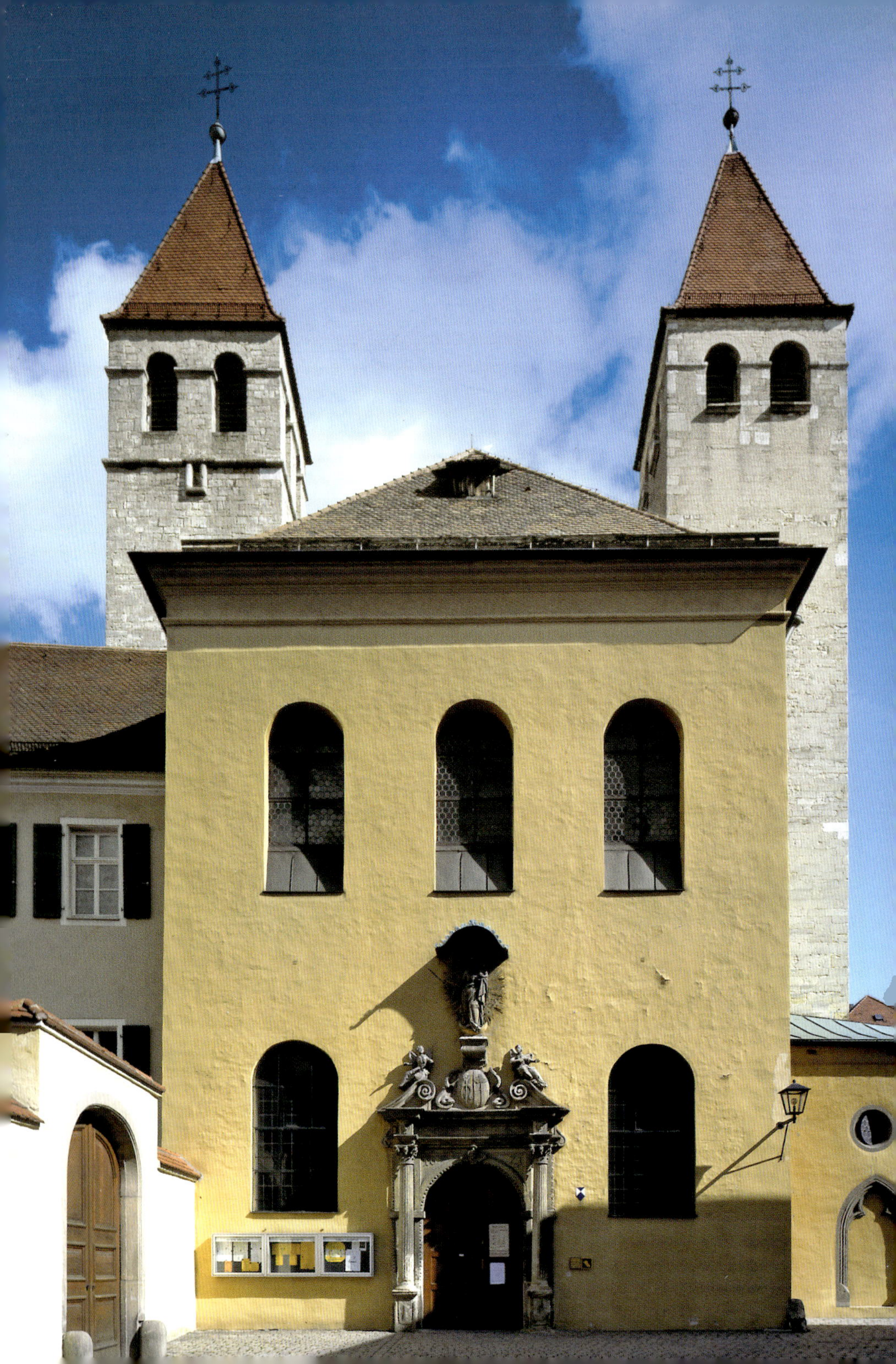

West front of the Lower Minster Church. The basilica's romanesque porch had a second storey added to it in the 17th century.

mid-12th century, its north wall was again constructed where the north wall of the Agilolfing church had stood. The building work was very probably carried out from 1146 on by craftsmen from the diocese of Como. Despite baroque alterations, the romanesque complex is clearly identifiable as such from both the outside and the inside.

The 1000-year history of the convent for noblewomen ended with the loss of its imperial status and the period of Secularisation in the early 19th century. Since 1821, the basilica has been the cathedral's parish church, whilst the convent buildings, renovated in the baroque period, have served as the bishop's residence.

Exterior

Towards the west, the building catches the eye because of its porch and the two high towers behind it. Whereas the 12th-century porch was renovated in the baroque period and had an upper storey added to it, the towers have retained their romanesque appearance, as have the facades of the nave and choir. However, all that can be seen from the street is the termination of the choir, built with large blocks of stone; its severe lines, unadorned by any decorative features, dominate Erhardigasse.

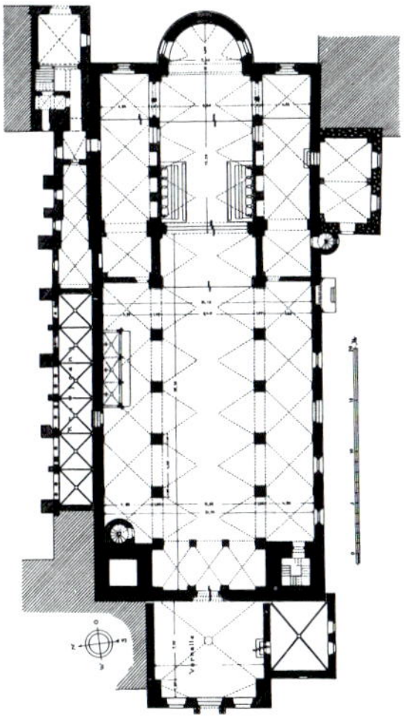

Interior

On entering the porch, one is surprised first of all by its unusual depth. On the walls at the sides, romanesque masonry and walled-up arcades are to be seen. The stonework is visible, too, in the facade with the entrance door, a stepped portal (c. 1150), which betrays the Upper Italian origin of its mason. The bronze rings on the door are a rarity; they were probably made in Northern Germany in the early 13th century.

The comparatively long pillared basilica has a nave and two aisles; with its round-arched arcades, the deep choir and, finally, the apse, it has retained its romanesque character to a great extent although it underwent two phases of renovation in the baroque period. In 1625, the flat ceilings were replaced by barrel vaulting with dormer vaults; at the same time, the organ loft was constructed at the west end, and the oratories above the arches in the east aisle were added, too. As a result, the two side choirs seem to be quire separate. The restrained stucco on the walls dates from about 1730. The only survivals of the romanesque wall decoration are the (much restored) paintings on the arch of the apse (knee-length portraits of apostles) and on the west wall (Majestas Domini).

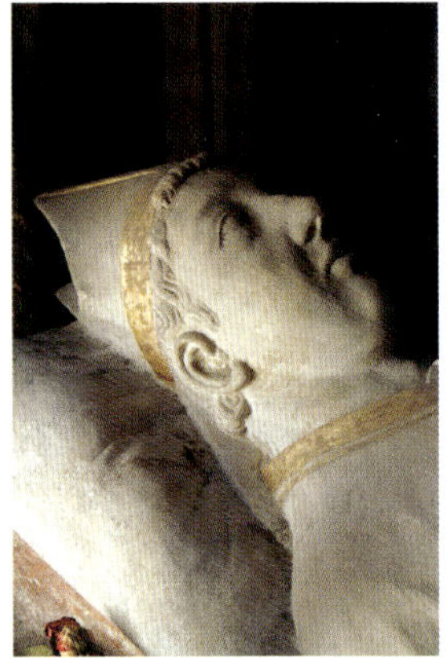

Furnishings

The altars are baroque. The most remarkable one is the marble high altar, designed by Jakob Mösl from Salzburg. The early baroque altar dedicated to the Virgin Mary in the north aisle includes a wooden figure showing the Mother of God enthroned; it is of the Byzantine Nikopoia type (early 13th cent.).

Above the lying figures of three bishops on floor slabs, also in the left aisle, is a stone canopy dating from c. 1325/30 with (much retouched) paintwork from the early 16th century. The oldest part of the ensemble is the figure of Erhard, which lies in the middle. The high-quality stone sculpture marks the position of the saint's grave beneath. The figure lying beside St Erhard dates from a few years later. It represents the Blessed Albert of Cashel, an Irish bishop who died in Regensburg, and was buried beside Erhard, while on his way home from a pilgrimage to the Holy Land – according to legend he died when he heard of the death of Erhard, his colleague and friend. The third figure is that of an unknown bishop. It was probably placed here in the 17th century for the sake of symmetry. However, an original component of the canopy group is the small figure of a female saint that is attached to the pillar at the left corner; this has been identified as Duchess Judith.

Lower Minster: small statue of a female saint (Abbess Judith?) on the canopy over St Erhard's grave (c. 1325/30)

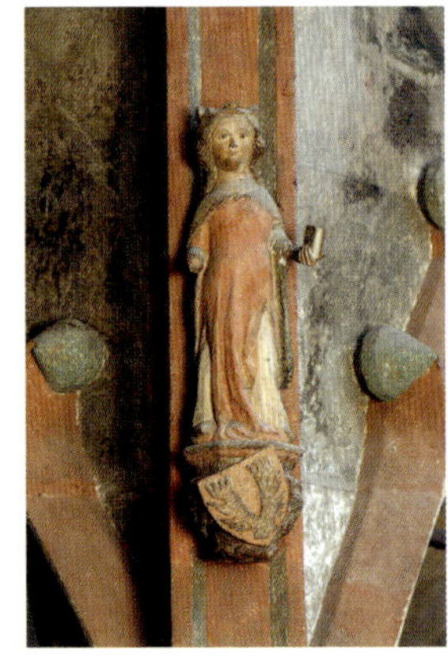

Other important early gothic works are the wooden crucifixion group (c. 1300) in the War Memorial Chapel that may be entered from the porch, as well as the stone figure of the Madonna on the south wall of the choir (1st half of the 14th cent.).

Lower Minster: gothic stone canopy over St Erhard's grave (c. 1325/30), the work of master masons from the cathedral

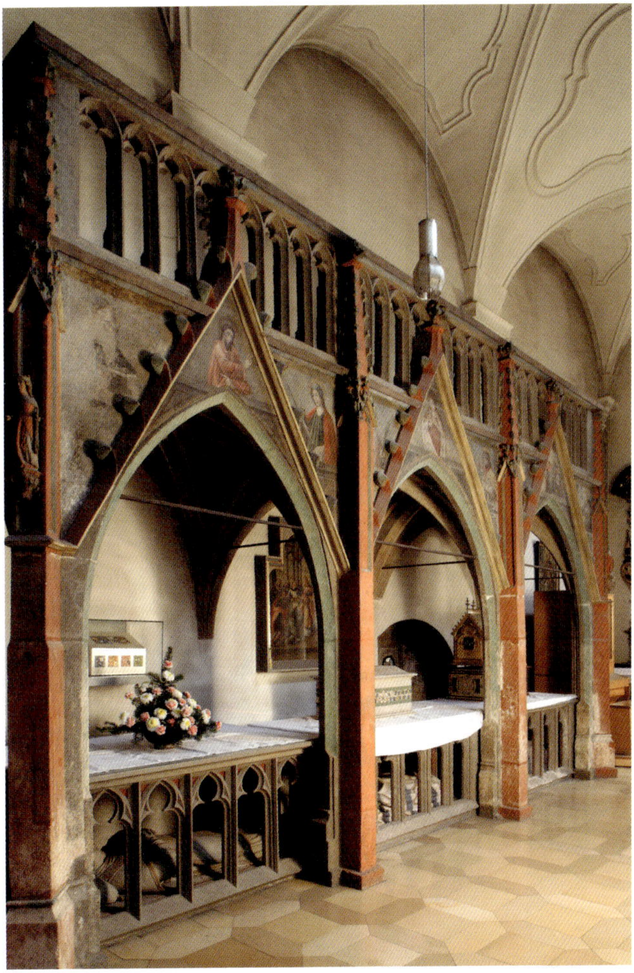

The ladies in the Lower Minster Convent could establish 'contact' with the saint by looking through the *fenestella* (little window) between the cloisters and St Erhard's grave.

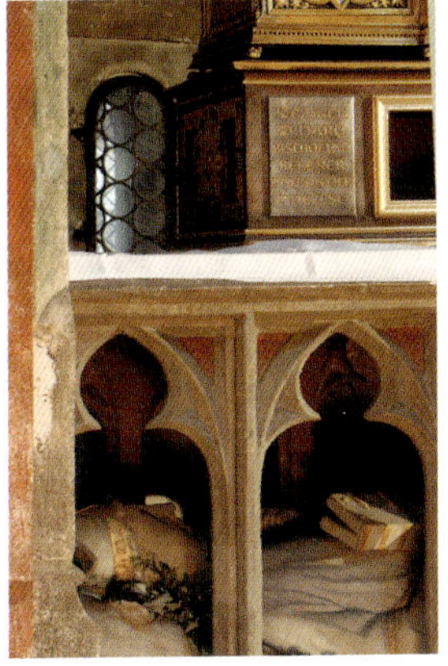

Opposite, on the north wall of the choir, are two excellent early baroque bronze sculptures showing, firstly, Christ Crucified and, secondly, the sorrowing Mary Magdalene; they were executed by Georg Petel (c. 1630). Originally, the group stood in the middle of the church, beneath the chancel arch. The memorial for Duchess Judith, which was erected in 1631 under the organ loft,

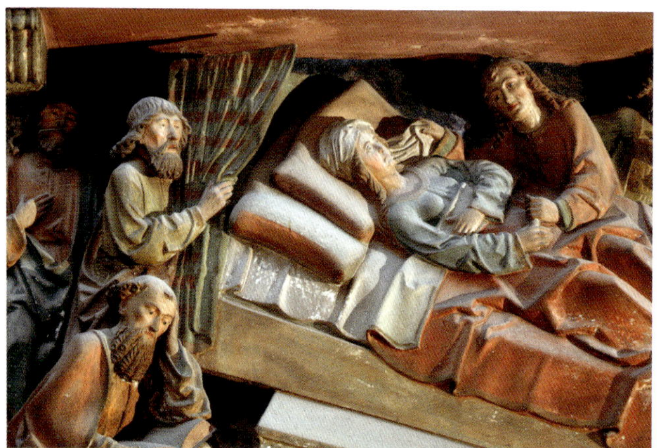

Lower Minster: relief showing the Virgin Mary's death (c. 1430) on the south wall of the choir

belongs to the same period. The convent's founder, who died in 986, is portrayed lying on the lid of the sarcophagus, recalling the figures on mediaeval tombs.

Archaeological Basement

From underneath the organ loft, it is possible to gain access to the remains of the previous buildings on this site, which were excavated in the 1960s. Thanks to suitable preparation by educational specialists, visitors can here – in an area measuring about 600 m² – experience the history of settlement on this spot, from the days of Roman soldiers' barracks, to the time of the Great Migrations and to the series of ecclesiastical buildings here, ranging from those in the 7th century up to the present-day romanesque minster.

From the minster it is only a few metres to Alter Kornmarkt, the former grain market. A short diversion leads through Pfluggasse into Erhardigasse, which, following the course of the Roman *via sagularis,* leads northwards along the wall of the legionary camp. The buildings along this narrow street are all closely linked with the history of the minster. Apart from the towering choir of the convent church on the west side of the street, the **Erhardi-**

kapelle/St Erhard's Chapel (7), is the most remarkable building. Hidden behind a neo-romanesque porch furnished with original sculptures from the cloisters of the Schottenkloster (Scots' Abbey; see p. 191) is one of the most mysterious sacred buildings in Regensburg. The small church, probably dating from the 10th century, which has a nave and two aisles, rests on slim pillars and was originally the ground floor of a two-storey construction. Near the chapel is the so-called St Erhard's Well, which, according to the first biography of the saint, written at the end of the 11th century, is supposed to have been dug by the holy man himself.

Returning to Alter Kornmarkt, one sees in Pfluggasse the north wall of the **Karmelitenkloster/Carmelite Monastery (8)**, which was founded by the Emperor Ferdinand II in 1634 to strengthen the Roman Catholic Church in the Protestant imperial city. The courts of the bishops of Bamberg and Freising had been located here in the Middle Ages. The laying of the foundation stone did not, however, take place until 1641, under Frederick III, and the building of the church was delayed until 1660. The facade of the church facing Alter Kornmarkt is similar to the facade designed by Ottaviano Mascherino for the order's mother church,

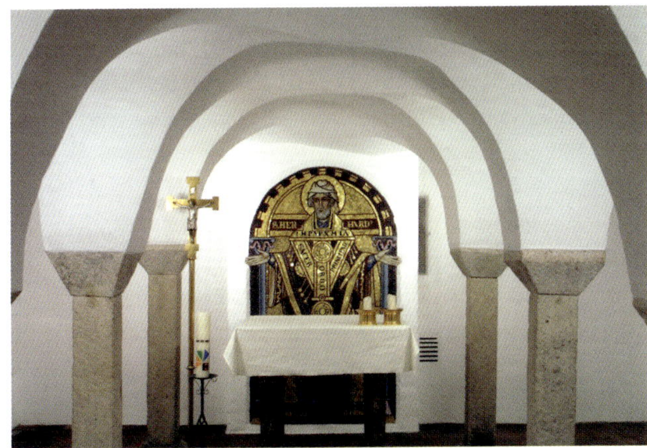

St Erhard's Chapel: the only part of the pre-romanesque Lower Minster complex to have been completely preserved. The decorations are neo-romanesque.

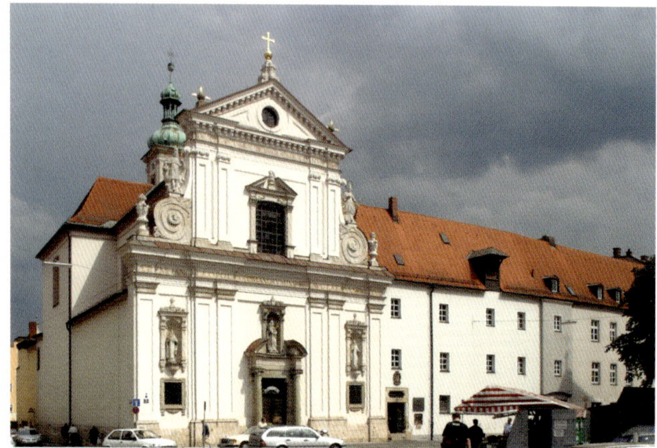

Carmelite church and monastery, built in the 17th cent. at the emperor's instigation, but to the displeasure of the Protestant imperial city.

S. Maria della Scala, in Rome. The monastery was dissolved in 1810 but was then re-founded by King Ludwig I in 1836, after which the church, which had been stripped of its furnishings, was furnished with baroque altars from other Regensburg churches. The high altar (1701) and the two altars in the transept (1624–27) came from the Cathedral, the altars in the side chapels from St Cassian's and from the Augustinian Church, which had been demolished in 1838.

Looking across Alter Kornmarkt from the Carmelite Church, one sees the **Herzogshof/Ducal Palace (9)** and the so-called **Römerturm/Roman Tower (10)**. The two buildings formed the north-eastern part of the Carolingian palace, which was occupied by the Bavarian dukes from 976 at the latest. After a major fire in the city in 1152, the buildings were greatly altered and extended. In 1196, members of the House of Wittelsbach moved into the palace and had it refurbished in imposing style. Thus, in about 1210, the massive residential tower was built on Carolingian foundations (Treasury). Later, the tower's huge stone blocks, which were reminiscent of those in the Roman walls, caused it to be referred to, misleadingly, as the Roman Tower. It consists of a really massive ground floor with a double wall made of granite blocks. Above it there rise four floors made of rough-hewn stone with blocks at each corner. The Roman Tower was the only residential tower in Regensburg whose upper floors could be heated.

The arch that links the tower with the ducal palace on the other side of Domstrasse dates from 1937, although it replaces an older crossing.

The present-day palace also results from a modernisation of the building undertaken by the Wittelsbach rulers in the early 13th century, although its appearance again changed greatly in 1936–40. After the western sections of the building had been demolished, all that remained of what was once a palace with four wings around a central courtyard was the palace hall. This, too, suffered major changes when part of a wall was knocked

The Ducal Palace and the so-called Roman Tower (early 13th cent.) were part of the Bavarian dukes' palace and are now also the Bavarian state's oldest surviving grand public buildings.

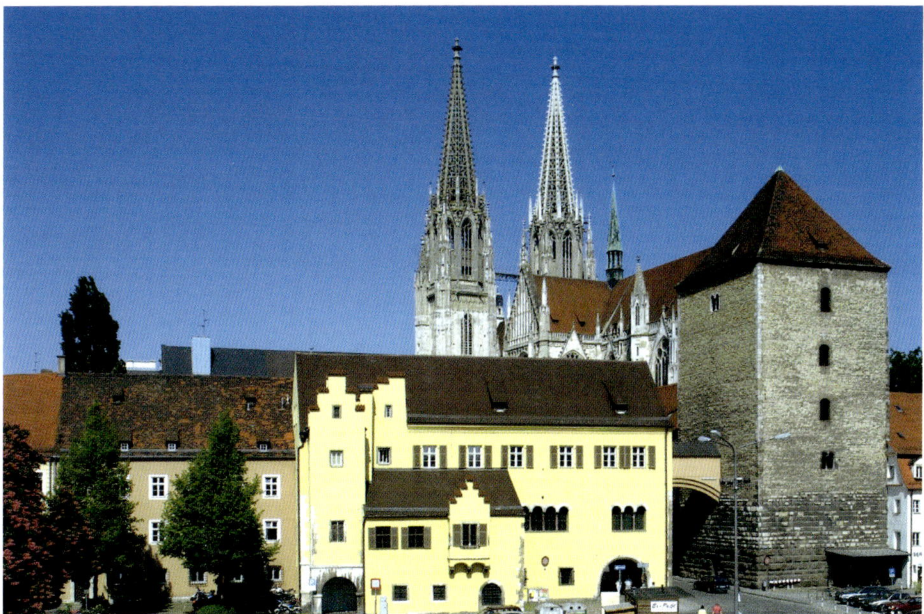

down to make a pedestrian passageway and when new windows were installed. During the same period, on the other hand, the ballroom, the so-called Duke's Hall, on the first floor was extensively restored, thus regaining its original appearance. The wooden ceiling with its heraldic symbols is painted to show how it looked in the 13th century. The square choir in the chapel that adjoins the hall to the south abuts onto a small tower with a crow-step gable that rises from the east facade of the duke's palace. In the south wall of the chapel, there are two round-arched windows with another small window above them, an arrangement that is characteristic of romanesque chapels in Regensburg.

Alte Kapelle

The **Alte Kapelle/Old Chapel (11)** stands across the southern end of Alter Kornmarkt. The origins of this church dedicated to Our Lady are surrounded by legends, some of which even claim it to be Bavaria's mother church. What is sure is that the Emperor Ludwig the German (826–876) had it rebuilt as his palace chapel, employing Roman building materials. He set up a collegiate foundation for the church, which has continued to exist ever since – nowadays the only surviving one from Carolingian times. The church quickly became dilapidated once, at the end of the 9th century, the palace had been moved to a site near St Emmeram's (see p. 138) under the Emperor Arnulf of Carinthia. By 976, what was now called the 'Old Chapel' was regarded as unsafe, but then the Emperor Henry II, a strong supporter of the collegiate foundation, had it fully renovated in 1002. It is not clear whether he oversaw the building of a new church or simply a complete refurbishment. Instead of the original central apse, this Carolingian-Ottonian basilica had a massive chancel added to it in 1441–52, donated by the Count Palatine Johann von Neumarkt. In 1747, in preparation for the 750th anniversary in

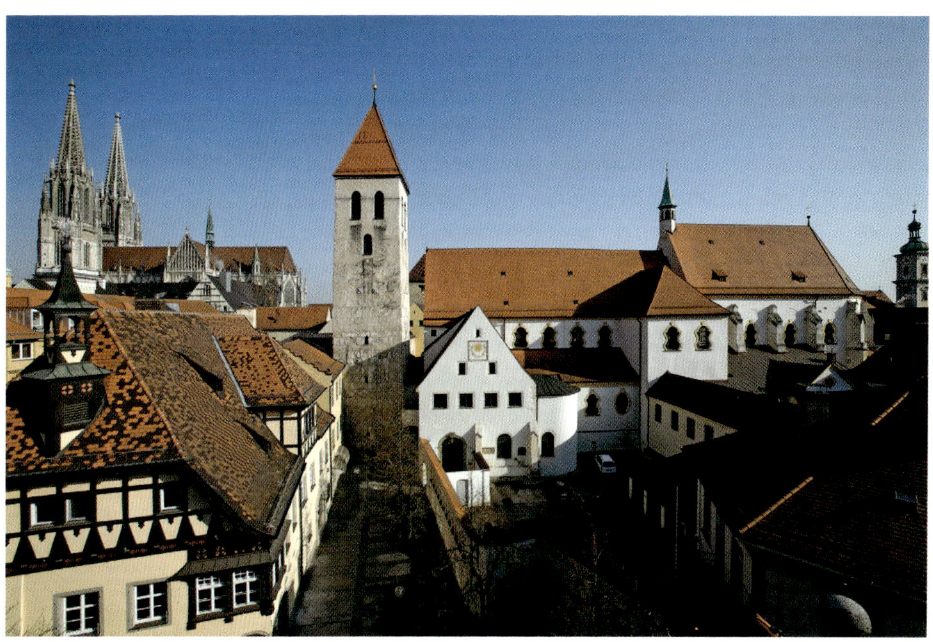

The Old Chapel from the south. As was usual with early mediaeval churches in Regensburg, it had a free-standing belltower.

1754 of the re-establishment of the collegiate foundation by the Emperor Henry II, work began on transforming the interior in the rococo style.

The Alte Kapelle is important for the history of mediaeval literature due to, of all things, love letters! In the early 12th century, the canons from the Alte Kapelle also used to teach female pupils at one of the two convents. From that time, some Latin verse has survived which the young girls and their teachers sent to each other. It includes expressions of affection, the first known love letters on German soil.

Exterior

From Alter Kornmarkt, it is easy to follow the historical development of the building. Right at the west end, there is the free-standing tower, which very probably goes back to the 9th century and which, in the Ottonian period and again in the 12th/13th centuries, had several storeys added to make a bell-tower. Blocks of Roman stone were used in its walls, just as they were used in the lower part of the walls of the Carolingian basilica that was renovated under Henry II. The basilica ends at the transept, which is only slightly wider than the nave. The high, late gothic chancel, which is broken up into sections by means of buttresses, is attached to the transept. The two very different sections of the building are formally connected by the line of windows shaped like bass viols, which allows one to anticipate the baroque unity of the interior, even from outside the church. The changes made in the 18th century are further illustrated by the facade with the porch and the main doorway (1752), which faces the square. In order to stress the venerable history of the building despite its 'modernisation', the baroque wall containing the doorway had mediaeval sculptures placed on it: a madonna holding a crown (c.1360/70), two flanking romanesque lions and, in the niches for figures at each side, two more romanesque sculptures whose original meaning is no longer clear.

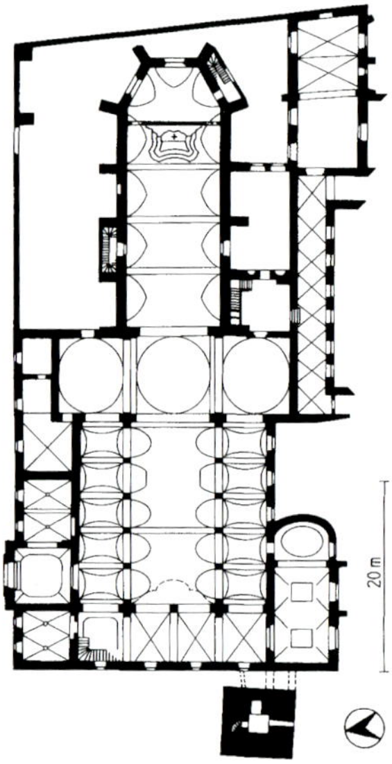

20 m

Interior

In the porch, one's glance falls on mediaeval additions on either side: to the left, the Vituskapelle/St Vitus' Chapel; built c. 1300, it was once the burial chapel of the Gumprechts, a patrician family, and later became the baptismal chapel for the collegiate foundation's parish. This use is indicated by a font (late 12th century), which was placed here later; a wooden madonna dating from 1270/80 is also noteworthy. On the west side of the porch, two windows allow one to look into a room that was once part of a two-storey chapel, but which has lost much of its historical atmosphere because it was hit by a bomb in 1944. This was formerly St Mary's Chapel 'sub gradu', i.e., it lay 'under the flight of steps' leading to St Erasmus' Chapel on the first floor. A tradition associated with the Alte Kapelle, but not documented until 1392, asserts that this tiny chapel dedicated to the Virgin is Bavaria's oldest church.

View of the choir of the Old Chapel. The late gothic building was refurbished in the 18th cent. and has one of Bavaria's most magnificent rococo interiors

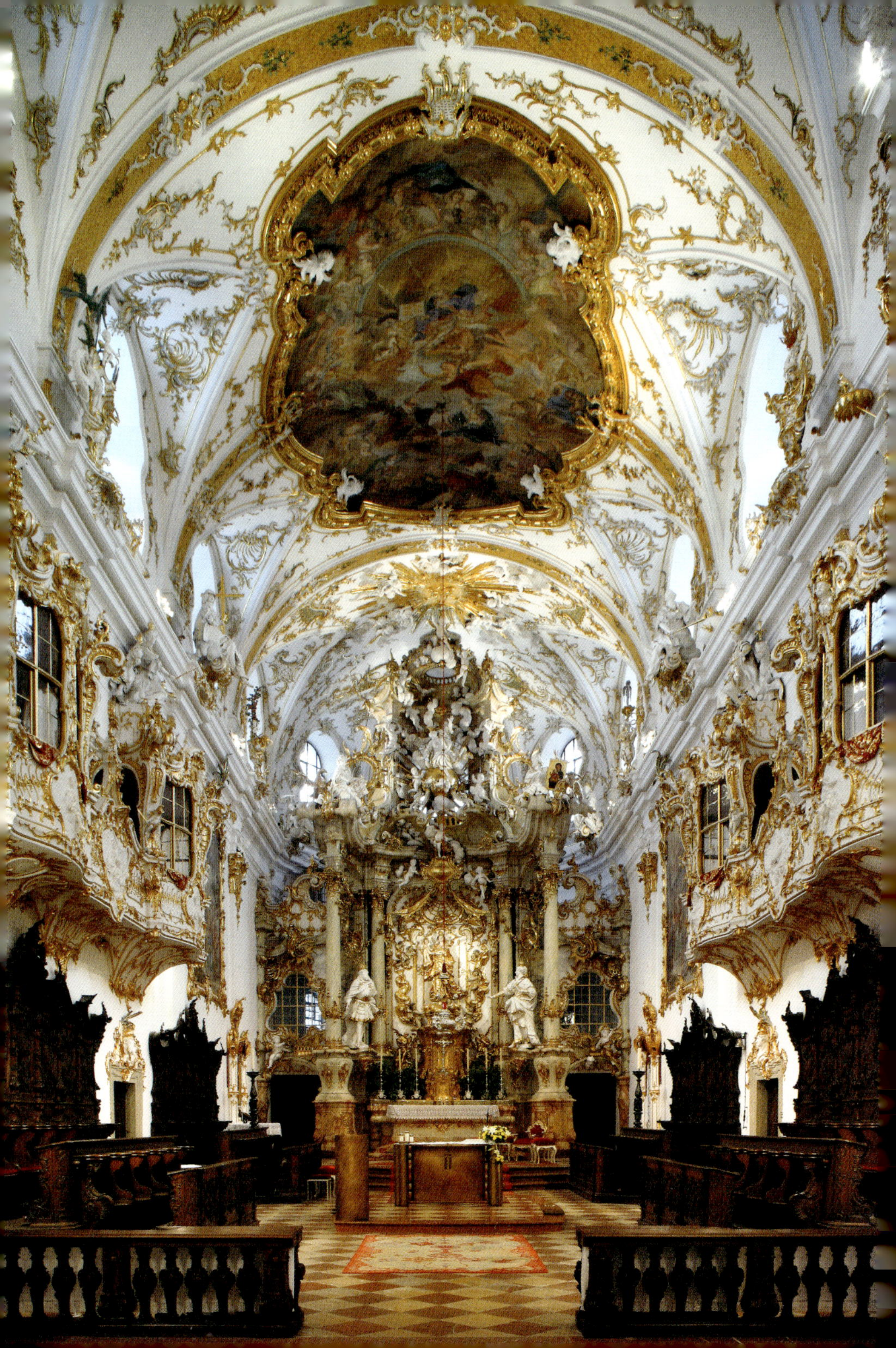

On entering the basilica, the visitor is overwhelmed by 18th-century magnificence. Yet, beneath the white and gold of the rococo, the nave and two aisles of the older pillared basilica with an east transept are still clearly perceptible. The wide nave is divided up into six bays, the westernmost one having been made wider so as to include the organ loft. To the east, the transept is followed by the four bays of the chancel, whose altar wall divides off the polygonal termination, which is used as the winter choir. Over the nave and chancel is a barrel vault with dormer vaults; the transept has shallow pendentives, the aisles flattened barrel vaulting.

Much as the 18th century respected the basic architectural ideas for the mediaeval structure of the building, it nevertheless evolved an extravagant brilliance regarding the details of the decoration in the church, a brilliance that was possible only then. A stucco specialist from Wessobrunn, Anton Landes, worked in the nave and the crossing and in the transept during the summers of 1750/52, and then in the aisles in 1754. The Augsburg artist Christoph Thomas Scheffler executed the wall and ceiling paintings in the nave and transept. The re-decoration of the chancel was not begun till 1761. By this time Scheffler had died, so now Gottfried Bernhard Göz, another painter from Augsburg, worked alongside Landes. In the year the latter died, 1764, the redecoration of the chancel reached its brilliant climax with the two double oratories, whose form seems to have been inspired by the splendid carriages of that time. They are adorned with magnificent reliefs (King David, St Cecilia, the cardinal virtues) and allegorical statues representing the four then known continents.

The frescoes further develop the by then twenty-year-old programme of decoration in St Emmeram's Church (see p. 151ff.), with the aim of achieving a more unified impression. On the walls of the nave here there are historical illustrations above every arcade – not just over every second one –, and the painted ceilings are all intended to be looked at from one angle. The content of all the paintings is designed to celebrate the collegiate foundation. The ten pictures in the nave show scenes from the lives of its founders, the Emperor Henry II and his consort Kunigunde, both of whom were later declared saints. On the other hand, the two frescoes on the ceiling of the nave refer to the foundation of the Alte Kapelle as 'Bavaria's Mother Church' and to the climax of its history, the bestowing of a miracle-working icon on Henry II by Pope Benedict VIII. The fresco in the cupola over the crossing shows the Virgin Mary as the Queen of Heaven; Henry and Kunigunde are included in the throng of saints surrounding her. This motif is then varied in the chancel fresco: as representatives of all earthly sovereigns, Henry and Kunigunde exchange their earthly crowns for the heavenly crown of eternal life on the Day of Judgement.

On the high altar, too, completed by Simon Sorg in 1776, St Henry and St Kunigunde appear as statues at each side, facing the Mother of God. Thus it is made clear that not only the programme of frescoes but also the sculptures in the basilica celebrate Henry and Kunigunde, above all. By this means, the 18th-century members of the collegiate foundation demonstrated its close links with the history of Bavaria and of the Holy Roman Empire.

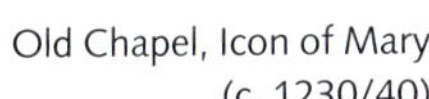
Old Chapel, Icon of Mary (c. 1230/40)

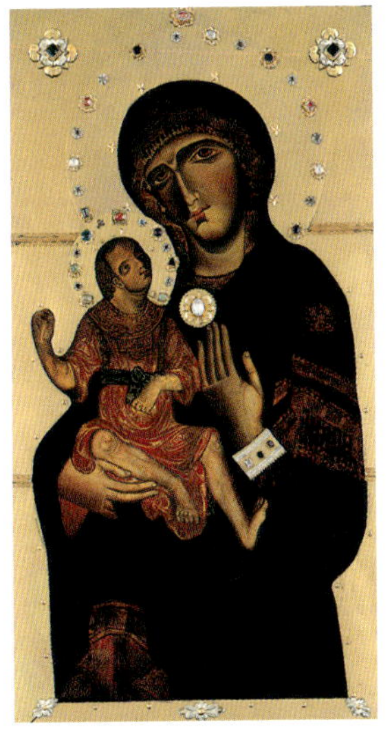

Chapel of Grace

A stepped portal (c.1200) in the south wall of the western bay of the nave leads into the Chapel of Grace. Originally dedicated to St James, the chapel was re-decorated in baroque style in 1693, when the miracle-working painting was placed there – it had previously stood on a side altar in the chancel. The picture, which, according to legend, was painted by St Luke, is a Byzantine icon of the so-called 'Dexiokratusa' type (Mary has her child on her right arm) and is said to have been a gift from the Emperor Henry II, who had received it from the Pope in 1014. In fact, however, the picture was not painted until c.1230/40, and it seems that the wooden panel was used in those days as the door of a small reliquary. In view of the painting's theme, it appears likely that this contained a relic of the Virgin Mary or an object connected with the worship of the Virgin. What is more, it is thus at least conceivable that this venerated object may have been the original icon donated by Henry II.

Romanesque tower house in Salzburgergasse; beside it, a Roman doorpost

If one leaves the Alte Kapelle via the Chapel of Grace and walks straight ahead through Kapellengasse, one reaches the street called Am Brixener Hof. After passing the site of the synagogue that was destroyed in 1938, one comes to the **Brixener Hof (12)**, a large house dating from the 11th century on the corner of Luzengasse. The Emperor Henry II presented the plot of land to Bishop Albuin von Brixen in 1002, so that the bishop and his successors would have somewhere to reside when they came to Regensburg for royal diets and similar assemblies. The property remained in the possession of the cathedral chapter in Brixen

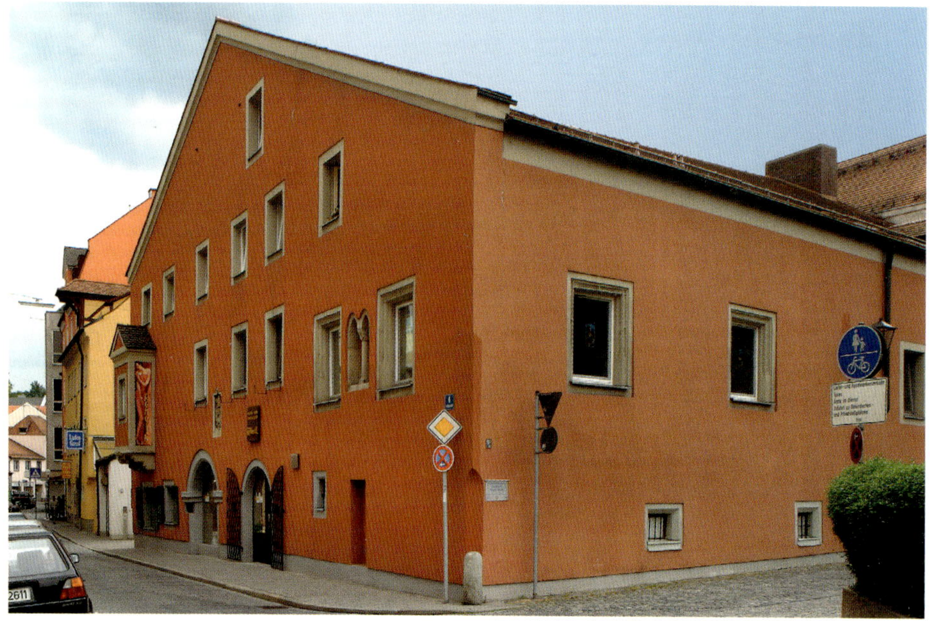

Brixener Hof, erected as the Bishop of Bressanone's residence in Regensburg in the early 11th cent.

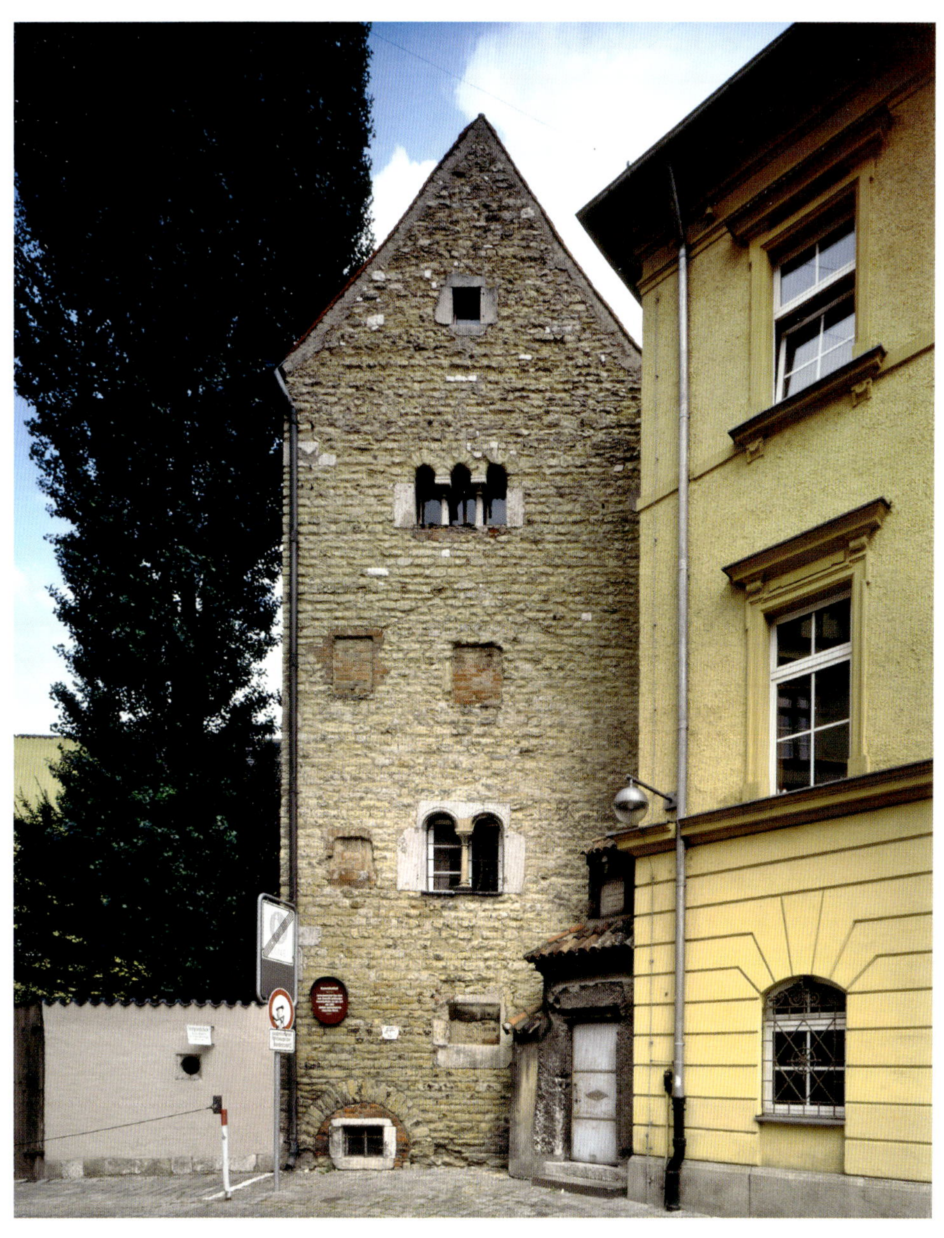

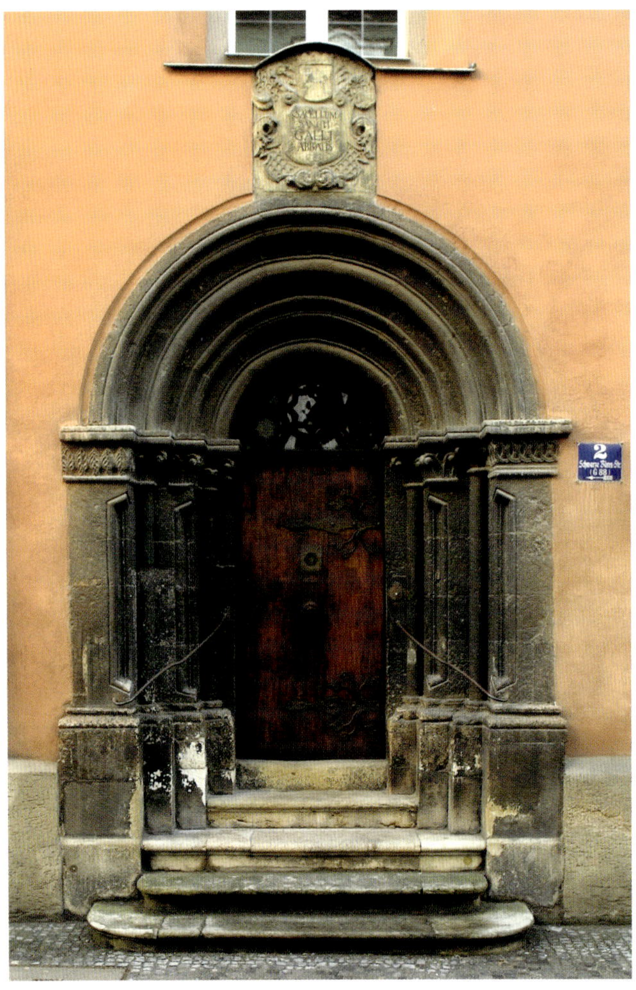

Former Ehrenfelser Hof; portal of the Gallus Chapel (c. 1210)

(Bressanone) until 1809. In spite of an extension added in the late 12th century, refurbishment in the late 15th century, and renovations of doubtful quality in 1969, the wide-fronted building with its low saddle roof is a good example of the high-mediaeval mansions used by visiting bishops, but is now the sole survivor of this type of 'court'.

Returning towards the Alte Kapelle, the route turns left into Schwarze-Bären-Strasse, which, in the high Middle Ages, was lined on both sides by these 'courts' occupied by church dignitaries. A short diversion into Salzburger Gasse is to be recommended. There, a Roman doorpost, which, when excavated, still stood upright in the ground, is now built on to the north side of No 1. Immediately next to that is a **romanesque tower house (13)**, which the dendrochronologists have dated at 1196. The building, which presumably used to be rendered, is in an excellent state of preservation and is impressive above all because of its considerable depth.

Back in the Schwarze-Bären-Strasse, one discovers at No 2, an 11th century cathedral canon's residence, the graduated round-arched doorway (c. 1210) of the former **Galluskapelle (14)**. This building, known as the Ehrenfelser Hof, was the home of Konrad von Megenberg, one of the most important scientists of his day. He lived here from 1348 until his death in 1374.

At the end of Schwarze-Bären-Strasse, one turns right into Pfauengasse and returns to Domplatz. Here, No 6, **the former residence of Prince-Bishop Dalberg (15)** is basically a gothic mansion – even as regards its roof structure – which Joseph Sorg converted into a residence for the cathedral provost in early neo-classical style between 1795 and 1800.

The arms of Joseph Carl von Lerchenfeld, the provost who commissioned the building, appear in the tympanum. Carl von Dalberg, Imperial Arch-Chancellor and Prince-Bishop, resided here from 1803–10. A plaque under the balcony recalls that Napoleon set up his headquarters here on April 24 and 25, 1809.

The **Collegiate Church of St John (16)** stands at the northern end of Domplatz. It developed from the originally north-south-oriented baptistry attached to the Carolingian cathedral. A foundation for Augustinian canons was established here in 1127; in 1290 this was turned into a collegiate foundation which still exists today. In the course of the construction of the gothic cathedral, the Carolingian church had to be demolished because it was in the way and a new church was built in 1380/81. With the exception of the tower, this building was completely renovated again in the 1760s, so that it now presents itself as a late-baroque hall church. Only fragments of the once extensive frescoes (1768) by Johann Nepomuk Schöpf from the royal court in Munich have been preserved, or have been revealed again, due to a fire in 1887. Schöpf was also the creator of the painting on the high altar (baptism of Jesus, 1769). The most important work among the church's fairly heterogeneous furnishings is Albrecht Altdorfer's painting of 'The Beautiful Madonna' (c. 1520; original in the Diocesan Museum) on the south wall of the chancel.

The complex of buildings directly north of St John's is the **Bischofshof/Bishop's Palace (17)**. It consists of four wings around a central courtyard and dates back to the early Middle

Former residence of Prince-Bishop Carl von Dalberg, created in the late 18th cent. when two mediaeval canons' mansions were converted into the cathedral provost's residence.

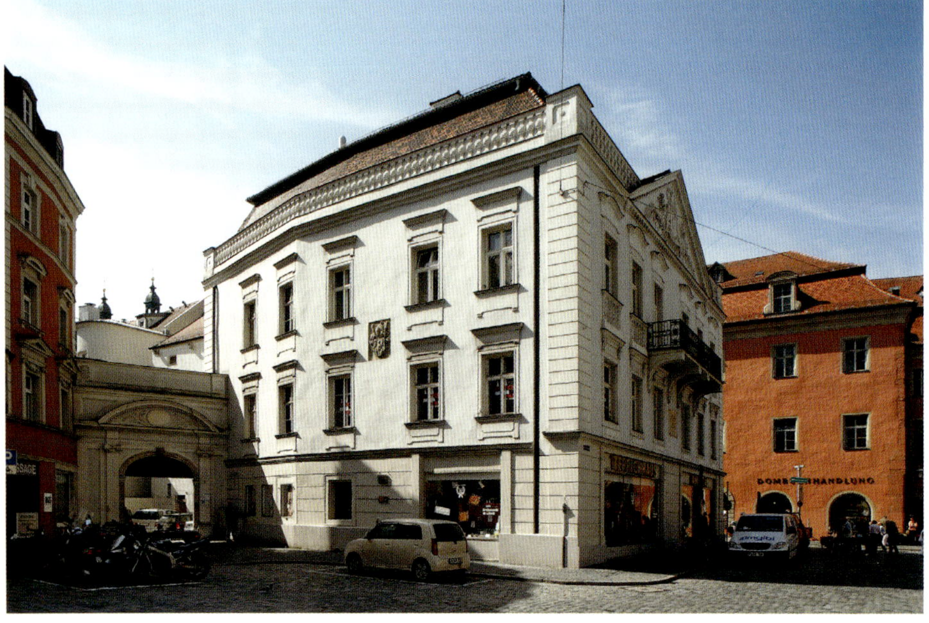

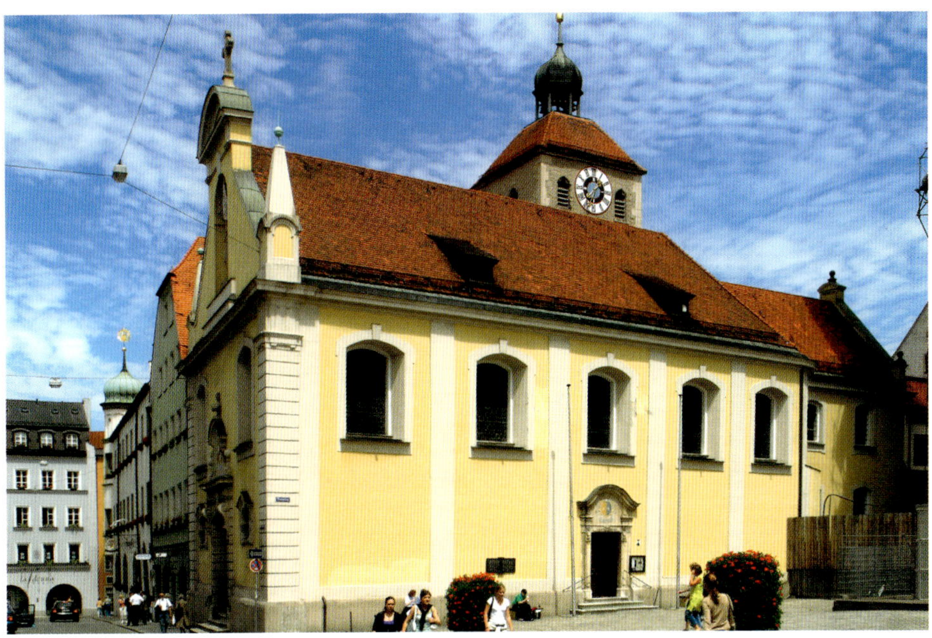

View of St John's Collegiate Church and Krauterermarkt

Ages. At that time a first episcopal residence developed. It included the Roman *Porta Praetoria* (see p. 24ff.); after the abandonment of the *Via Praetoria* and due to the need to accommodate the new buildings connected with the cathedral, the bishop's palace expanded further and further westwards. At the same time, the course of the walls of the legionary camp dictated the northern limit of the palace. After the fire in 1273, which also destroyed the cathedral, a new palace was erected, and further building work was carried out in the 15th and 16th centuries. In those days, the palace also provided accommodation for the emperor when he visited Regensburg. As a result of Secularisation (1803), the palace no longer needed to function as an official residence; after 1910, the complex was converted into a restaurant and hotel.

The oldest part of the complex is the east wing, which is still basically romanesque. It contained the so-called Emperor's Baths, which Albrecht Altdorfer decorated with wall-paintings in 1532

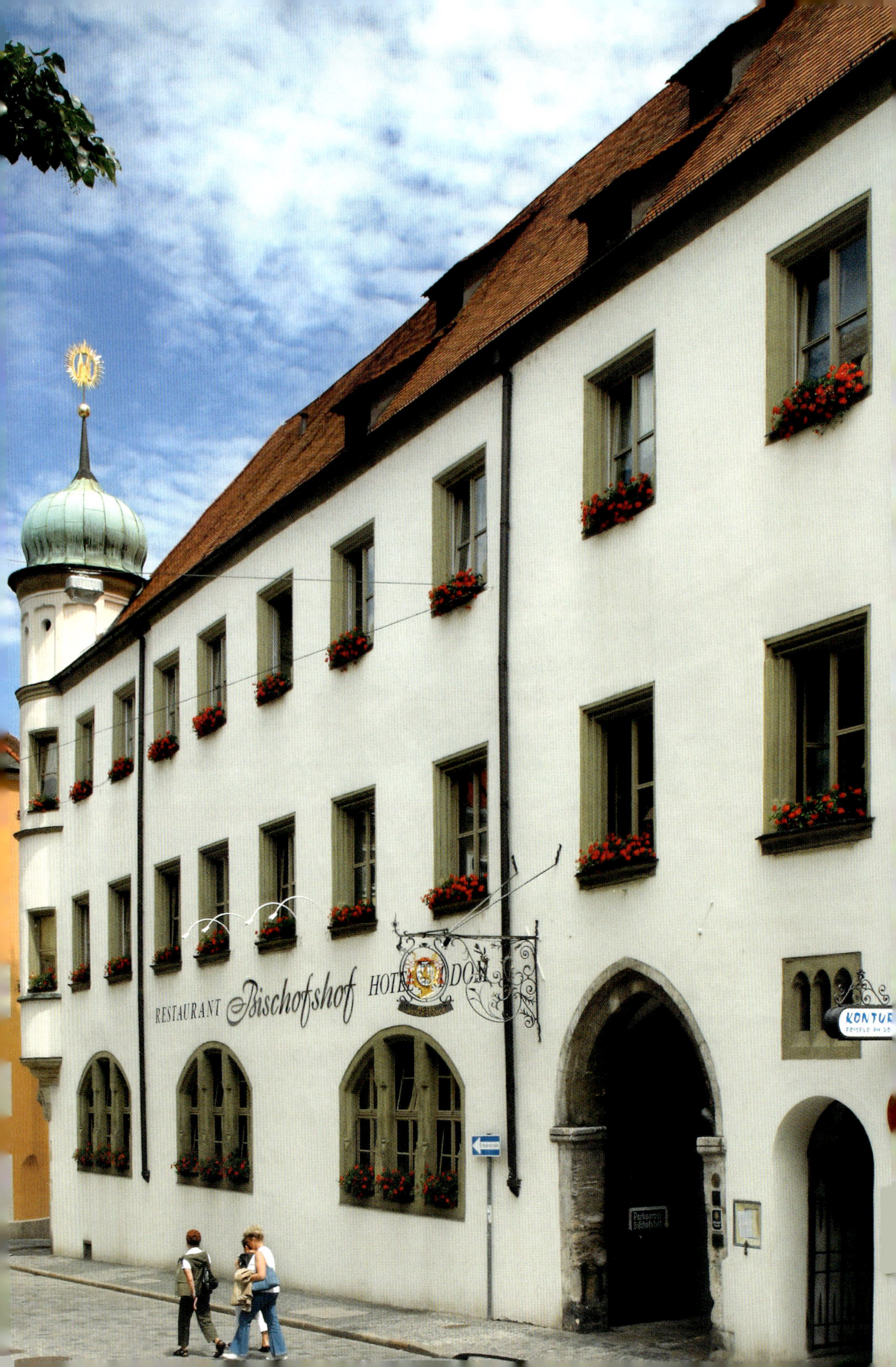
RESTAURANT Bischofshof
KONTUR

West wing of the former bishop's palace in Krauterermarkt. The early gothic doorway (c. 1230) survived when the palace was refurbished during the Renaissance.

or shortly afterwards. Nowadays, unfortunately, only a few fragments removed from the walls (most of them now in Regensburg's Museum of History) as well as the preliminary sketch preserved in the Uffizi Galleries provide evidence of these room decorations in Renaissance style. For his motifs, Altdorfer clearly relied on the frescoes by Romanino in the Castel del Buonconsiglio in Trento, which had just been completed.

The basic fabric of the north, south and west wings dates from the 13th–15th centuries, but they were later frequently altered. The conversion into a grand house in Renaissance-style, carried out by the Episcopal Administrator Johann, son of Elector Philipp von der Pfalz (1507–38), is still reflected in the three-storey, originally open courtyard arcades in the north wing. In contrast, the round tower with bay windows that characterises the outer north-western corner of the bishop's palace was added in the second major phase of modernisation in the 16th century under the direction of Bishop David Kölderer von Burgstall.

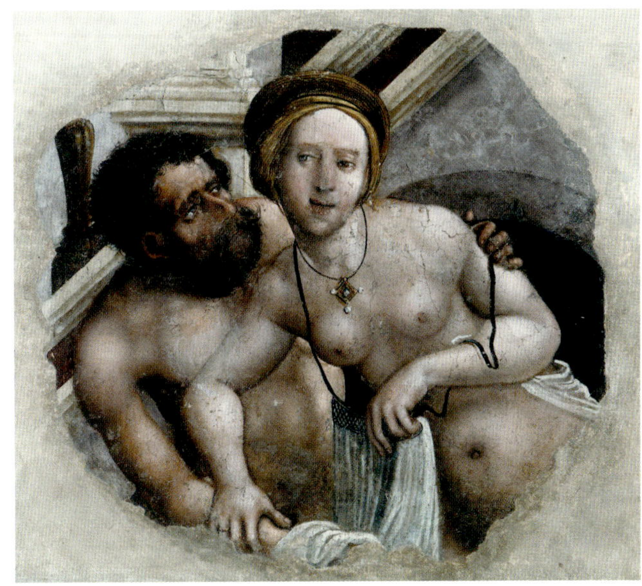

Fragment of Altdorfer's wall paintings in the so-called Emperor's Baths in the bishop's palace (Museum of Regensburg History)

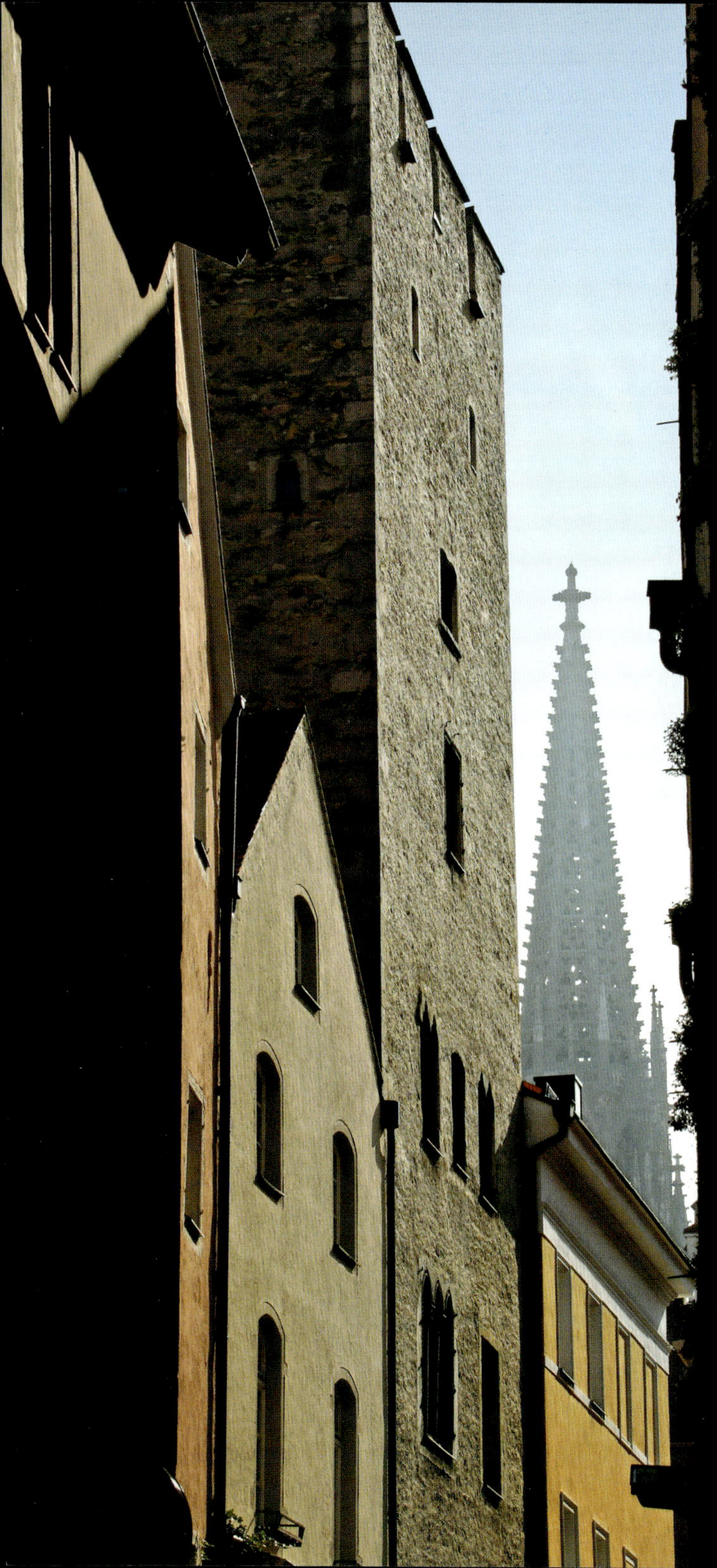

The City of Merchants and Burghers

From the early Middle Ages, merchants settled in the area to the west of the former legionary camp where the Roman civilian population had lived. Thanks to Regensburg's political significance, and to the efforts of bishops based here to Christianise the east, the conditions for the establishment of a trading centre of continental significance were ideal. Mainly due to its role as an entrepôt for luxury goods from Venice and Byzantium, furs from Russia and wine from Tyrol, the settlement outside the western wall of the Roman camp – this wall most probably existed until the 10th century – began to acquire the appearance of a town. Duke Arnulf of Bavaria had this *urbs nova* (New Town) fortified in about 920. This was the first extension to a town created anywhere north of the Alps. In the south, it included St Emmeram's Abbey and, in the north-west, reached as far as present-day Weissgerbergraben. By about 1200 Regensburg was the largest city in Southern Germany.

From the 12th century, the *pagus mercatorum*, the merchants' district, acquired its still characteristic architectural profile due to its stone-built merchants' and burghers' mansions, many of them with imposing towers. Comparable towns can be found only in Northern and Central Italy. A typical feature of secular architecture in mediaeval Regensburg is also the wealth of private chapels. Following the introduction of the Reformation in Regensburg in 1542, these rooms for private worship were de-consecrated. Many of them are now used as shops or restaurants and thus accessible for the general public.

Altes Rathaus

The starting point for this tour is the **Altes Rathaus/Old Town Hall (1)**. In 1213, there was a first attempt by Regensburg's citizens to build a town hall as an expression of their power in the city. At the behest of the bishop, however, the building which the duke had approved was pulled down even before it was finished. It was not until Regensburg was made a free imperial city in 1245 that it also acquired the right to govern itself at the communal level. For that purpose, appropriate

The seven-storey tower that belonged to the Loibl family is somewhat hidden away in Hinter der Grieb, but is extremely well preserved.

rooms were necessary and, above all, a large hall in which the city council could assemble. To that end, a site in the centre of the merchants' district was selected.

A tower dating from the mid-13th century and the building adjoining it to the west form the core of the group of buildings, which was gradually extended between the 13th and 18th centuries and which today still remains the seat of the city administration. Around 1325/30, a striking building containing a large hall was erected at the western end of the square: this was to become the preferred meeting-place for imperial assemblies. After 1594, these assemblies met exclusively in Regensburg – from 1663 until 1806 in the form of the Perpetual Imperial Diet, to which the emperor and princes sent permanent representatives. Gradually, this assembly of ambassadors acquired the form of a parliament for the estates of the empire. Together with Vienna, the emperor's chief residence,

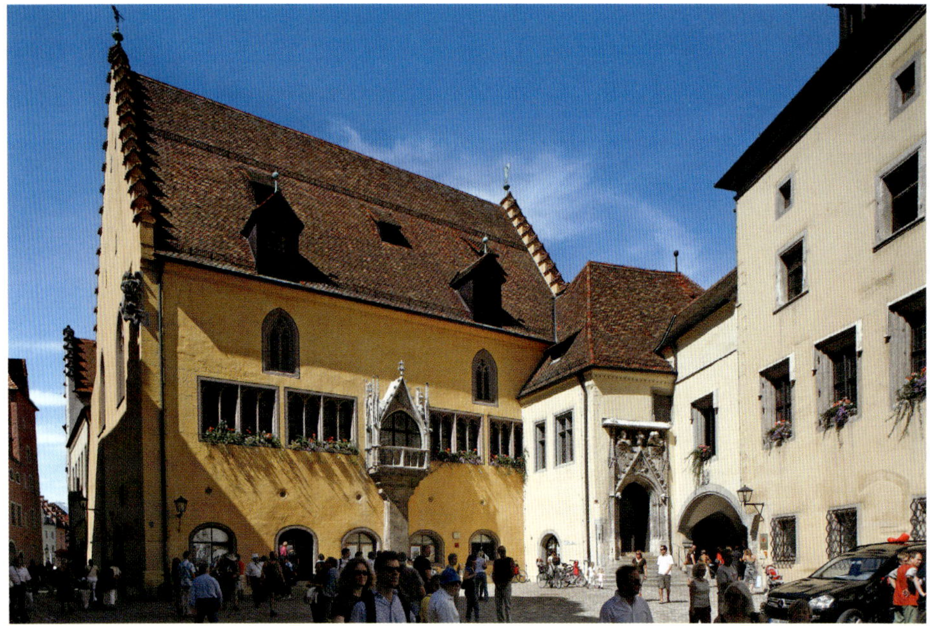

The group of buildings that make up the Old Town Hall. Right, the original 14th-century building; left, the hall erected in 1325/30. Adjoining this is the staircase with its decorative portal (1410/20) and an archway with a covered passage over it (1481).

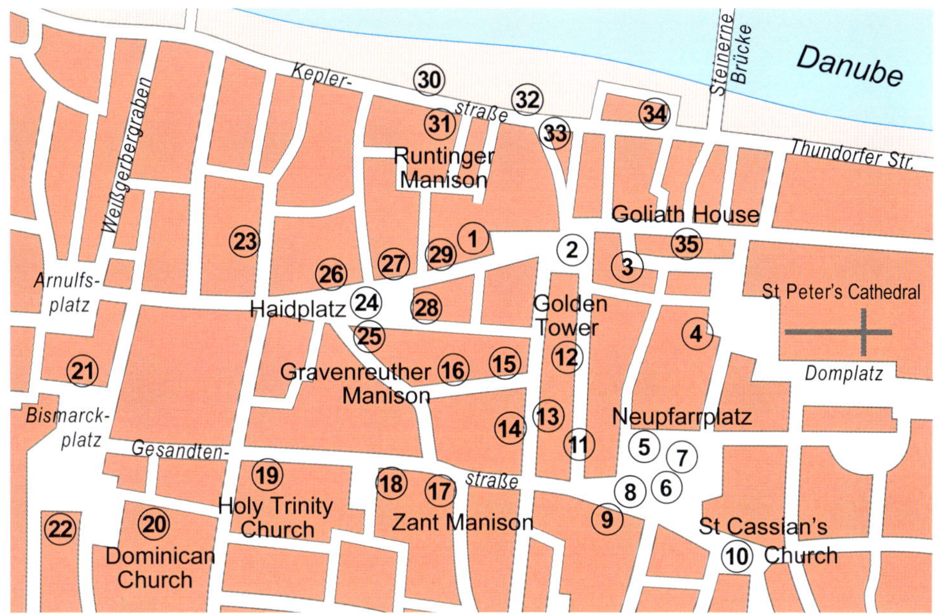

Regensburg became the most important political centre in the Holy Roman Empire.

Due to the increasing need for space for the Imperial Diet's staff, the city administration was squeezed out into the sections of the complex that lay further east, which led to extensive building operations there in the 17th and 18th-centuries. In this process, all traces were removed of Aha Church, first mentioned in 1002. It was entirely absorbed into the baroque town hall.

Imperial Diet Chamber Building (M)

The two-storey arrangement, with shops and courtrooms in the lower storey and a large hall on the first floor, reflects a quite widespread design for Gothic town halls. What is special about Regensburg's building is, above all, the oriel window which dominates the facade facing the square; it was erected about 1330 by

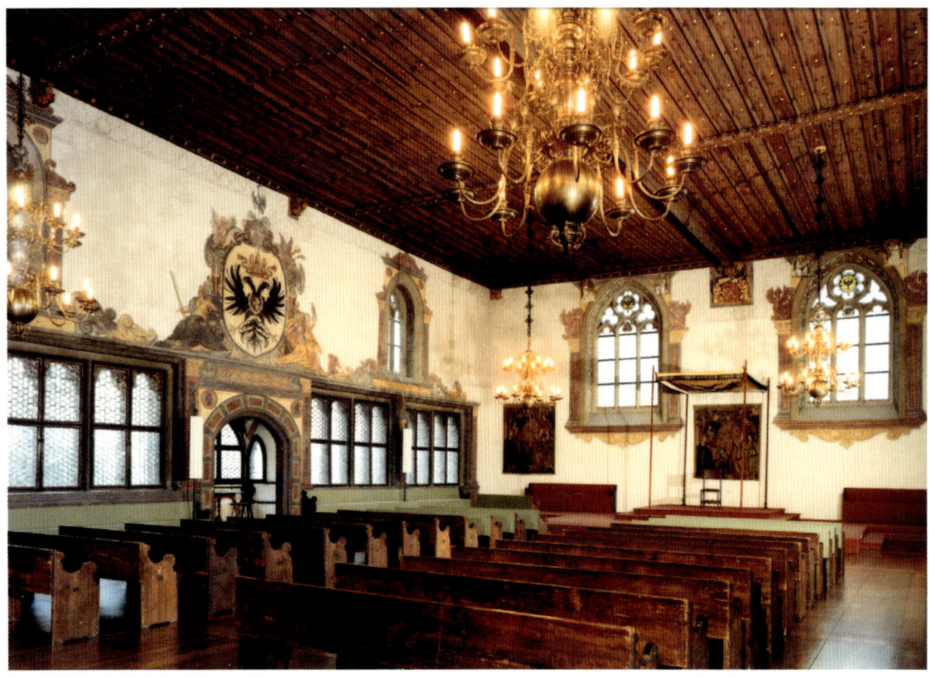

Old Town Hall: Imperial Hall. Originally intended as a venue for social functions for Regensburg's citizens, the hall was used for all imperial assemblies from 1594 and, from 1663 until 1806, for the Perpetual Imperial Diet.

masons from the cathedral workshop. Another link with the building of the cathedral came about a good hundred years later, when a new, free-hanging ceiling was constructed in the hall in 1446. The decision to do without any supports that would divide up the room, a feature which was so important for the appearance of the imposing hall, was made possible by taking over a new construction technique that had been developed a few years earlier for the roof of the cathedral nave.

Unlike the main facade, the two shorter side walls, which both have impressive crow-step gables, have not however retained, or have only partially retained their original appearance. Since 1564 at the latest, the entrance to the great hall has been in the north facade, which has had other buildings adjoining it since the early 15th century. The south facade, on the other hand, adjoined a gatehouse which closed off the market area to the west and was not demolished until 1611. Inside the gate was the chapel of St Simon and St Judas, consecrated by Pope Leo IX in 1052. Only after the demolition of the gatehouse did the facade acquire its second (western) traceried window, which was made identical to the existing one for reasons of symmetry.

Staircase and Portal

Only in the course of the 15th and 16th centuries was the building containing the Diet Chamber linked in several stages to the core building of the Town Hall. In 1481, for instance, an archway was built over the Gasse zum Roten Herzfleck, and then, in 1564, the approach to the Diet Chamber was made more imposing. For this purpose, a stairway was built leading to a hall on the first floor, although both of these – either for reasons of stylistic homogeneity or for the purpose of historical legitimation – were given a definitely archaic appearance despite the involvement of Renaissance architects. Thus, the decorative portal dating from 1410/20, with the allegorical figures of two watchmen 'Schutz' (Defence) and 'Trutz' (Defiance) was re-erected, and inside, a pseudo-gothic balustrade with tracery was built for the staircase.

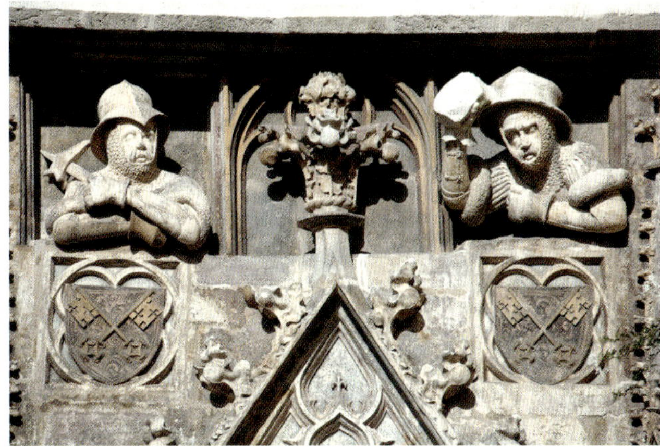

Old Town Hall: decorated doorway for the staircase into the Imperial Hall; two figures (nicknamed 'Defence' and 'Defiance') personifying the city leaders' readiness to defend their rights are the work of masons from the Cathedral (c. 1410/20).

Original Building and Tower

The eight-storey tower and, to the west, the adjacent building with three wings reflects the grand architecture favoured by Regensburg's patricians about the middle of the 13th century. It is conceivable that these two buildings were in fact erected for the purpose of impressing people. Typical of such an aim is the (now walled-up) loggia on the first floor of the tower. After a fire in 1360, the tower had been rebuilt by 1363. There was a further change in baroque days, when the present-day roof was constructed instead of the original battlements. The coachman's entrance leads into a courtyard which was open to the public; against its back wall is the Peace Well by Leoprand Hilmer (1661). The allegorical sculptures of seated figures at each side represent four allegorical Virtues and were originally to have been placed beside the portals of Holy Trinity Church (see p. 108ff.). They are the work of Leonhard Kern, a sculptor from Schwäbisch Hall (1630–32).

Baroque Town Hall

The south facade (1721/23), which develops strictly symmetrically between two corner projections with a rusticated base, has such a uniform appearance that one would no longer suspect that this eastern section of the Town Hall has such a complicated history. The central axis is emphasised by means of a pillared doorway with allegorical figures representing Justice and Wisdom on top of it; the rest of the decoration is painted on the facade. The same is true of the east facade in Zieroldsplatz, a small square; here the sculptures over the doorway represent two other Virtues, Fortitude and Moderation. In the idyllic arcaded courtyard, there is a fountain against the wall with a stone figure of Neptune by Leoprand Hilmer (1662). Nothing is visible of the important mediaeval buildings that once stood here – neither of the Market Tower, first mentioned in 1347 and burned down in 1706, nor of Aha Church, first

View across Kohlenmarkt to the Town Hall complex. Right, the building newly erected in the baroque period; behind it the tower (reconstructed after a fire in 1360) and part of the great hall (c. 1325/30).

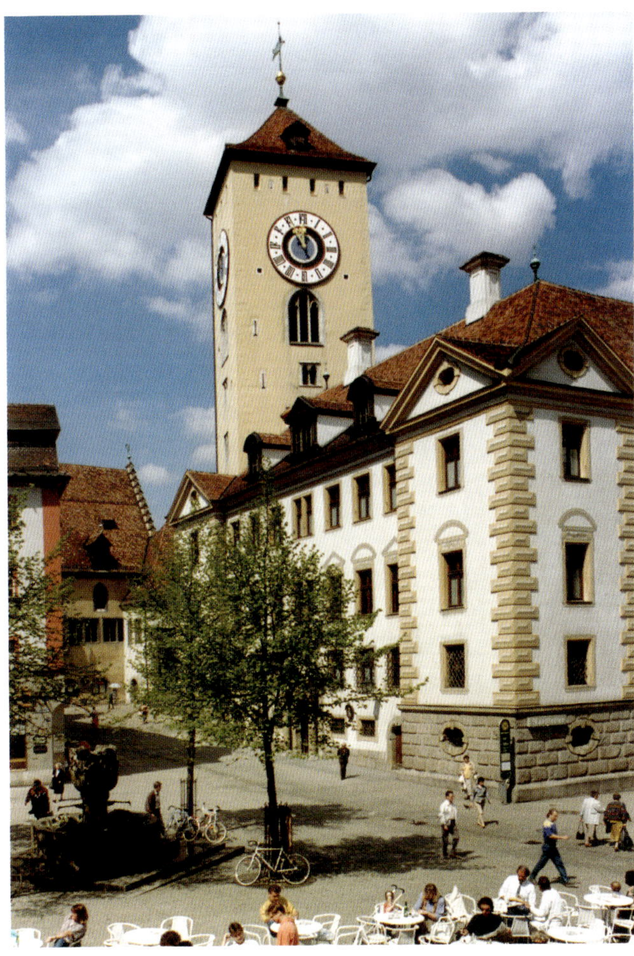

mentioned in 1002, which was dedicated to St Bartholomew. Its strange name is explained by its waterside position (*aha* meant water in Old High German).

To the east of Rathausplatz is **Kohlenmarkt/Coal Market (2)**. It evolved just outside the still traceable north-west corner of the Roman legionary camp. Goliathstrasse, running eastwards from here, marks the northern wall of the camp; Wahlenstrasse, running southwards, follows its western side. The square already played a central role in city life long before the year 1000. Its importance as a burial ground, proved to have been its function in late Roman and early mediaeval times, was limited in the high Middle Ages to the area around Aha Church (see above). In the 8th/9th centuries, major excavations were undertaken here to divert the Vitus Stream, which continued to flow through an open gutter till modern times. The square's use as a market is first documented in 934, and by about 1000, it already had some stone buildings.

Whereas the fountain by Günther Mauermann, which was placed here in 1984, picks up the tradition of the Market Fountain removed in 1780, the trees that were planted simultaneously represent a modern, urban feature.

The early gothic Baumburger Tower in Watmarkt. Erected in a conspicuous place in the city, it once had a loggia that opened out onto the street.

Looking south from Kohlenmarkt, one gets a good view of Wahlenstrasse and the Golden Tower (see. p. 102ff.). First, however, the route continues straight ahead, turns right at the corner of Goliathstrasse and goes slightly uphill into Watmarkt. Here one enters the area of the former legionary camp. The first thing that catches the eye is the seven-storey **Baumburger Turm/Baumburg Tower (3)**, one of the most impressive and best preserved towers built by Regensburg patricians. Erected in the third quarter of the 13th century, the tower has always remained the same height. The two-bayed room on the ground floor, now a restaurant, was once a private chapel. The balcony on the first floor is a later addition. Instead, there was once one of the open loggias that were characteristic of many of Regensburg's patrician towers. It was, however, as in all similar instances, walled up, for climatic reasons, before the end of the Middle Ages. The adjoining residential wing to the east dates from the 15th century.

Although some of the buildings on the north side of Watmarkt were extensively rebuilt between the 18th and

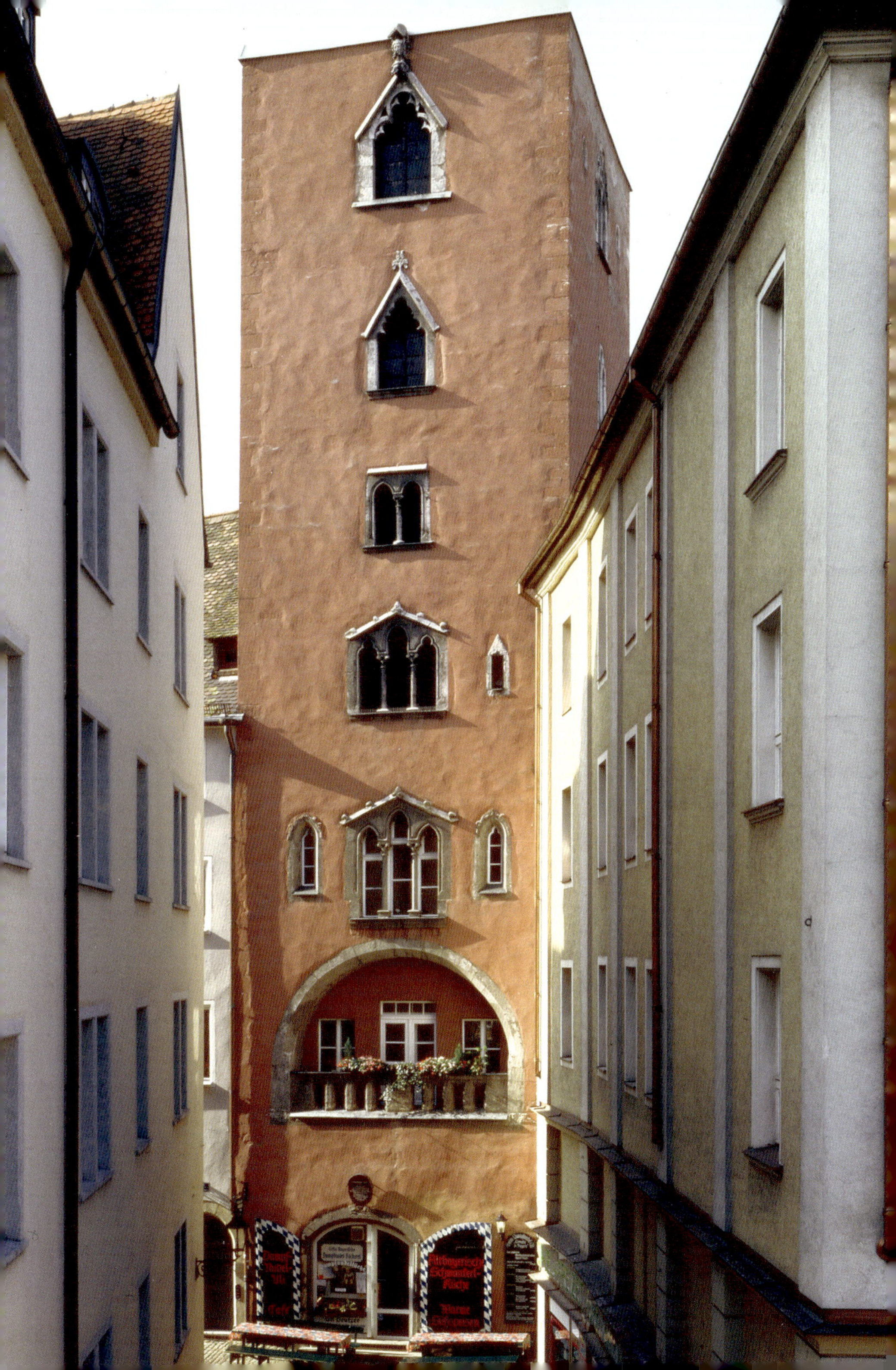

20th centuries, the alley once inhabited by cloth merchants and clothiers is still impressive because of all the patrician mansions in it. No 6 still has magnificent gothic masonry. It has a residential wing (c. 1320) on the corner of Tändlergasse and a tower (c. 1200) adjoining it to the east; the latter originally had six floors plus battlements, but these were removed when more storeys were added in the 17th century. Opposite, an elegantly structured oriel window on the south facade of the Goliathhaus (24) catches the eye. It was constructed in the early 14th century, when the previously existing loggia was walled up. No 7 was built in the 1250s, replacing a previous building that had burned down. Despite major changes in the baroque period, nearly all the masonry in all the storeys has survived. The trees whose wood was used for the ceiling beams and boards were felled in 1251.

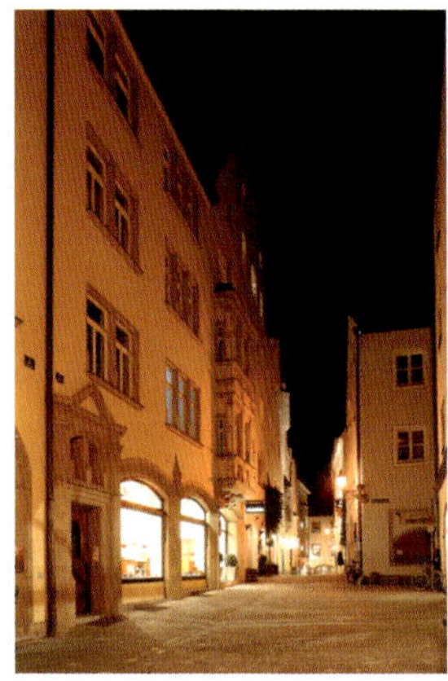

Despite major alterations in c. 1900, Watmarkt retains important examples of gothic patrician architecture and the character of a mediaeval street market.

At the end of Watmarkt is the more open Krauterermarkt, which, to the south, leads seamlessly into Domplatz. Where the two squares merge, opposite the majestic facade of the cathedral (see p. 44ff.), one finds the Imperial Fountain, the first of six similar fountains with which the imperial city of Regensburg expressed its confident view of itself in monumental form. A very ornate pillar in the centre of the hexagonal basin has, on top of it, a golden orb with an eagle sitting on it, the symbol of the emperor's global power.

Behind the fountain, forming the western end of Domplatz, is **Haus Heuport/Heuport House (4)**, an imposing patrician mansion, to which the building at the corner of Kramgasse (Hotel Kaiserhof) also used to belong. This northern section of the complex, which also includes the base of a late romanesque tower, dates back to the 12th century; the southern section was started about 1300. Whereas the striking row of gothic windows in the first storey was reconstructed in 1934, the unusual entrance arrangement from the early 14th century has been preserved. Access to the gothic banqueting hall on the first floor is via an open-air gothic staircase in the courtyard. On the right, next to the stairs, there is still a stone block with three holes in it, which were used for extinguishing torches. Climbing the stairs, one sees, on the left, two allegorical figures: a young girl expectantly faces a man, whose intention to seduce her is underlined by the apple he holds in his right hand. His back, however, which is concealed from the girl's view, is full of vermin. He is Satan personified.

From Krauterermarkt, one can enter Kramgasse, a narrow alley leading into the heart of a still completely intact mediaeval quarter. Nearly all the houses here still possess remarkable romanesque and gothic building fabric, some, even, still have traces of gothic fittings. This applies particularly to No 8, which looks virtually as it did in the 14th century, thanks to the recent reconstruction of its decorated facade on the basis of expert findings. At the end of the right-hand row of houses, on the corner of

The Heuport Mansion originally included the two parts of the building now painted in different colours. The name recalls the former Hay Gate, which once lay south of it and led to the Jewish ghetto; it is also a reminder of the hay market held in front of it.

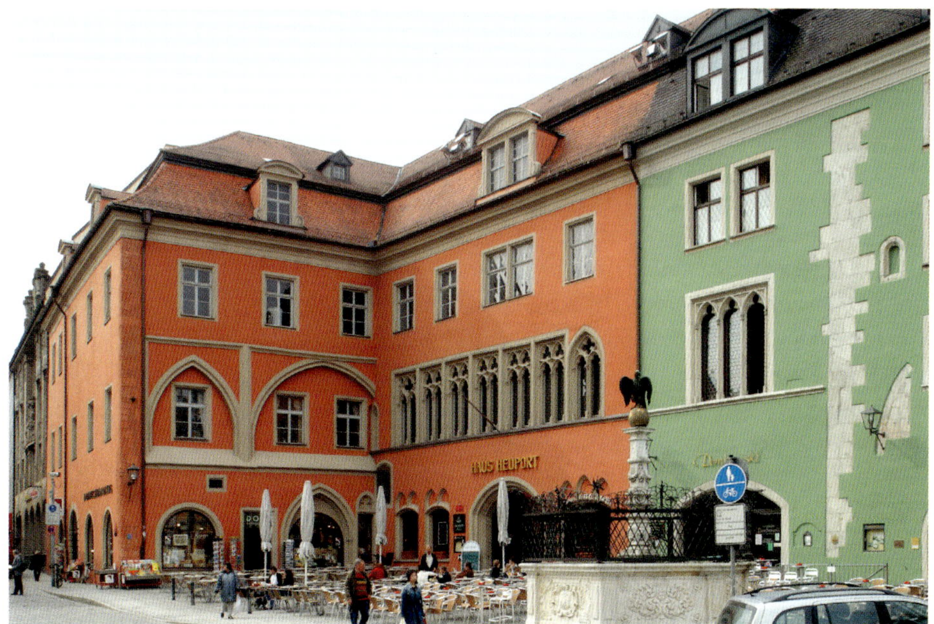

Tändlergasse, are the remains of a gothic tower belonging to No 1 Tändlergasse. The part of the building facing Kramgasse was the birthplace in 1547 of the illegitimate son of the Emperor Charles V and Barbara Blomberg, the daughter of a Regensburg craftsman. As Don Juan d'Austria, this child was to be the victorious commander of the Christian fleet at the battle of Lepanto against the Turks in 1571 and would thus go down in history as the saviour of Western civilisation.

The route now leads left into Tändlergasse, at the end of which one enters, quite suddenly, a large, open square.

Neupfarrplatz came into being when the ghetto was destroyed in 1519 and is now dominated by Neupfarrkirche, the New Parish Church

Neupfarrplatz

Neupfarrplatz (5) seems completely out of place in the otherwise mediaeval city layout, not only because several of the buildings in it are modern but also because of its straight sides, which do not seem to reflect organic growth. In fact, this square did not develop naturally in the course of history, but was, rather, a piece of open land created by the destruction of the Jewish ghetto in 1519. Only the houses facing on to the south side, which were no longer part of the ghetto, are of mediaeval origin, although here, too, the facades date from later periods.

Although the existence of Regensburg's Jewish community is first documented from the third quarter of the 10th century, its history certainly goes back further. The main evidence of this is the fact that the Jews, who normally had to settle near the city walls, had their district within the Roman walls, which ceased to form the city boundary in 920. Enjoying the protection of the duke, the king and, from the 13th century, the imperial city, the Jewish community in Regensburg was able to develop in relatively peaceful fashion.

Not until the mid-15th century did Antisemitism increase perceptibly due to the city's economic decline. Anti-Jewish feeling reached it regrettable climax in 1519, when the Empire's Jews no longer had a protector for a while after the death of the

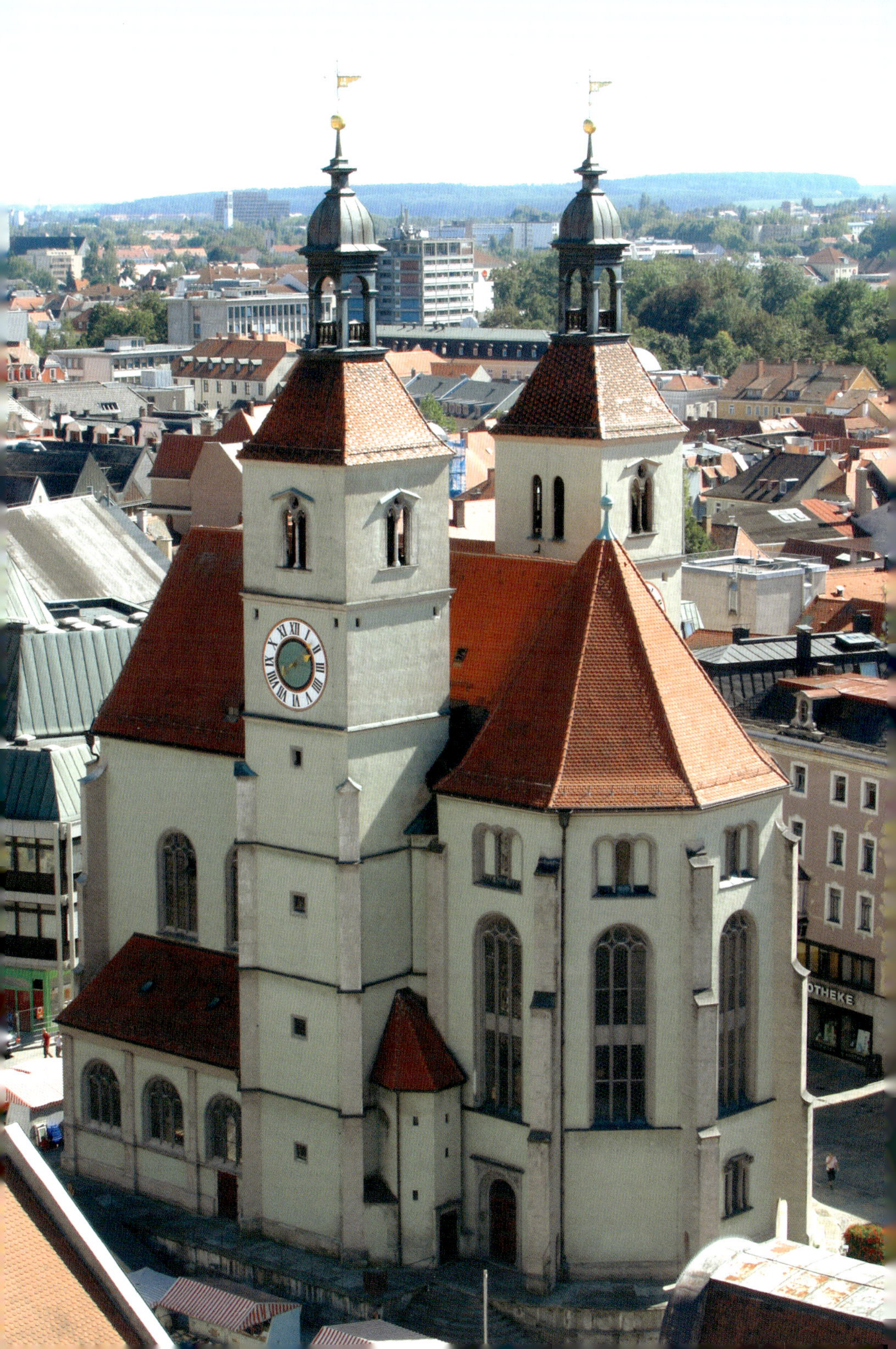
OTHEKE

Emperor Maximilian I. The city council immediately decided to expel them as well as to destroy the synagogue and the entire ghetto. In order to make this decision irreversible, the temporary recovery of a workman who had had been seriously injured during the demolition of the synagogue was represented as a miracle and ascribed to the Virgin Mary. Symbolically, a chapel dedicated to the Virgin was erected on the ruins of the synagogue in March 1519 already, and this became the destination for a quickly increasing stream of pilgrims. People flocked here from all over Europe to worship the 'Beautiful Madonna of Regensburg'.

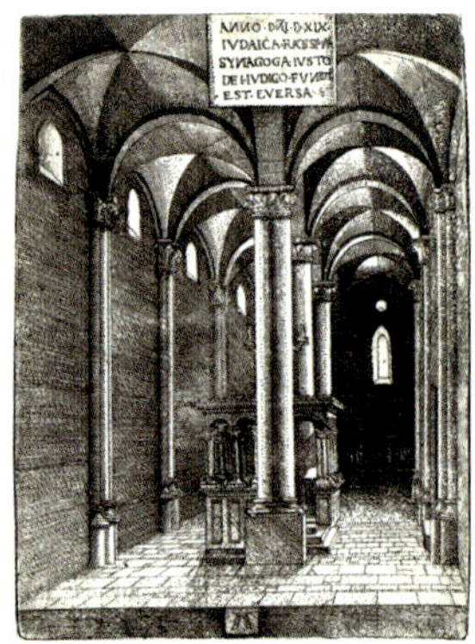

The interior of the synagogue was portrayed by Albrecht Altdorfer just before its destruction on Feb. 21, 1519 (etching, Museum of Regensburg History).

Pilgrimage Church of the Beautiful Madonna – New Parish Church

As a result, the city council laid the foundation stone for a magnificent pilgrimage church in September 1519. The present-day **Neupfarrkirche/New Parish Church (6)** represents what was realised of that ambitious project. According to the model in the Museum of Regensburg History made by the Renaissance architect Hans Hieber from Augsburg, the long choir at the west end, which is flanked by two towers, was to have been adjoined by a huge hexagonal building, which, as the true centre of the pilgrimage, would have housed the miracle-working picture. However, after just a few years, the number of pilgrims fell rapidly owing to the influence of Lutheran doctrine; thus the source of finance for the ambitious project also dried up. The choir was consecrated in 1540 and the west end of the building provisionally completed. When Regensburg's city council decided to convert to the Lutheran faith in 1542, this torso became the city's first Protestant church. Not until 1860–63 did the Munich architect Ludwig Foltz construct the choir at the west end, thus achieving an aesthetically satisfying conclusion to the long and varied history of the church's construction.

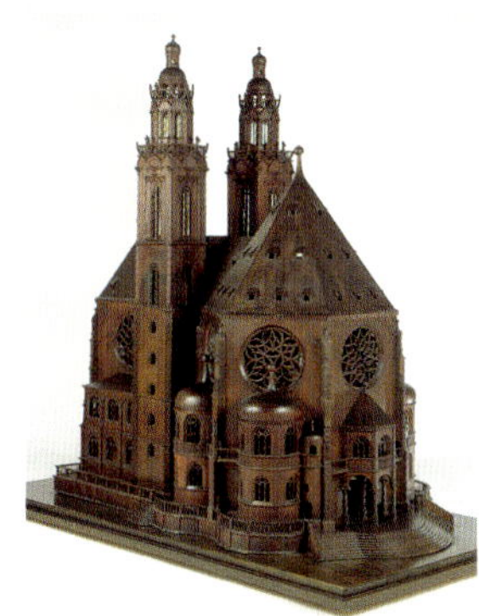

Model of the Pilgrimage Church of the Beautiful Madonna (c. 1521, Museum of Regensburg History), revealing the enormous size of the building planned by Hans Hieber.

Exterior

Like the cathedral, the church stands on a high base that runs all around it. The choir, which is closed on three sides and has stepped buttresses, still owes a lot to late Gothic tradition, although the large, round-arched traceried windows show signs of Renaissance influence. Its modern ideas, as a comparison with the model indicates, would have been realised primarily in the central-plan building, which was never erected. And the extensions flanking the choir, and the towers, too, were executed only in a very reduced and largely conventional form. It remains uncertain whether the four early gothic biforium windows were re-used in order to save money when the north tower was provisionally completed in 1595, or whether these were, so to speak, trophies from a demolished Jewish house. At all events, Foltz had similar windows built in to the south tower when he completed it. Moreover, he designed identical helm roofs for both towers. Foltz also followed the principle of stylistic appropriateness when building the west choir.

Interior

Because of the absence of the west end and because of the considerably reduced size of the side chapels, it is hardly possible to say what impression Hieber wanted the interior of his church to make. The architect's creative ideas can be judged only through details such as the unusual capitals on the hemispherical wall columns or the double-helix spiral staircase in the south tower.

The high altar designed by Albrecht Altdorfer for the pilgrimage church was never realised, and the winged altar created by Michael Ostendorfer after the change of denomination in 1553–55, of great interest because of its Protestant programme of images, now stands in the Museum of Regensburg History. Today, the church has a simple baroque pillared retable with a painting of the Crucifixion by Johann Hermann Wiwernitz (c. 1650).

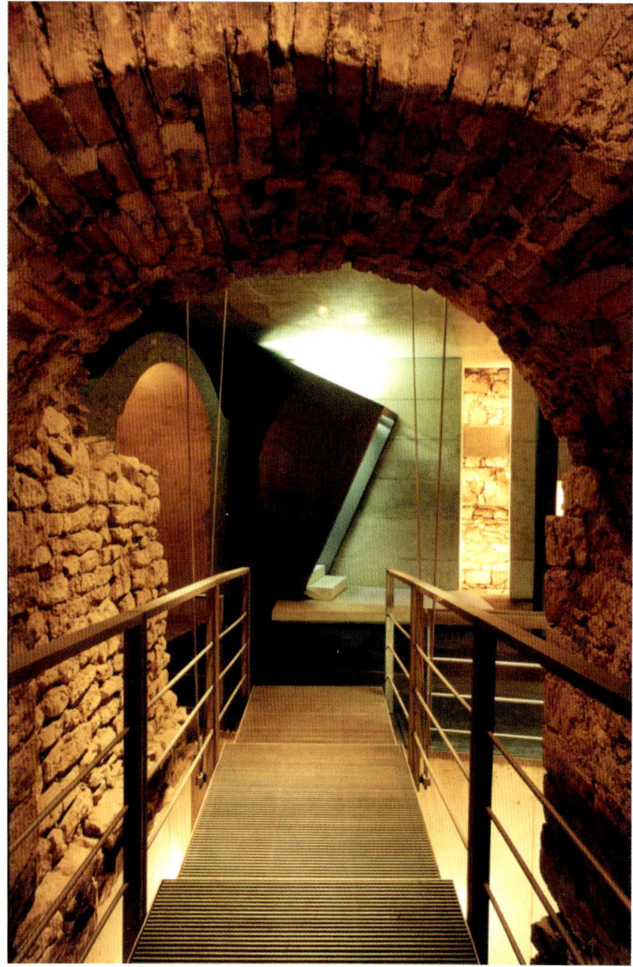

'*document* Neupfarrplatz', an instructive exhibition, relates the history of Neupfarrplatz through its archaeology.

North of the church is the entrance to the so-called ***document* Neupfarrplatz (7, [M])**, an underground archaeological display that was created during excavations from 1995–2001. Access to some of the cellars in the mediaeval Jewish quarter is again possible. Furthermore, some stretches of Roman wall, as well as a ring bunker dating from the National Socialist period, have been exposed, so that the very special historical narrative hidden here beneath more than 6 metres of cultural rubble is now revealed to visitors.

At the west end of Neupfarrplatz, where the central-plan nave of the pilgrimage church was to have stood, passers-by can walk around a **relief (8)** set into the paving stones to show the ground-plan of the destroyed late gothic synagogue beneath. The relief shows that the building had a nave and one aisle, separated by three columns. The synagogue was constructed, using fabric from its smaller predecessor, along the lines of the synagogue in Worms, and acted in turn as the model for the building of the Altneuschul in Prague and for the second Viennese synagogue.

In 1995, when – thanks to the archaeological excavations – the location and ground-plan of the synagogue destroyed in

The location of the old synagogue in the city is revealed again by Dani Karavan's 'Place for Thought' in Neupfarrplatz.

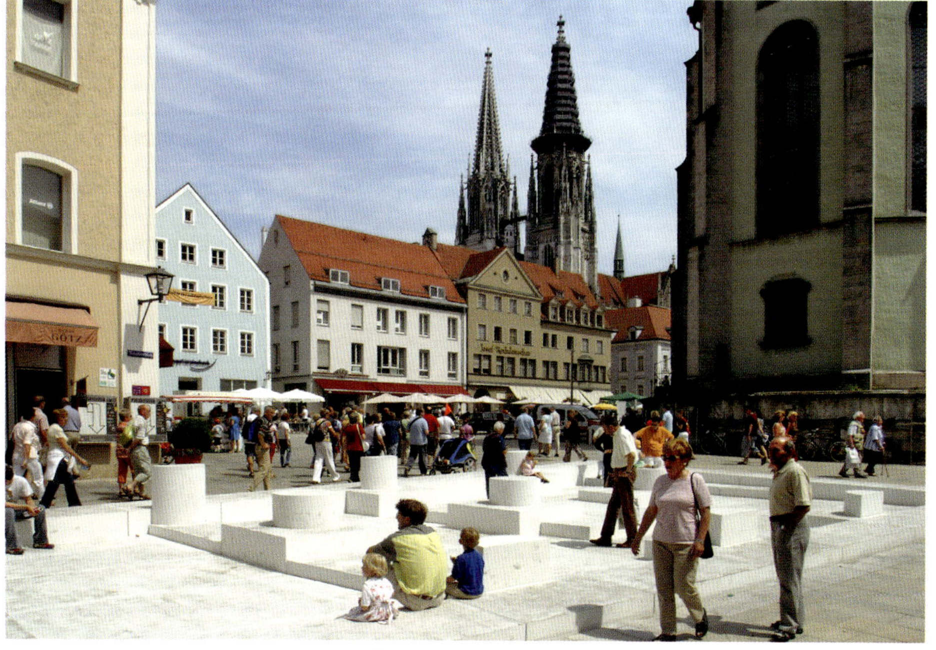

1519 had been revealed, it was decided that the imperial city fountain that had been erected here subsequently should be shifted westwards so as to be able to restyle the site above the former synagogue. For that purpose, the Israeli artist Dani Karavan designed the pavement relief (completed in 2005), which is intentionally not a memorial but a sunken seating area

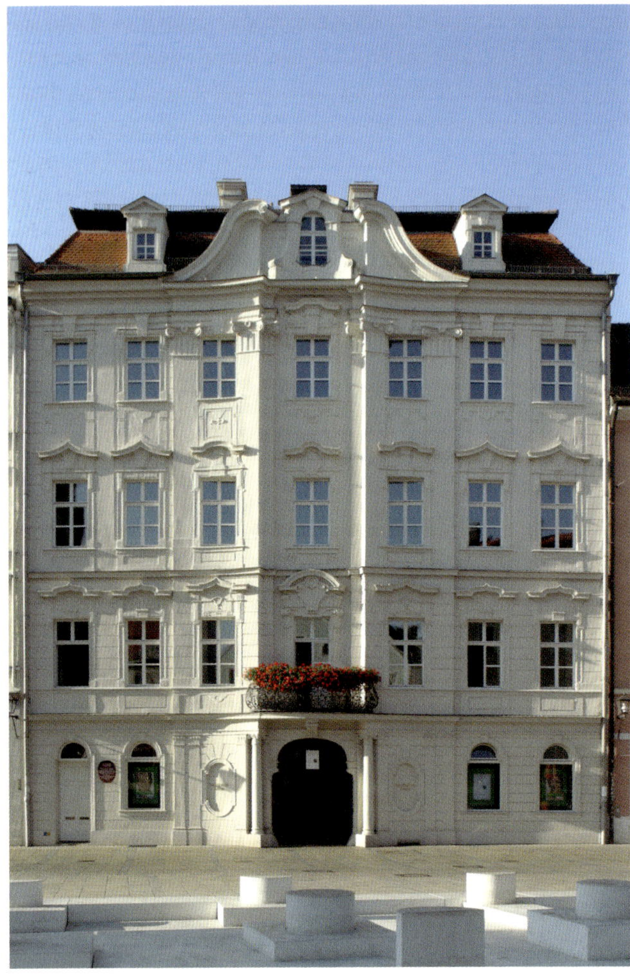

The Löschenkohl Mansion (1731–33) is the architectural highlight of the south side of Neupfarrplatz.

which invites passers-by to rest for a while and by this means integrates this historic, sacred site into its urban surroundings once more.

From here there is a good view of the **Palais Löschenkohl/ Löschenkohl Mansion (9)**, which the merchant and banker Hieronymus Löschenkohl employed Michel Prunner, an architect from Linz, to build in 1731/33. The facade visible from the square is one of the best examples of late baroque secular architecture in Regensburg: it has seven naturally formed bays and the three-bay central projection is concave at the sides and has a concave surface again at the front. Architecturally, the mansion – apart from models in Prague and Vienna – has close connections with the Löschenkohl Villa (P. 211f.), also erected by Prunner. After the decline of the Löschenkohl family business in 1743, the house became the residence of the Elector of Saxony's ambassador until the end of the Holy Roman Empire in 1806.

As one walks along the south side of Neupfarrplatz, a short detour to the east is to be recommended, passing various alterations made by planners and architects in the last third of the 20th century.

St Cassian's Church

St. Kassian/St Cassian's Church (10), a rather inconspicuous building, is one of the oldest churches in Regensburg. First mentioned in 885, it belonged to the palace in Alter Kornmarkt. Yet, unlike the Alte Kapelle (see p. 66ff.), which served as the palace church for the king and his court, St Cassian's was the church for the king's officials in those times. The church is still the parish church for the collegiate foundation at the Alte Kapelle.

The choice of St Cassian as patron saint is unusual north of the Alps and results from Regensburg's early association with the patriarchy of Aquileia and the once close relations between the Regenburg church and the Diocese of Bressanone, which venerates St Cassian of Imola as its first bishop. The building, which used to be surrounded by a graveyard, seems much more recent from the outside. It was in fact rebuilt on Carolingian foundations by master masons from the cathedral workshop in the early 14th century, extended westwards in 1477, and refurbished in the 18th century.

The floor in the interior lies noticeably lower than the present-day street-level, but all the same considerably higher than the gothic and, above all, Carolingian floor-levels recently established after excavations. Thus the height of the church has changed greatly in comparison with the then lofty new gothic building erected shortly after 1300. The pillars now seem to be squat, the arches strikingly wide.

The two eastern bays, with their columns and wide arcades, are survivals from the building erected at the start of the 14th century on the Carolingian foundations, whereas the two bays in the nave were built at the time of the late Gothic extension. The original Carolingian building, too, had a nave and two aisles and its nave still lies underneath the present-day one. The aisles were, however, considerably narrower; their apses were located where the eastern pillars of the present church stand today.

The stucco work in the nave and choir was executed by Anton Landes, who had previously worked in the Alte Kapelle. At the same time, Otto Gebhard was working in the nave on the large ceiling fresco, in the centre of which Peter is portrayed as a fisher of men. However, the commission for the remaining frescoes, completed by 1758, was given, for unknown reasons, to Gottfried Bernhard Göz. The walls of the nave have scenes from the Old Testament and from the life of the Virgin Mary painted on them in typological combination. The paintings on the ceiling of the north aisle show episodes from St Cassian's life, those in the south aisle refer to the building's history.

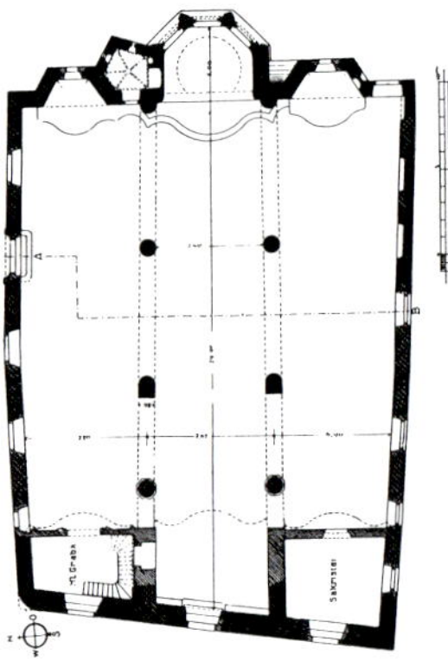

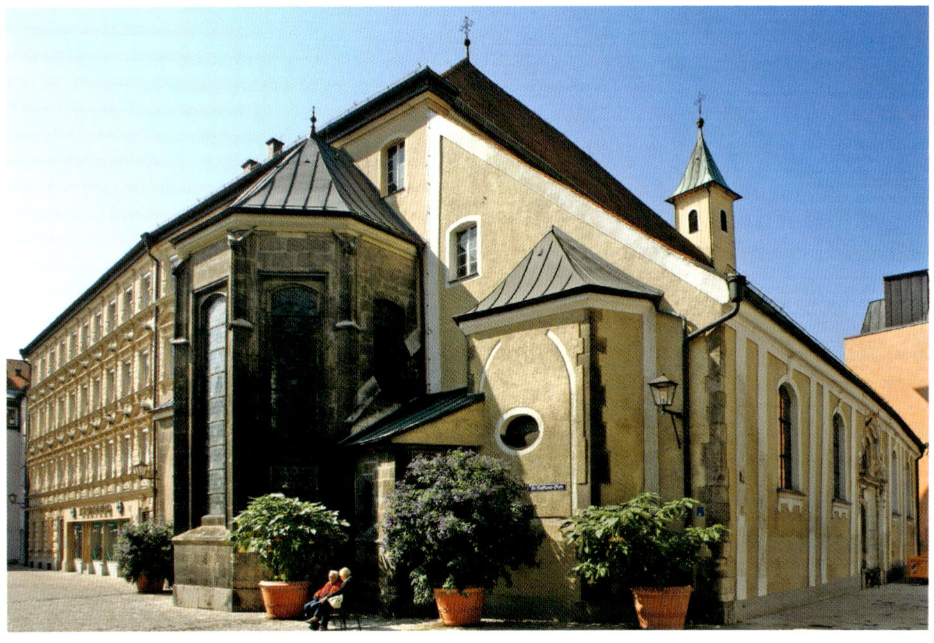

St Cassian's Church from the north-east

Whereas in the other mediaeval churches in Regensburg that were refurbished in the 17th /18th centuries, their original architectural design can still be clearly perceived, the character of St Cassian's interior was lastingly changed – not only as a result of the floor-level being raised, but also because the arches in the nave arcades were artificially lowered using half-timbering techniques. By this means, space was created, on the one hand, for the enormous cartouches in the clerestory but, on the other hand, the church acquired – intentionally or unintentionally – a very antiquated quality because the columns looked so squat.

Hans Leinberger's statue of the 'Beautiful Madonna' (c.1520) was placed on the southern side altar in 1747 in the hope of reviving the pilgrimage (see p. 94), which had come to an end in the 16th century. The statue had once adorned the altar in the wooden chapel in Neupfarrplatz. Against the wall in the southern aisle is the former late gothic high altar, a winged retable, made, probably, by a Lower Bavarian master craftsman in 1498, with the figure of St Cassian enthroned in its shrine.

The route leads back across Neupfarrplatz, past Karavan's relief and the imperial city fountain, now in its new position, and turns into **Wahlenstrasse (11)**. Its former name *inter latinos*, which is known to have been used as early as 1135, indicates that Italian merchants had their establishments here. The German name for the street was derived from these '*Welschen*', a German word for foreigners. Its relatively great width bears witness to the desire to impress displayed by its residents, who built substantial houses here. Numerous goldsmiths had their workshops in Wahlenstrasse in the 14th and 15th centuries. From 1481 at the latest, according to a regulation, these workshops had to be easy to see into, so that they could be better supervised.

Many of the facades were modernised after the end of the Middle Ages, but the fabric of the houses is, almost without exception, still largely mediaeval. This is proved, not least, by the extensive romanesque and gothic cellars, which were used not only as store-rooms but also as sales rooms. For this reason, they had separate entrances reached via stairs that led directly to the street. Some of these former entrances can still be located by means of the trapdoors in the pavement.

On the left, when one comes from Neupfarrplatz, is the tower of the mansion, dating from the second half of the 13th century, that belonged to the Kastenmayer family. The arch in the wall on the first floor indicates that there was once an open loggia here; the arch higher up was for reinforcement. Particularly remarkable are the two rooms on the ground-floor, both of which once had two bays. The northern one, sometimes said to be a former chapel, is in its original form still and has elaborate cross-vaulting. – No 23 was, from 1563–81, the residence of Ulrich Schmidl, co-founder of Buenos Aires and previously the historian of the region on the Rio de la Plata. –

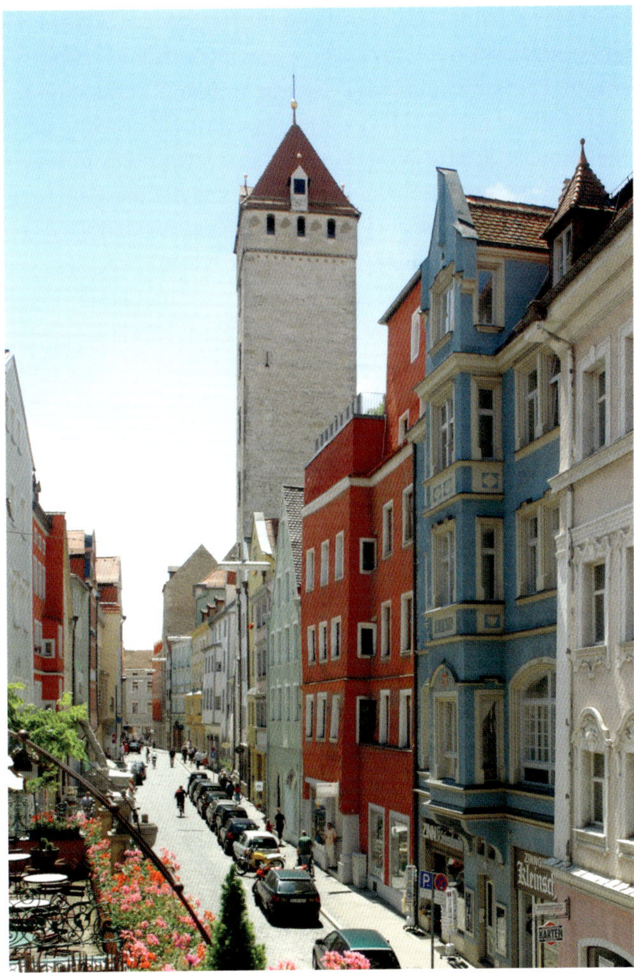

View of Wahlenstrasse, looking south. In the centre of the picture is the early gothic Golden Tower. Nearly 50 metres high, it is the most impressive of Regensburg's tower houses.

At No 20, the romanesque tower (albeit greatly altered in late gothic days and in the 19th century) and the more recent living quarters can still be seen. The essentially romanesque tower of the Degginger family's mansion (No 17) is set back from the street and therefore not visible. The facade of the part of the building used as a residence had a traceried gallery added to it in 1314, when members of the cathedral masons' lodge carried out major refurbishments. A decorative element like this gallery was in fact unusual in secular buildings in Regensburg but it had the effect of making the two hitherto differing parts of the house appear uniform. The bay window was probably added in the early 15th century. – Opposite is the **Goldene Turm/Golden Tower (12)**. Erected about 1250, it originally had only four storeys, but was extended to its present-day height as early as c. 1300. Ever since, it has been Regensburg's tallest patrician tower. The present pyramid roof unfortunately replaced the original battlements in about 1600. Nobody has yet been able to prove conclusively whether the embrasures on the north and south sides were intended for defensive purposes or not.

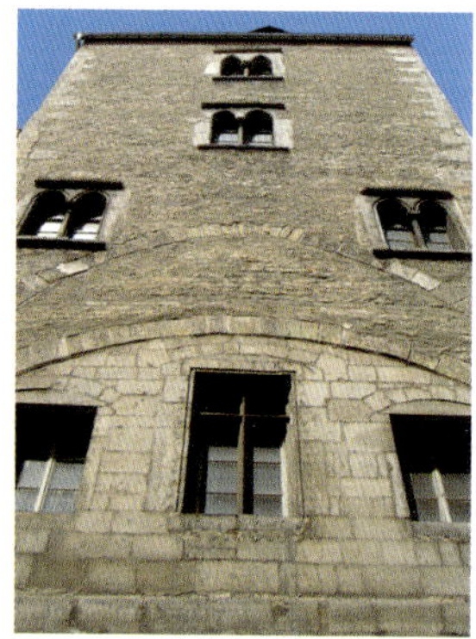

The tower of the Kastenmeyer Mansion in Wahlenstrasse with its bricked-up loggia

Through the inner courtyard, rebuilt during the Renaissance, of the complex attached to the Golden Tower, one reaches Untere Bachgasse, along which the Vitus Stream used to flow until it was diverted underground in 1837. The tradesmen who settled here because of the stream in the early Middle Ages, were soon driven further west to the edge of the city. The reason for this was probably primarily the offensive smells, particularly those caused by tanneries. In the following years, splendid romanesque and gothic houses were built along Bachgasse. Of particular interest is **No 13 Untere Bachgasse (13)** with a tower that was erected in 1102 or soon afterwards. Although some windows were modernised in gothic times, the romanesque facade of this residential tower has survived in unusually pure form.

The **Lyskirchnerhaus/Lyskirchner Mansion (14)** opposite, at No 10 Untere Bachgasse, looks today as it did after it was converted in late gothic style in the second half of the 15th century. That was also when the lavish coachman's entrance and vestibule were built. It had two bays, a popular means of impressing people that was employed by Regensburg architects designing dwelling houses at that time.

The Lyskirchner Mansion, No 10 Untere Bachgasse, is a typical late gothic patrician residence in Regensburg. Tower houses were already a thing of the past.

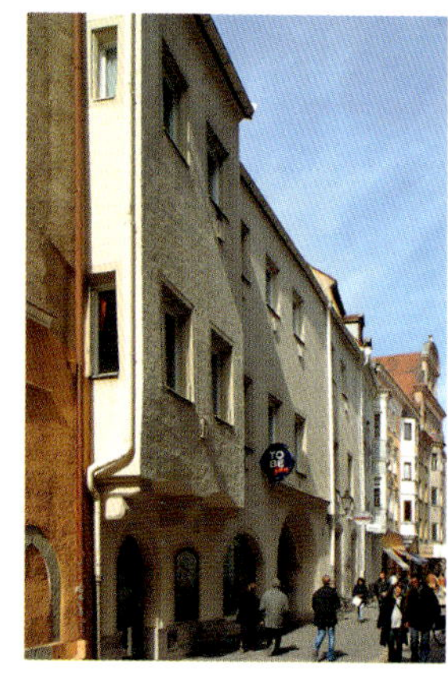

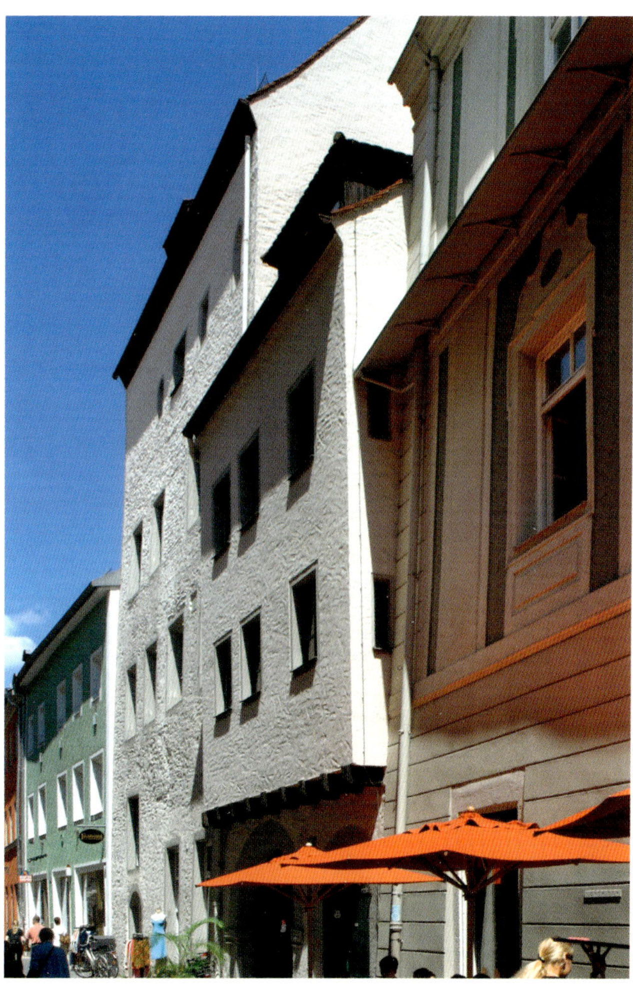

No 13 Untere Bachgasse: built in the early 12th cent. and thus probably Regensburg's oldest surviving tower house

A few steps further north is the narrow street called Hinter der Grieb. On the right is the **Löblturm/Löbl Tower (15)**, erected about 1270, and still in an excellent state of preservation. From its cellar up to the battlements, it still conveys a very authentic idea of what high gothic patrician towers looked like. The room on the ground-floor with its two bays and cross-vaulting was once the Löbl family's private chapel, as is still shown by the keystone with the family arms on it. The further course of the alley is dominated by the **Gravenreutherhaus/Gravenreuther Mansion (16)**, which comprises several buildings which were linked together between about 1200 and the early 14th century to form an extensive complex. The lack of unity affects the appearance of the facade. At the eastern end of this elaborately structured facade, one can see a loggia which was walled up in the late gothic period already; in the west wing, an oriel window with three bays hints at the existence of a magnificent public room behind it. The two towers belonging to the complex are visible only from the inner courtyard. While the east tower dates from about 1250, the west tower was not erected until the early 14th century, relatively late for a patrician tower in Regensburg. On its ground-floor is the former private chapel, a room

The alley called Hinter der Grieb is distinguished by the bay window of the Gravenreuther Mansion and by the 7-storey tower once owned by the Loibls, a patrician family.

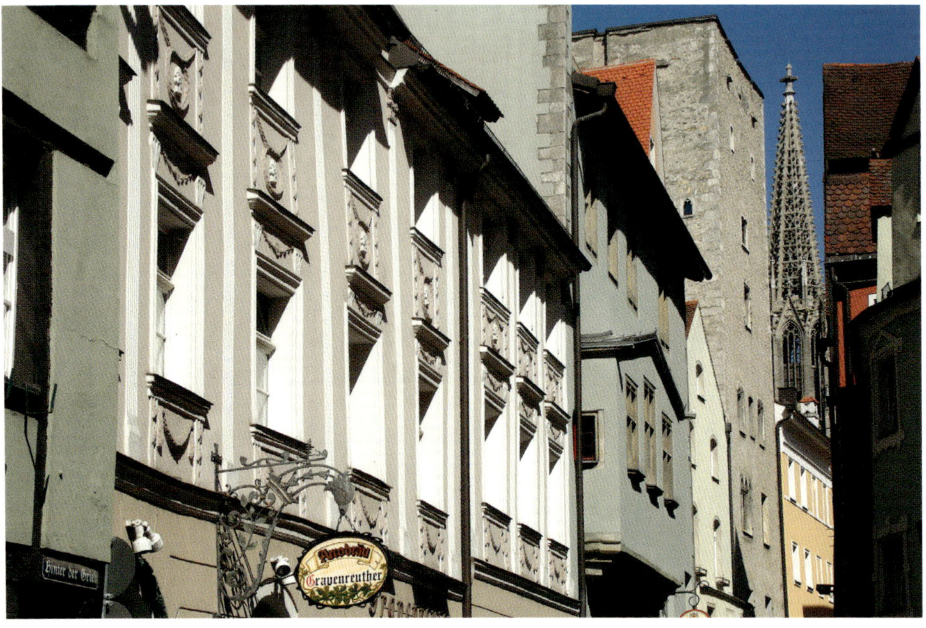

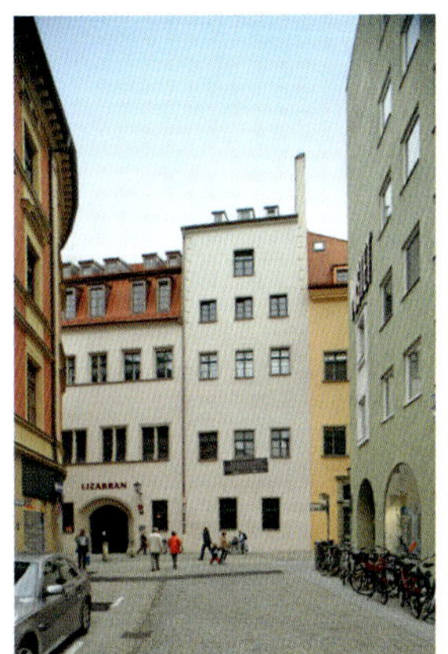

View through Roter-Hahnen-Gasse to the castle-like mansion erected by the patrician Zant family from the 12th cent.

with two bays which has five-section ribbed vaults and thus belongs to a small group of churches and chapels in Regensburg which were obviously intended to be set apart by this elaborate form of vaulting. The ultimate models for this decorative motif are to be found in the chapels in cathedral ambulatories of the early gothic period in France.

Looking through Rote-Hahnen-Gasse at the end of Hinter der Grieb, one catches sight of another imposing mansion. It was used as a tobacco factory from 1812 until the year 2000, which is why people in Regensburg generally refer to it as the 'Snuff Tobacco Factory'. The complex combines two houses that belonged to the Zandt (No 3 Gesandtenstrasse) and Ingolstetter (No 5 Gesandtenstrasse) families and which were not joined together until 1898. The **Zanthaus/Zant Mansion (17)**, to the east on the corner of Spiegelgasse, developed in turn from two dwelling-houses, each of which had its own tower and chapel. The Zants, one of Regensburg's richest families in the 13th/14th centuries, obviously had a great desire to impress and this is still clear today, above all in the two-bay entrance hall spanned by five ribbed vaults. Unfortunately, the sense of the original width of the room is seriously impaired because the left-hand bay has been partitioned off in the meantime. To the east of the entrance hall is the oldest part of the complex, a 12th-century tower, which, however, is no longer visible from Gesandtenstrasse, particularly since its upper floors were demolished in 1718; three small romanesque round-arched windows are the only evidence of it that remains. To the left of them, there is a walled-up doorway with a pointed arch; this was once the entrance to the chapel of St Pancras and St Pantaleon, mentioned in 1328, which lay to the east, adjacent to Spiegelgasse. There, a pointed arch still marks the spot where the chapel's oriel window projected over the street. To the right, a stone shield shows the Zants' arms, a lion. The second tower of the Zant Mansion stands at the western end; it has survived in its full height and is thus easily recognisable. Adjacent to it is the late gothic **Ingolstetter-haus/ Ingolstetter Mansion (18)**, which also contains masonry from a previous romanesque house on its site. What strikes one first about the facade, when one comes from the east, are sculptures (lions with human heads, grotesque masks), once part of a 14th-century doorway. Beside it is the driveway into the entrance hall, which had two bays, as in the Zant Mansion. The section of the building to the west has 12th-century masonry in the cellar and on the ground-floor. The two-storey bay window on the corner of Gutenbergplatz dates from 16th-century renovations.

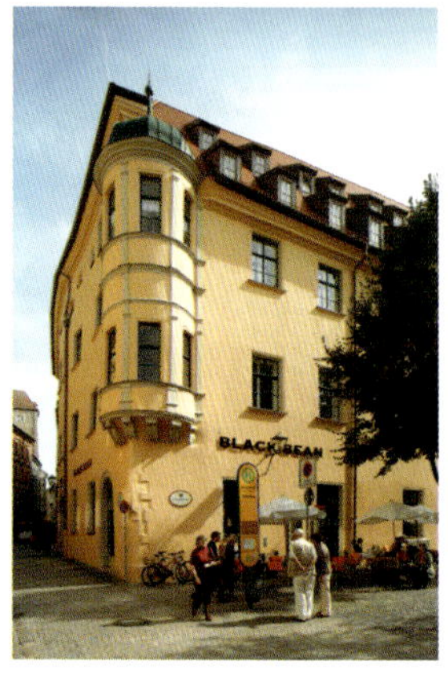

The late gothic Ingolstetter Mansion has had a Renaissance bay-window as its dominant feature since the 16th cent.

After standing empty for years and falling into disrepair, the Zant and Ingolstetter Mansions were refurbished in 2005/07. The main difficulty was to preserve these important mediaeval houses, including the alterations made in the Renaissance and baroque periods, while also taking their significance as an industrial monument into account. For this reason, some of the production machinery was left in situ and made accessible to the public in a museum (M).

Holy Trinity Church

Following Gesandtenstrasse westwards, one sees **Dreieinigkeitskirche/Holy Trinity Church (19)** on the left. Members of the Protestant parish, ordinary burghers, had it built from 1627–31 on city-owned land, after an imperial decree of 1626 made it impossible for them to share the use of the Dominican Church (see p. 112ff.) with its Roman Catholic congregation any longer. Holy Trinity was thus the first church in Regensburg that, from the start, was oriented to the requirements of a Protestant parish in its architecture and furnishings. The commission for the church's construction was given to Johann Carl from Nuremberg, an expert on building fortifications. He built the first Protestant church in Bavaria, apart from the court church in Neuburg an der Donau. When Joseph Furttenbach from Ulm published his ideal design for a Protestant church in 1649, this followed Holy Trinity Church in every detail.

Exterior

The massive building has a saddle roof, a rectangular choir narrower than the nave, and towers (the south one unfinished) placed in the spandrel between the nave and the choir. It is impressive due to the contrast between the smoothly plastered walls and the ashlar masonry in the lower part of the walls, at the rusticated corners, round the window frames and the doorways. The unusual arrangement of horizontal oval windows with large round-headed windows above them prepares the visitor for the two-level structure within the church. The lack of any sort of decorative figures does not accord with the original plans. In fact,

Holy Trinity Church, erected between 1627 and 1631 on a site of very limited size surrounded by mediaeval houses and streets, was built for Regensburg's Protestant citizens.

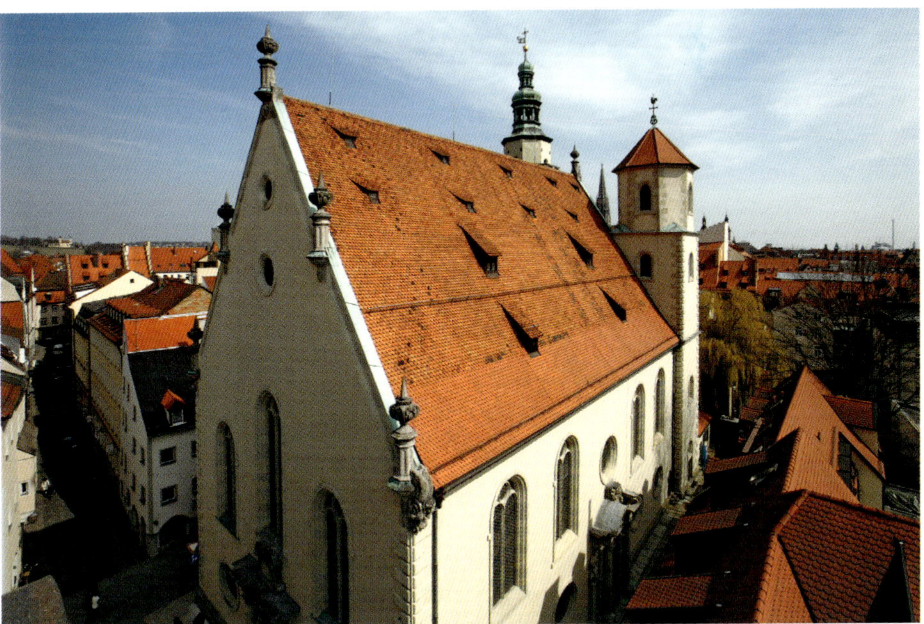

Leonhard Kern, a sculptor from Schwäbisch Hall, was commissioned in 1630 to create six allegorical figures of the cardinal virtues, which were to be placed in pairs on either side of the broken pediments over the north and south doorways as well as over the west door. The sculptures turned out to be too massive, however, and they were never placed in the intended position. The personifications of Fides, Spes, Justitia and Prudentia were placed in the courtyard of the Town Hall (see p. 86), the allegory of Caritas was discovered only in the 1930s, when sewers were being repaired in Adolf-Schmetzer-Strasse; the sixth figure is still missing.

Interior

The wide hall of the nave is spanned, like the choir, by a lengthwise barrel vault that appears to be resting only on consoles. In fact, the two wooden barrel vaults are suspended from the roof beams, the work of Lorenz Friedrich, a master carpenter employed by the city of Regensburg . The ceiling in the nave is decorated with a star pattern, that in the choir with a gothic-style net vault. The ribs are made of stucco and have no function in the construction. Rather, especially in the choir, they provide a formal link with the tradition of gothic vaulting. This sort of conservatism, which is relatively typical of Regensburg church-building (by both denominations) at that time, was, however, unacceptable where the walls were concerned. Because of the low gallery, which runs round three sides of the nave and permits a good view of the pulpit and the single altar, there was the problem of ensuring sufficient light everywhere. Carl solved the dilemma by installing horizontal oval windows in order to illuminate the darker zone under the gallery. In this respect, the requirements of Protestant worship found their expression in the architecture here.

Furnishings

The aedicule altar with its four pillars was set up in 1637; it had been made in Regensburg by Georg Stellenberger to a design by Georg Jakob Wolff. The angel that crowns it is by Leonhard Kern.

The programme of paintings is restricted to the two sacraments of the Protestant church, Baptism (predella) and Communion (central panel). The portrayal of Christ's baptism is by a Regensburg artist, Johann Paul Schwendtner, the Communion painting is thought to be from Augsburg. The arms above the altar painting are those of the altar's donor, Duke Franz Albert von Sachsen-Lauenburg, who had been sent to Regensburg as a secret negotiator by Wallenstein in 1634.

Typical of an early baroque church built by its parishioners is also the seating, which has been preserved in the original form. The splendid carved stalls in the choir were reserved for the

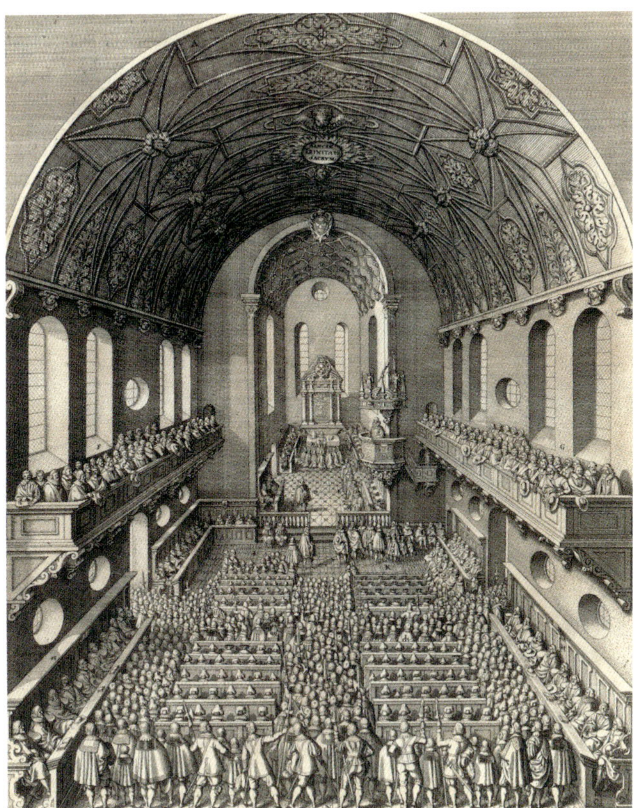

The consecration of Holy Trinity Church on Dec. 5, 1631 (copper engraving by Merian, Museum of Regensburg History). The vaulting is, formally, in the gothic tradition.

members of the city's Inner Council, the gentlemen of the Outer Council had their places in the side pews along the outside walls of the church. Aristocratic ladies and 'honourable citizens' sat in the rows of pews in the centre. Only aristocratic gentlemen, distinguished citizens and learned persons were allowed to to sit in the gallery. In 1755, members of Regensburg's municipal authority and Protestant ambassadors to the Imperial Diet were given their private oratories at the eastern ends of the gallery. The oratory in the centre of the gallery, beneath the organ, was constructed in 1790 for Duchess Therese of Mecklenburg-Strelitz, the wife of Karl Alexander of Thurn and Taxis. Documents relating to the history of Holy Trinity, as well as items from the church treasury are on show in this part of the gallery.

Outside, on the southern and eastern sides of the church, is the small, yet atmospheric graveyard in which Protestant ambassadors to the Imperial Diet and also Austrian Protestant aristocrats who died in exile in Regensburg found their last resting-place. The majority of the monuments date from the second half of the 17th century and the first third of the 18th century.

Dominican Church

The former **Domanikerkanerkirche St Blasius/Dominican Church of St Blasius (20)** stands just a few metres southwest of Holy Trinity Church. Whereas its choir faces the street called Am Ölberg, the huge nave runs westwards along Predigergasse. Together with the Minorite Church (see p.196ff.), the Dominican Church was the second large church built by a mendicant order in Regensburg and was also one of the earliest and largest buildings erected by the Dominicans in the German-speaking area. The church is also of supra-regional importance in the development of high gothic architecture.

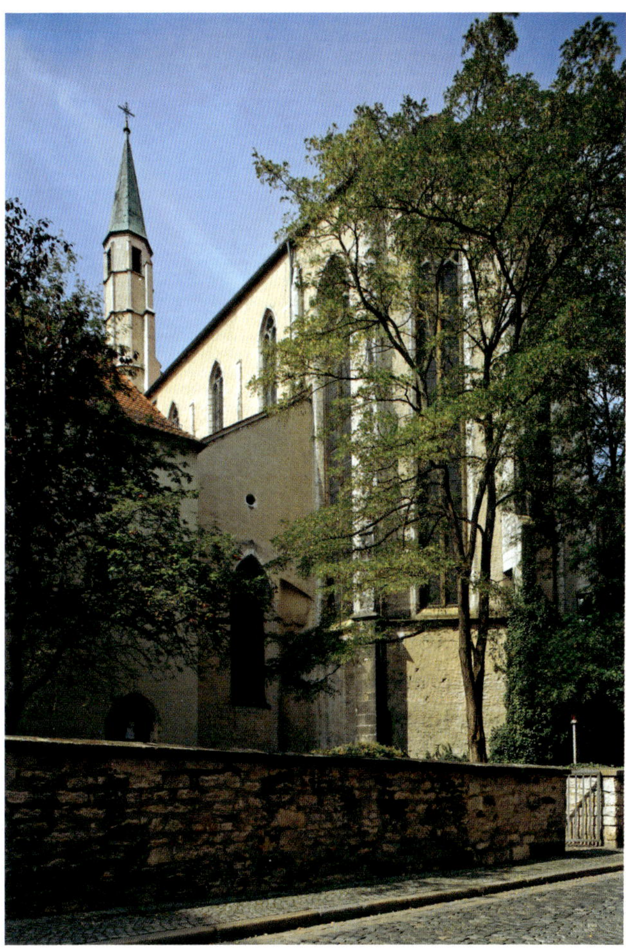

The choir of the Dominican Church (before 1246–54). In 1271/72, Regensburg's Dominican friary oversaw the founding of the Dominican communities in Landshut, Eichstätt and Bolzano.

The first mention of a Dominican house in Regensburg comes in 1229. The monastery experienced an early intellectual flowering from 1237 until 1240, when St Albertus Magnus taught here. At this time – certainly before 1246 – building work began on the eastern parts of the church. In 1254, the first altars were consecrated. The nave was erected after 1271 and was used for liturgical purposes at the start of the 14th century. During the

Reformation, the church, which traditionally had close links with Regensburg's patricians, was taken over by the City Council for certain periods in order to hold Protestant services in the nave, while the choir was left to the monks. The consequence of the 1626 ban on the simultaneous use of the church by both denominations was the construction of Holy Trinity Church (see p. 108ff.).

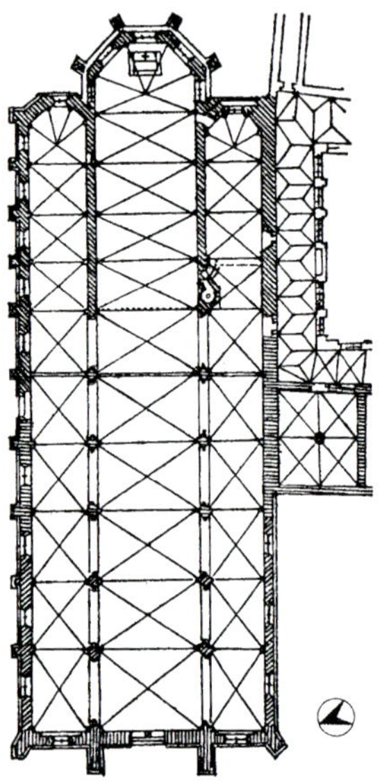

Exterior

The very long building with a saddle roof extending over both the nave and the choir is impressive because of its homogeneous appearance. Only the slim belfry that rises on the south side, a replacement for an earlier ridge turret, is a post-mediaeval element. The polygonal termination of the choir, just like the nave, seems to rise even higher because there are no protruding buttresses. Only the main choir, closed on three sides, is accentuated by corner buttresses with several steps. These are broken through at the level of the window-ledge cornice, so that a walkway can run all along above the windowless base. The walls of the sides of the choir have little masonry in them because of the two-light traceried windows. Simple, inconspicuous buttresses are also found in strict regularity on the north facade, in the middle of which there is a side doorway. The main doorway is in the west front, which is divided horizontally by a cornice in the area of the nave. The portal consists of a double-arched door with a round-headed blind arch and a trefoil frame above it. A statue of St Dominic was placed in the originally undecorated tympanum about 1400. Above the cornice is a large, six-light traceried window, which takes as its the model the clerestory windows at St Urbain's in Troyes (completed in 1286).

Interior

Even more than the exterior, the inside of the building is striking for its austere monumentality and the virtually complete absence of decoration. The principles of architecture propounded by the

The simplicity of the vast interior of the Dominican Church is emphasised by this view trough the nave to the choir at the east end.

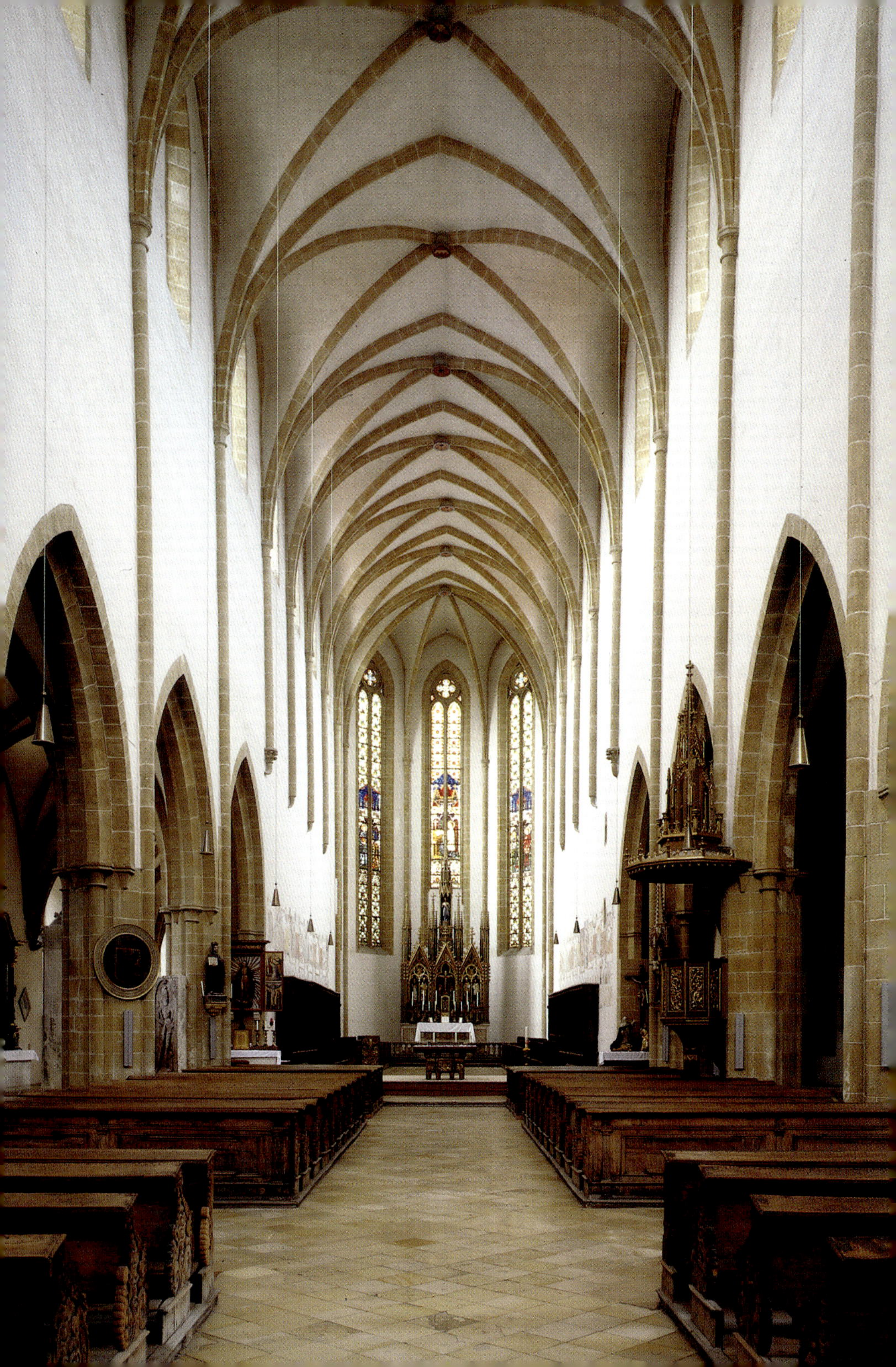

mendicant orders are thus far realised. Unusual, on the other hand, are the cross-ribbed vaulting in the whole of the six-bayed church and the considerable height of its nave. This is followed, for the first time in the history of mendicant order architecture in Germany, by a four-bay choir with a polygonal apse termination. The idea behind this was to combine the monks' choir with the room for services and the room for preaching. In the northern choir chapel, there are three shaft capitals decorated with figures. One of them shows a master builder, who is the bearer of a crocket capital; his name is given as 'Brother Dietmar'. It is, of course, not certain whether he may be seen as the architect of the church, or simply as the site manager.

Despite the sparsity of sculptures and the loss of nearly all the original furnishings, the church interior must clearly have looked magnificent in the Middle Ages. On the one hand, there are indications that all the windows had stained glass in them; on the other hand, the remains of fine wall-paintings have survived. Initially, the stone blocks in the walls in the choir were painted, quite normally for the churches of mendicant orders, in monochrome grey with white grouting. The south wall of the northern chapel in the choir was later given a frieze with coats of arms and crosses, showing the names of those buried there. At the beginning of the 14th century, the main choir was decorated with a frieze that looks like imaginary architecture and contains the names of the friaries in the German Dominican province; a decorative tapestry hangs below this. As several meetings of all the chapters in the province took place in the Regensburg friary before the Reformation, it may be assumed that, until the choir stalls were acquired (c. 1490/1500), the names of the friaries indicated where their priors sat. Towards the very end of the 15th century, paintings based on the Book of Hours, showing scenes from the Passion, were added above the frieze and these, in turn, are linked by a tapestry held by angels. – Particularly noteworthy among the other wall-paintings are the frieze (dated 1331) in the south aisle showing the

14 Holy Helpers, one of the first large-scale portrayals of this theme (see p. 50, 210), and a very fine painting of the scene on the Mount of Olives (2nd quarter of the 14th century) in the north aisle.

Among the other interesting items in the church, the sacramental altar on the northern wall of the main choir is especially remarkable: it has a statue of the Madonna wearing a mantle which she holds protectively around numerous representatives of the three political estates (clergy, nobility and burghers).The statue (c. 1460/70) still has its original colouring. The sculpture is also a reminder that veneration for the Madonna of Mercy with her protective mantle was especially propagated by the Dominicans in the Middle Ages.

The cloisters adjoin the church to the south. They were built, including the three-light traceried arcades, at the time the friary was founded in the 13th century. The wings, which probably had flat ceilings originally, were decorated with rib vaulting around 1424. Since 1624, what was presumably a mediaeval lecture hall in the west wing of the cloisters has contained the Albertus Magnus Chapel (extensively restored 1896/97). In it there is a two-level teacher's desk, in which the upper seat was for the 'master', whereas the 'baccalaureus' (bachelor) sat below him during disputations On the back of the desk, there is a portrait of the Dominican friar Vinzenz Ferrer, who was canonised in 1455. Some of the benches around the walls of the room also date from the second half of the 15th century.

Neoclassical Bismarckplatz

The mediaeval city appears to end abruptly west of the Dominican Church. This impression is the result of changes made to the layout of the area, which began in 1803 under Carl von Dalberg, Imperial Arch-Chancellor, who was then Regensburg's ruler. He had two hitherto largely undeveloped squares, Oberer and Unterer Jakobsplatz (now Arnulfsplatz and Bismarckplatz) completely re-designed by his court architect, Emanuel von Herigoyen, who had been born in Portugal and trained in Paris and Vienna. First of all, Herigoyen had to plan the **theatre and assembly rooms (21)**. In order to make room for the theatre, the former arsenal had to be demolished, but this seemed to be superfluous now that Regensburg was politically neutral. What was new about the building, which was already opened on September 2, 1804, was the very progressive combination of a theatre with a public hall, restaurant, café and private function rooms. Secondly, the complex – which burnt down in 1849 and was re-built by the Prince of Thurn and Taxis' architect, Karl Victor Keim – introduced to Regensburg a form of neoclassicism which no longer modified baroque traditions in neoclassical style, but broke with them entirely.

The city's theatre was erected as a theatre and assembly rooms in 1804 and rebuilt in slightly altered form after a fire in 1849.

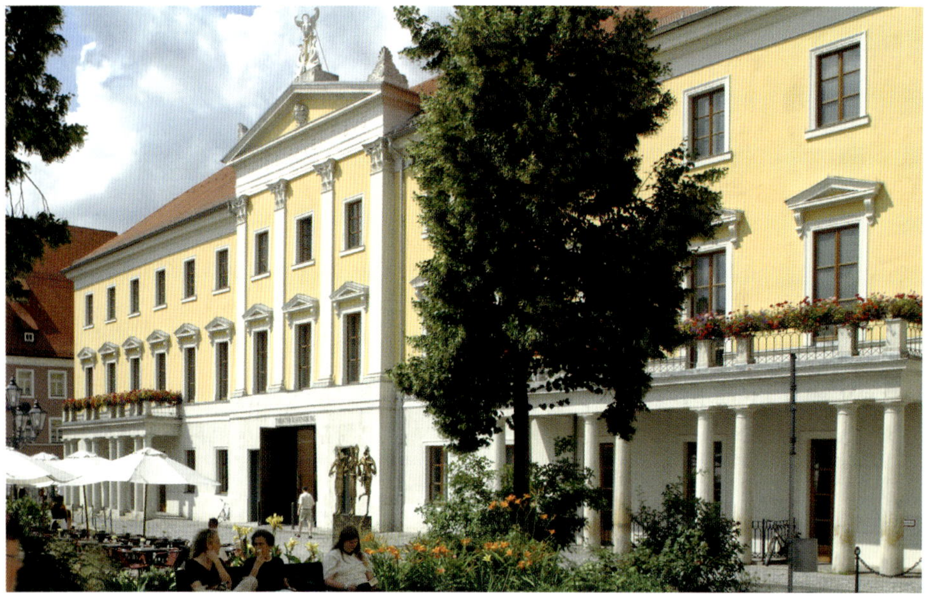

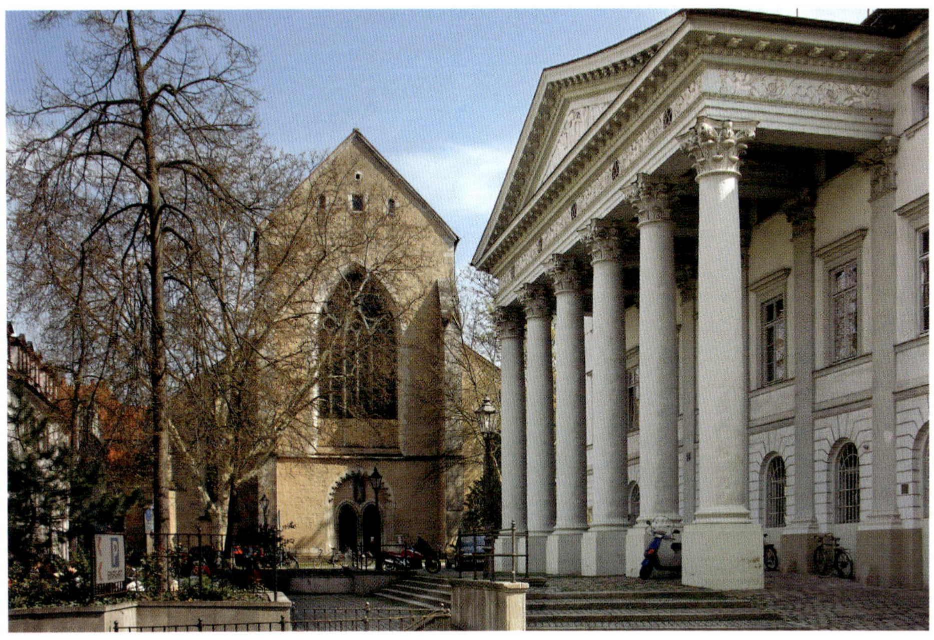

View past the former French Embassy (1804/05) to the west front of the Dominican Church (13th/14th cent.)

The theatre and assembly rooms were not even finished when Dalberg commissioned Herigoyen to design an imposing mansion for the **French Embassy (22)** at the southern end of the square. The municipal grain store and stables had to make way for the new building (1804/05). With its huge six-columned portico facing the square, the facade brought an impressive new architectural motif to Regensburg. The choice of the Corinthian, i.e. the imperial, Order makes it seem likely that Dalberg wanted to pay homage to Napoleon with this building.

Walking past the east side of the theatre, one reaches Ludwigstrasse via Drei-Mohren-Strasse. Despite its considerably more modern appearance, Ludwigstrasse is the western section of a traffic axis that had been established by about 920, and led through the merchants' quarter from Kohlenmarkt in an east-west direction. Some of the buildings still have a substantial amount of romanesque and gothic fabric. For instance, the eastern section of the house on the corner of Drei-Mohren-Strasse, which is so untypical of Regensburg because of its visible timber frame, has a romanesque core. This earlier part of the building, constructed solely in stone, can easily be recognised because of the lack of half-timbering. The next house but one (No 3) has a much higher, tower-like tract with a crow-stepped gable that is obviously gothic. The same applies to the former Elephant Pharmacy a few metres eastwards, whose late gothic crow-stepped gable dominates the corner of Glockengasse.

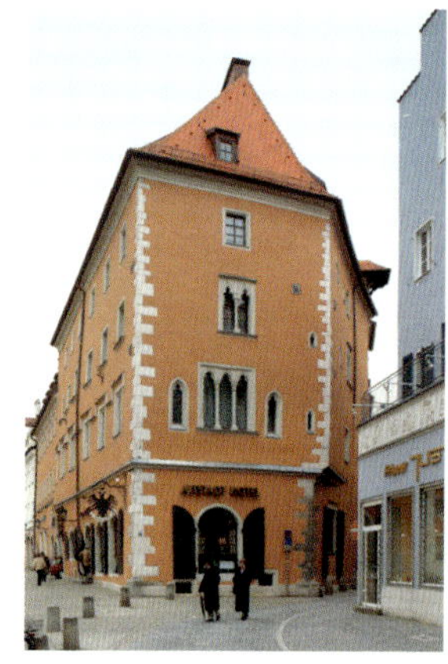

The narrow west facade of the 'Arch' (late 13th cent.)

Before one continues to Haidplatz, which opens up like a funnel, it is advisable to make a detour into Am Römling, a street running northwards. On its left side is a conspicuous building, the **Thomaskapelle/St Thomas' Chapel (23)**, dating from about 1300. It is part of the extensive complex of buildings that belonged to the Auer family, then one of the most powerful patrician families in the city. Since the regrettable demolition of several wings of the building in 1888/89, only the north-eastern section of the romanesque-gothic complex has remained. The northern part of what has survived forms, as it were, the shell of the chapel, which is the only private chapel in Regensburg to be visible from the street because its three-sided termination juts out into the roadway. Although the chapel was de-consecrated during the Reformation and forfeited its original height of 11m when a false ceiling was installed in 1646, the impression conveyed by the room is still extraordinary. Eight ribs with deep hollow moulding spring from one central compound pier without dividing capitals and then combine to form a star vault. Against the walls, this rests on consoles, which – like the keystones – are decorated with wonderful carvings. All this blends together into a whole, making the Auer Chapel (now a restaurant) one of the great achievements of religious architecture in early 13th-century Regensburg.

Haidplatz

From Ludwigstrasse, it is only a few steps to **Haidplatz/Haid Square (24)**, which is impressive not only because of its triangular shape but also because of the buildings that frame it. In late Roman/early mediaeval times, the site was part of the cemetery

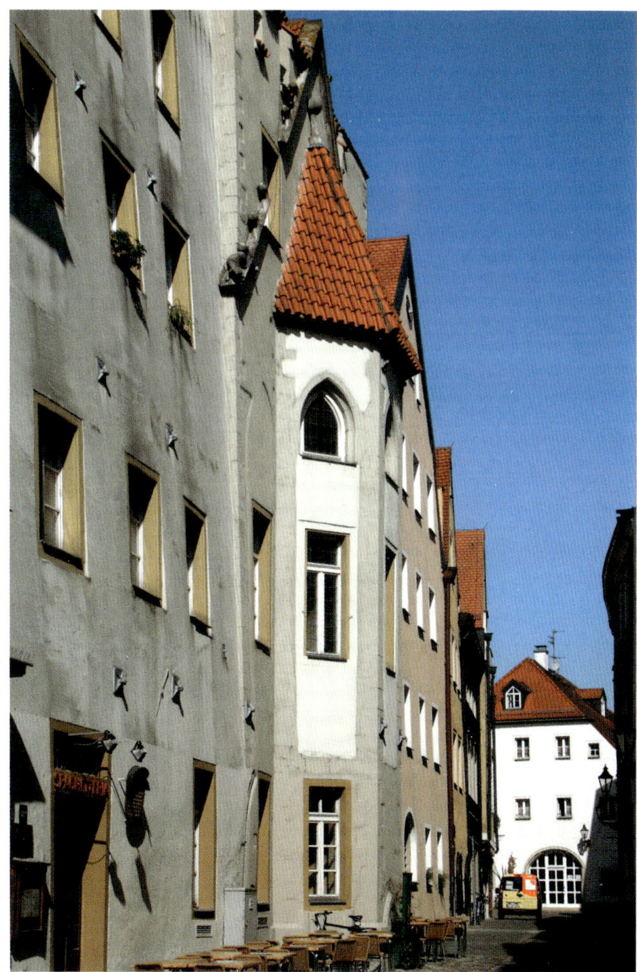

View of the street called Am Römling. Left, the surviving section of the Auer Mansion with the choir of St Thomas' Chapel (c. 1300)

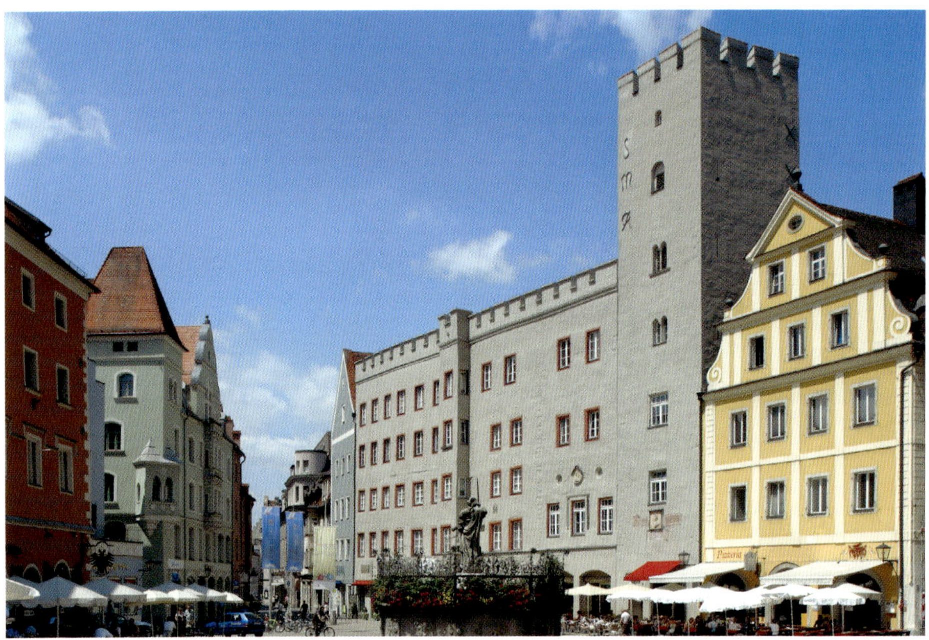

Looking across Haidplatz to the west: left, part of the 'Arch', right, the Golden Cross, in the centre the Justitia Fountain

that stretched westwards from the north-western corner of the Roman camp, but in the 10th century, wooden buildings are known to have stood here, at least on the south side of the square. From the 12th century, the term 'Haid' (heath) is known to have been used to describe this relatively large area of undeveloped land. Beginning from the 13th century, imposing houses were erected around the open space by the city's patricians. The Justice Fountain was built in the centre in 1656; through its reference to Justice, a virtue associated with rulers, it was one of the series of allegorical fountains in the imperial city.

The Ark

The so-called **Arch/Ark (25)** is a very striking gothic mansion on the south side of Haidplatz. The special thing about this complex, which was constructed in the late 13th century and which has no adjoining buildings on three sides, is its trapeze-shaped ground-plan. The reason for this is the location of Roten-Hahnen-Gasse, which branches off here and which had a branch of the Vitus Stream (see p. 104) flowing through it until the 19th century. The narrow west facade, the bows of the Ark, so to speak, is given emphasis by a triple and a double arcade as well as by ashlar at the corners. At street level on the north side, facing the square, there was once a probably romanesque public chapel dedicated to St Laurence, but this was built over when the 'Ark' was erected.

Golden Cross

The opposite side of the square is dominated by the so-called **Kaiserherberge Goldenes Kreuz/Golden Cross Imperial Hotel (26)**, which was originally a mid-13th-century patrician mansion. The early gothic core consists of a seven-storey tower and the adjoining residential building. The oriel window, however, already belonged to the neighbouring house; not until 1862 was the latter refurbished and made to look as if it was part of the Golden Cross. The extension reflected the last great period of prosperity then being enjoyed by the traditional hotel, which had accommodated many crowned heads. The use of the property as a hotel for the nobility began as early as the 15th century. The Emperor Charles V stayed at the Golden Cross three times; here, in 1546, he had his affair with Barbara Blomberg (see p. 92). The ground-floor room in the old residential quarters has a slightly domed ceiling made of beams decorated with late gothic tendril designs, which are now concealed in order to preserve them since the room is used as a café. Above it, on the first floor, as indicated from outside by three similar windows, is the mediaeval hall, which was extensively refurbished in baroque style in the 17th century and altered again in the 19th century. The former chapel of St Leonhard on the ground-floor at the back of the house has, on the other hand, retained its original mediaeval appearance. The chapel has a single central pillar and cross-rib vaulting. It is likely that it was originally constructed for secular

The neoclassical Thon Dittmer Mansion conceals remains of its gothic predecessors on this site

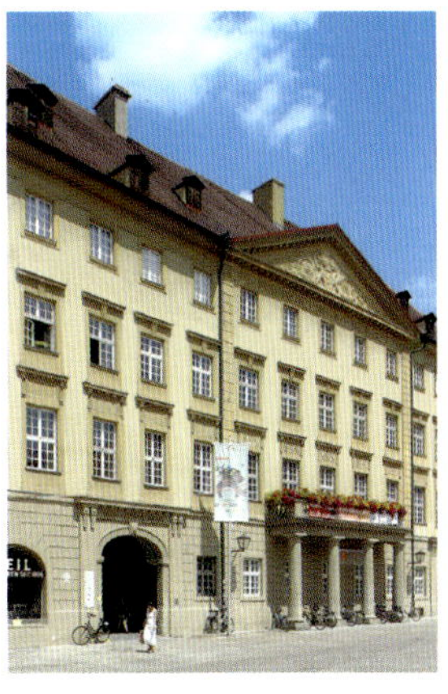

purposes and not converted into a chapel until the 15th century. This was the place where, on Maundy Thursday in 1541, the Emperor Charles V ceremonially washed the feet of twelve elderly men.

Thon Dittmer Mansion

The **Thon-Dittmer-Palais/Thon Dittmer Mansion (27)**, the second major building on the north side of the square, replaced a gothic building that had been refurbished in baroque times. The new mansion was erected by Georg Friedrich Dittmer, a merchant and banker, between 1781 and 1785. The early neo-classical building was extended in 1808/09 by Herigoyen, who created the present 15-bay facade. The symmetry of this facade successfully conceals the complicated history of the building; yet, when one takes a look at the interior courtyard surrounded by the mansion's four wings, its mediaeval roots are still perceptible. Above the gateway through which coaches used to enter, there is an oriel window (c. 1380) with a clock-face on it. It is supported by a richly decorated console with the figures of two lovers on it. The presumably allegorical significance of the sculpture was taken up again in the 17th century, when a statue personifying Transience was added. To the east of the gateway is the former private chapel dedicated to St Sigismund (c. 1380), a room with two bays and some interesting sculptures.

New Weigh House

The entire eastern side of the square is taken up by the **Neue Waag/New Weigh-House (28)**, a building consisting of four wings around a central courtyard. It developed from a patrician mansion on this site which was erected about 1300. All that remains of that building is the north wing and the tower with the private chapel – once dedicated to St Christopher but now used as a shop – on the ground-floor. The other parts of the building were added in the 15th century, although the Renaissance-style arcaded courtyard did not acquire its present-day form until

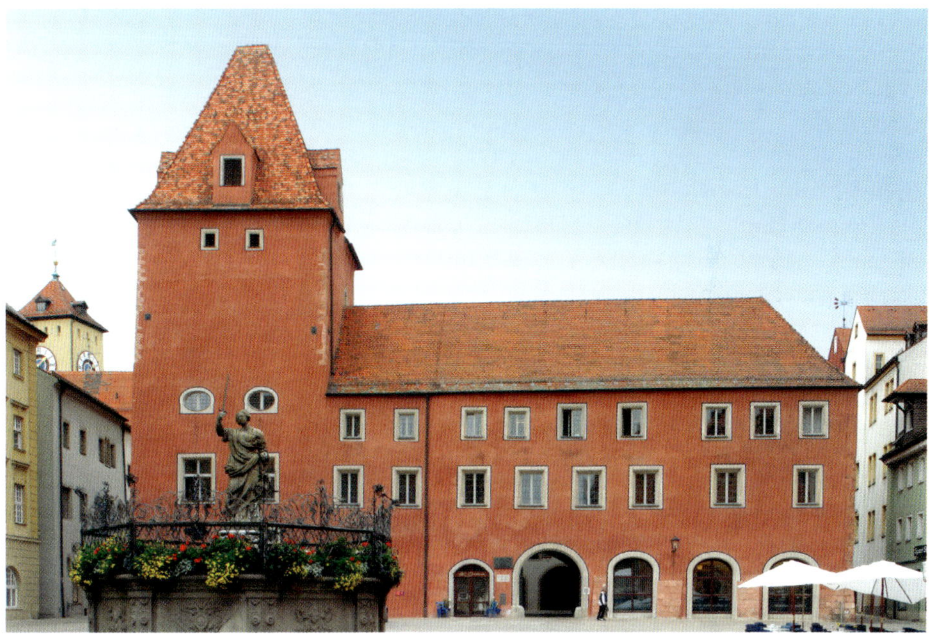

The New Weigh House on the east side of Haidplatz; in the foreground, the Justitia Fountain

1573. Because of its central position, the building was obviously suited for official use. Thus, the imperial city purchased it in 1441 and installed the public scales there, which had formerly been somewhat hidden from view in St.-Albans-Gasse. The building also accommodated the so-called 'Gentlemen's Drinking Parlour', where the city's patricians used to foregather. This was also the building where, in 1541, a so-called religious disputation was organised, under the aegis of the Emperor Charles V, with the aim of reversing the secession of the Protestant Christians. In 1782, the imperial city's library was set up on the first floor of the tower and the north wing. For this purpose, the gothic hall was sacrificed.

Rathausplatz is only a few steps away. On the way there, is the **Altmannsches Haus/Altmann Mansion (29)**, on which triforium windows (c.1060/80), a survival from the original early

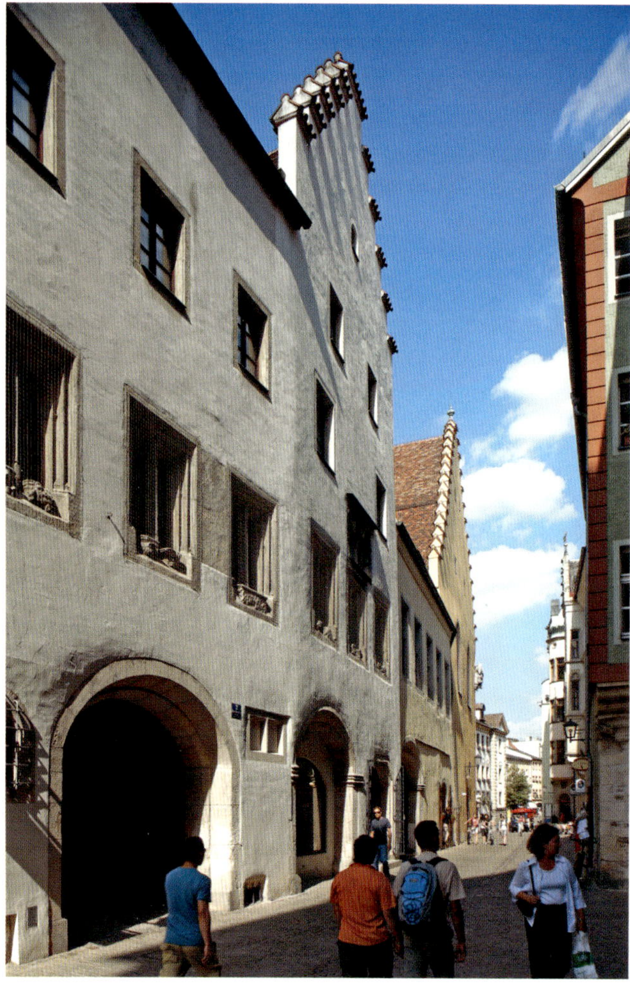

The Altmann Mansion, whose eastern tract (with a reconstructed crow-step gable) is first documented in 1052. Behind it is the gabled south facade of the Imperial Hall.

romanesque house, have been revealed between the first and second floors. However, the visitor is recommended to turn northwards from Haidplatz into Weingasse, which once led to the wine market in Keplerstrasse. From the corner of Scheugässchen, there is a good view over an open patch of land, created when buildings were demolished at the end of the 1950s, to the early gothic towers of the mansions lining Keplerstrasse. In this road, which runs parallel to the Danube, the closeness of the river is noticeable. On the north side of the road, for example, there are large buildings which have stood there ever since they were erected in the Middle Ages in connection with trade on the river. The huge **Weinstadel/Wine Store (30)** was built in 1527, according to Albrecht Altdorfer's design, as a place where barrels of wine unloaded on the quayside behind it could be stored and inspected by customs officials. Part of the 14th-century city walls are integrated into the northern facade of the store, which must have replaced a mediaeval predecessor. The mediaeval Weintor (Wine Gate), which used to provide direct access from the street to the quayside, had to be demolished when the western extension to the store (Keplerstrasse 16) was added in 1849/50. Beside the Weinstadel, to the east, is the Mauttor (Toll Gate) from 1611, with the adjoining Mauthaus. This was also

The Weinstadel, built in 1527 as a store for the wine brought by ship to Regensburg

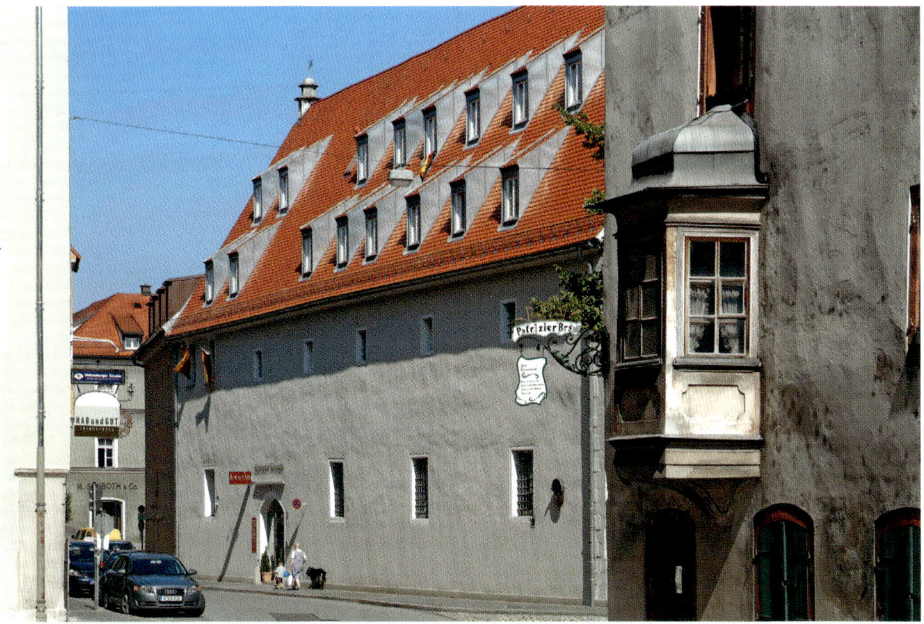

built as a warehouse in the 15th/16th centuries, incorporating a tower in the city walls dating from the first third of the 14th century. The building was extended towards the street in 1611.

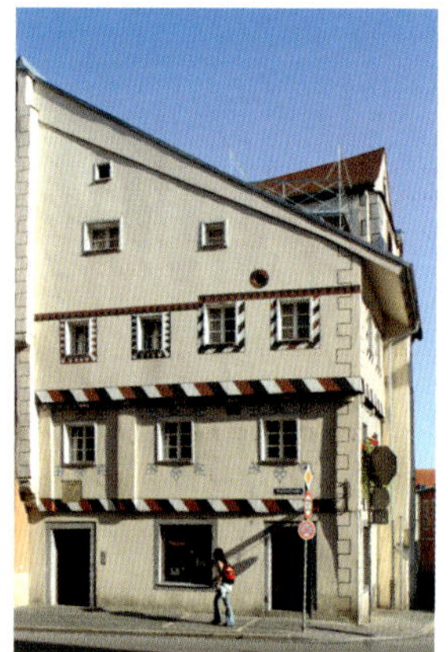

No 2 Keplerstrasse: the tower-like stone building towers over the adjoining wooden house erected in c. 1250.

Runtinger Mansion

The other side of the road, opposite the Weinstadel, is dominated by an imposing merchant's mansion, the **Runtingerhaus/Runtinger Mansion (31)**. The Runtinger family, which had amassed great wealth, above all through the trade with Venice, purchased the eastern part of the complex in 1367 and the western part in 1399 and converted it into a single impressive dwelling. The original part of the building was a tower-house at the eastern end dating from about 1200, which was remodelled and provided with a western extension in the second half of the 13th century. That was when the elaborate window arcades and the crenellated roof were added, as well as a first-floor loggia; this was, however, closed up again for climatic reasons in about 1330, when three rectangular windows were constructed. The western extension with its crenellations did not acquire its present-day appearance until about 1400, after the Runtingers had bought it. The fact that the building underwent refurbishment in the 1960s/70s involving 'free reconstruction' means that the interior conveys an only partially authentic picture. Nevertheless, characteristic features of the mediaeval merchant's mansion have been preserved, such as the vaulted store-rooms on the ground floor and, above them, the room that once lay behind the loggia as well as the adjoining hall (c. 1400). Its ceiling planks rest on an octagonal supporting pillar, as used to be the case in the gothic hall in the Neue Waag as well (p. 125). The now revealed wall paintings derive from various periods. On the west wall is a sinopia (a preparatory sketch for frescoes) dating from about 1340; it shows a line of dogs which are chained together, as well as crests and names of important families, and may refer to the mediaeval hunting poetry of the Minnesinger Hademar von Laber. The most remarkable feature on the second floor is the room panelled with broad planks dating from about 1440.

On the northern side of the street, on the corner of the alley called Am Schallern, is an early gothic house, **Keplerstrasse 2 (32)**, in which the astronomer Johannes Kepler lived with his

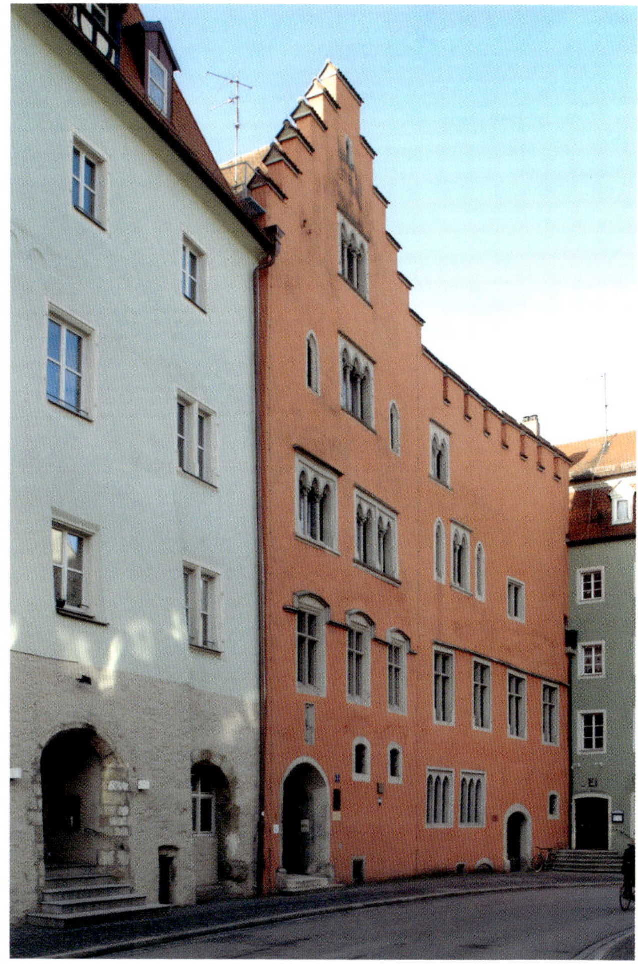

The early gothic facade of the Runtinger Mansion. The eastern tract, with its crow-step gable, started out as a romanesque tower house.

family from 1626–28. The tower-like stone building on the northern side and, south of it, the striking three-storey wooden building on the corner were both built in about 1250 over a shared cellar. The wooden house is one of the oldest of its kind in Germany. Of interest regarding building techniques are the surviving rectangular tiles under the plasterwork, which were mounted at the time the house was built, both as a base for the plaster and for insulation purposes. The painting on the facades is a reconstruction of the 13th-century decorations and was undertaken after examining the remnants of the original plaster and paint.

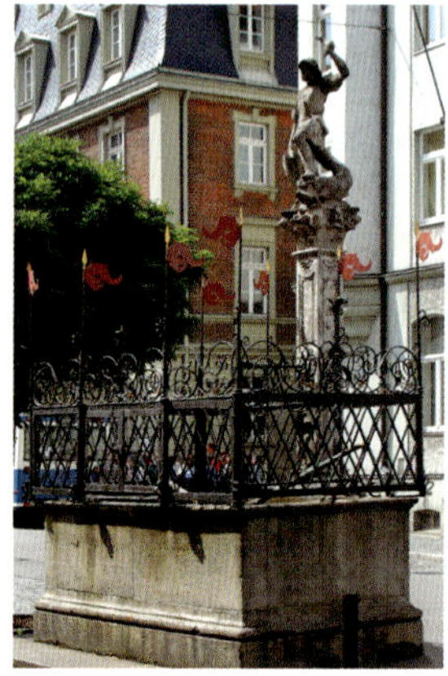

The fountain in Fischmarkt, from the south-east

At this point Keplerstrasse opens out into **Fischmarkt/ Fish Market (33)**, which, historically speaking, it would be more correct to call the meat market. In the Middle Ages, namely, meat, offal and game were sold here and in the nearby alleys, whereas the fishmongers had their stalls in various places in the city. Not until 1529 was the eastern part of the square designated as the central fish-market and, accordingly, paved. The fountain, which dates back to 1610 in its present form, seems, to judge by the attributes of the statue on it, to refer to the fish trade; in fact, the figure was probably originally an allegory of virtue of the type usual on fountains in the imperial city but, in the course of a later restoration, the figure mistakenly had a fish placed in its hand instead of the original sword (?).

The Mediaeval Port

Eastwards, the Fischmarkt leads into Goldene-Bären-Strasse. Here, the buildings on the north side of the street are separated, like islands. Behind them, towards the Danube is the alley called Am Wiedfang. Its name, deriving from Middle High German *witfend,* i.e. wood storage area, still recalls the mediaeval port layout, which also explains the unusual appearance of the street. The reason for this was that, after the Stone Bridge had been built, a canal became necessary so that shipping could

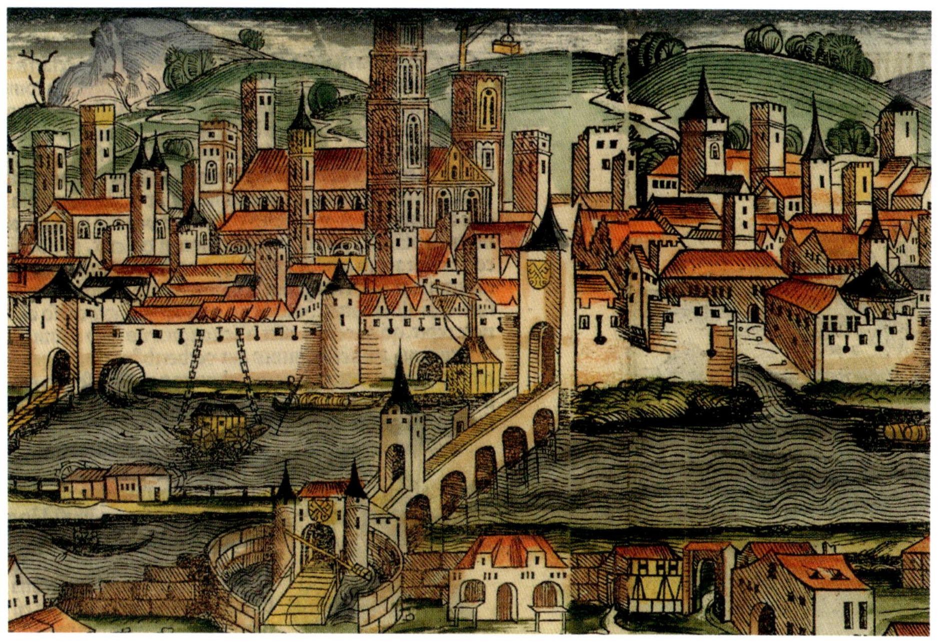

Regensburg from the north. Detail from a woodcut by Michael Wolgemut in Hartmann Schedel's 'Chronicle of the World' (1493, Museum of Regensburg History). It shows clearly where the port canal left and rejoined the Danube.

avoid the resulting dangerous currents and eddies. This canal began next to No 1 Am Wiedfang and flowed into the Danube again just below the bridge, which it passed through via the southernmost arch (now bricked up again). The canal was only 3 metres wide, but this was just sufficient for the then usual salt barges; it was filled in again in the first half of the 16th century at the latest. Presumably, its usefulness was out of all proportion to that of the commercially significant buildings planned at the foot of the Stone Bridge. The place where the canal entered the quayside area can still be deduced from the pointed north-eastern end of No 1 Am Wiedfang and from the empty plot beside it, on which part of the city wall, which was closed up again in 1528, is exposed to view.

The **Kapelle St. Georg/Chapel of St George am Wiedfang (34)** was built in the second half of the 12th century in the middle of this port area, directly beside the canal.

Although it was de-consecrated during the Reformation and converted into a dwelling-house (No 7 Goldene-Bären-Strasse), architectural features of the two-storey church are still visible. Towards Goldene-Bären-Strasse, the romanesque doorway is preserved, while on the east side of the house, the unplastered apse built of small stone-blocks can be seen. The fact that this apse was raised beyond the height of the first storey in the 18th century was a result of its being mistaken for a turret. Inside the building, the hall church with its nave and two aisles and its three bays can still be recognised; its vaults rest on four cruciform pillars, the first time that these appear in Regensburg. A staircase leads up to the upper floor through the thick west wall; furthermore, there used to be a link between the two storeys in the middle bay. The construction of St George's as a two-storey chapel suggests that it was intended for two different groups of people or functions. What is interesting in this context is the fact that, just a few metres further eastwards, there was also the octagonal St Margaret's Chapel, which was de-consecrated during the Reformation as well. No trace of this presumably late romanesque central-plan building now remains, but a knowledge of its existence is important for imagining the mediaeval port in Regensburg.

At the end of Goldene-Bären-Strasse, the approach road to the Stone Bridge (see p. 223ff.) turns off to the left, while Brückstrasse on the right leads into the city centre. The tradesmen that lived here in the Middle Ages catered to the needs of travellers, who could, for instance, have their worn-out shoes repaired as soon as they arrived in the city. Indeed, three of Regensburg's four cobblers had their workshops here in 1319. The formerly close links between the bridge and this street are also clear from the fact that most of the houses in Brückstrasse paid their dues to the bridge-master until 1366.The mediaeval appearance of the street has been altered due to various con-

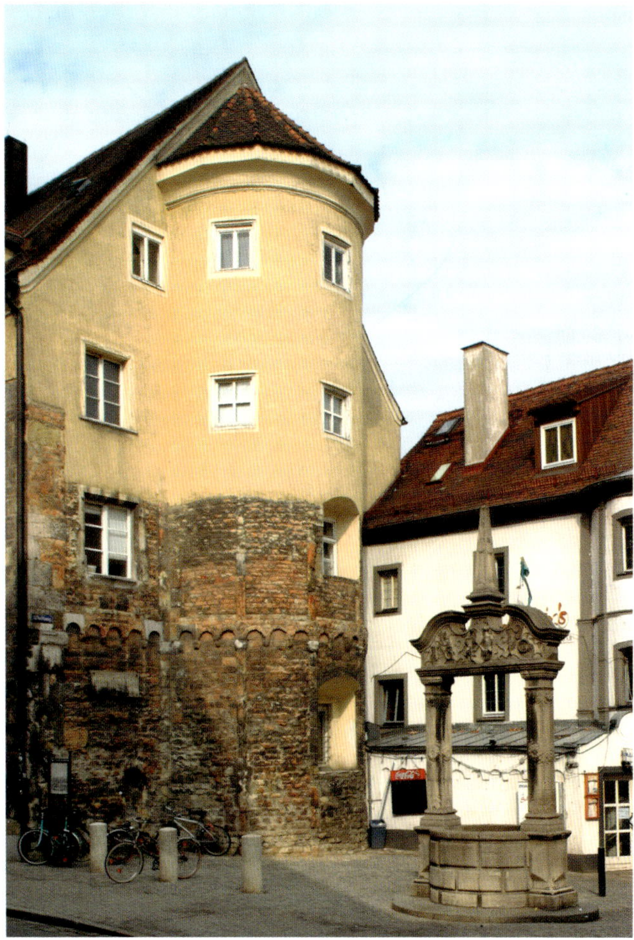

The former St George's Chapel in Am Wiedfang (12th cent.), from the south-east. In front of it is a Renaissance fountain dating from 1610.

versions and new buildings. What is striking are the overhanging upper-storeys on several houses, by means of which the size of the rooms in them could be increased. On the right, moreover, the now only five-storey remainder of a once larger tower dating from about 1220 can be seen as part of No. 4. The building it formed part of was owned by the Benedictine abbey in Kastl before 1255.

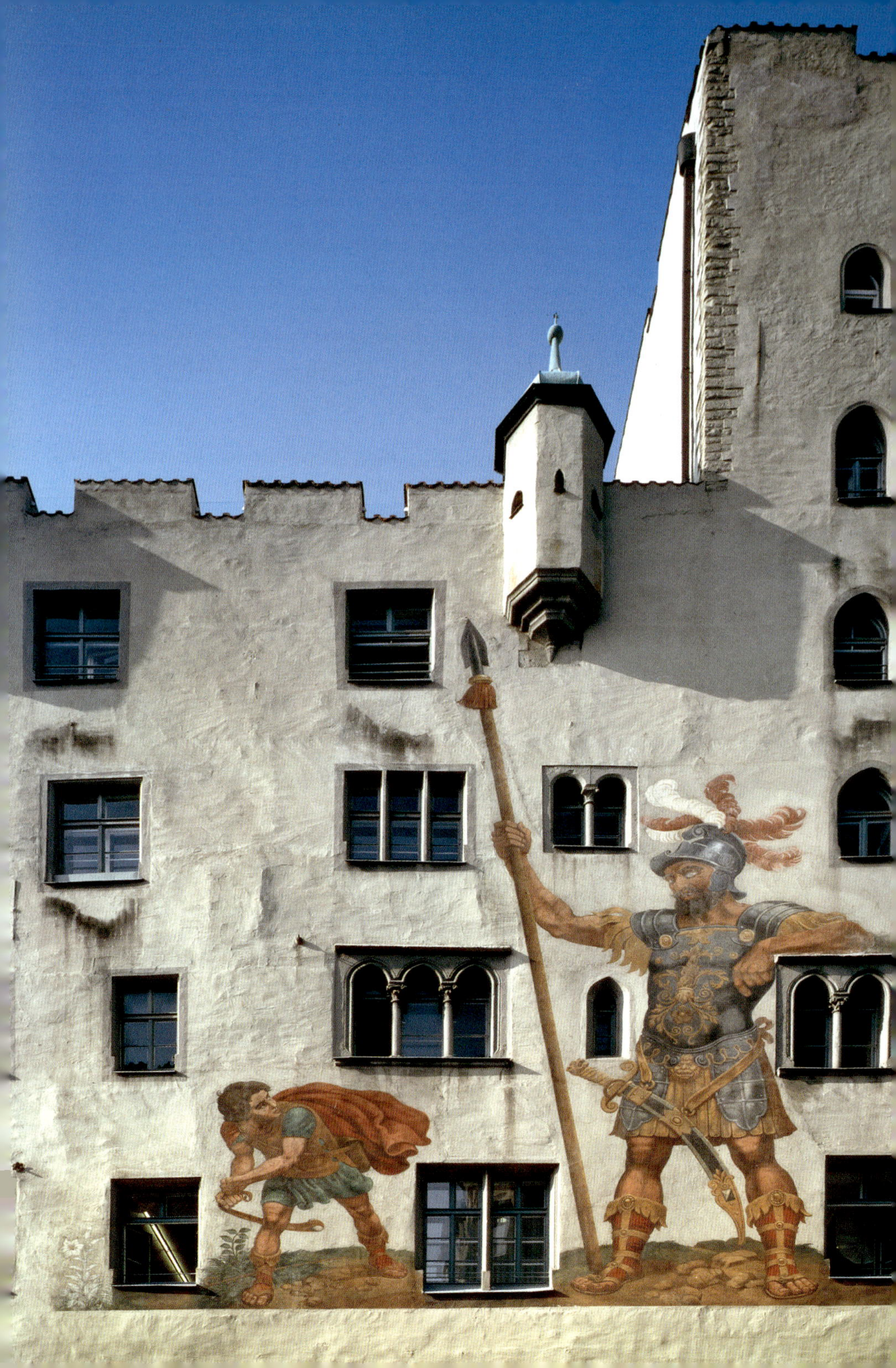

View up Brückstrasse to the Goliath House (13th cent.). Mural on the facade by Melchior Bocksberger (c. 1570/80)

From Brückstrasse, one's gaze falls on an impressive early gothic facade decorated with an enormous depiction of the battle between David and Goliath. This patrician mansion acquired the name **Goliathhaus/Goliath House (35)** due to this painting, which was originally executed between 1570 and 1580 by Melchior Bocksberger but has been altered several times since. The house, like its neighbours, is on the site of the northern wall of the Roman legionary camp. It was built in the first half of the 13th century, probably by the Thundorfer family, who owned it until 1290. With its tower to the right – from the observer's point of view – of the living quarters, the Goliath House embodies the 'classical' type of imposing Regensburg patrician mansion. This is reinforced by the crenellations on the roof and the polyhedral corner turrets, both expressing a willingness to fight. The symbolic nature of these ornaments, which were hardly suitable for military purposes, is particularly clear in this case, as there was never a walkway behind the battlements.

From the Goliath House, it is then only a few steps back to Kohlenmarkt and Rathausplatz.

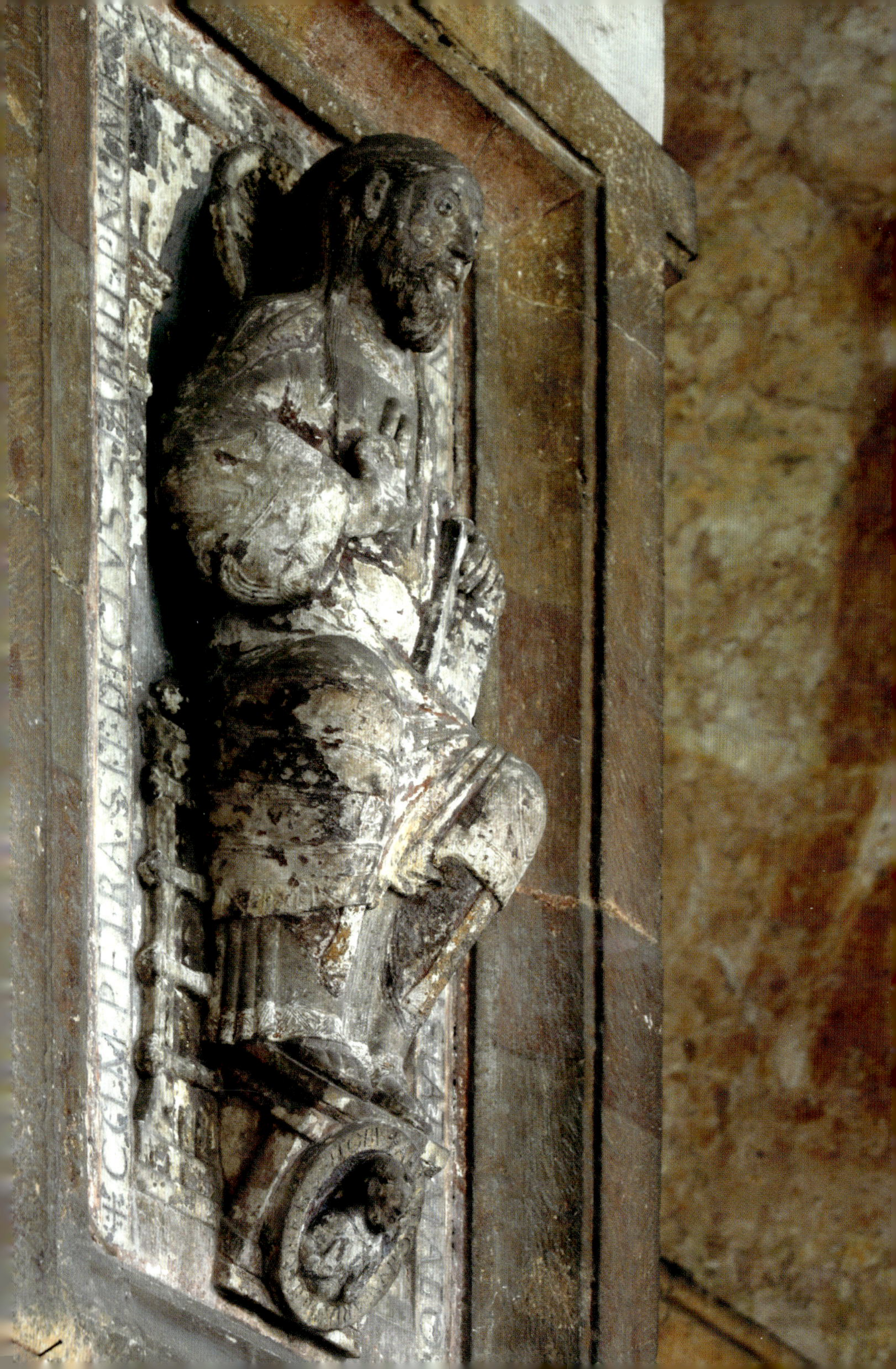

From Abbey to Palace: St Emmeram's

When Duke Arnulf of Bavaria had the newer part of Regensburg fortified about 920, St Emmeram's Abbey and the land around it, which lay in its southernmost corner, was surrounded by the ring-wall as well. St Emmeram's, the oldest and most influential monastic community in the city, was in existence as early as 740, after the martyr Emmeram had been buried here in 700. His first grave was probably in St George's Church, which stood on the site of a late-Roman cemetery but has now disappeared without trace.

Emmeram, who came from Poitiers in Western France, seems to have been a bishop at the court of Theodo, an early Bavarian duke. Legend says that the duke's daughter Uta had an affair with a judge's son. When the consequences of this love-affair could no longer be concealed and the couple confided in Emmeram, the latter is said to have tried to save the young people by suggesting that they should blame the pregnancy on him. He himself then set off on an already planned pilgrimage to Rome. It is also said that the duke's son, wanting to take revenge for his sister's disgrace, caught up with Emmeram three days later in Kleinhelfendorf (south of Munich), where he had the bishop tied to a ladder and cruelly tortured. The dying man is supposed to have uttered the wish to be buried in Regensburg. After he died, it rained steadily for 40 days and thus, in order to put an end to the flooding, the Bavarians granted his wish and had him brought by boat along the Isar and the Danube to Regensburg, where the townspeople gave him a triumphant welcome.

In view of the historical rivalry between the Agilolfing-Bavarian ducal family and the Frankish royal family, it seems fairly likely that Emmeram's murder – made public by means of an imaginative legend – served to place the blame for a bishop's death on the Agilolfings. In this case, Emmeram's canonisation by Bishop Gaubald, appointed by Boniface in 739, must also be seen as a political act directed against the Agilolfing dukedom.

St Emmeram's porch: relief showing Christ the Saviour enthroned, and a portrait of the benefactor (1049–60). This sculpture, together with the reliefs of SS. Emmeram and Denis on either side, is among the first examples of romanesque portal sculpture in Germany.

The Carolingian abbey church with the still preserved ring crypt that encircles St Emmeram's grave was erected under Abbot Sintpert

(768–791). The subsequent rapid rise of the monastery, whose abbots were also Bishops of Regensburg until 975, to a centre of art and culture was accompanied by the encouragement of the cult surrounding Emmeram by the Carolingian kings. In the end, the Emperor Arnulf of Carinthia made Emmeram the patron saint of the East Frankish Empire and had a new royal palace built near the martyr's grave. Moreover, he planned to make the church the royal family's burial place. These efforts to make St Emmeram's Abbey, and with it the city of Regensburg, into the political and cultural centre of the empire ceased when the Carolingian dynasty came to an end in 911 on the death of Ludwig the Child. Although the Ottonian emperors took up the cult of St Emmeram again for a while in the second half of the 10th century, and resided in the palace beside St Emmeram's when they held court in Regensburg, Henry II finally moved the royal palace back to Alter Kornmarkt.

Despite the political changes in the empire, however, the rise of the abbey, which had begun in 975, when St Wolfgang brought Abbot Ramwold from Trier, continued and reached its climax in the 11th century. At that time, masterpieces of book illumination were being created in St Emmeram's, and – not least because of its magnificent library – the abbey came to be a cultural centre of European rank. In 1052, Pope Leo IX visited the abbey and dedicated the just completed crypt to St Wolfgang in the presence of the Emperor Henry III. Only four years later, another pope, Victor II, visited St Emmeram's.

Until the death in 1164 of Bishop Hartwig, who had All Saints' Chapel (see p. 52ff.) built as his mausoleum, the bishops of Regensburg were buried in St Emmeram's. A devastating fire in 1166 led to the basilica, and the recently erected parish church of St Rupert, being rebuilt almost from the foundations. The lettering accompanying the pictures then painted on the walls of the church has survived, so that the programme of frescoes can be reconstructed. Inspired presumably by the terrible conflagration, Abbot Peringer II (1177–1201) had lead pipes laid from Dechbetten to the abbey to provide a water supply. It was a masterpiece of engineering.

When quarrels with the bishops of Regensburg became increasingly bitter in the 13th century, the abbey produced a brilliantly forged docu-

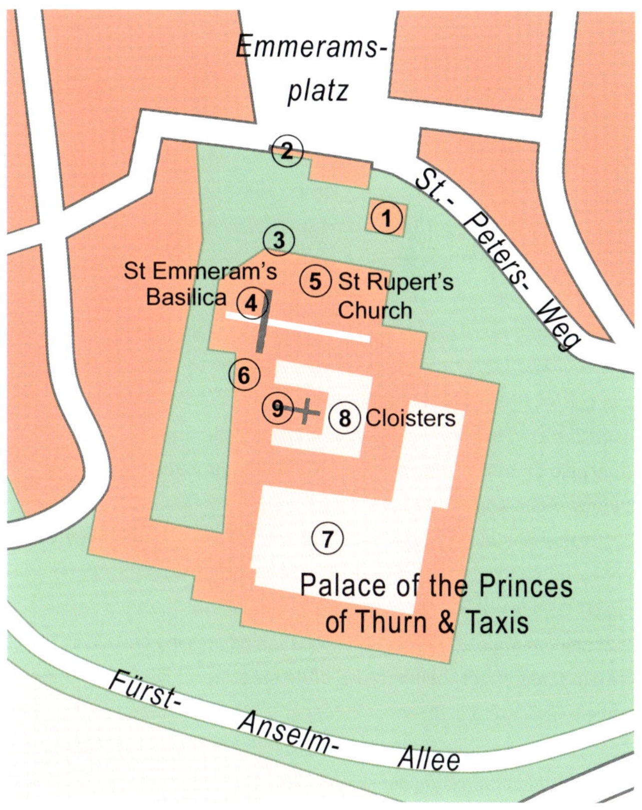

ment according to which Ludwig the Child, the East Frankish monarch buried in St Emmeram's in 911, had guaranteed it the status of an imperial abbey, answerable to no one save the emperor, and other privileges. The confirmation of this diploma by King Adolf of Nassau in 1295 had far-reaching consequences. The abbot of St Emmeram's became an imperial prince, and the abbey was placed under the direct supervision of the papal curia.

The library having been constantly enlarged, St Emmeram's developed into a centre of Humanism in the early 16th century. The abbey survived the turbulences of the Reformation almost unscathed, but suffered greatly in the Thirty Years' War. In 1633, after Regensburg's capture by the Duke of Weimar, the monastery buildings were damaged and looted. The worst blow, however, was the loss of the silver high altar dating from the first third of the 10th century, which the monks had to have melted down in order to be able to pay contributions to the victors. A fire that started due to negligence in 1642 also had devastating consequences for, among other things, the roof of the basilica. On that occasion, the painted romanesque coffered ceiling was finally destroyed.

In spite of the heavy losses sustained by the abbey in the first half of the 17th century, its last great period of eminence followed just a few decades later. This is due to the achievements of a series of great abbots. The first in this group was Coelestin Vogl (1655–91), who made good use of the abbey's money and was, moreover, an outstanding historian. He thus laid the foundation for St Emmeram's role as a centre of critical historiography. Throughout the 18th century, the abbey remained a widely known stronghold of research and was an important source of materials for the Bavarian Academy of Science when it was founded in Munich in 1759. The self-confident abbots had a highly developed urge to impress and this led, moreover, to numerous measures to improve and beautify the abbey buildings, the artistic climax of these efforts being the refurbishment of the church and the library by the Asam Brothers.

The political upheavals at the beginning of the 19th century put an end to this glorious era. As a result of the decree terminating the Holy Roman Empire, the Abbey was handed over to Prince-Bishop Carl von Dalberg, who initially enabled the monks to continue their pastoral and scholarly activities. When, however, Dalberg's principality was incorporated into the Kingdom of Bavaria in 1810, the full force of secularisation was felt. The abbey church became a parish church and the mediaeval art treasures which the abbey had preserved, above all works dating from Carolingian and Ottonian times (e.g., the Codex Aureus created for the Emperor Charles the Bald in c. 870, the portable altar that belonged to the Emperor Arnulf of Carinthia and also the Emperor Henry II's Sacramentary from the early 11th century) were all carried away to Munich. The monastery buildings, unused after the monks

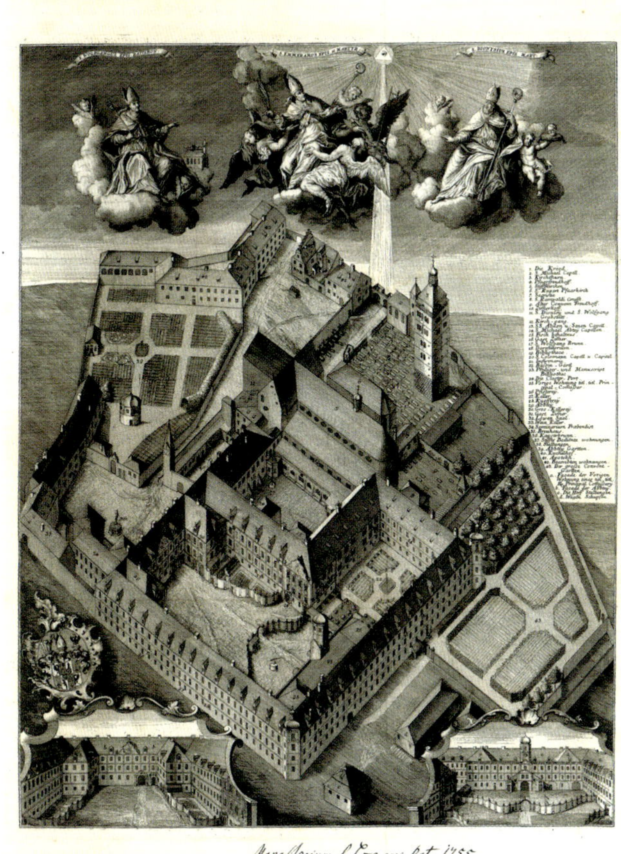

A bird's eye view of the former St Emmeram's Abbey, from the south-east. Copper engraving, c. 1750 (Museum of Regensburg History)

had been expelled, were handed over to the House of Thurn and Taxis in 1812 to compensate it for the loss of the postal monopoly.

Although their principal residence was, at that time, still in Frankfurt, the Princes of Thurn and Taxis had already been in Regensburg since 1748, when the emperor had bestowed on them the hereditary office of imperial representative at the Perpetual Imperial Diet. The princes transferred their family seat to Regensburg only after they had been given St Emmeram's, the former imperial abbey. Thus, in the early 19th century, a complex of monastic buildings that had had great significance for imperial history was transformed into a magnificent palace, which in turn ranked among the greatest in Europe. In spite of the change in ownership as a result of the period of Secularisation, the Princes of Thurn and Taxis maintained a sense of obligation towards the 1200–year-old tradition of St Emmeram's until the 20th century. The history of the Holy Roman Empire with its many religious and worldly facets can still be experienced there in its original surroundings.

From Emmeramsplatz, only the impressive **bell-tower (1)** announces the extensive complex of former monastery buildings. Free-standing like the towers of the Alte Kapelle (see p. 67f.) and of the Obermünster (destroyed in 1945), the campanile was probably constructed in the 10th century, using Roman stone-blocks. In 1575–79, the old tower was encased in another layer of stones and decorated with statues that had particular connections with St Emmeram. This unusual project has to be seen in connection with the mood of the Counter-Reformation. Instead of the old tower, which had become unsightly due to various kinds of damage, the abbey erected, within the boundaries of the Protestant imperial free city, a tower which was in effect a monument to its own historically legitimated importance. This is also the explanation for the strikingly conservative style of architecture, e.g., the apparently gothic canopies over the statues and the pairs of romanesque-style round-arched windows.

Access to the extensive complex of former abbey buildings is through a gothic **portal facade (2)**. It is the only section completed of a portal with a porch on a rectangular base, which was probably begun at the beginning of the 1250s and would have had two storeys. This building was to replace an older, probably Carolingian, porch on the same site. The two doors with their pointed arches reflect the intention to build a porch

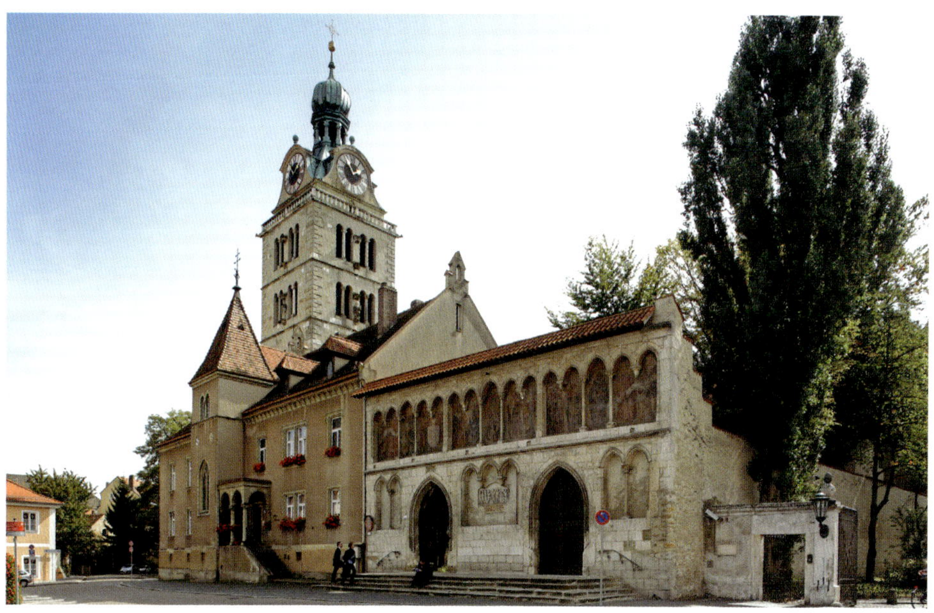

View of St Emmeram's gateway from the north-west. Left, beside it, the priest's house, built in 1890 on the foundations of the romanesque St Michael's Chapel; behind it, the free-standing bell-tower

with two bays. According to the inscription, a relief showing the first station of the Way of the Cross (Jesus is sentenced to death by Pontius Pilate; Jesus takes the cross upon his shoulders) was placed in the blind arcade between the portals in 1511. This is very early evidence of the custom, which evolved in the late Middle Ages, of portraying Christ's passion against the background of the Via Dolorosa in Jerusalem. The paintings in the upper blind arcades also go back to mediaeval times, but have been restored several times since.

Behind this wall with its doorways are the **churchyard and porch (3)** of the basilica. On the site of this idyllic churchyard with its greenery, there was, probably from the 11th century on, a two-aisle hall linking the basilica and the gateway. The two aisles were necessary due to the church's double portals. The hall was re-erected after the fire in 1166. Although only the two southern bays closest to the church have survived, the pillars attached to the west wall of the churchyard and the blind arcades there show that the hall originally had seven bays. It is not clear whether the hall collapsed after a short time or whether it was demolished. In this context, Conrad IV, the Staufer king, comes to mind. He had several buildings pulled down in revenge for an attempt to assassinate him in St Emmeram's Church in 1250.

It is still possible to get an idea of the architecture of the porch in the two surviving bays as the high-mediaeval floor-level has been retained. The transverse and ridge-ribs of the groin-vaulting rested on massive free-standing pillars, which divided the two aisles, and pillars attached to the walls. The half-columns in front of the pillars have capitals with convex moulding with various kinds of ornamentation; in their style and in their motifs, they show similarities to those in the the nave of the Scots' Church (p. 188f.).

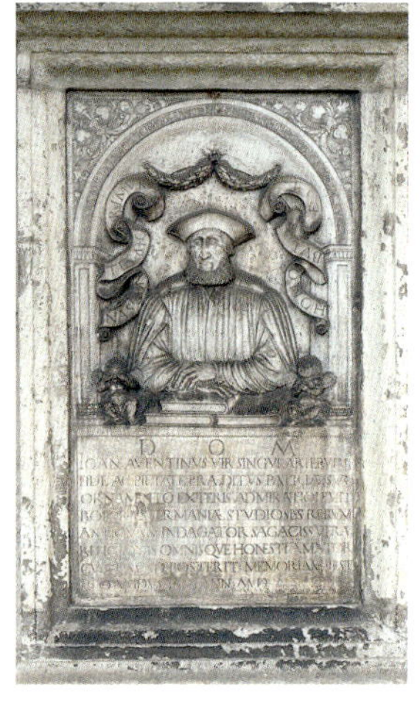

Memorial to the Bavarian historian Aventinus in the churchyard at St Emmeram's

There are numerous stone pictures and memorials in the churchyard and porch; particularly remarkable are, firstly, the relief portraying the scene in the Mount of Olives, which was probably created by a master mason from the cathedral and which is to be found on the eastern pillar on the wall of the porch, and, secondly, the Renaissance memorial (on the western wall of the porch) for the great Bavarian historian and philologist Johann Turmair, known as Aventinus, (1477–1534), who was a frequent visitor to the abbey's library.

The Basilica

Exterior

Due to the building's situation and the limited access to it, the visitor can always glimpse only parts of the **basilica's (4)** exterior. (see also p. 156). The church lacks a really impressive facade. Yet the entrance is splendid. Two apsis-like, round-arched niches with rectangular doors fitted into them are to

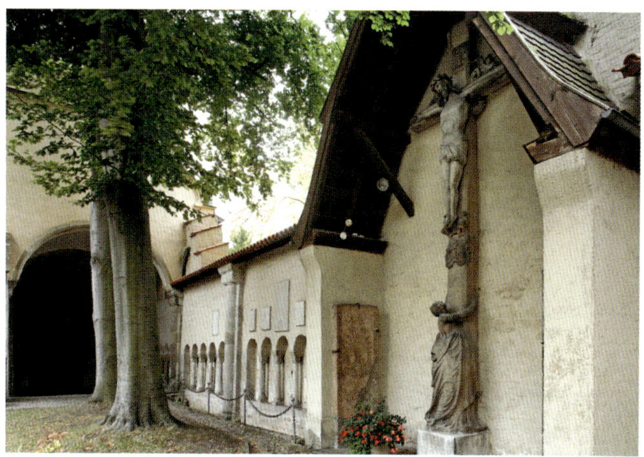

St Emmeram's: west wall of the churchyard, with its romanesque divisions

be seen in the south wall of the porch. The niches are framed by pillars with sculptures on them that signal the beginning of the use of portal sculptures north of the Alps. There are three limestone reliefs with figures that are almost three-dimensional: in the centre, Christ enthroned, on the left, St Emmeram and, on the right, St Dionysius (Denis). Below the figure of Christ is a portrait of Abbot Reginward with the dedication inscription. According to this, the doorway was erected between 1049 and 1060. This date has been confirmed by the dendrochronological examination of wood used when building it.

The unusual form of the so-called 'double-niche doorway' was possibly intended as a reference to the monumental niche in the west-work of the palace chapel in Aachen, thus expressing St Emmeram's claim to be a prestige building for the Carolingian kingdom. The choice of sculptures can also be seen in this light: the veneration of the Saviour was encouraged by Carolingian rulers, St Emmeram had enjoyed the rank of an imperial saint since the days of the Emperor Arnulf, while St Dionysius was the special saint for the Frankish monarchs. At the very time when the portal was being constructed, St Em-

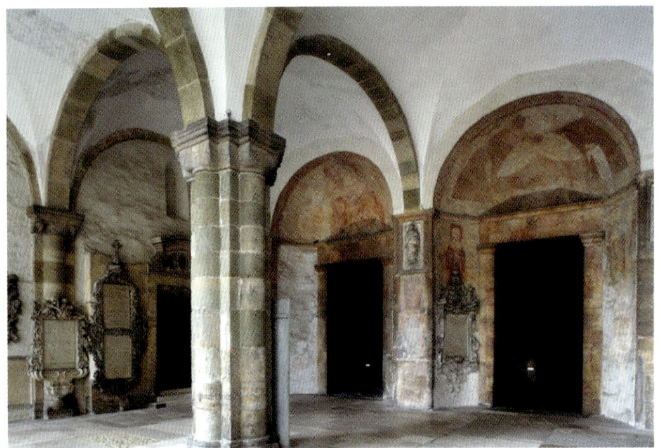

St Emmeram's: looking through the porch to the portal with its two niches, constructed 1049–60.

meram's Abbey emphatically claimed to own relics of this saint, which the Emperor Arnulf reputedly had had stolen from St Denis near Paris.

Interior

Whereas the right-hand entrance leads into the west transept, the left-hand one takes one into the actual basilica. At first sight, this appears to be baroque, but when one looks through the nave to the high altar, one can still clearly perceive – beneath the splendid gown of stucco and paintings – the original architecture of the tenth-century pillared basilica with a nave and two aisles but no transept. This had grown out of an 8th-century core and had been extended in the 11th century. What is striking in a pre-romanesque church is, above all, the unusually wide nave. Merely its remarkable dimensions make St Emmeram's obviously important for the history of architecture in Southern Germany.

In order to discover St Emmeram's architectural origins, it is necessary to go into the north choir, where the plaster has been removed to reveal two Ottonian (?) pillars, as well as romanesque masonry with double arcades inserted into it. Here, too, is the entrance to the 8th century **ring crypt**

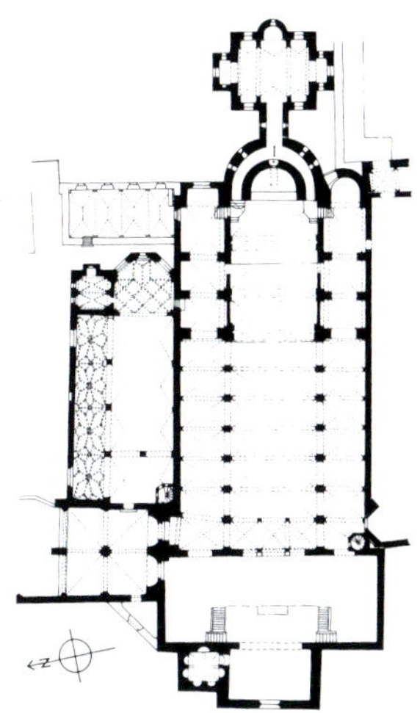

(before 791), which lies beneath the choir. This consists of a barrel-vaulted passage that forms a semi-circle around St Emmeram's grave, which lies directly beneath the high altar, and once enclosed the outer wall of the Carolingian choir – a highly unusual feature. At the top of the semi-circle, on the inside, there is a niche with a so-called fenestella, an opening that once permitted believers to peep at the sarcophagus containing the saint's bones. *Confessio*-structures of this kind, accessible via a semi-circular passage, were quite common in Carolingian architecture; they were all imitations of the ring-crypt that was constructed around St Peter's grave in Rome in 590. The inscriptions and wall paintings, only some of which have been revealed, are probably survivals from the time the crypt was built. They were influenced by the Anglo-Saxon art of the time and also have parallels in the abbey's Carolingian illuminated books.

From the top of the semi-circle, on the outside, it is possible to go through a barrel-vaulted passage leading off to the east into an **outside crypt**, which Abbot Ramwold had had constructed as a *crypta ecclesia*, i.e., a church that lay partly underground, obviously a reminiscence of his earlier abbey, St Maximin in Trier. The building, which was consecrated by St Wolf-

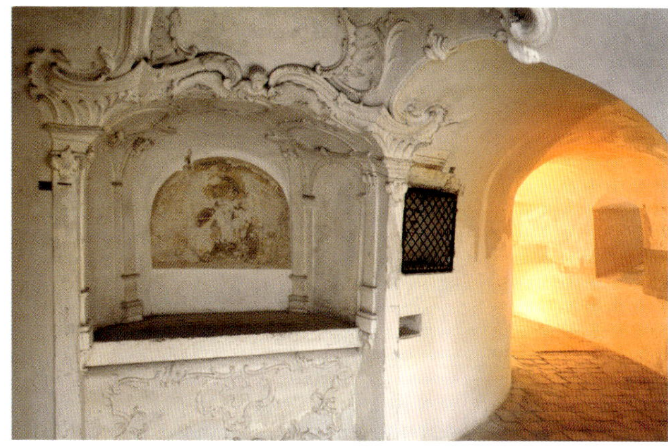

St Emmeram's: ring crypt (8th cent.): the *fenestella*, which once permitted pilgrims to glimpse the saint's sarcophagus, was closed by means of a stone slab early on and decorated with stucco in the 18th cent.

gang in 980, has a square ground-plan, to which in the east an apse and in the north and south an annex were added. In the southern annex stands Ramwold's sarcophagus, which was presumably also the architect's intention, such outer crypts often being used for the burial of ecclesiastical dignitaries. On the other hand, the room no longer has its original layout. Until it was altered in 1773/75, the crypt was divided by means of two pillars into two aisles with three bays each. This presumed hall-like room was one of the first of its kind in Germany. A survival of this earlier layout is the capital placed in front of the pillar on the south-western wall. The original plan was further altered in Ramwold's lifetime already. Even before the building was finished, the idea of constructing a two-storey crypt had been abandoned, perhaps because of structural problems.

The fragment of a painting (c. 980), discovered on the north wall of the passage connecting the ring crypt with the outside crypt, indicates that, when the latter was built, there was a depiction of the Last Judgement here.

The **west transept** with its rectangular choir, which was added in the mid-11th century, rises at the west end of the basilica, but was, unfortunately, separated from it optically when the baroque organ-loft was constructed. The west transept gives a clear impression of the monumental quality of the basilica when it was built. The triumphal arch at the threshold of the choir corresponds in its dimensions to the arch which, until the organ-loft was installed, framed the approach to the nave of the basilica from the west transept, The archaic severity of this architecture is enlivened by the choir platform with a flight of steps at each side. Underneath this platform is **St Wolfgang's Crypt**. Consecrated by Pope Leo IX in 1052, this is a hall-like room with a nave, four aisles and four bays that has an exceptionally harmonious atmosphere. This impression is reinforced by the fact that the nave and all four aisles end in rounded niches in the west wall, and the three western bays in similar niches in the side walls. Round or, in the nave, octagonal

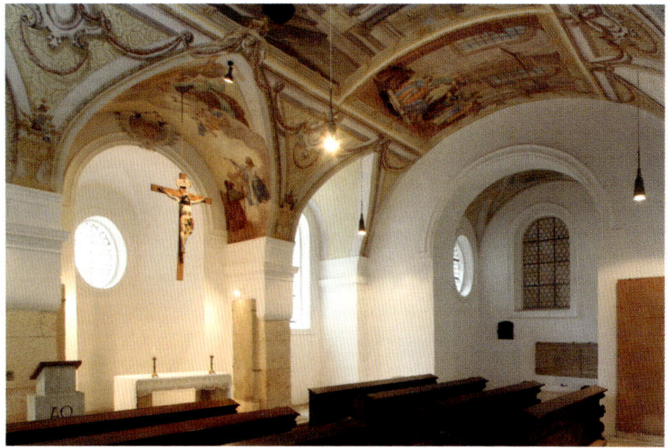

St Emmeram's: Ramwold's Crypt (consecrated in 980). The appearance of the room underwent major changes in 1773–75.

pillars, some of them with ornamented tetrahedral capitals, support the groin vaults. Their size varies slightly, the purpose of this variation being the creation of an exactly square vault, like a canopy, above St Wolfgang's Altar. Behind this, the fourth bay has been bricked up and contains three burial chambers, one above the other, which contained the bones of St Wolfgang and the alleged relics of St Dionysius. The uppermost burial chamber, which is higher than the crypt, carries the table of the Dionysius (now Holy Cross) Altar, consecrated in 1211. To the east, it is connected with a devotional niche that can be entered from the transept. This very original *confessio* was obviously restored when the altar was consecrated in c. 1211.

The huge dimensions of the west transept and the west choir become obvious only in connection with St Wolfgang's Crypt, the new centre of worship that was created in about 1052. Architecturally, the abbey thus became able to compete with the cathedral, which had also acquired an enormous westwork just a few decades earlier. What was at least as important was the parallel to the Abbey Church of St Denis near Paris, which also had a comparable west transept. Since St Emmeram's claimed at that time to have St Dionysius' relics (previously stolen from St.Denis' Abbey) in its safekeeping, the ab-

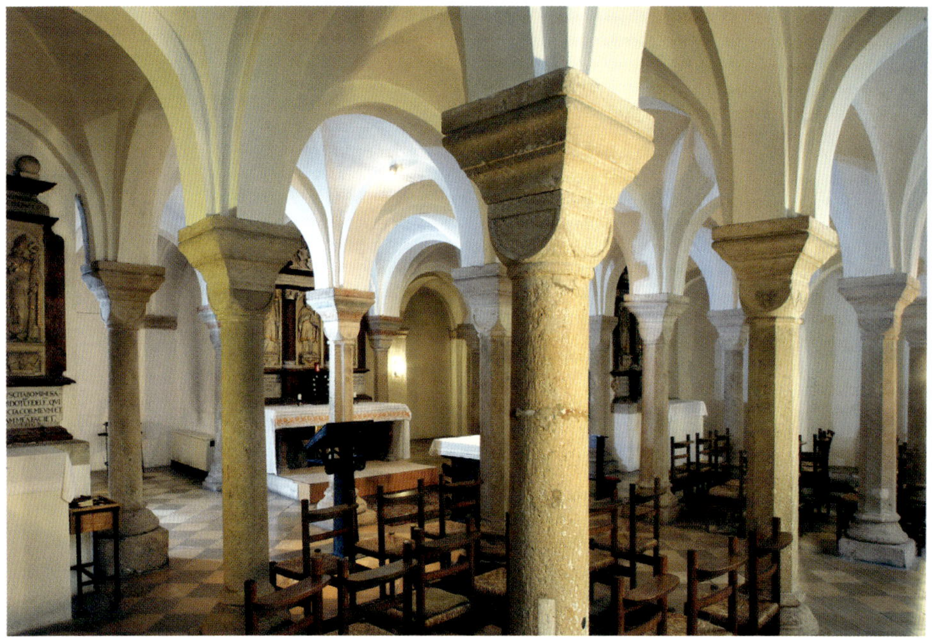

St Emmeram's: Wolfgang's Crypt (consecrated in 1052). 16 columns and pillars support the vaulting in this harmonious room.

bey's intention in building the west transept was obviously to show that it subscribed to the tradition of the ancient royal monastery of the Frankish kings. Significantly, the altar in the west choir was dedicated to St Dionysius.

The **Chapel of St Mary Magdalene** lies in the northern spandrel between the choir and the transept. It is in the base of a projected tower, which was presumably to have had a counterpart on the south side of the choir, thus making the west transept appear even more massive. The Magdalene Chapel is a square room with rounded niches in the walls, rather like those in St Wolfgang's Crypt, and is exceptionally beautiful. This is underlined by the wall-paintings, whose oldest layer dates from the period after the fire in 1166. In the lower storey of the chapel, or rather, of the planned tower, there is a room with a single pillar that is accessible from St Wolfgang's Crypt.

Baroque Decorations

Unlike the west transept and the crypts, the main basilica in St Emmeram's was completely refurbished from 1731 on under Abbot Anselm Godin. Johann Michael Prunner, an architect from Linz, covered up the pillars, structured the nave by means of pilasters along the walls and inserted a barrel vault with transverse ribs and dormer vaults underneath the flat romanesque ceiling. This interior shell is decorated with paintings and stucco work by the brothers Cosmas Damian and Egid Quirin Asam. What is remarkable is that the basilica's basic architectural plan, which dates back to the early Middle Ages, is not concealed by illusionistic alterations, as often happened during similar baroque transformations. In keeping with this policy, the themes of the programme of frescoes and statues are designed to glorify the abbey's great mediaeval history. For instance, the stucco figures above the arcades in the nave and above the oratories in the chancel portray, without exception, mediaeval saints and holy men who are connected with St Emmeram's. The paintings which decorate the walls of the nave, alternating with statues, illustrate scenes from Emmeram's life. Due to the way the stucco is used to frame and slightly tilt the surface of the pictures, the artist intentionally creates the impression that these are historical paintings hanging on the walls. The ceiling fresco in the nave, painted so that it can be looked at from two directions, once again illustrates the abbey's early history. Looking eastwards, one sees the legendary 'Martyrs' Hill' near the abbey; it was named after early Christians in Regensburg who are alleged to have been murdered there. To the west, one sees Pope Leo III, who, by handing the Exemption Bull to monks from St Emmeram's, is said to have freed the abbey from the authority of the Bishop of Regensburg. The fresco in the chancel, alone, – appropriately for its liturgically significant position – is devoted to a purely religious topic, the glorification of St Benedict and his importance as a missionary.

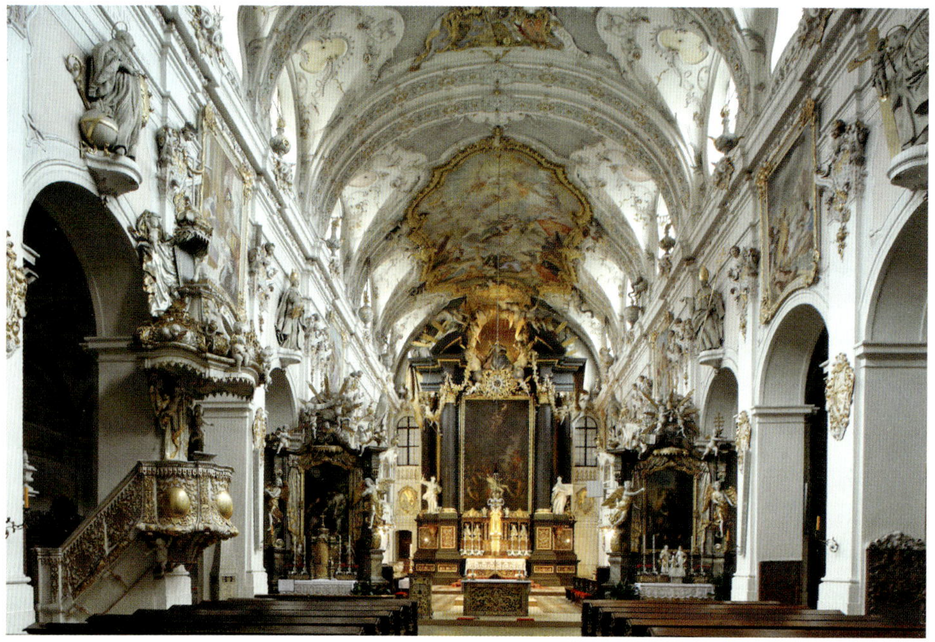

St Emmeram's: despite the baroque refurbishment of the basilica, its romanesque structure is still clearly visible. The paintings and stucco are by the Asam Brothers (1731–33)

Furnishings

The majority of the altars date from the 18th century. The high altar, with four columns and a retable showing St Emmeram's martyrdom, by Joachim von Sandrart (1666), goes back to the 17th century, but was re-modelled by Egid Quirin Asam. Beneath the mensa, there is a silver reliquary made soon after 1423 to hold the alleged relics of St Dionysius. With its rich, partially gilded relief decoration, it is one of the masterpieces of the goldsmith's art from 15th-century Regensburg. Abbot Wolfhart Strauss, who commissioned the reliquary, also donated a painted panel showing *Maria lactans*, which is kept in a baroque showcase on the Holy Trinity Altar in the north aisle. This painting, which shows the Madonna on her throne being crowned by angels, was probably the work of an unknown master about 1440 and shows similarities to Dutch paintings of that time.

Memorials and Monuments

St Emmeram's has an exceptionally rich and varied collection of sepulchral sculpture. Particularly noteworthy are the mediaeval tombs in the eastern part of the basilica, memorials to ecclesiastical and, above all, secular dignitaries, the majority of whom are not, however, buried in St Emmeram's. This, too, reflects how the abbey regarded itself and how it expected others to see it.

Whereas since the fire in 1642 only an inscription in the floor of the choir has commemorated the Emperor Arnulf of Carinthia, who presumably really was buried in St Emmeram's in 899, the table-like tomb for Abbot-Bishop Tuto (d. 930), which stands in the south aisle, marks the start of a series of closely related monuments. At the end of the 13th century and in the first half of the 14th century, the neutral table-style tomb was combined with individually sculpted effigies of the dead persons. The most valuable of these idealised portraits, qualitatively speaking, was created about 1280/90 and depicts a queen or empress, who is traditionally identified with Hemma (d. 876), the consort of King Ludwig the German. The recumbent statue, which still has traces of original colouring, was regrettably placed in a standing position in the wall in the 17th century, after the other parts of the tomb had obviously collapsed at that time.

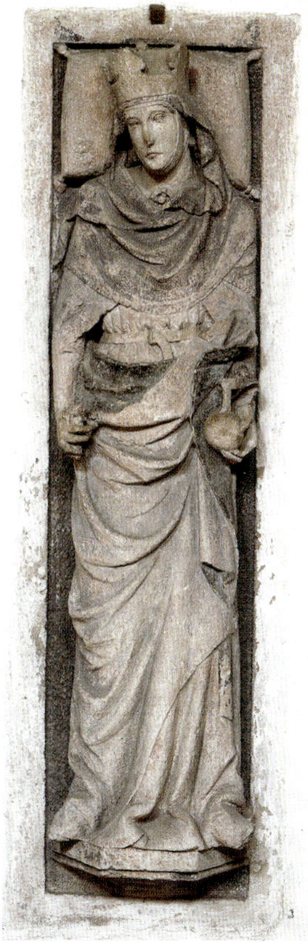

St. Emmeram's: Queen Hemma's memorial slab

St Rupert's Church

Built on to the basilica and accessible via its porch, **St Rupert's Church (5)** was the abbey's parish church until 1812. The building, which used to have only a nave, was rebuilt after the fire in 1166 and acquired its choir – closed on three sides – in 1405. St Mary's Chapel was built on to the north side in 1431, before a north aisle was then added in 1474. Its easternmost bay was used by Regensburg's goldsmiths as their guild chapel; west of it was the chapel for carpenters and cartwrights.

After the wooden coffered roof in the nave collapsed in 1765, the roof and all the decorative painting in the church were renewed in rococo style, although the mediaeval architectural elements were incorporated into the new design. For instance, delicate rocailles in the aisle are in harmony with the slender late gothic stellar vaults. Furthermore, some of the mediaeval furnishings were retained, for example, the mid-15th -century tabernacle with a tall finial on it decorated with painted figures of saints. Another remarkable feature is the stone half-length figure on a romanesque pillar, depicting the Madonna with a clothed child (c. 1330).

The painting on the baroque high altar (c. 1690) is by Johann Heiß, a painter from Augsburg, and shows the baptism of Theodo, the early Bavarian duke, by St Rupert. Otto Gebhard's painted ceiling (1765?) in the nave also celebrates the triumph of Christianity over heathendom in early mediaeval Bavaria.

Until the present-day sacristy of St Emmeram's was built in 1615, a chapel dedicated to St Zeno of Verona, which was probably built in the 8th century, stood on the same site, behind the choir of St Rupert's Church. This chapel was one of the earliest religious buildings in Regensburg and the most northerly place of veneration for St Zeno.

The Former Abbey

Opposite St Rupert's, in the west wall of the porch, there is a passageway leading to the site of the former abbey, although the buildings on it now reveal little, at first sight, of the nature of the mediaeval abbey. Instead, a courtly atmosphere has dominated here since the arrival of the Princes of Thurn and Taxis in 1812, and it is the grand buildings erected in the 19th century that are mainly responsible for this impression. South of the former Treasury beside Emmeramsplatz, on the site of

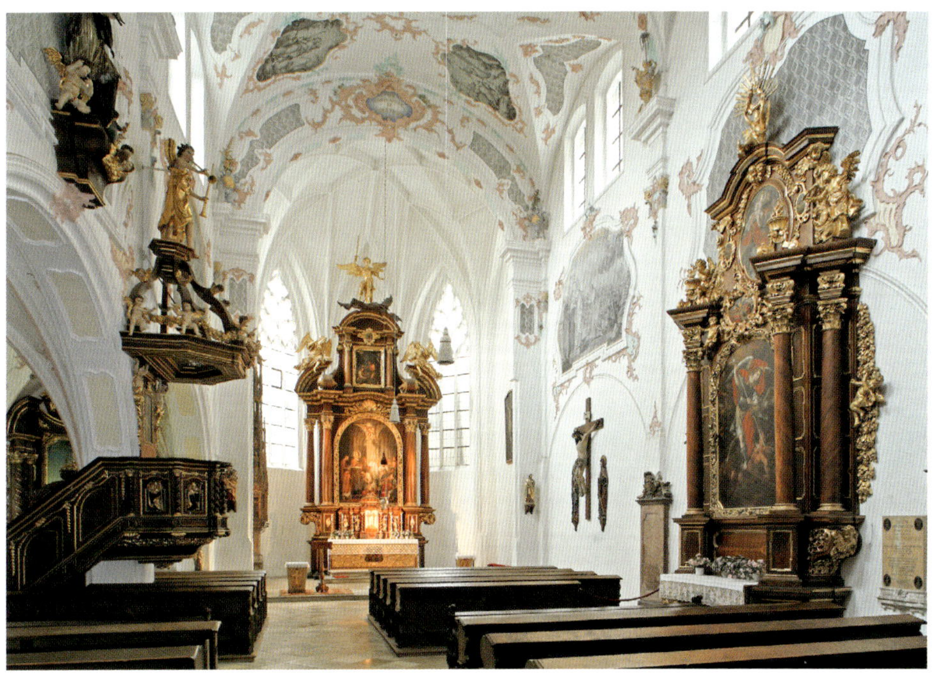

St Rupert's, the parish church for St Emmeram's Abbey until 1812, was built in the 12th cent. and provided with baroque vaulting in 1765.

the former monastery garden, is the stable complex (🏛M), built by Jean-Baptiste Métivier in 1828–31. The two wings of this neoclassical building provided accommodation for horses and coaches, while the main building behind the courtyard was used as an indoor riding-school.

The west transept of St Emmeram's rises impressively on the eastern side of the roadway. The **Old Monastery (6, 🏛M)**, which adjoins it to the south, was rebuilt after the fire in 1166. The ground-floor of the west wing, visible from the road, contained the rooms needed to cater for the monks: the kitchen, the larder and the refectory. Whereas the latter was refurbished in baroque style in 1689, the romanesque kitchen with its two bays has been preserved, as well as the larder, also a romanesque room with one central support. On this building, the 12th-century masonry has been left unplastered so that the public can see it. In front of these rooms was once the walled kitchen-courtyard, which was probably a herb-garden. In the 18th century, a building that included the coachman's entrance to the **palace courtyard (7)** was erected immediately next to the west wing. The architectural framework of the courtyard sums up St Emmeram's history, as it were: to the left, there is, first of all, the romanesque south wing of the Old Monastery, then its east wing, set back to the north; this was refurbished by Johann Michael Prunner in 1732–37, and contains – above the former chapter-house – the magnificent library, which has frescoes executed by Cosmas Damian Asam in 1737; to the north-east, around the so-called David's Courtyard, is the New Monastery, added on in 1666; furthest east is the outer east wing, built on late-mediaeval foundations and altered in the 18th century and again in the 19th – this was the residence of the Imperial Principal Commissioner from 1740–42; to the south is the 165m-long outer south wing, rebuilt by Max Schultze, architect

St Emmeram's: the west choir and transept. The romanesque west wing of the Old Monastery adjoins it to the south.

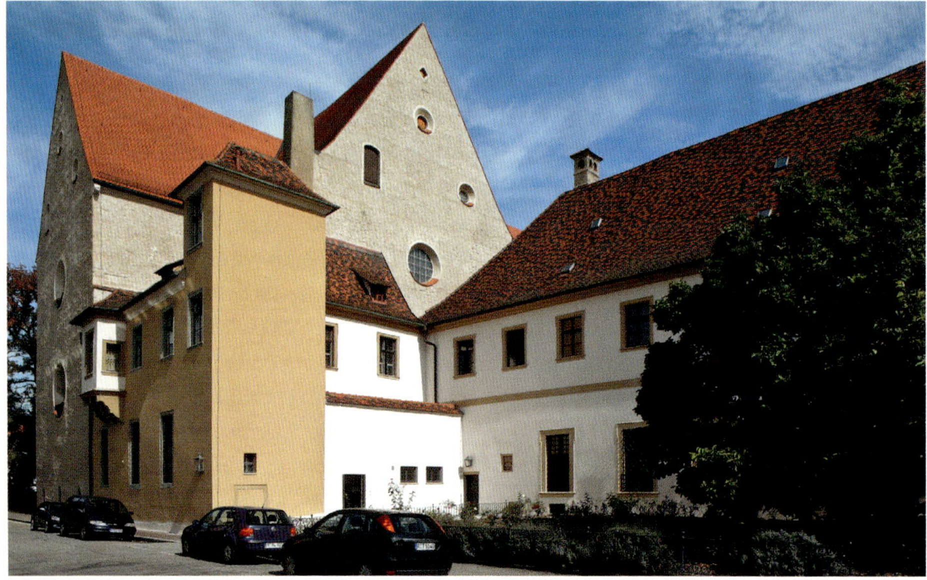

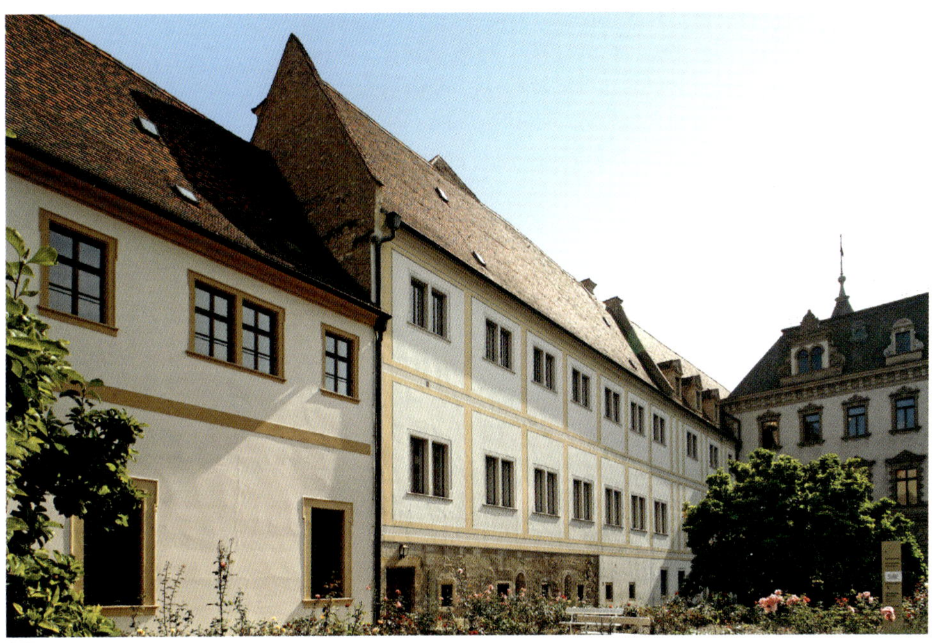

The former Abbey of St Emmeram, now the Palace of Thurn and Taxis: the west wing of the Old Monastery (12th cent.). The outer south wing of the Palace stands at a right angle to it (1883–91).

to the Prince of Thurn and Taxis, in 1883–91 – once a brilliant masterpiece of historicist pomp in the harmony of its architecture and furnishings. The Elector's Fountain has stood in the middle of the courtyard since 1889. It was placed first in what was then the front courtyard of the abbey and served, like the statues decorating the campanile, to show the Imperial City of Regensburg just how important the abbey considered itself to be. The kings chosen by the electoral princes (from the 13th century) were guarantors of the close alliance between the abbey and the empire. The Emperor Arnulf of Carinthia, as the ancestor of these kings, stands on the fountain; he, of course, had even built his palace next to St Emmeram's.

The Cloisters

The buildings of the old monastery surround the **cloisters (8, M)**, whose northern wing adjoins the church. Constructed over a long period between about 1220 and the end of the 14th century, they offer a fascinating picture of the stylistic development of gothic art in Regensburg. However, they also contain interesting remains of previous buildings on the site. For example, the bay in the corner furthest north-east is the last remnant of a chapel dedicated to St Benedict that was mentioned in 996 and restored about 1064. It once stretched further east from here, but was obviously not rebuilt after the 1166 fire. In contrast, the three bays that adjoin the corner bay to the west, are part of the dormitory which was located here until 1166. The monks could go straight through the door in the middle bay into the basilica for their nightly services. Some remains of the romanesque cloisters, which were erected about 1170, after the fire, and were already as large as the present-day complex, have also been preserved: above all, the two four-arched arcades in the east wing, which once enabled the monks to look across to the chapter-house. Windows of this kind between chapter-house and cloisters are a characteristic of mediaeval monasteries. Apart from having the practical purpose of letting light into the chapter-house, this was probably a formal reminder of the original function of chapter-houses as a place of penance and of judgement, as the antechamber to holiness, so to speak. In addition, there are suggestions that the monks in the chapter-house liked to keep an eye on what was happening in the cloisters.

In about 1230, an architect from the Cistercian sphere, and ornament sculptors trained in Northern France were engaged to restore the cloisters in gothic style. They began work in the north wing, without, however, touching the three dormitory bays. The latter were incorporated into the new cloisters despite the differing level of the floors and the dividing arch for the doorway. The seven bays added by c. 1240 – making eight altogether, with the western corner-bay, – display a wealth of early gothic detail in their sculptures. The

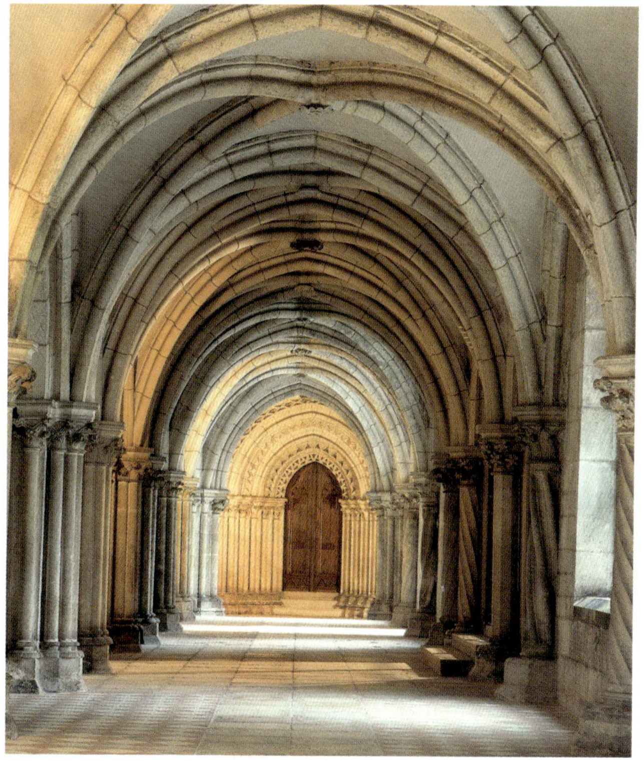

The former Abbey of St Emmeram, now the Palace of Thurn and Taxis: looking north through the west wing of the cloisters. The doorway (c. 1220) leads into the basilica.

architect's Cistercian training is recalled, for instance, by the preference for tripartite windows (symbol of God's trinity) and the allocation of this wing of the cloisters as a place for reading. This is indicated even today by the benches on the north wall as well as by the fact that the arcades looking out on the courtyard all face the centre bay, where the abbot and the reader had their seats. They sat against the suitably impressive background of a five-arched arcade with wheel windows above it. Both the arcade's pointed arches and the circle of the wheel window are surrounded by dog-tooth moulding. This decorative motif, with many variations, also dominates the pointed-arched archivolt of the pillared doorway with its seven contours that leads into the basilica from the corner-bay. The full effect of the depth created by this portal can be felt only when looking at it from the west wing, which had been gothicised, step by step from north to south, by the end of the 13th century. Trefoil and curved-dagger ornaments were now used in the window tracery. Masons from the cathedral were at work here, as they were in the south wing, which, with its naturalistic foliate capitals, is already high gothic. Building work continued here right through the 14th century, as shown by the portraits of abbots on the keystones. After that, the period of gothic restoration came to an end. In 1573, Hans Bocksberger painted frescoes in the romanesque east wing, which was completely refurbished in baroque style in 1732/33. Sections of these paintings as well as the already mentioned windows in the romanesque chapter-house have been visible since 1972.

The Thurn and Taxis Crypt Chapel

The original appearance of the cloister garden was changed almost completely when Maximilian Karl of Thurn and Taxis commissioned his architect, Karl Victor Keim, to construct a **crypt chapel (9, M)** for members of the princely family. Seen in its own right, the neogothic building, which was inspired by mediaeval castle chapels and completed in 1841, is one of the most important historicist family mausoleums in Germany; owing to its enormous proportions, however, it degrades the cloisters to an unimportant covered walk. What is more, among other things, the late-romanesque pump room which marked the end of the water conduit laid by Abbot Peringer II had to make way for the crypt chapel.

Access to the two-storey mausoleum is from the west wing. Whereas a flight of steps at one side leads down into the crypt, a gently ascending staircase provides access to the chapel. The rather dark room with a nave and two aisles has stellar vaulting that rests on slender marble columns; this room then opens to

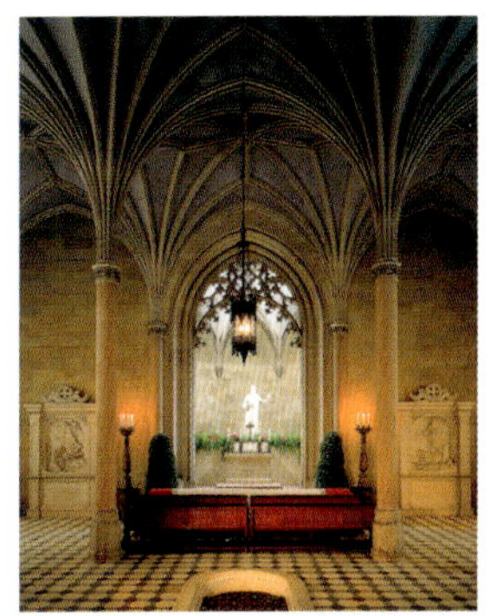

The former Abbey of St Emmeram, now the Palace of Thurn and Taxis: the Thurn and Taxis Crypt Chapel (1836). On the altar, a statue of Christ by Johann Heinrich Dannecker (1832)

the east into a light-filled choir. In it one sees a statue of Christ by Johann Heinrich von Dannecker, a sculptor from Stuttgart, which is placed above the simple altar on a revolving plinth. The theatrical presentation of this marble statue, which was completed in 1832 and whose gestures are illustrated by the inscription on the base 'Through me to the Father', is to be explained by the fact that this figure – whose first version had gone to the court of the Russian czar in 1824 – was considered by the German Romantics to represent a successful attempt to perpetuate the traditions of the mediaeval heyday of Christian sculpture.

The stained glass (1836–40) executed by Franz Josef Sauterleute for the side windows rounds off the gothic impression the chapel was intended to convey.

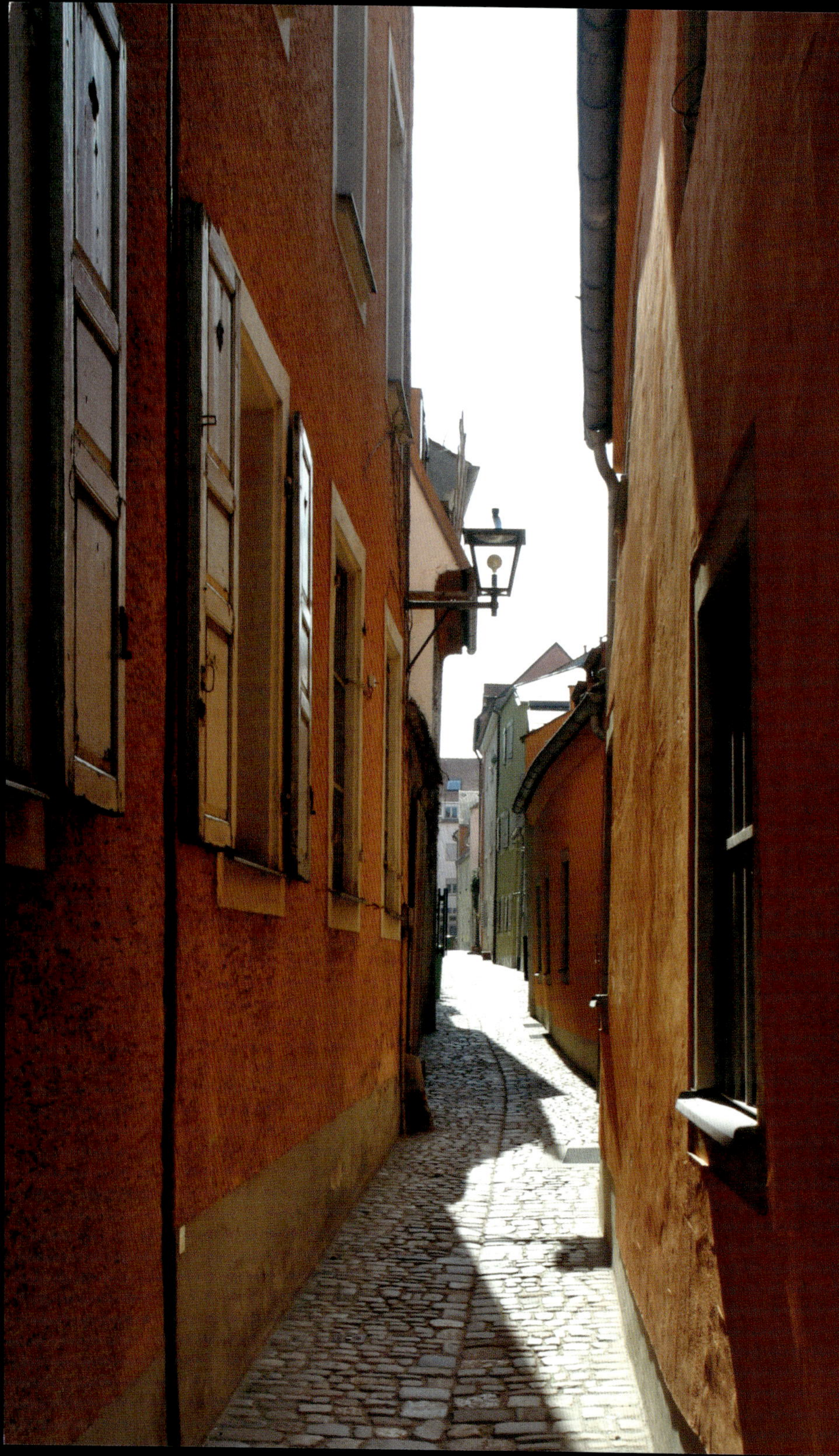

Westnerwacht, the Western Quarter

After Duke Arnulf had had the merchants' quarter and the site of St Emmeram's Abbey incorporated into Regensburg's ring of fortifications in about 920, the western city boundary ran where, even today, Weissgerbergraben, Arnulfsplatz and Bismarckplatz mark a caesura in the urban layout. As early as the 11th century, however, the urban settlement spread beyond this boundary and stretched southwards from Brunnleite, beside the Danube, as far as St James' (Jacob's) Benedictine monastery, founded c. 1100. Thus, by the mid-12th century, it seemed to be time to fortify this suburb with its impressive and massive buildings as well. The defences that were then erected, a roughstone wall with two ditches outside it, have left no visible traces in the modern city; only archaeological evidence of them has been found in the area of Rote-Löwen-Strasse and Fidelgasse. Furthermore, the new fortification did not really take into account the rapid growth the city was undergoing in Lederergasse, at that time the main road out of Regensburg in the direction of Nuremberg; the fortifications thus had to be extended still further westwards. By 1233 at the latest, the area as far as the then recently founded Dominican Convent was protected by a double wall. In 1284, finally, the authorities began to bring the whole of the western suburb, now known as the Westnerwacht, into the ring of defensive walls around the city. The former suburb had thus become an inner-city quarter with its own watchman. The building of the complete wall, which was a great financial strain on the city, reached its westernmost point with the erection of the Prebrunn Gate in 1293 and came to an end in the early 14th century, when the wall along the Danube was built. Thus, the mediaeval fortification of Regensburg in the west of the city, too, had reached the limits which are still marked today by the course of Regensburg's 'green belt', the tree-lined avenue around the city. There were political reasons for the fact that Prebrunn, a suburb that lay still further west and was economically important as the potters' settlement, was not included within the ring-wall. Since 1181, namely, the Duke of Bavaria had exercised political power there.

Westnerwacht: looking through Fidelgasse

Until the 19th century, the pattern of settlement in the western quarter was very heterogeneous. In the area nearer the inner city, as well as along Wollwirkergasse and, in particular, Lederergasse, there was dense building activity, with some quite impressive craftsmen's dwellings, while in the other areas, there was a large proportion of small houses as well as private and church-owned gardens. In the Middle Ages, metal-workers and leather-workers were concentrated in this district. The tanners had not been tolerated in the city at all for many years because of the unpleasant smells they caused, and so, since the 10th century, they had moved further westward every time the city was extended, until, after the last fortification of the western suburb in the late 13th century, they were at last able to settle down within the walls. The weavers and clothiers were primarily active in Westnerwacht. The proportion of brewers was also relatively high. In addition, there were all sorts of small tradesmen, quite a few day-labourers, a few smallholders and, not to be forgotten, the houses of three religious orders.

The economic development of the western quarter suffered a heavy blow when, in the late 15th century, the trade route to Nuremberg was moved to the northern bank of the Danube. Lederergasse thus lost its significance as a regional traffic artery. Then, when a bastion was built outside the Prebrunn Gate during the Thirty Years' War, thus causing it to be permanently closed, the tradesmen and craftsmen in Westnerwacht were completely isolated. The quietness of the area may even have led Albrecht Altdorfer, the Regensburg councillor and painter, to purchase a house in the middle of a large garden here six years before he died. The great master of the so-called Danube School thus began a tradition which reached its climax in the 18th and early 19th centuries, when some large houses with gardens were built on the outermost edge of the western quarter, thus bringing a patrician lifestyle to parts of a district inhabited by less wealthy people.

There was, however, no real change in the social structure until the refurbishment of the whole quarter was begun systematically in 1986, turning Westnerwacht into a popular residential area. Today, the craftsmen and tradesmen have nearly all disappeared.

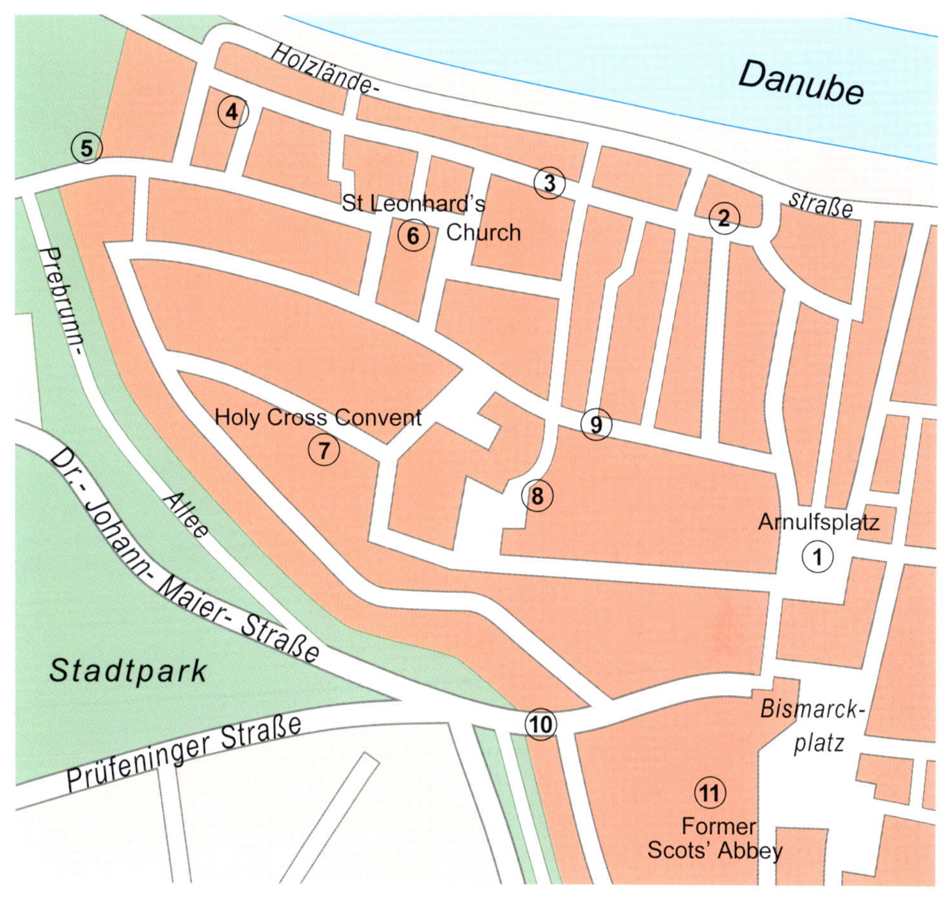

Arnulfsplatz

Arnulfsplatz (1), already an important road junction in Roman times and the site of an altar dedicated to Vulcan, the god of fire, is also the ideal historical starting point for exploring the mediaeval western quarter. From about 920 until 1830, the so-called Ruozanburg Gate stood on the east side of the square, at the end of Ludwigstrasse. This was the western gate of the city extension undertaken by the Bavarian Duke Arnulf. Before that, the street forked west and south-west, while Weissgerbergraben, which leads directly northwards to the Danube, still follows the line of Arnulf's city moat. To be quite precise, there were actually two parallel ditches with a rampart between them.

From the 10th century on, the rows of houses on the west side of Arnulfsplatz and west of Weissgerbergraben marked the beginning of the suburb. Although historicist facades – with the exception of the solid baroque Kneitinger Brewery and Restaurant – dominate the west side of the square today, this picture is deceptive in that most of the cellars of these houses are romanesque. For instance, the romanesque Arnulf's Tower stood south of Kneitinger's inn, on the other side of Kreuzgasse, until it collapsed in 1648; further north, where Wollwirkergasse begins, there are still the remains of a building dating back to the 11th century. These early stone buildings prove that this western suburb of Regensburg was not a district only for poor people but that some quite wealthy families, obviously those prepared to defend themselves, also settled here, especially in the part of Westnerwacht closest to the city. In the 13th/14th centuries, this area was called *vor burgh* – an expression that survives in the French word *faubourg* (=suburb).

Apart from Weissgerbergraben, two other streets lead northwards from Arnulfsplatz: Strasse zur Schönen Gelegenheit and Rote-Löwen-Strasse. Although the former is fairly wide by mediaeval standards and was thus called simply *ampla strata* (1266) or *weite strazze* (1325) (its present-day name dates back to c. 1700 and refers to the name of a house), the narrow Rote-Löwen-Strasse was, until the late 15th century, the more important street down to the Danube and the main road to Nuremberg. The house at No 1 Rote-Löwen-Strasse, which partially blocks the roadway, dates from this time, although the oldest parts of it – up as far as the ground-floor – are romanesque. The door-splays round the indoor entrance

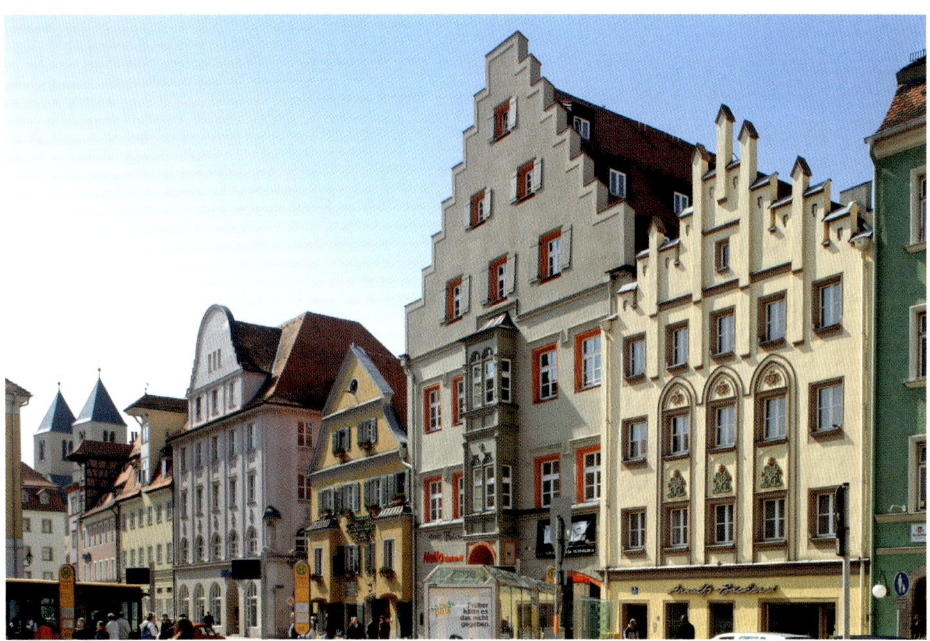

The line of houses on the west side of Arnulfsplatz. This was where the suburb began to develop from the 10th cent. Far left, the towers of St James' Scots Abbey Church.

to the main cellar were hewn from Roman stone-blocks. The upper floors were ravaged by fire in the 14th century. A dendrochronological examination has shown that the wooden beams used to rebuild the ceilings and roof were felled in 1354.

From here, the road continues to the left, past baroque warehouses and No 6 Weintingergasse, a dwelling-house with a romanesque core, to **Brunnleite (2)**. This square beside the Danube lies at a point where the river once formed a bay and is first mentioned in a document in 1007, when the Emperor Henry II gave two farms here to the diocese of Bamberg. No trace remains of these two properties, which were part of the western suburb included in the first western extension between 1125 and 1156. There was also a small church dedicated to St Matthew in Brunnleite; it is mentioned several times in 1253, but had probably been consecrated before 1155, in fact. The foundations of this romanesque building are to be found in the house at No 4, which faces the Danube, i.e., in a very busy place between Lederergasse and the banks of the Danube, with, running eastwards, the Holzlände. This stretch of quayside, where the wood market was held, has buildings dating back to the late Middle Ages. At the rear of No 5 Holzländestrasse, the stone-built core of the building erected in the 14th century contains a Jewish ritual bath dating from the late-18th century.

Lederergasse

Lederergasse (3) begins in Brunnleite; until the late 15th century this was the chief link between the city centre and the main road to Nuremberg. It got its name from the 'red' tanners, leather-workers who produced harder leather for shoe-soles and suchlike from cowhides, as opposed to the softer, more supple leather produced by 'white' tanners from the hides of calves, goats, sheep and other animals. The local name *unter den Lederern* (among the tanners) occurs for the first time in 1251, but the traces of their settlement go back to the early Middle Ages. At first, wooden houses were built on this land, but the earliest stone buildings appeared at the end of the 11th century – along with the still visible division into plots.

No 1 Lederergasse immediately offers an authentic picture of the early stone buildings in this long street. Whereas the eastern part of the building adjoining Brunnleite was erected in gothic style already in the second half of the 13th century, the nucleus of the building to the west is 12th century. From the cellar up to the first-floor, it still has romanesque barrel and rib vaults. Archaeological excavations, moreover, uncovered remains of the late 13th-century furnaces in which the tanners heated animal hides in order to speed up the rotting process and thus the loosening of the hairs.

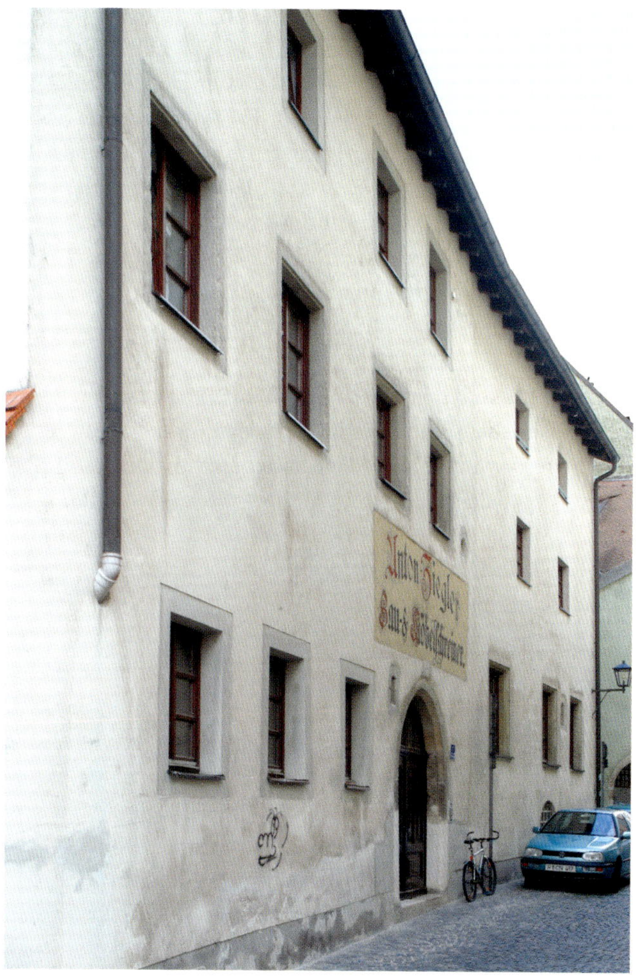

No 1 Lederergasse, one of the oldest tradesmen's houses in the street. The 13th cent. extension is at the front while the original 12th cent. building stands behind it.

Further along Lederergasse, numerous old gables for hoists bear witness to the former commercial use of these properties. Despite later conversions, nearly every house has mediaeval cellars. Even the former brewery and inn at No 9, which was completely refurbished in the Renaissance, still has a two-storey 12th-century core in the south-western part of the building. No 25, another former brewery, was also renovated in the Renaissance; the building consists of a south-eastern nucleus dating from the 12th century, of which only the stone-built cellar has survived, and a four-storey tower with cellars to the west, which was built in the second half of the 13th century. Such examples show that, when these sometimes quite wealthy inhabitants of the western suburb built houses on their land, they often took the design of burghers' houses in the city centre as their model.

Herrenplatz

Lederergasse leads into **Herrenplatz (4)**, a square which seems idyllic because of the trees in it, but which at the same time appears somewhat out of place in its small-scale suburban surroundings because of its wide, regular layout. It is not, in fact, a square with a long history. Until the late 15th century, the land was built on, in the same style as in the streets around it.

After the imperial city had placed itself under the rule of Albrecht IV, the Bavarian duke, for economic reasons, the duke started to build himself a palace in 1489. The new residence for the Wittelsbach rulers was to be erected in addition to the old Ducal Palace in the city centre (see p. 64ff.). A number of buildings at the western end of Lederergasse and in the parallel street to the south, Gerbergasse, were demolished to make room for the new building. This, however, was nowhere near finished when, pressure having been exerted by the emperor, the duke again had to recognise Regensburg as a free imperial city. Thus it came about that a representative of the emperor took up residence in the completed part of the palace instead of the duke. When this imperial employee moved out in 1510, the unfinished building began to fall into disrepair.

The house at No 2 Herrenplatz on the north side of the square survived the 15th-century demolition process. Its nu-

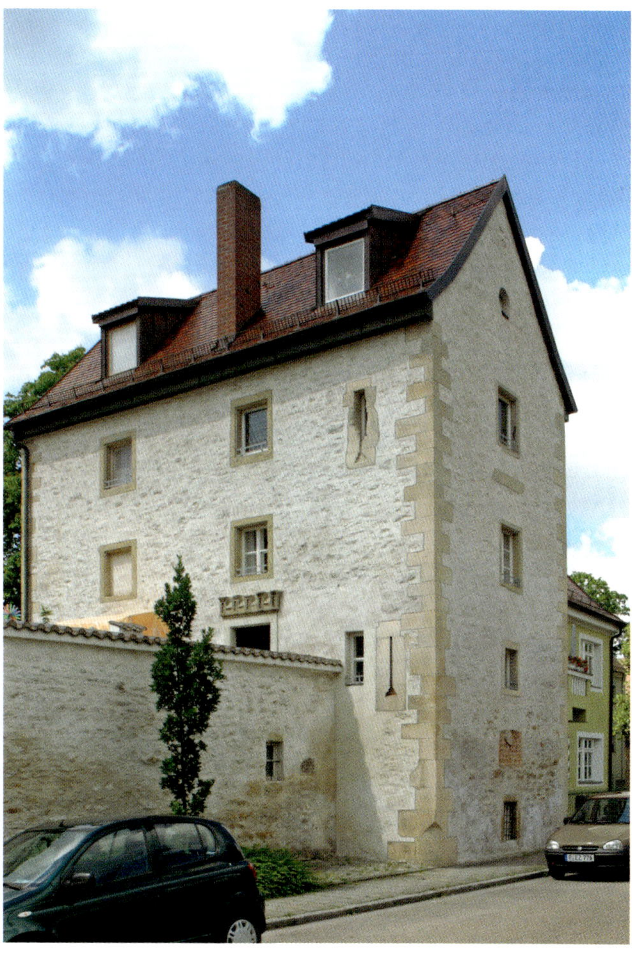

View of No 2 Herrenplatz from Holzlände. The core of the building is formed by a tower dating from 1320 that was part of the city walls.

cleus is a tower built as part of the city walls in 1320. A Latin inscription on its north side commemorates the beginning of the last section of the wall around the Westnerwacht, the stretch along the Danube. One of the earliest representations of Regensburg's crossed city keys was to be seen on the gothic coat of arms here, but it is now very badly weathered. Like many of the other towers in the walls here, this tower was probably used as a dwelling-house from an early stage. It was extended southwards in the 15th century, so that the tower just looks like a house that has turned out rather too tall.

In the south-west corner of the square, a striking tower-like construction on the houses built in the 1990s is a reminder of a tower that used to stand here, probably a relic of the palace built by Duke Albrecht. This late gothic tower had been created by adding further storeys to a 12th-century romanesque tower-house, remains of which are still preserved in the cellar and on the ground-floor of the present building. Before the northern part of the building (No 4 Herrenplatz) was constructed, archaeological investigations revealed the same type of romanesque heating system as was found at No 1 Lederergasse and ascribed to the tanning trade.

South-west of Herrenplatz is the square called Am Singrün, whose name – documented since the late Middle Ages – presumably indicates that *Singrün* (lesser periwinkle), an evergreen plant, once flourished in this area. The spirit of neoclassicism took root here in the furthest corner of Westnerwacht at the beginning of the 19th century. In 1804, a summer residence and a porcelain factory were built in the outer ward of the city walls to plans drawn up by Dalberg's architect, Emanuel von Herigoyen. The two buildings illustrate, even today, how the city wall complex was gradually converted into buildings and gardens in the south and west of Regensburg from the late 18th century on.

The summer residence, now known as the **Württembergisches Palais/Württemberg Mansion (5, M)** and used as the city's natural history museum, was built for Georg Friedrich von Müller, an adviser to the Princes of Thurn and Taxis. It was designed by Emanuel von Herigoyen and constructed in 1804–06 on the former site of a tower in the city walls. After von Müller's death, ownership passed to Princess Sophie of Thurn and Taxis, wife of Duke Paul of Württemberg. Typical of neoclassicism in Regensburg are the relief friezes showing figures on the south and west facades; they are probably the work of the sculptor Christoph Ittlsberger. The interior of the house still contains some interesting elements of the neoclassical furnishings and fittings, including an elegant spiral staircase.

On the way back to the centre of Westnerwacht, the visitor first passes, on the right, the neoclassical mansion-like building that contained the aforementioned porcelain works (No 1 Am Singrün).The building was unfortunately altered in 1908. Then, on the south side of Herrenplatz, there is the extensive complex of St Michael's Old People's Home, once a baroque

The so-called Württemberg Mansion (1804–06) reflects the architectural and horticultural transformation of the former mediaeval defences in the early 19th cent.

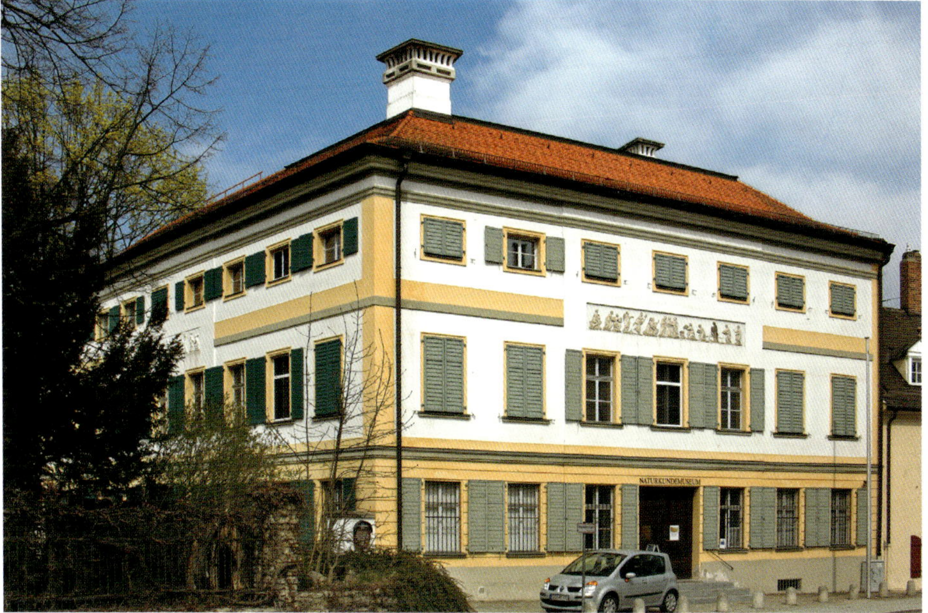

villa. At the entrance to Gerbergasse (Tanners' Street), whose name, again, is a reminder of the quarter's traditional crafts and trades, there stands a tower-like house built in 2001 to plans by Manfred Blasch, the latest contribution to the architectural history of Westnerwacht.

St Leonhard's Church

Gerbergasse runs towards **St Leonhard's Church (6)**, a very remarkable romanesque church dating from 1130–50, which used to belong to the Order of St John of Malta. It is not known who had it erected in the suburb, around which the wall had not yet been built. The church at the former Benedictine monastery at Prüll, south of the city, which was consecrated in 1110, seems to have provided the inspiration for St Leonhard's, an early hall church with a nave and two aisles. Not until a century later did St Leonhard's come into the possession of the Order of St John, which, as an order of knights, originally cared for the safety of pilgrims in the Holy Land. Its Regensburg commandery, or branch, had financial problems in the Middle Ages already and then, increasingly, suffered recruitment problems, as well. For some time in the second half of the 16th century, the church was used for Protestant services, and was then badly damaged in the Thirty Years' War. After that, the commandery barely managed to survive until it was dissolved in 1810. A breath of splendour entered the church again only when the Pustets, a family that own a publishing-house in Regensburg, commissioned an extensive programme of 'restoration' from 1883 to 1895. The artistic director of this project was a Cathedral clergyman, Georg Dengler, who – as diocesan artistic adviser – refurbished many churches in the See of Regensburg in mediaeval style during the last quarter of the 19th century. St Leonhard's is thus both a significant example of original romanesque architecture and an impressive specimen of neoromanesque church art.

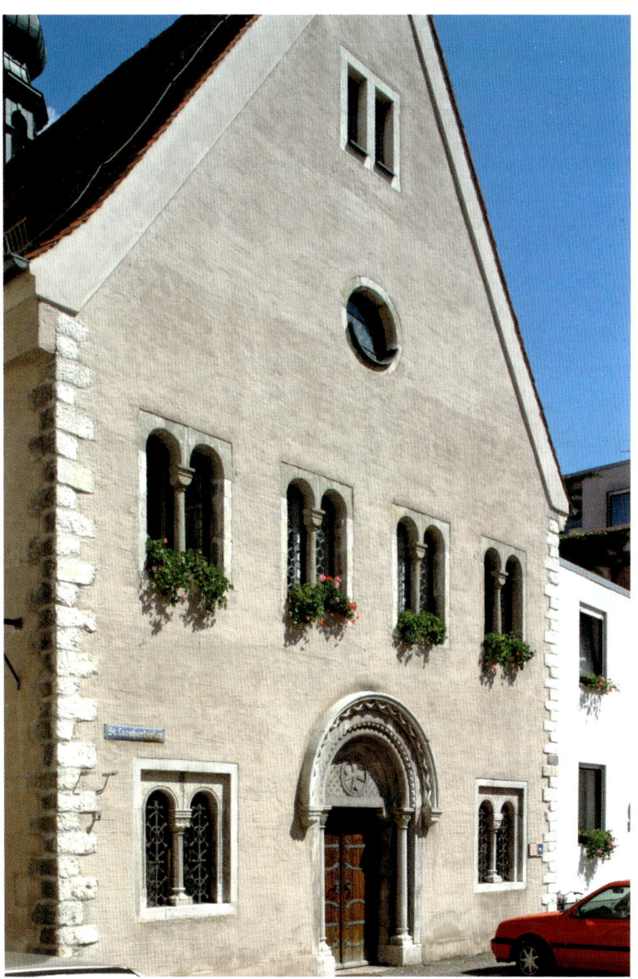

St Leonhard's, formerly owned by the Order of St John of Malta. The neoromanesque facade conceals a fine 12th cent. hall church.

The west front was designed by Dengler. With a row of windows in the upper storey and the steep gable, it looks almost like the facade of a private house; only the doorway with the rounded arch and the Maltese cross in the tympanum betray the ecclesiastical character of the building and its earlier use by the order of knights. The two biforium windows in the lower storey have original 12th-century mullions. The use of such remnants of older buildings – these come from the cloisters of the former St James' Monastery – is characteristic of Dengler's 'restorations'.

The west door leads into the lower porch, which evolved as a result of the extension of the romanesque gallery towards the west. The reason for doing that was the opening, in 1886, of St Leonhard's Children's Home, which is run by nuns. In contrast, the romanesque hall church with its nave and two aisles and rib vaulting is impressive because of its height. This impression used to be even stronger as the floor was once lower. Since Dengler's terrazzo flooring was installed, the bases of the columns and of the pillars attached to the walls have no longer been visible. This impairment of the original quality of the room is scarcely made up for by the fact that the terrazzo floor with its inlaid mosaic figures and Latin inscriptions is an important example of neoromanesque church art. The floor was complemented by a retable that imitates the late-Carolingian ciborium associated with Arnulf, a crown-like chandelier hanging in the nave and, not least, by wall-paintings (destroyed in 1970).

By far the greatest treasures in St Leonhard's are, however, its two gothic side altars. That in the north aisle is a winged retable altar, with paintings only, that was produced in about 1430 by a craftsman trained in either the Upper or the Central Rhine region. The middle section of the triptych portrays Calvary, the wings to the left and right each show two scenes from the Passion. The outer sides of the wings portray the Annunciation, the birth of Christ, the three kings worshipping Christ and the presentation in the Temple. The side altar on the south side, the former high altar, is a retable dated 1505 and probably created in Regensburg, which has a wooden statue of the Madonna in its shrine. The four reliefs on the inner side of the wings illustrate scenes from the life of the Virgin Mary. The outer sides of the wings are painted with portraits of the Man of Sorrows and the Mater Dolorosa, flanked by St John the Baptist and St Leonhard. The four figures stand on illusionistic plinths and are obviously supposed to look like sculptures.

From St Leonhard's, the route leads southwards through St-Leonhards-Gasse and then eastwards into Weitoldstrasse. On the left, here, the eye is caught by the idiosyncratic baroque building of the Malteser Inn with its five-storey tower; to the right lies Am Judenstein, an elongated open space. This derives its name from a Jewish gravestone dating from 1374, which was brought here in 1519, the year the Jews were driven out of Regensburg. The stone can be seen on the north-east corner of the school, built in 1870, which now dominates the square. Being so huge, the building in round-arch style is quite out of proportion to its surroundings; what is more, first the garden and then, because of an extension added in 1909, the whole of Albrecht Altdorfer's summer residence had to make way for the school.

On the west side of the square stands Herz Jesu (Sacred Heart) Parish Church. This was planned in 1926 and built from 1928 on and, although it is again a massive building, it is much better integrated into its smaller-scale environment. The architect was Carl Schad, who worked for the Princes of Thurn and Taxis, and in the interior, above all, it is clear that his intention was to combine the creative principles of New Functionalism with the mediaeval traditions of the location. The stone reliefs on the altar, as well as the terracotta figures above the nave arcades, were made by the sculptor Margarethe of Thurn and Taxis at her own expense.

Convent of the Holy Cross

South-east of Am Judenstein is the **Kloster Heilig Kreuz/ Holy Cross Convent (7)**, a Dominican convent. The foundation started out as a community of pious women who

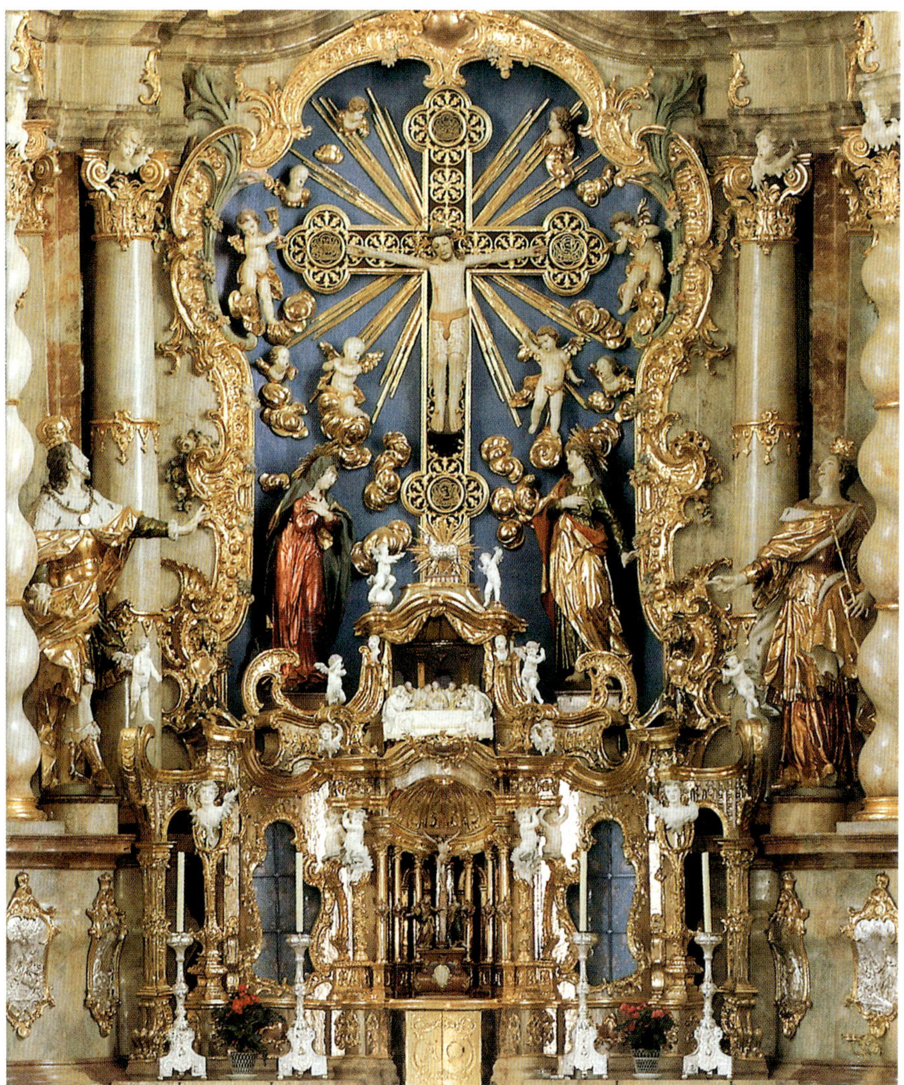

wanted to live in monastic surroundings according to the Rule of St Augustine and the regulations that St Dominic had issued to the nuns of St Sixtus in Rome in 1220. In 1233,

High altar in the Dominican convent church: late romanesque crucifix from the time the convent was founded

they were presented with the site for their convent by Regensburg citizens. The document recording this donation reveals that the city wall on the landward side of Westnerwacht already reached as far as this plot of land. Thanks to a period of rapid expansion, which continued throughout the 13th and 14th centuries, the church was consecrated as early as 1244. Apart from a fire which destroyed some of the early convent buildings in 1547, there were no great changes to the buildings until baroque times. Despite the contemplative nature of their order, the nuns averted the dissolution of their convent in 1803 by agreeing to provide schooling for the Catholic girls in the Upper City (i.e., the West End). Thus, Heilig Kreuz is the oldest Dominican convent in existence in Germany today.

Since the church in the north-east corner of the convent site has no really impressive facade, what strikes the visitor first is the modern footbridge over Nonnenplatz, linking the convent and the school. This enables the nuns to teach in the school without actually leaving their cloister. The outer walls of the convent and of the immediately adjacent chapter-house to the west are part of the original building consecrated in 1244. This was, however, refurbished in baroque style between 1742 and 1751. This is why the north facade, which faces the road, is characterised by curved, round-arched windows, and, beneath the middle window, a doorway which is reached via a double flight of steps; on the canopy over the door there is a statue of St Helena holding a cross.

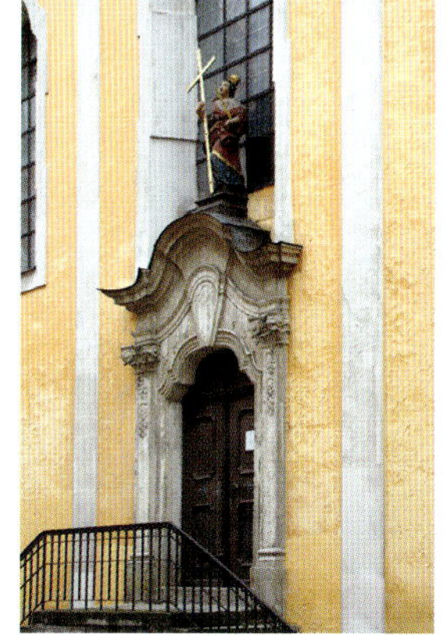

The Dominican Holy Cross Convent: the main doorway (c. 1755)

The interior of the church, once just a nave with a wooden ceiling, lost all traces of its early gothic appearance in the 18th century and has presented itself ever since as a very fine rococo interior with rounded corners. The end of the choir, tetrahedral outside, is also rounded inside. The decorations were the work of the Modlers, an Oberpfalz family specialising in stucco-work, Simon Sorg, a sculptor from Regensburg, and Otto Gebhard, a painter from nearby Prüfening. All that

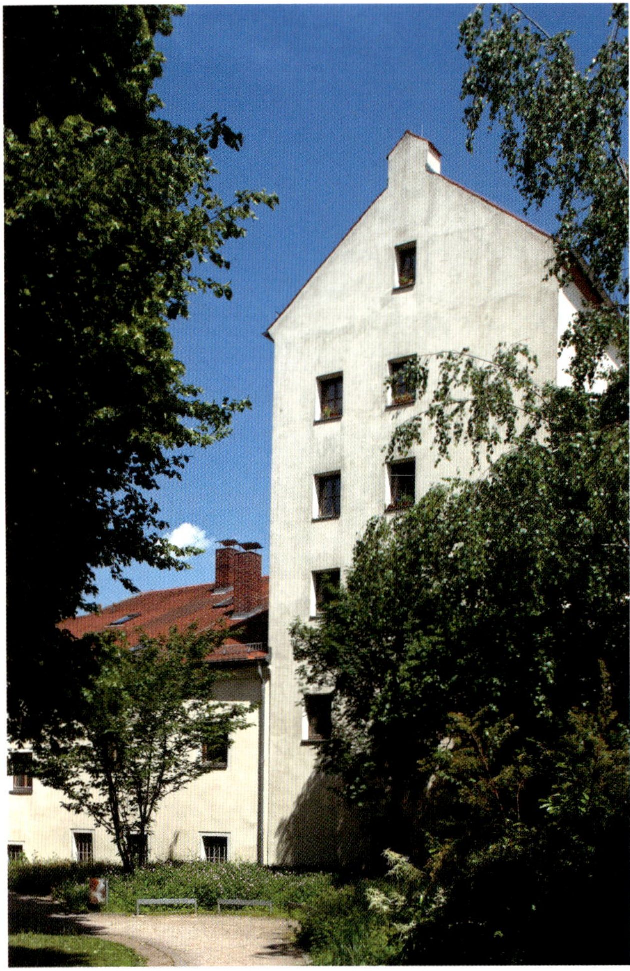

The Ehscheider Tower still contains romanesque fabric.

remains from the period of the convent's foundation is the late romanesque crucifix on the high altar. It stands, as it were, for Christ's cross, which legend says was found by Helena, the mother of the Emperor Constantine, and to which the church is dedicated. Its veneration, especially by the Dominican Order, is the theme of the large fresco over the nave.

In Kreuzgasse, named after the convent, there stands, somewhat overshadowed by the Herz Jesu Church, the so-called **Ehscheider Tower**, one of the most interesting secular buildings in Westnerwacht. To judge by its name, it must have been the residence of a land steward, a judge in lawsuits about land-ownership. The cellar and parts of the ground-floor go back to the 12th century, the vaulting on the ground-floor and first floor dates from 1230/40. The other floors were repeatedly altered between the 16th century and 1825. The two northern extensions, as well, – the living quarters and a former warehouse – still contain significant amounts of mediaeval fabric despite modern conversions.

Wollwirkergasse

The narrow passage between the Ehscheider Tower and the choir of Herz Jesu leads into **Wollwirkergasse (9)**, which runs eastwards, back to Arnulfsplatz. After Ledererergasse, this

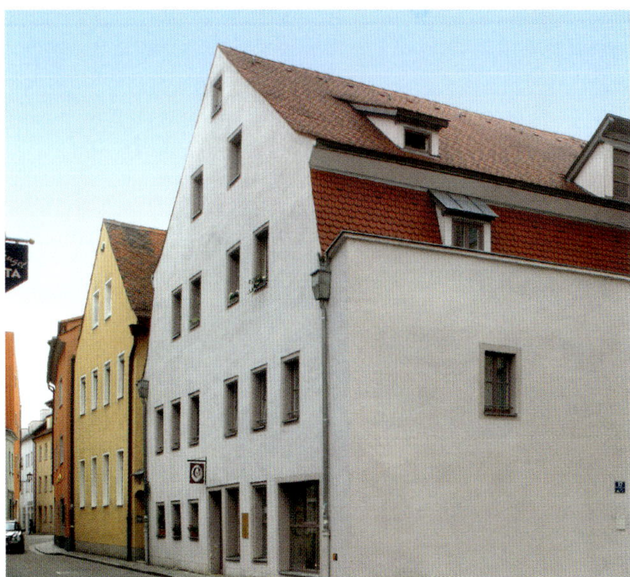

No 17 Wollwirkergasse: a 14th cent. core lies hidden behind the baroque exterior.

was the second most important thoroughfare in mediaeval Westnerwacht. The fact that the very first house on the right (No. 19), a faceless building dating from 1954, is set back from the line of facades is a reminder of city planning schemes in the 1950s, when Wollwirkergasse was to be widened to ensure a better traffic flow. Fortunately, the project came to nothing and only this one house was demolished. The demolition was, however, all the more painful since it involved one of the finest mediaeval craftsmen's houses in the quarter. The building, which dated essentially from about 1200, had a late Gothic oriel window looking out onto the street.

The facade of the next-door house (No 17) was also elaborately decorated in about the mid-15th century. The building, which dates back to the 14th century, is distinguished today by its baroque mansard roof. It originally had a lean-to roof over the first-floor in the western half of the facade and this joined up with the higher eastern part of the building. The gable on the western side was decorated with figurative paintings of high quality. These depicted the rather strange combination of the then popular legend of a maiden with a unicorn and a very secular commercial scene, probably a reference to the cloth merchant's business in the house. The paintings were discovered and examined in 1997, but then placed under a layer of protective plaster again to conserve them.

The facade of No 5 has a Roman wall in its foundations, while experts have proved that there was a Roman road a few metres further south. The visitor can get an idea of the number of Roman finds in this part of the suburban settlement outside the Roman camp by going to the archaeological exhibition room that has been opened in the former velodrome (No 4b Arnulfsplatz; M).

A romanesque wall with stones arranged in a herringbone pattern has been integrated into the modern buildings that mark the transition from Wollwirkergasse to Arnulfs-

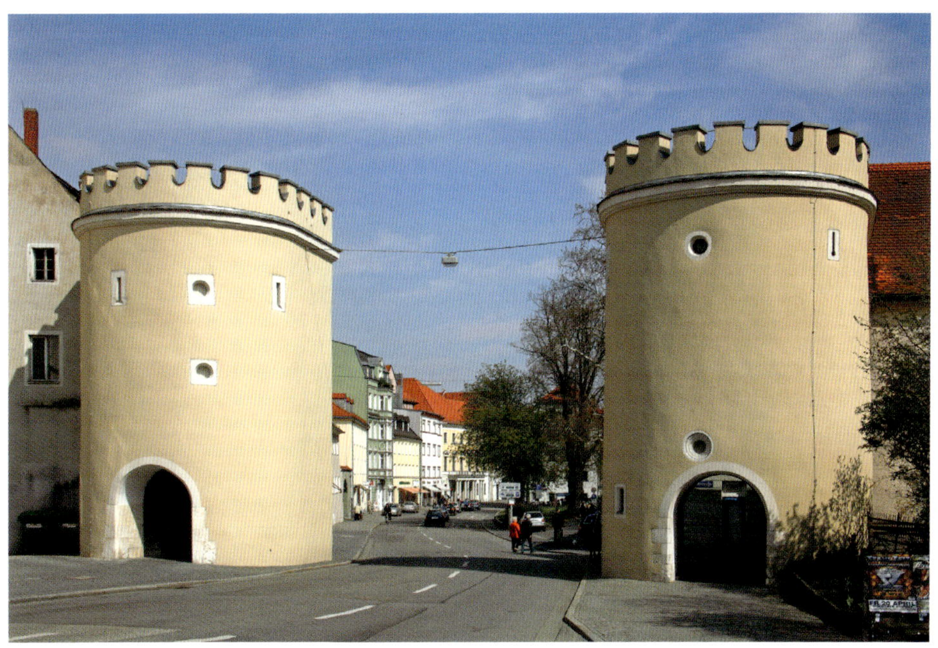

The so-called Jakobstor. In fact, these are merely the flanking towers that stood outside the gate-tower that was demolished in the 19th cent.

platz. This arrangement of stones, which goes back to Roman *opus spicatum,* was used in Regensburg for outbuildings from the 12th to 14th centuries. In this case, too, at No 1 Wollwirkergasse, the building concerned was a barn. It was gutted in 1976 and partly demolished in 1992. Since then, together with the neighbouring house, No 8 Arnulfsplatz (built in the 11th/12th centuries), it has constituted a pitiful relic of early post-Roman secular architecture in the western suburb.

From Arnulfsplatz, the short Neuhausstrasse leads to Jakobstrasse, which runs in a south-westerly direction. At the end of the latter, **Jakobstor/St James' Gate (10)** stood from the late 13th century until it was virtually demolished after 1812. It had provided a second means of access to the city from the west, along with the more important Prebrunn Gate. Nowadays, only the two towers that flanked the outwork survive. The gothic gateway stood near the junction of Stahlzwingerweg and Jakobstrasse.

The Former Scots' Abbey

The part of Westnerwacht that lies south of Jakobstrasse is taken up almost entirely by the land belonging to what was formerly the **Benedictine Abbey of St James (or St Jacob) (11)**. The abbey was founded about 1100, after Regensburg's burgrave and 16 wealthy citizens had presented a Irish monastic community, active in the city for nearly three decades and constantly expanding, with the land necessary for erecting the buildings its members needed. The first church was consecrated in 1111; a year later the Emperor Henry IV placed the abbey under royal protection. The result was a period of extraordinary expansion, so that, by 1170, branches of the Regensburg community had been founded in Würzburg, Erfurt, Nuremberg, Constance, Vienna, Eichstätt and Memmingen. When internal quarrels raised the spectre of the dissolution of the abbey in 1514, two Scottish clerics living in Rome succeeded in convincing Pope Leo X of their nation's claim to St James'. This was possible since mediaeval Latin sources described both Irish and Scots as *scoti.* What now became the Scots' Abbey had an extremely varied history and was even able to avoid being dissolved during the period of Secularisation in the 19th century by having itself declared British property. In 1862, however, it was dissolved by Pope Pius IX because of recruiting problems. The diocesan seminary moved into the buildings.

The strip of grass and trees which provides a pleasant 'buffer zone' between busy Jakobstrasse and the north facade of the former abbey church served as the cemetery for the abbey parish (founded in 1156) from the mid-12th century

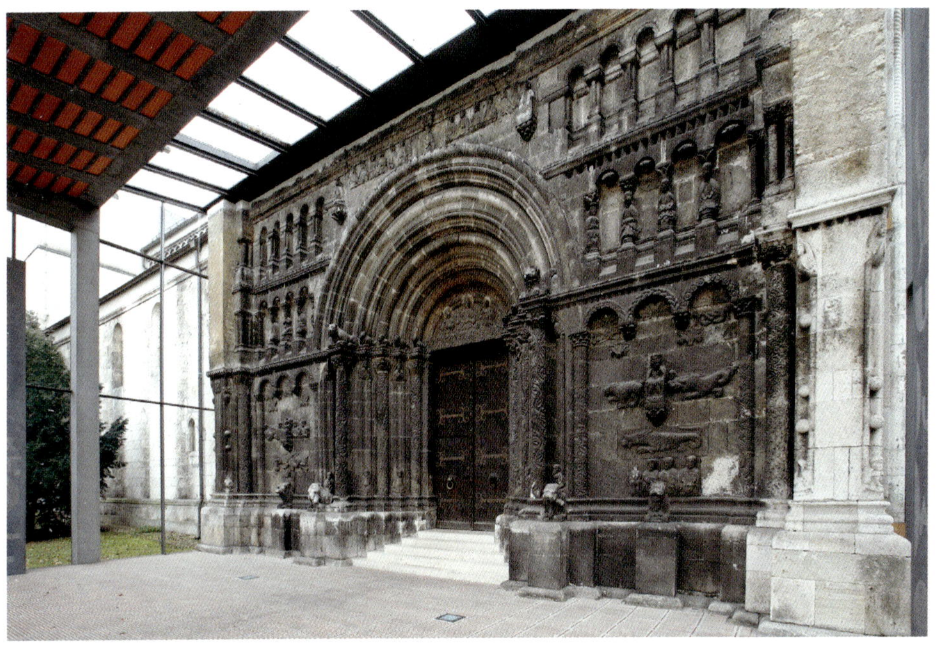

The former Scots' Abbey of St James: the romanesque portal wall (c.1170/80) has been protected by a porch since 1999.

until 1827. St Nicholas', the abbey parish church, which had a nave and one aisle, stood at the eastern end of the cemetery until 1560. The demolition of St Nicholas' and the removal of the cemetery wall have left almost the whole length of the romanesque complex of St James' visible. This building was erected on the site between about 1150 and 1180, replacing the abbey church consecrated in 1111, which had become too small.

The Exterior

The basilica's oldest parts are at the east end. Both the two side choirs and the towers above them were part of the earlier church. The choir with its apse, as well as the nave and two aisles, form a great contrast to the ancient fabric because of their unplastered walls built of skilfully dressed blocks of lime-stone. At the west end, there is a massive transept with

The former Scots Abbey of St James: looking east through the nave

triangular gables; this does not, however, extend beyond the walls of the aisles. A frieze of round arches runs all around the building beneath the cornice round the eaves. The main apse is also decorated with blind arcades. Apart from this, all the ornamentation of the facades is concentrated in the western half of the wall of the north aisle, which has been made into a magnificent showpiece with a wealth of architectural sculpture. Here, and not in the west front, is the main entrance to the church – the famous so-called 'Scots' Portal'.

The round-arched recessed doorway with several archivolts is in the centre of the symmetrically arranged facade. The tympanum contains three half-length figures with nimbuses: in the centre is Christ, raising his hand in blessing, on either side two unidentifiable saints. Lions crouch on the imposts of the columns, which are set into the jambs, and on the jutting-out corners of the imposts above the columns. The line of the imposts is continued as a cornice on each side of the doorway, so that the facade is divided horizontally. In the lower zone, there are, on each side of the doorway, to the left and the right, areas framed by three-quarter pillars and three-arched blind arcades; in the centre of each field is a group of figures in high relief. On the left, that is, to the right of Christ, there appear, above a lion that lies near the base of the column, a siren and a winged dragon holding prisoner a lion and a human figure. Above them sits the Mother of God, enthroned and with her child on her lap. She is flanked by two pairs of intertwined human beings. In the right-hand field, a group of three monks and a siren as well as a dragon with a ball in front of its snout appear above the lion. The figure of Mary enthroned in the left-hand field has a male counterpart here, a figure on a throne flanked by a griffin and a man-eating creature. The upper zone of the facade, again divided horizontally, consists of two rows of blind arcades. The supports in the lower row take the form of human figures, those in the upper row are in the form of compound pillars. Right at the top, over

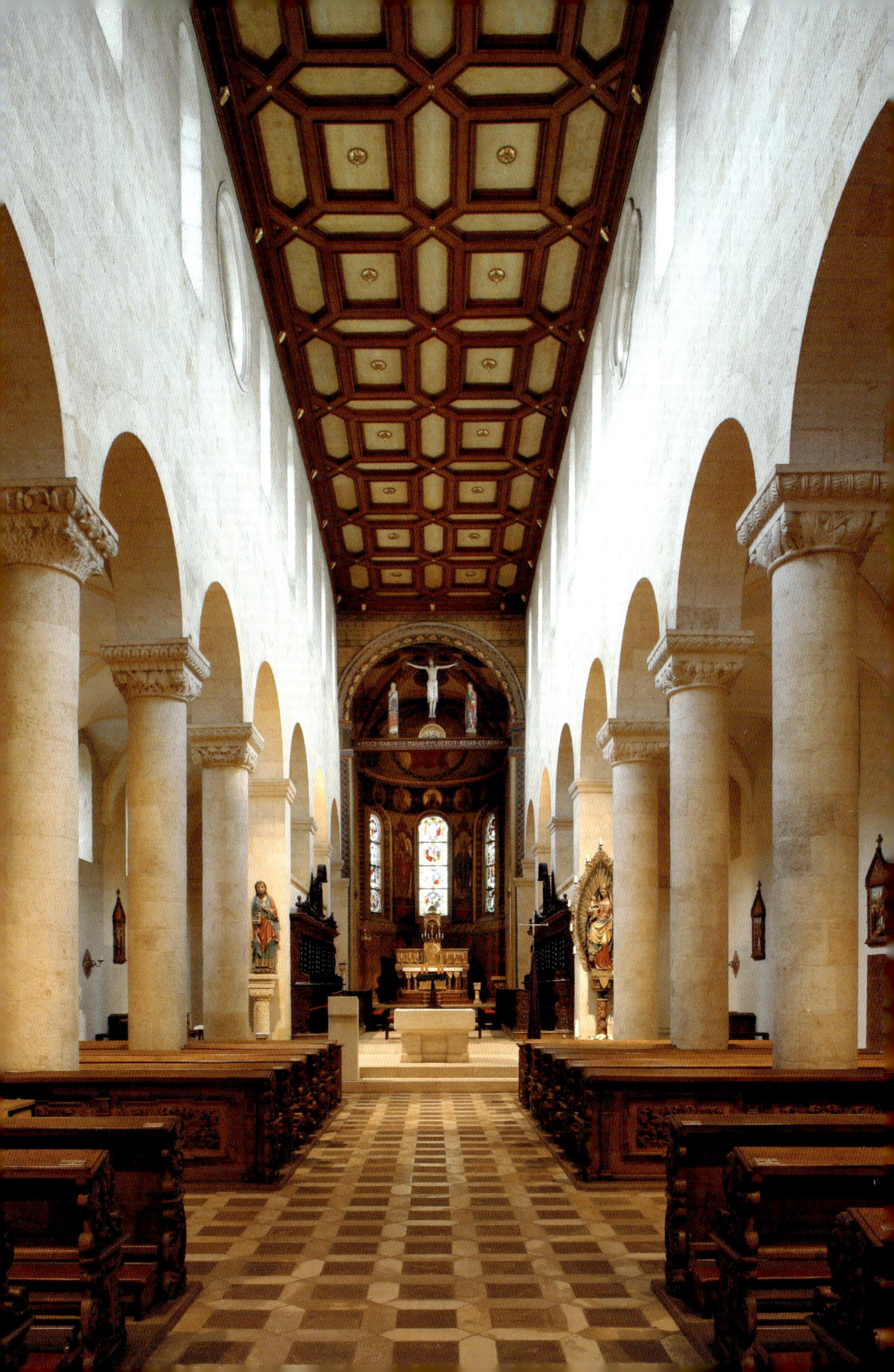
ECCE·THRONVS·MAGNI·FVLGESCIT·REGIS·ET·AGNI

the top of the doorway arch, there is, between two unidentifiable human figures, a frieze showing Christ and the twelve apostles as half-length figures.

This mystifying collection of images on the 'Scots' Portal' has given rise to diverse attempts to interpret it. With regard to its style and its presentation in the context of an elaborately designed facade, it stands alone in the field of German portal sculpture in the 12th century. The overall impression is reminiscent of the portal facades of romanesque churches in Catalonia (Ripoll, Santa Maria) and Western France (Poitiers, Notre-Dame-la-Grande), whereas comparable examples of architectural sculpture – for example, the two-dimensional foliate ornaments on the column shafts – are most likely to be found in the Rhine-Maas region. The illuminated books and miniatures from the Irish home of these Regensburg monks may well have played a role as a source for the idiosyncratic assortment of motifs on the 'Scots' Portal'.

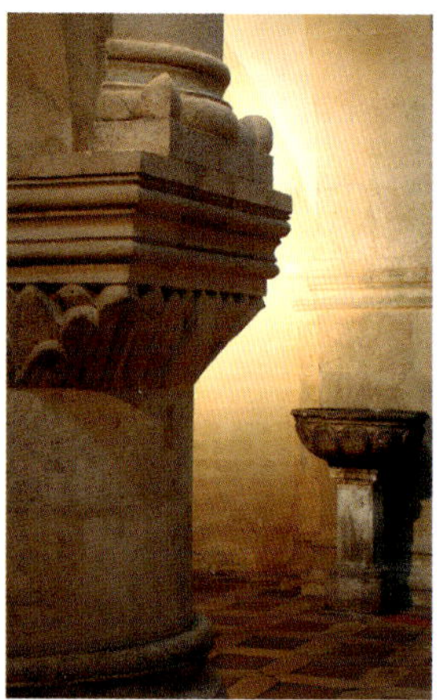

The former Scots Abbey of St James: pillar under the gallery at the west end. The half-column in front of it supports the first nave arcade.

Details of the building indicate that it was intended from the start that the portal facade, like that at St Emmeram's, was to have a porch. However, this apparently did not materialise in the Middle Ages. In 1999, a glass porch was erected to protect the facade.

Interior

The basilica with a nave and two aisles is a surprise, above all, because of the lofty proportions of the nave. In the western half, its arcades rest on ashlar columns; in the eastern half, which is separated from the rest by means of a choir screen to form the monks' choir, the arcades have rectangular pillars. The easternmost bay lies beyond the triumphal arch, so that the choir bay in the chancel opens into the side choirs, on the model of the reforming monastery in Hirsau. The transept which completes the basilica at the west end takes the form of a massive, two-storey construction. The columns supporting the cross-vaulting that carries the gallery are noticeably squat.

The exceptional wealth of ornamentation, especially in the western half of the church, the part used by the laity, contrasts greatly with the sobriety of the architecture. Above all, the capitals of the ten columns are decorated with a variety of ornaments, plants and figures alternately. A romanesque relief placed in the wall beside the north door depicts the horizontally 'hovering' figure of a monk, who is called Rydan in an inscription and thus becomes a historical person. Equipped with a key and a bar, he was obviously the abbey's porter.

The former Scots' Abbey of St James: relief figure of the porter Brother Rydan. Behind, in the jamb, the support for the beam with which the door was barred.

Furnishings

The high altar and the two side altars were made in 1874, to designs by Dengler (see p. 174), using the original *mensae* as well as mediaeval items from the abbey cloisters. Much more important, however, than these historicist products are sev-

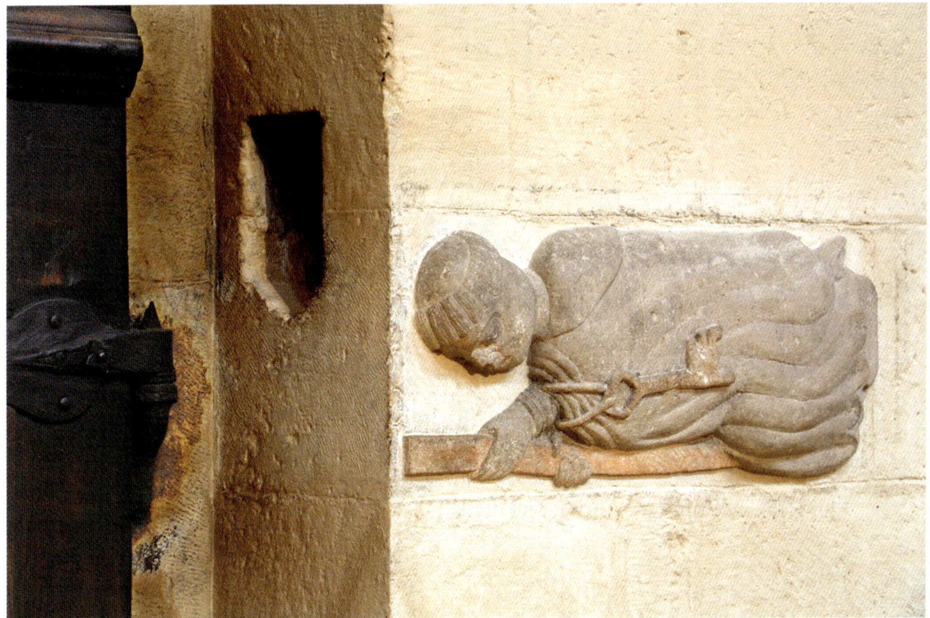

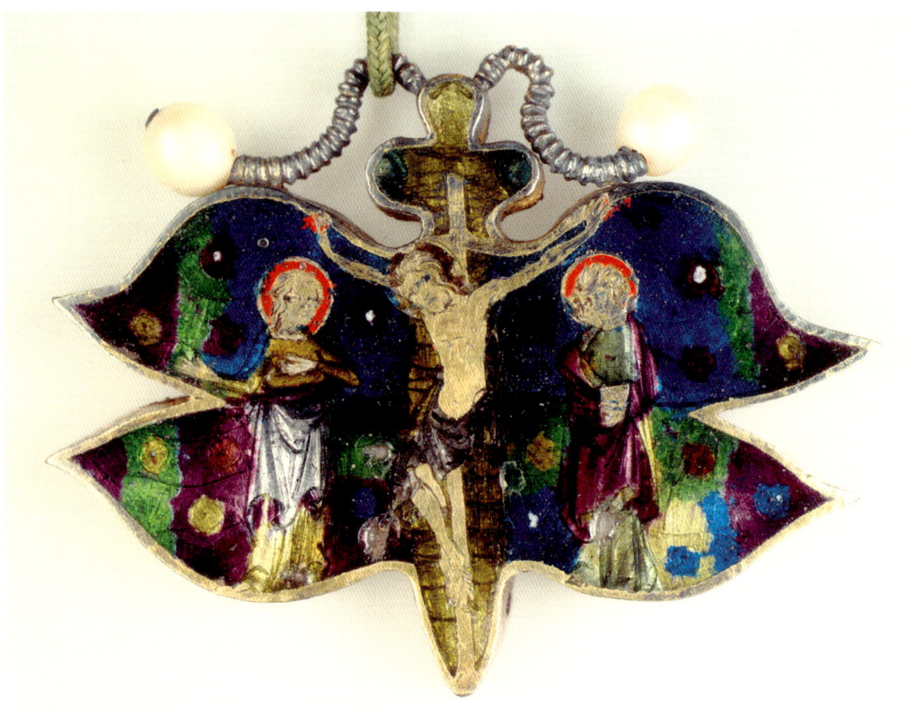

eral romanesque and gothic art works. Since 1893, a late gothic crucifixion group consisting of life-sized wooden figures has hung beneath the triumphal arch; probably it was originally on the rood screen. On the wall of the south aisle there is a painted crucifix (c. 1370). When it was restored (from 1989), a magnificent silver reliquary (c. 1310/20) shaped like a butterfly and with coloured enamel on it, was found in the back of the head of the Christ figure; this is now one of the greatest treasures in the Diocesan Museum in St Ulrich's Church (see p.55). Remarkable, too, are the two stone sculptures displayed in front of the choir pillars: left, St James the Elder (c. 1315/20); right, a Madonna with the clothed Christ child in her arms (c. 1360).

A cross reliquary in the shape of a butterfly (c. 1310/20), originally kept in the head of the figure on the crucifix that hung on St James' south wall (Regensburg, St Ulrich's Diocesan Museum).

In the south aisle, on the right of the door leading into the cloisters, is the memorial to Abbot Ninian Vinzet (d. 1592), who, before coming to Regensburg in 1578, had gone down in history as Father Confessor to Mary Stuart and adversary of John Knox, the Scottish reformer. In the north aisle stands the memorial to Bishop Ignatius von Senestréy (d. 1906), who had the seminary set up here after the dissolution of the Scots' Abbey. The sculpture, by Georg Busch the Younger, an artist from Munich, shows the bishop seated on his throne and holding a model of Regensburg Cathedral, the completion of which was, for Senestréy, a symbol of powerful Roman Catholicism.

The cloisters, south of the church, are not open to the public as a rule because they are part of the seminary. Although numerous pillars and capitals were removed from them, especially in the last quarter of the 19th century, in order to be used as *spolia* in various churches in Regensburg (see p.63, 175f.), the remaining portals and capitals bear witness to the formerly splendid ornamentation.

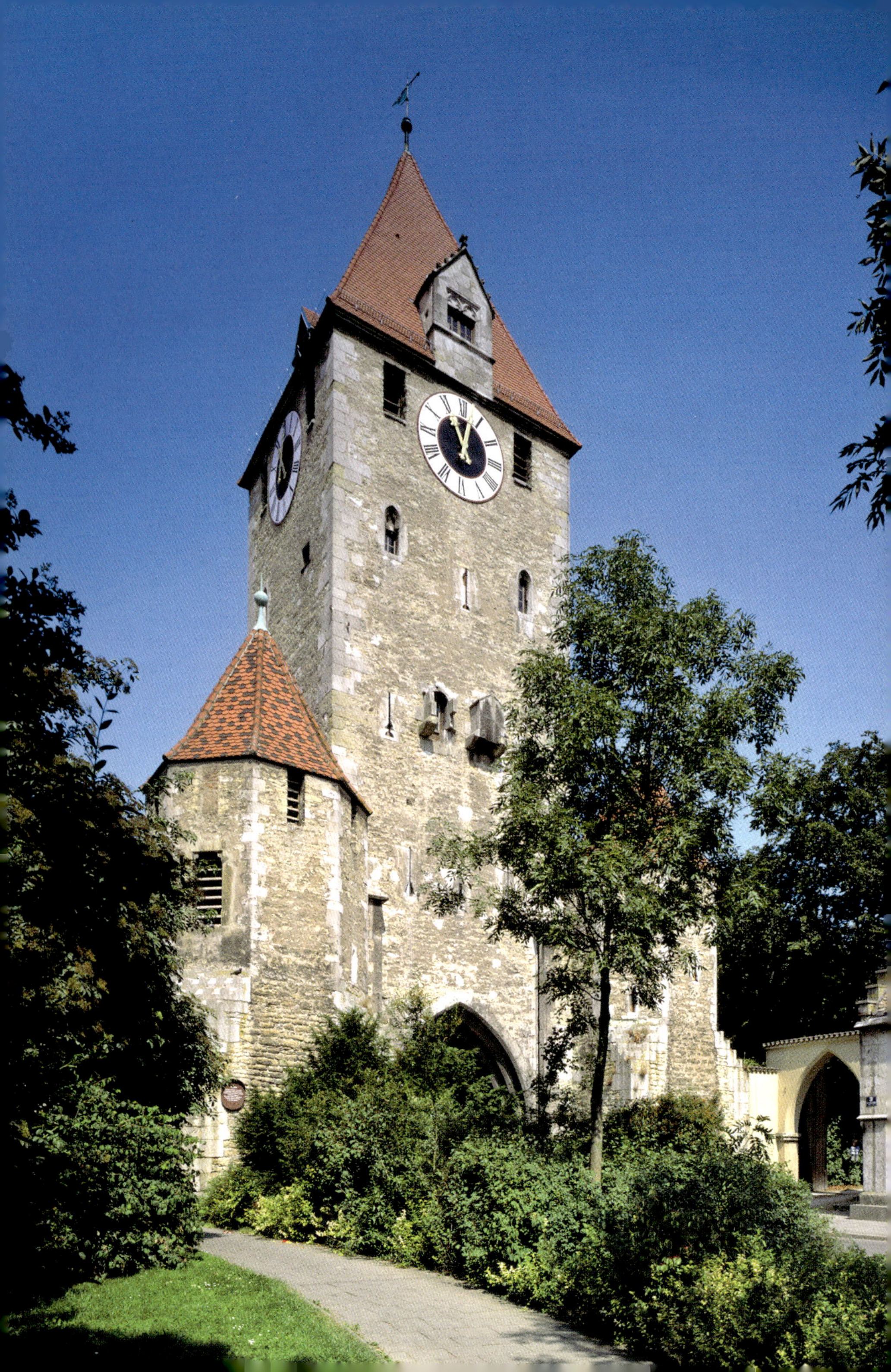

Ostnerwacht, the Eastern Quarter

Like Westnerwacht, Regensburg's eastern suburb was not brought entirely within the city's defensive ring until the early 14th century. Yet, unlike Westnerwacht, which developed as the continuation of Regensburg's 'new town', which had been fortified as early as 920, under Duke Arnulf, and had already developed a long way westwards, Ostnerwacht came into being almost directly outside the walls of the Roman legionary camp. Arnulf's early 10th-century city moat lay right outside the Roman fortifications. The consequences are visible, even today, in the city's layout and appearance here. The impressive political and ecclesiastical buildings that were erected within the walls of the Roman fort lie adjacent to the settlements in the suburb; there is no transitional area. Only the Minorite Friary, constructed in the 13th/14th centuries outside the – now demolished – Schwarzes Burgtor (Black Castle Gate), the successor to the Romans' east gate, represented a sort of link between the two so different areas of town due to its sheer size.

In Roman times already, there was a civilian settlement *extra muros* on the eastern side of the city, though a much smaller one than that to the west of the legionary camp. Mediaeval building activity was concentrated around present-day Ostengasse, then the main road out of the city in the direction of Straubing and Vienna. There were houses beside the road as early as 1000. Further south, in the area of the later Minorite Friary, was St Saviour's Chapel, known to have existed by 1024.

In the course of the Middle Ages, the commercial centre of the mediaeval suburb grew up along both sides of Ostengasse, from Donaulände on the banks of the Danube as far as the axis of Bertoldstrasse and Heiliggeistgasse. To the south of this quarter, with its warehouses, inns and tradesmen's houses, an extensive monastery complex developed after the Minorite (Franciscan) Brothers had come to Regensburg. From about 1228, a community of penitent women, so-called Sisters of Magdalene, who joined the Order of St Clare in 1296, settled in their neighbourhood. The convent of the 'Poor Clares' stood, until the buildings were destroyed in 1809, more or less on the site of Dachauplatz today.

View of the Ostentor (East Gate) and its two flanking towers (c. 1300) from outside the city. Right, the neogothic gatekeeper's house (1840) and the entrance to the Royal Villa park.

To the east of the two monastic communities, the land had only few buildings on it and was devoted mainly to farming and horticulture. Until the early 19th century, the Stärzenbach, the eastern arm of the stream that flowed through the city centre, crossed this land; it now runs exclusively underground.

Towards the mid-13th century, the eastern suburb became part of the city's system of watches. The first mention of the *vigilia orientis*, the eastern watch, can be dated to 1251. It may be assumed that the building of the wall around the suburb also began at this time. The fortifications reached their outermost point with the Ostentor (East Gate), erected about 1300. By about 1320, the whole of the eastern quarter, like the western quarter, had been included within Regensburg's late mediaeval defensive ring.

In early modern times, the Capuchin Order, another mendicant order, settled at the far end of Ostengasse, thus again increasing the strongly ecclesiastical nature of Ostnerwacht, which it had had since the Middle Ages. This tendency was to be seen in various smaller charitable institutions as well as in farms belonging to the convent for noble ladies at Niedermünster and to the collegiate foundation attached to the Alte Kapelle.

A number of summer residences were built here in the middle of the fields during the baroque period; among these, the villa belonging to the banker Löschenkohl was the most striking because of its size and ambitious architecture. In 1854/55, the City of Regensburg erected a summer residence for King Maximilian II in the furthest north-eastern corner of the district, literally on the bastions there. Thus, for the first time, Ostnerwacht had a secular building of massive dimensions. However, due to its position on the fringes of the city, the so-called Royal Villa can be perceived as part of the cityscape only from the banks of the Danube.

Between 1865 and 1898, three city schools were built in the eastern part of Ostnerwacht and these huge buildings represented new dominating features among the otherwise small-scale buildings. To a certain extent, these new proportions were adopted by the new houses built

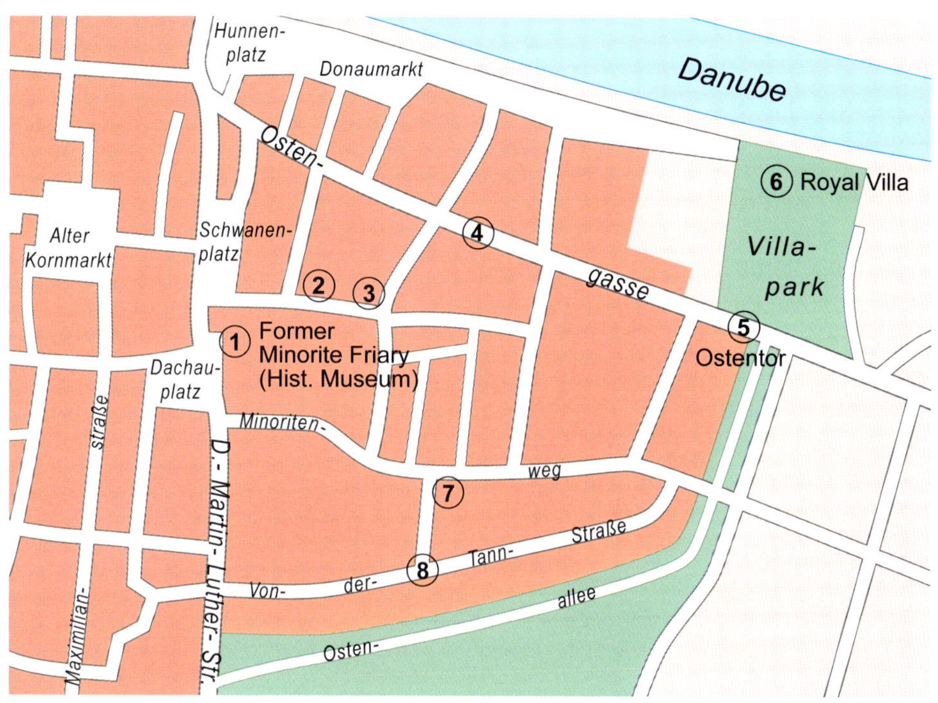

along Von-der-Tann-Strasse around the end of the 19th century. They were also basically in keeping with the architectural ideas of National Socialism, which left its mark for posterity on Minoritenweg in the form of administrative buildings. The multi-storey buildings erected subsequently in the 21st century, in turn, also adopted these dimensions. Thus the small-scale mediaeval development of individual plots has been gradually abandoned in the last 150 years. On top of that, a large number of buildings have been demolished since the Second World War, leaving terrible scars that are still visible today in the once densely built-up north-eastern corner of Ostnerwacht. The road between the Eiserne Brücke (Iron Bridge) and Dachauplatz was also widened to four lanes, causing the disruption to the layout of the city which is responsible for the fact that Ostnerwacht is sometimes no longer regarded as part of the ancient city centre.

Looking from the Great Cloisters of the former Minorite Friary (now the Museum of Regensburg History) towards the church, which was consecrated in 1286 or soon after. The choir was enlarged in the 1340s.

Dachauplatz is a good starting-point for a walk around Ostnerwacht. On its north side, Drei-Kronen-Gasse, running westwards, links up with the centre of the city. The so-called Schwarzes Burgtor, which replaced the Roman *porta principalis dextra*, stood at the eastern end of this street. It was part of the city fortifications constructed in 920 and – together with the Hallertor, also now demolished – was one of the city's two east gates in the Middle Ages. Although they became obsolete as city gates when the Ostentor was built about 1300, they remained in existence until the 19th century. The Schwarzes Burgtor was pulled down in 1812, the Hallertor, which stood further north between St.-Georgen-Platz and Hunnenplatz, was not demolished until 1868.

Since St Clare's Convent, which once adjoined the Schwarzes Burgtor and covered a large part of present-day Dachauplatz, was bombarded and set on fire by Napoleon's forces in 1809, it has disappeared entirely from the cityscape. In contrast, its older male counterpart, the Minorite Friary, still dominates the north-east corner of the square. Nowadays, it houses the Museum of Regensburg History (M).

The Former Minorite Friary

In 1221, that is, at a time when St Francis of Assisi was still alive, a group of his 'Lesser Brothers' came to Regensburg. They impressed the local people through their exemplary behaviour and excellent sermons, with the result that, in 1226, Bishop Conrad IV allowed them to use St Saviour's Chapel, just to the east of the city, and two other buildings. In 1233, Count Albert IV from Bogen presented them with a nearby house owned by his family. In addition to that, there were a whole series of other gifts from citizens, dukes and even kings in the following years, all of which had the aim of ensuring that the **Minorite Friary (1)** was on a secure financial footing and that the friars could thus continue

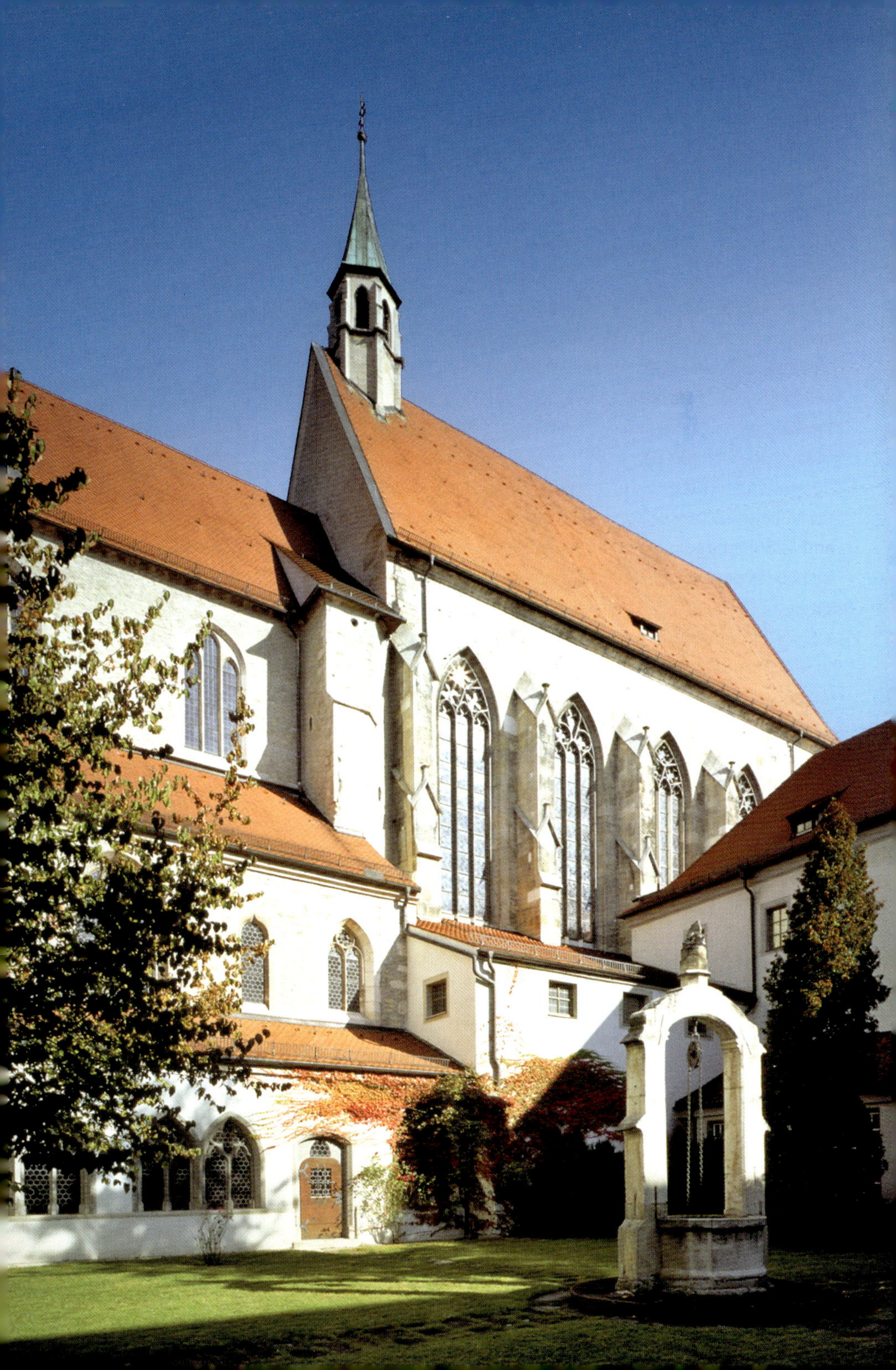

indefinitely to offer pastoral care that was not limited to parish boundaries.

In a spiritual respect, too, the friary in Regensburg experienced a period of great fame before the end of the 13th century. The highly reputed preachers David von Augsburg and Berthold von Regensburg were active, and the poet Lamprecht von Regensburg translated Tommaso da Celano's 'Life of St Francis' into German.

Not surprisingly, the Minorites in Regensburg very soon saw that it was necessary to build a large church. Between c. 1250/60 and 1286, a huge basilica with a nave and two aisles was therefore built in place of St Saviour's Chapel, although the new church was dedicated to the same patron saint. Yet, again, the choir soon seemed too small, so that that was rebuilt before 1347. The Minorite Friary Church thus became the largest church owned by a mendicant order in Southern Germany.

After the dissolution of the friary, the church was de-consecrated and its furnishings sold for a pittance. The magnificent stained glass from the choir (c. 1360/70) ended up in Munich and is now in the Bavarian National Museum (a small part of it is on permanent loan to the Museum of Regensburg History). From 1810, the friary served initially as barracks; the smaller cloister complex was demolished. The City of Regensburg purchased the buildings in 1931 in order to turn them into a museum.

Exterior

From the point of view of the city's buildings, the Minorite Church is the eastern counterpart of the Dominican Church, which had been begun a few years earlier. It is characterised by the absence of a tower, a typical feature of churches belonging to mendicant orders. Instead there is a gable turret on the west gable of the long choir with its four bays. In the east, the choir, whose walls between the pier buttresses are almost completely replaced by traceried windows with four lights, ends in five sides of an octagon. To the west of the choir is the older nave with its two aisles;

in its austerity, this nave with its seven-bay facade made of rough undressed stone masonry corresponds very closely to the architectural ideal of the mendicant orders. The simple west front reflects the basilica structure of the nave. There are pier buttresses where the aisles join the nave. The three doorways – the two outer ones are bricked up – illustrate the change of style from romanesque to gothic. Thus, the centre one is still round-arched, while the side ones already have pointed arches. There are in each case, windows with three lights above the cornice of the doorway area, which is stepped towards the centre.

Today, the church is part of the Museum of Regensburg History. One enters it through the surviving wing of the otherwise demolished Little Cloisters. The tympanum (c.1280/90) in the wall above the entrance to the church comes from the Augustinian Church, demolished in 1838. It has a vine motif which can be understood as a symbol of Christ.

Interior

The interior of the church is impressive because of its enormous size. Columns with undecorated bases and imposts carry the pointed-arch arcades in the nave. Instead of the flat ceilings they now have, the nave and aisles all had an open roof construction (similar to a hammer-beam roof) in the Middle Ages. The organ loft was added in 1724. To the east, the nave is adjoined by the more recent choir, which is several steps higher and has cross vaulting. Since there are no side choirs, as there are, for instance, in the Cathedral or in the Dominican Church, the masonry in the walls at each side, as well as in the choir termination, has been largely replaced with windows. The sense of space achieved by this is remarkable enough today; before the stained-glass windows were removed, it must have been overwhelming. The colouring on the architectural elements dates back to the late gothic period, when the choir was decorated with figures of the saints (1499) and the nave with the Apostles' Creed (1492). The original colour of the paint on the

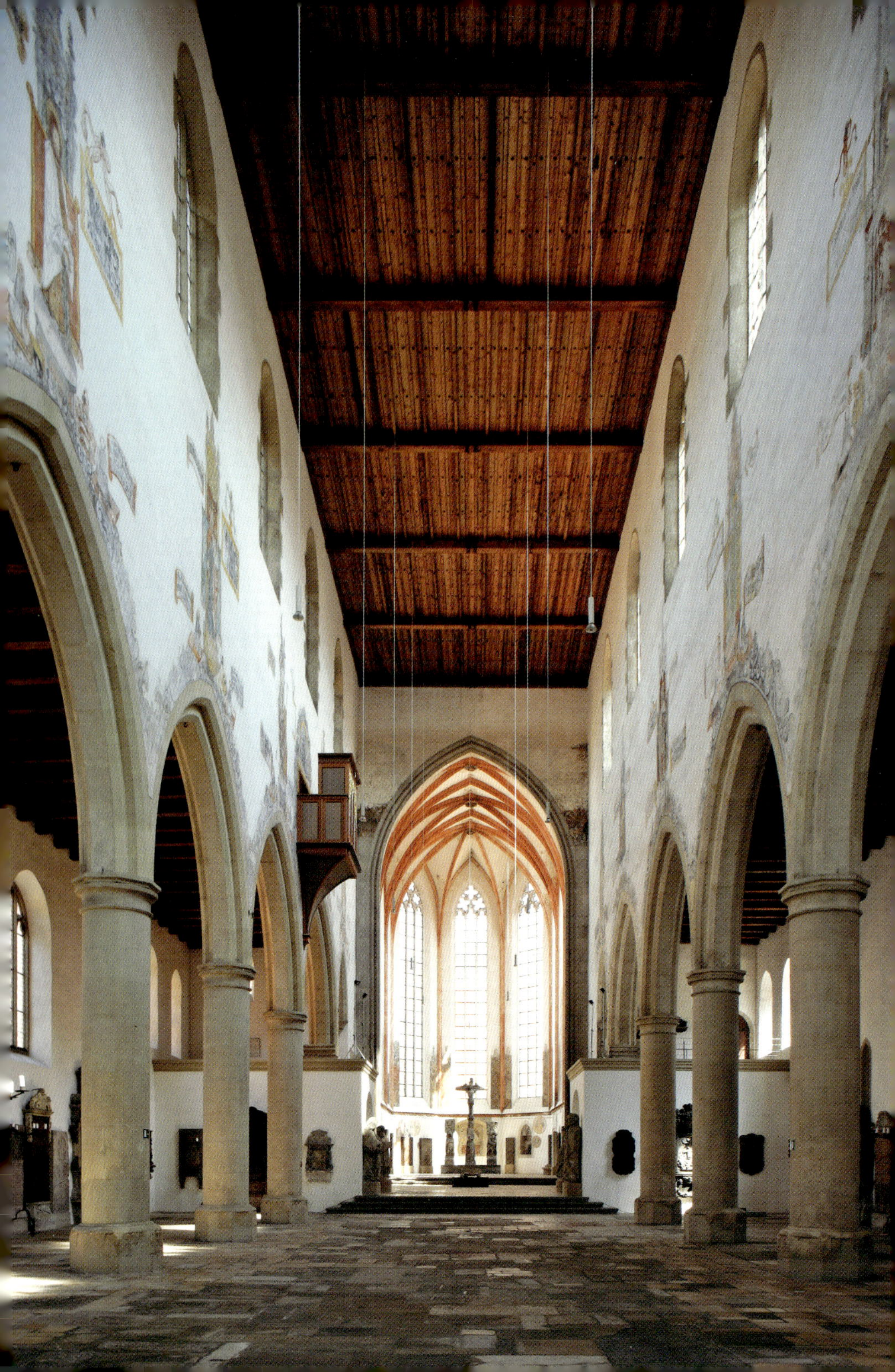

The former Minorite Friary: view of the nave with the remains of the gothic rood screen at the end of it.

walls was chalk-white, apart from the apostles' crosses. There is a fresco – badly damaged, unfortunately – on the south wall of the nave. Dating from the first third of the 14th century, it shows the 14 Holy Helpers, and is one of the earliest large-scale portrayals of this theme (see pp. 50, 117).

Furnishings

The Minorite Church is the only church in Regensburg where at least parts of the gothic rood screen have survived in their original position. Although it was dismantled in the nave in 1724, the wings at the sides were then turned into pulpits and still function as dividers between the nave and the choir. The movable furnishings in the church were sold off after 1810. Parts of the windows from the choir and the winged altar produced in Albrecht Altdorfer's workshop in 1517 are now in the Museum of Regensburg History, and thus at least now in rooms that belonged to the former Minorite Friary. The swallow's nest organ attached to the north wall of the nave was reconstructed in 1989 according to a design made in 1583 by Caspar Sturm, an organ-builder in the free imperial city.

The presence of numerous memorials on the walls is the result of the church being used as a museum. These memorials (14th –19th century) come from various Regensburg churches and cemeteries.

Some mediaeval fabric from the friary has been preserved to the south of the church. East of the above-mentioned remains of the Little Cloisters (1461/63), are the Great Cloisters, whose north and west wings date from the early 15th century. The builder of these cloisters, Thomas Schmuck, who also worked on the cloisters of the Dominican Church, has left a portrait of himself for posterity on one of the keystones in the west wing. Only the western bay of the south wing has survived; the rest of it was, like the entire east wing, destroyed in the 19th century and rebuilt in a different form in 1933, when the building was con-

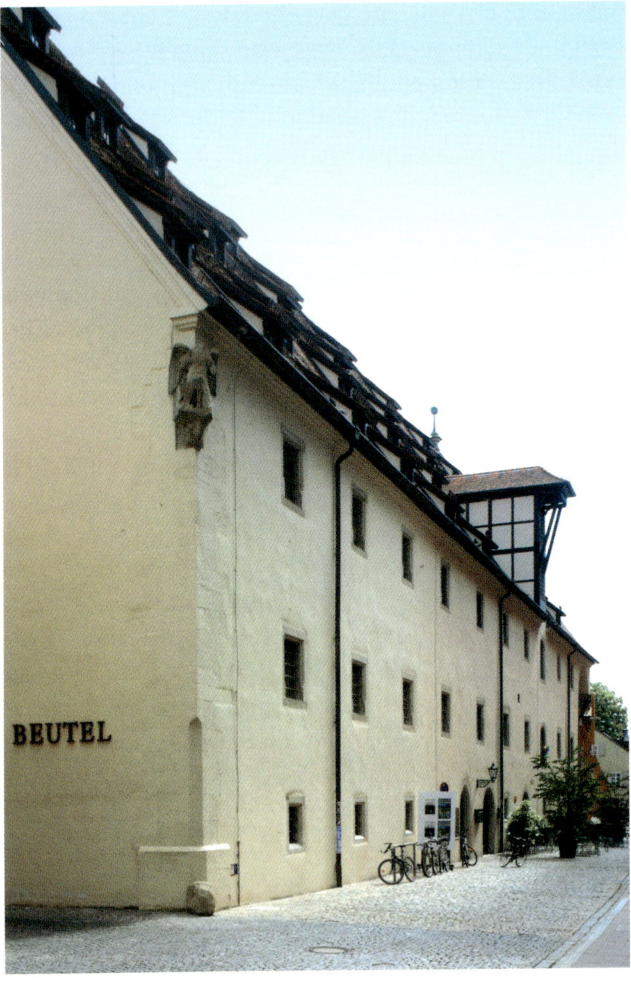

The Leerer Beutel (Empty Purse), the municipal grain store, erected c.1600.

verted into a museum. That was also the time when the well was placed in the centre of the cloister garden; it came from a building in Gesandtenstrasse.

The north wing of the cloisters leads to the former Chapel of St Onophrius, where Brother Berthold was buried (his gravestone is in the choir of the church). Restored in the 14th and 15th centuries, the chapel has, since then, had a nave and one aisle with a single supporting pillar in the centre. Via the Large Sacristy, which adjoins it to the east and has cross vaults resting on two free-standing pillars, one enters the former Paulsdorf Chapel. This noble family were among the major patrons of the Minorites, which is why they had the privilege of erecting their burial chapel in the cloisters. The room has had its present-day appearance since the late 16th century; the romanesque window arcade in its south wall came from the Salzburger Hof and was not brought here until the 1930s. Evidence of the former function as a family chapel is provided by the double memorial slab for the brothers Heinrich and Wilhelm von Paulsdorf, who died in 1467 and 1478 respectively, and by a tournament saddle which belonged to the Paulsdorfs and is also preserved here.

Bertoldstrasse runs along the north wall of the Minorite Church to the building that was once the city grain-store and is now known as the **Leerer Beutel/Empty Purse**. The previous building on this site also bore this strange name (*laerenpaeutel)*; it was a grain barn acquired by the city before 1471. The current building was constructed in two stages: the eastern section in 1597/98 and the western one in 1606/07. The huge three-storey building has a steep four-storey saddle- roof with a dormer for a hoist on the south side. The importance of the former grain-store is also indicated by the sculptures, unusually elaborate for a warehouse, which were made by Michael Dietlmaier. The cornice along the eaves is supported on three corners of the building by figures of angels holding the arms of the imperial city.

Next to the Leerer Beutel, going east, is the **Haus zum Steinsberg (3)**, an originally romanesque house which the Dollingers, a patrician family, made into a dwelling-house in the 14th century.

The – sadly only fragmentary – pointed-arch biforium windows on the first-floor date from this period.

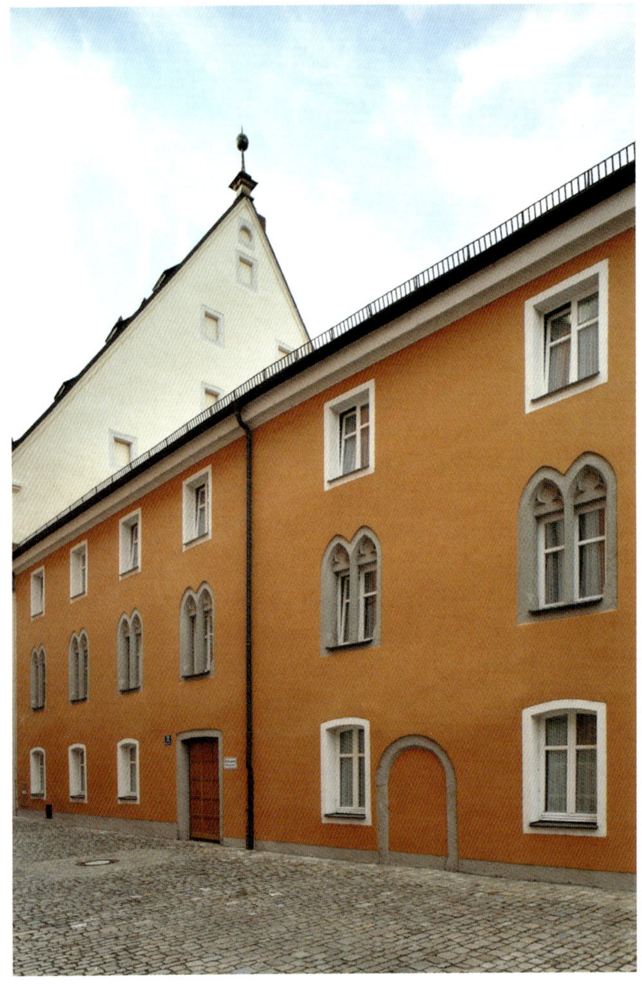

The Haus zum Steinsberg from the east. In the background, the east gable of the Leerer Beutel.

Hallergasse, which forks off northwards here, leads to **Ostengasse (4)**, historically the main street in Ostnerwacht. The stretch of road which runs almost straight ahead to the Ostentor looks rather unexciting in parts and conveys little idea of the formerly bustling thoroughfare. Only its width indicates the importance of this street in earlier days. As early as 1300, there seem to have been houses all along the road, although of a very heterogeneous nature. In the typical manner of a suburb, grand inns alternated with humble tradesmen's dwellings, ecclesiastical buildings and charitable institutions. At least towards the end of the Middle Ages, the street accommodated several makers of casks, barrels and so on, craftsmen who all produced containers for the storing and transport of wine, foodstuffs and other wares.

The old mixed economic structure has survived, more or less. For instance, three of the four buildings at the corner of the junction of Ostengasse and Hallergasse, and Schattenhofergasse – its northerly continuation – are relics of the once-flourishing brewery trade here. Whereas the south-western building (No 14 Ostengasse) was rebuilt in 1913/14 in a mixture of art nouveau and *Heimat* styles, the north-western house (No 13 Ostengasse) retains a considerable amount of mediaeval fabric behind its early neoclassical facade (1789). The original 12th-century romanesque building is to be found in the western third of the building and reaches from the cellar to the second floor. The house on the south-east corner, finally, betrays its mediaeval origins in its exterior as well. The former inn, known to Regensburg's inhabitants as *Brandlbräu*, dates back to the second half of the 13th century. The gateway for wagons and the early gothic triforium windows above it date from that time, whereas the rest of the building was completely modernised in 1596. A painting on the facade showing a chained bear and the former name of the inn 'The Bear on the Chain' result from further renovations in 1758. (Actually, the chain was not there to tether a bear, but to close off Hallergasse when there were great crowds of people in Ostengasse – for instance, when the emperor visited Regensburg or troops marched through the city.)

Further out of town, on the left-hand side (No 31 Ostengasse) lies the early baroque group of buildings that housed the Capuchin monastery, founded at the wish of the Emperor Mathias in 1613. After the monastery's dissolution in 1810, the nuns from

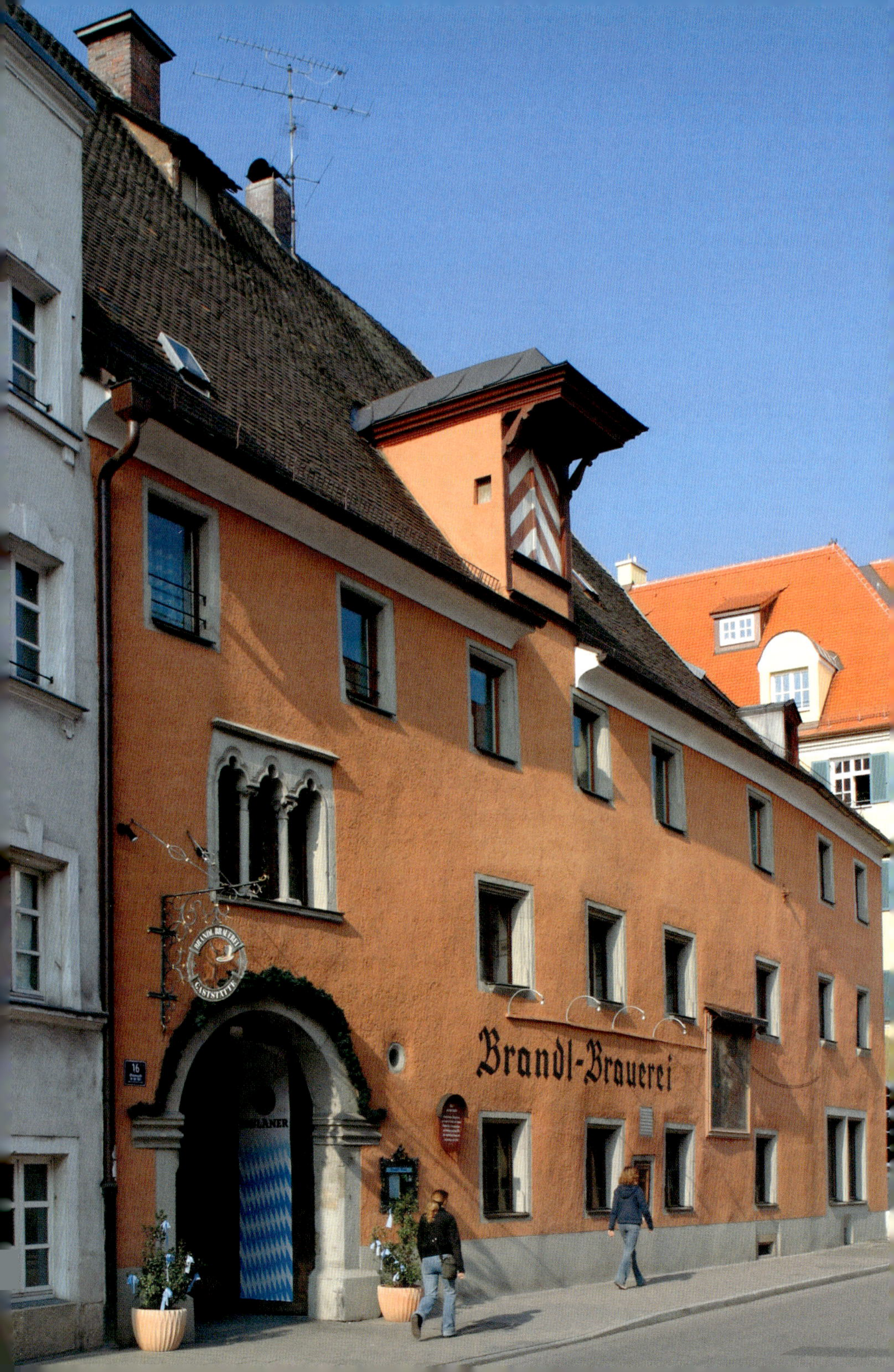
Brandl-Brauerei

No 16 Ostengasse, a gothic building and one of the old public house in Ostengasse

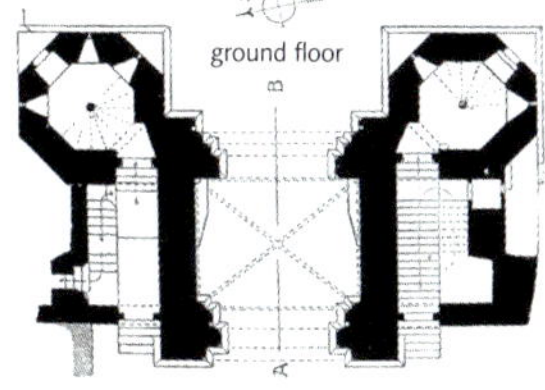

St Clare's were able to take over the complex, thus ensuring, for the moment, the survival of their convent, which had been in Regensburg since the 13th century but whose building in present-day Dachauplatz had been destroyed in 1809. The convent was not finally closed down until 1974.

From here, it is only a few steps to the **Ostentor/East Gate (5)**, which marked the easternmost point of the city from the time it was built until the 19th century. Formerly, quite large fortifications stood on this site but of these only the gate-tower flanked by two adjoining smaller towers has survived. A barbican with a walkway around its battlements used to stand outside the gate but was taken down in 1830. Despite this loss, the Ostentor, built with masterly perfection by masons from the cathedral, is one of the best preserved gothic city gates in Germany. Over the roadway through the five-storey gate there is cross-rib vaulting and an inscription dating from 1300 which records the start of construction work on the bailey wall. On the east side of the gate, which would have faced the enemy, are two embrasures at second-storey level through which pitch or boiling oil could be poured on attackers who had reached the gate. The two octagonal flanking towers were originally crenellated, as can still be seen; the high helm roofs were added after the Middle Ages. The pedestrian passageway through the north flanking tower was not created until 1936.

The drive leading to the **Königliche Villa/Royal Villa (6)** turns off northwards beyond the Ostentor. The neogothic mansion was built from 1854–56 to plans by Ludwig Foltz in order to provide a summer residence for King Maximilian II of Bavaria. In its exposed position on the former eastern bastion, the building bears witness to the Romantics' re-interpretation of the ancient city fortifications. These no longer marked the boundary between city and countryside, but the transition from the city to the open landscape, which is emphasised by means of captivat-

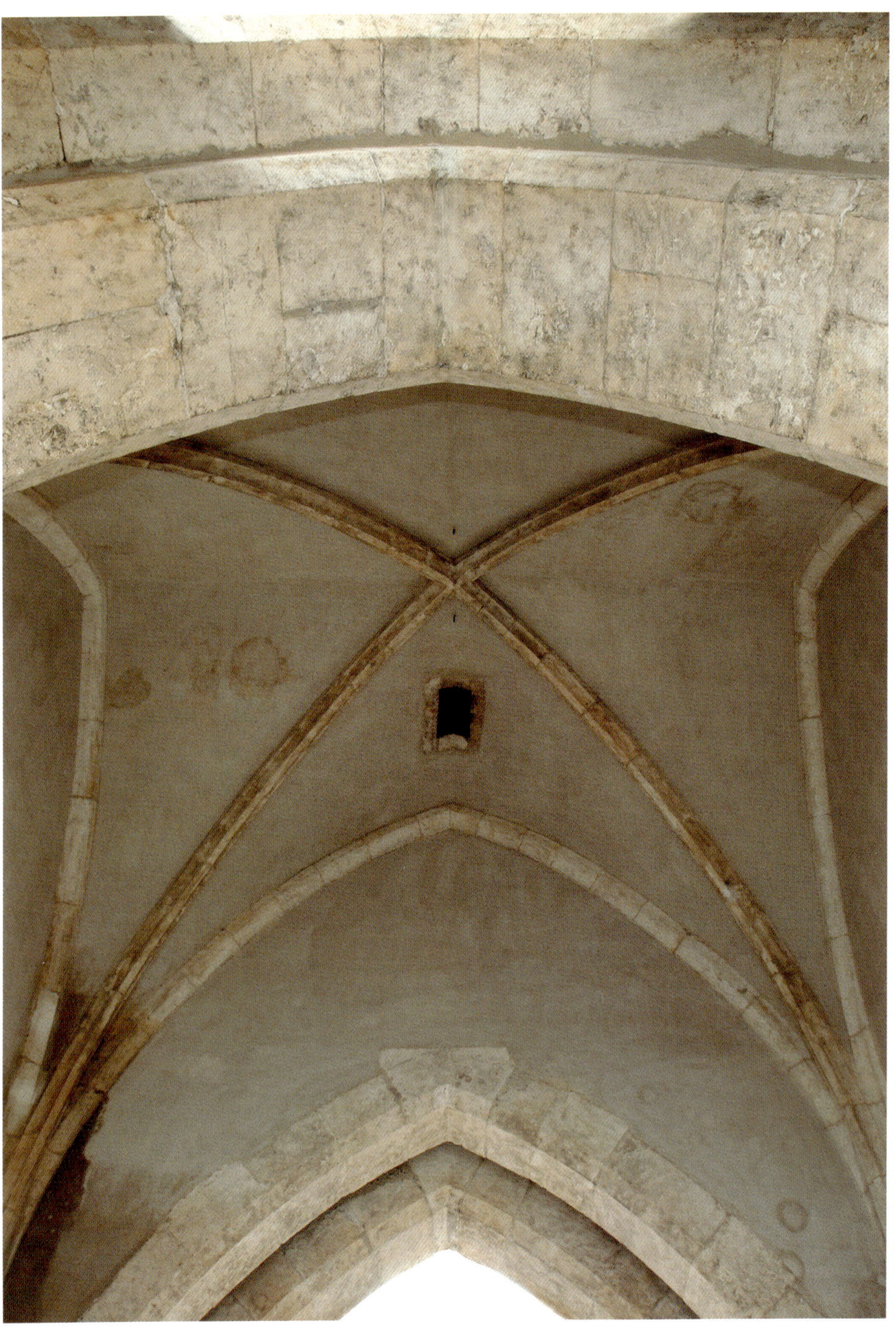

The Ostentor (East Gate): the archway. Inscription dating from 1300, commemorating the start of building operations for the adjacent outer ward.

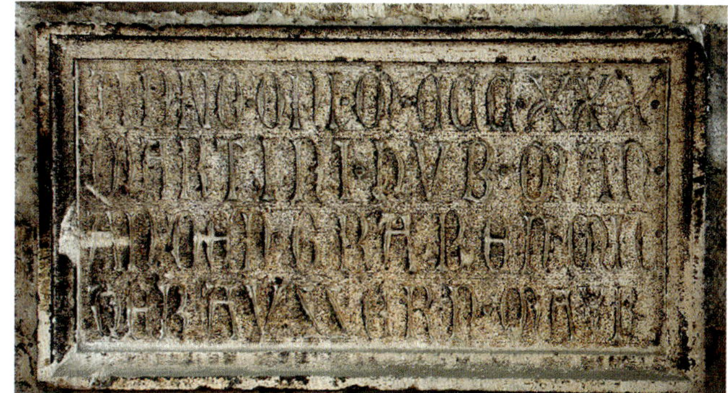

ing views. This is why the lofty building has oriel windows with lots of windows in them, while the projecting central section of the north facade, which overlooks the Danube, consists almost entirely of glass. From here, the panoramic view reaches from the silhouette of the mediaeval city in the west to the neoclassical Walhalla in the east. In this way, the Royal Villa, regarded as the finest example of the so-called Maximilian style outside Munich, became, as it were, the royal Belvedere, looking out over the monuments that Maximilian's father, Ludwig I, had erected around Regensburg.

Back in Ostengasse, one turns left into the street called Am Stärzenbach. Its name recalls the fact that the open bed of the eastern branch of the river that used to flow through Regensburg ran through Ostnerwacht. In the Middle Ages this street was the continuation of Minoritenweg and ran northwards to Ostentor. This old layout changed only when Minoritenweg was extended directly eastwards in 1889 in order to provide a better connection with the city centre for the residential area then growing up around Reichsstrasse. In the Middle Ages, the district around Am Stärzenbach and what became the outer Minoritenweg was settled mainly by market-gardeners. This is why the number of stone-built houses is relatively small: apart from No 2 Am Stärzenbach, which still has a gothic cellar, the most interesting house is

Vaulting in the archway under the East Gate

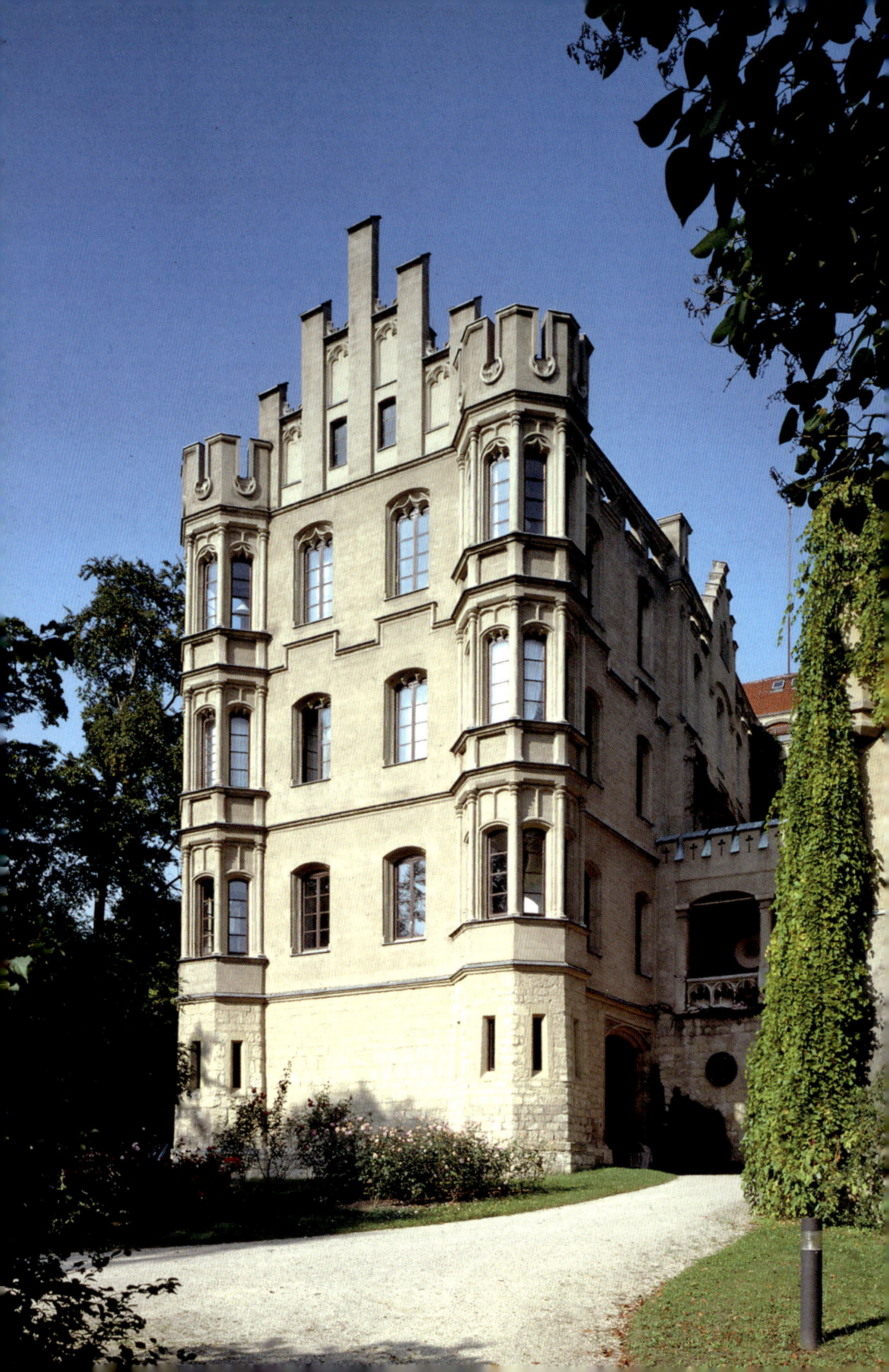

The villa erected (1854–56) for King Maximilian II of Bavaria on the site of the eastern bastion.

No 8, which again has romanesque origins; biforium windows dating from the second quarter of the 13th century have been revealed in its facade.

Beside the junction with Minoritenweg, there stands – hidden by No 27 – House No 29, the larger, eastern part of which dates back to the 13th/14th centuries. The original building must have looked like a tower. This house did not achieve fame in the history of the city, however, until the late 18th and early 19th centuries, when its then owners, an art-loving family of chandlers called Kränner, established a collection of paintings that was well-known far beyond the confines of the city.

Following Minoritenweg into the city, one passes a 15th -century house, No 21, on the right. The building was very splendid in the context of the late mediaeval settlement in the southern part of Ostnerwacht, and was owned by the von Hochholding family (their arms are on the bay window); it now looks almost out of place beside its much more recent neighbours. This also applies to the baroque **Gartenpalais Löschenkohl/ Löschenkohl Villa (7)**, which bears really impressive architectural witness to the tradition, traceable in this part of Ostnerwacht from the early 17th century, of using the numerous grassed-over areas not only for providing the population with food, but also for creating flower-gardens. Hieronymus Löschenkohl, a banker, had it built between 1730 and 1735 by Johann Michael Prunner, who was also the architect of the Löschenkohls' mansion (see p. 99) in Neupfarrplatz. The very imposing five-bay street facade is clearly structured at the elevated ground level and the *piano nobile* by a cornice running round it. This splendid impression is created mainly by the contrast between the rendered stonework – grooved at ground-floor level – and the openings in the facade, which are artistically framed in hewn stone. The dormer windows in the roof with their pointed gables also contribute to the overall impression. The most characteristic aspect of the villa is, however, its south facade, which faces what was once the garden and has a three-

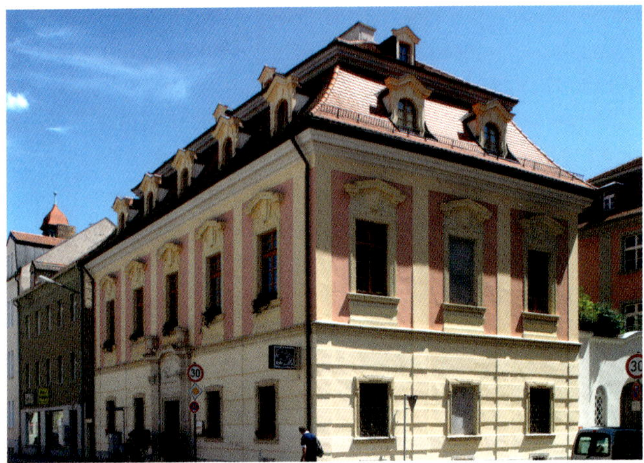

The late baroque Löschenkohl Villa (No 20 Minoritenweg), the work of Johann Michel Prunner, an architect from Linz

sided projection in the middle of it. This reflects Prunner's artistic origins in that it shows a close relationship with large Viennese villas, and also to the mansion at Pürkelgut, which Prunner himself built outside the gates of Regensburg in 1728; there the projection is semi-circular. This well-tried trick made it possible to view the 'artistically natural' garden from the ballroom on the first-floor from several different angles.

Kirschgäßchen, which turns off southwards just beside the villa leads, a few metres further on, into **Von-der-Tann-Strasse (8)**. This street of petit bourgeois houses divided up into flats, which were built in the late 19th and early 20th centuries, no longer reveals any traces of mediaeval Ostnerwacht. Nor were there any previous buildings here to speak of, as there had been numerous market-gardens on this land since the Middle Ages. These were joined only in the late 18th century by the Löschenkohls' garden and, right in the east, by the Kränner family's wax-bleaching premises. The 14th-century city wall ran along the south side of the street, which, until 1885, was called Krautererweg, a reference to the German name for market-gardeners. When the first houses were erected on the south side of

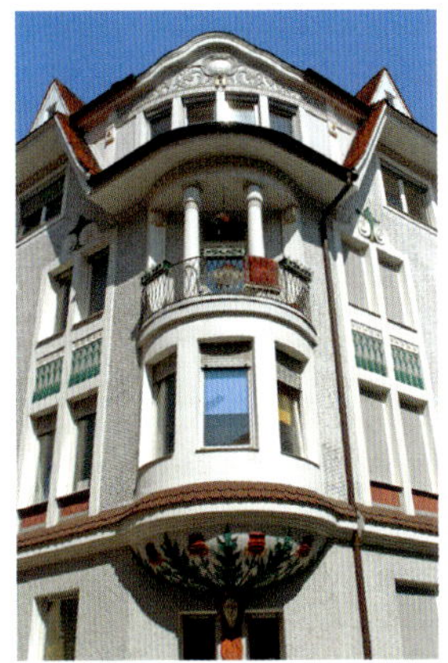

No 17 Von-der-Tann-Strasse, built in 1907, is one of the finest examples of 'Jugendstil' there.

the street from the 1860s on, remains of the mediaeval fortifications were incorporated into the new buildings. The facades facing the street still follow the line of the walls, while the facades looking out over the gardens at the back follow the line of the outer ward. Some houses are striking because of their art nouveau decorations, for instance the house on the corner of Kirschgäßchen (No 17), and a pair of houses (Nos 10/12).

At its western end, Von-der-Tann-Strasse leads to D. Martin-Luther-Strasse, which has cut through the mediaeval fortifications here since 1865. The so-called Klarenanger once lay north of here; it was named after St Clare's Convent, which was founded here in the 13th century and destroyed in 1809 (see p. 193). The surroundings here are dominated by the Neues Rathaus (New Town Hall), an example of National Socialist town planning, and a multi-storey car park built in 1971. At the end of this tour of Ostnerwacht, these massive, monolithic buildings – so completely out of proportion, historically speaking – again make the visitor realise what damage short-sighted planning can do to an urban landscape which has grown organically over centuries.

To the north of the car-park is a stela, made by Richard Triebe in 1978 as a memorial to Dr Johann Maier, a Cathedral clergyman, and his supporters, Josef Zirkl and Michael Lottner, who pleaded that the city should surrender to the Americans without any resistance on April 23, 1945. The National Socialists accused the three men of being saboteurs and murdered them.

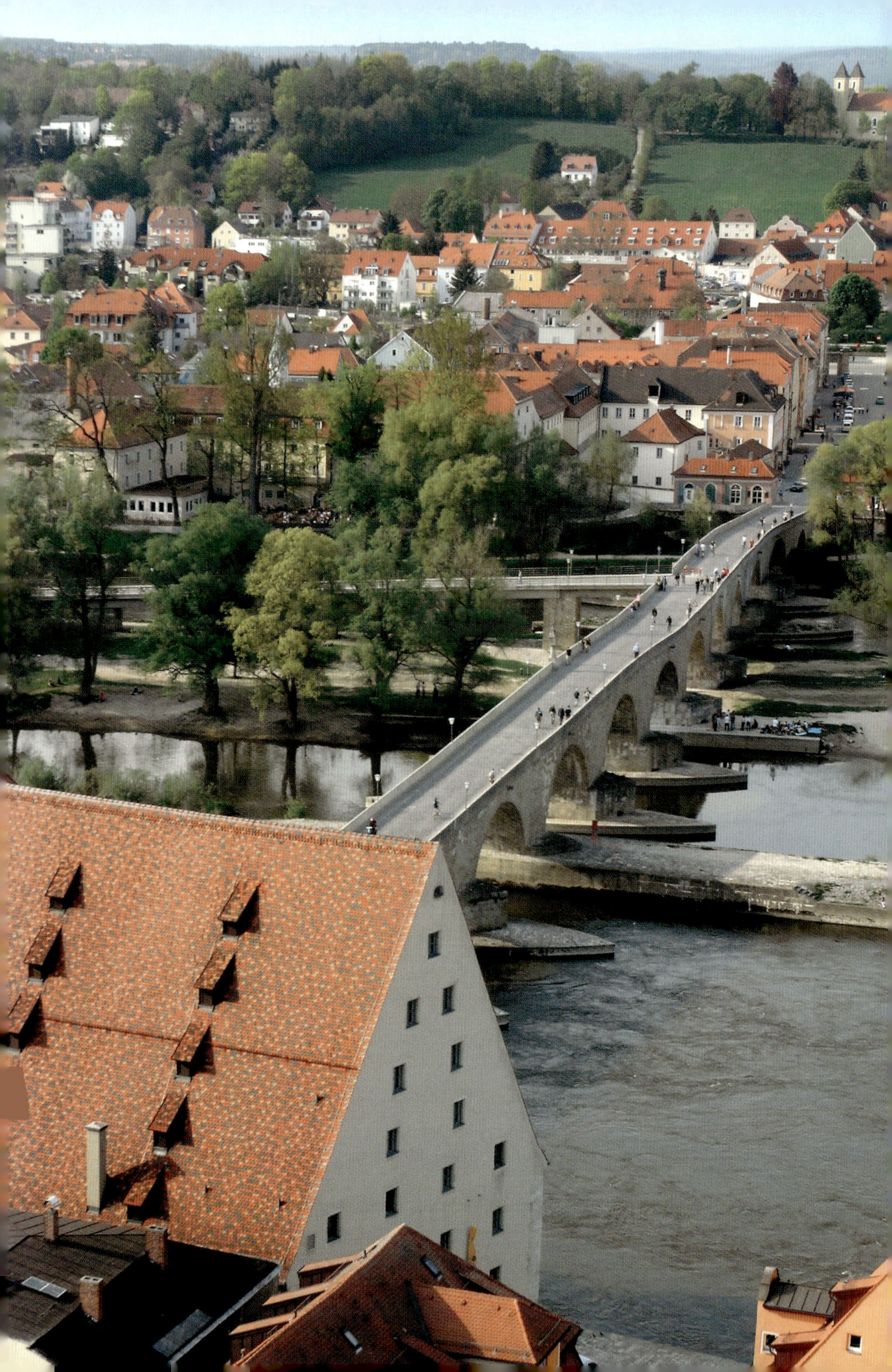

Stone Bridge, Stadtamhof and the Danube Islands

The Romans did not see any need to build a bridge to connect their legionary camp with the enemy territory north of the Danube. With Regensburg's rise in political and economic importance in the early Middle Ages, however, the problem of crossing the river became more and more pressing. Major continental trade routes met here, at the northernmost point of the Danube. Charlemagne already had a pontoon bridge set up across the river, starting from the then still functional north gate of the Roman camp. Presumably it did not stand up to the annual floods for very long, so that ferries alone once more had to cope with the steadily increasing passenger and goods traffic.

Constructing a permanent bridge over the Danube outside the gates of the international trading metropolis of Regensburg became one of the greatest challenges connected with traffic in the Middle Ages. It is not known when and on whose behalf planning for the building of a stone bridge was begun. At all events, the very low water-level resulting from the extremely hot and dry summer of 1135 provided the opportunity for starting work on the foundations. By 1146, the huge bridge had been completed. It was 350m long, and 16 arches were necessary to span the Danube. A 20m-long ramp linked the northern end of the bridge with Stadtamhof's present-day main street.

The bridge-builders' feat of engineering is all the more admirable insofar as the technical knowledge possessed by Roman builders of waterways and bridges first had to be re-learnt in mediaeval times. Not for nothing was the bridge over the Danube in Regensburg considered by contemporaries to be a spectacular achievement, something unique in Germany. In the Middle Ages, it was the only completely stone-built crossing over the Danube east of Ulm, and for 800 years it remained the only bridge in Regensburg that spanned the whole width of the river.

The significance of the bridge is reflected in its legal status. In 1182, the Emperor Frederick I, Barbarossa, decreed, at the wish of Regensburg's citizens, that access to the bridge and the crossing of it must be toll-free. However, the great cost of maintaining the bridge led in the

View from the north tower of the cathedral over the roof of the imperial city's salt store to the Stone Bridge and Stadtamhof. In the distance, outside the World Heritage zone, are Steinweg and the Dreifaltigkeitsberg.

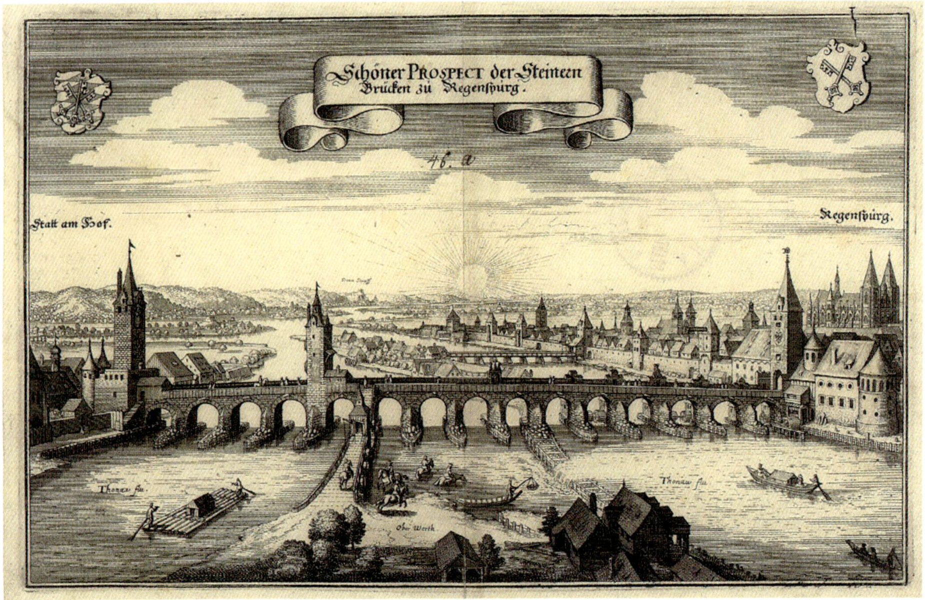

The Stone Bridge with its original three towers, view from the west. Copper engraving by Matthäus Merian, 1644 (Museum of Regensburg History). The Upper Wöhrd is in the foreground, the Lower Wöhrd and old wooden bridge in the distance.

14th century to a special tax on wine, mead and woollen goods. A bridge toll was introduced for carts in 1514.

Its economic importance and its function as a convenient means of access to the city soon made it necessary for the bridge to be fortified. For this purpose, three towers were erected – one at each end and one over the twelfth pillar – in the late 12th and in the 13th centuries. This characteristic silhouette determined the appearance of the bridge for almost 500 years and made it the city's most famous landmark, along with the cathedral. Only the southern tower on the bridge has survived. The middle one had to be taken down due to terrible damage caused by the masses of ice in the Danube in 1784, and the so-called Black Tower at the northern end was demolished in 1810 after it had been bombarded and set on fire by Austrian troops the previous year.

In the late 19th century, as a result of the Danube developing into a European waterway and of the increasing amount of road traffic, there

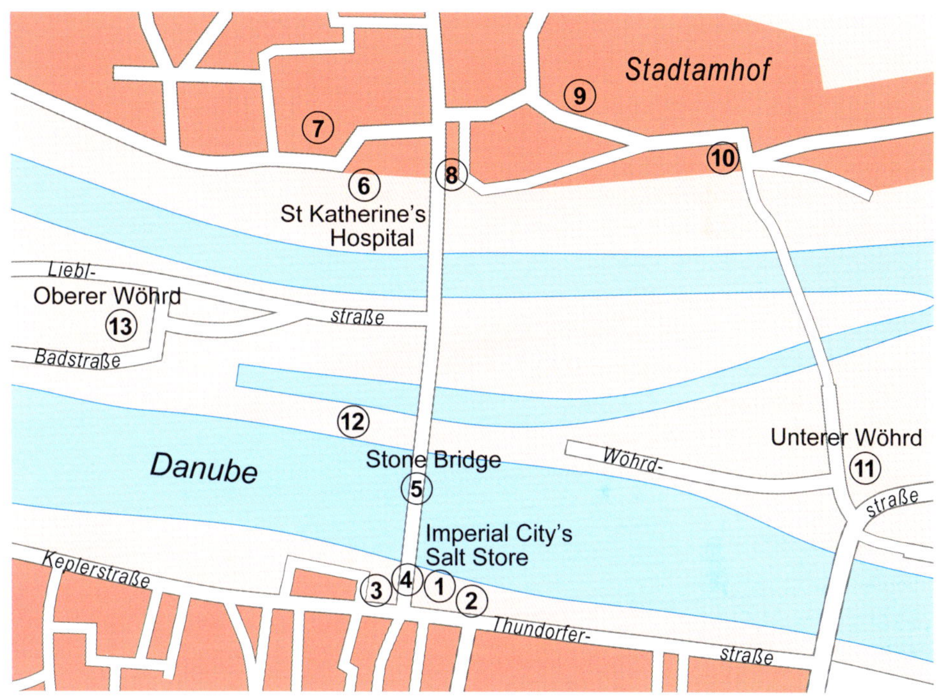

were demands for the bridge to be pulled down. Concrete plans for a new bridge were made at the beginning of the 20th century. It was due to the untiring efforts of the committed citizens who fought against the project that this unique example of bridge-building was not sacrificed to the belief in progress.

There are very close links between the bridge and the settlement to the north of it, Stadtamhof. Although its origins are sometimes traced back to *Skierstatt*, a royal farm sold to St Emmeram's Imperial Abbey in 981, and even to the Romans, merely the position of its main street, built in the 14th /15th centuries, demonstrates its dependence on the Stone Bridge.

Politically, however, Stadtamhof was never part of the free imperial city. In the mid-12th century already, it had come under the sway of the Bavarian dukes, and when Regensburg acquired its status as a free imperial city in 1245, the political boundary between Regensburg (which also owned the Stone Bridge as well as St Katherine's Hospital to the north west of the bridge) and Stadtamhof, a Wittelsbach territory, was determined for centuries to come. This frontier situation continued until Regensburg became part of the Kingdom of Bavaria in 1810. Yet, even then, Stadtamhof retained its municipal independence for a while; it was not absorbed into Regensburg until 1924.

There is almost no architectural evidence of Stadtamhof's mediaeval history. The Thirty Years' War caused severe damage, and then the Austrian army bombarded the little town and burnt it down on April 23, 1809, while fleeing from Napoleon's troops. The next morning, 95 houses and St Katherine's Hospital had been reduced to rubble.

Unlike Stadtamhof, the two islands in the Danube – Oberer Wöhrd and Unterer Wöhrd (Upper and Lower Wöhrd) – always belonged to Regensburg. They were of great importance for the imperial city's food supply, being the site of watermills and the home of fishermen. In addition, the long islands, above all Unterer Wöhrd, had plenty of room for storing materials of all kinds and for other functions requiring a lot of space. It was only in the post-mediaeval period that they became more important as places to go for a walk and to relax in.

At the Southern End of the Bridge

On the south bank of the Danube, the access ramp to the Stone Bridge is flanked by two enormous warehouses. The one on the right is the former **reichstädtische Salzstadel/ the Imperial City's Salt Store (1)**. It was erected between 1616 and 1620 in place of some mediaeval buildings – a bath-house, a cook-shop and a port-crane. Since it has a ground-floor, two upper floors and five storeys under the roof, the store is strikingly high, especially when seen from the east. Owing to the enormous loads and the marshy terrain near the mediaeval port canal (see p. 131), the rubble foundations had to be placed upon oaken posts and had lime mortar poured over them. Inside, the width of the building is impressive; the ground-floor is divided into three bays by means of stone pillars. Wood was the only material used in the construction of the upper floors. When the salt store was restored (1988/91), an attempt was made to preserve the original impression which this bold architecture conveyed by separating the modern metal and glass fittings from the historical fabric.

Beside the salt store, to the east, is the so-called **Wurstkuchl/Sausage Kitchen (2)**, which was erected instead of the cook-shop demolished when the salt store was built in 1615. On its north side, the single-storey building is attached to the 14th-century city wall, which has survived here. The interior still has the original arrangement of rooms – to the west, the smoky kitchen with an open fire; to the east, the dining-

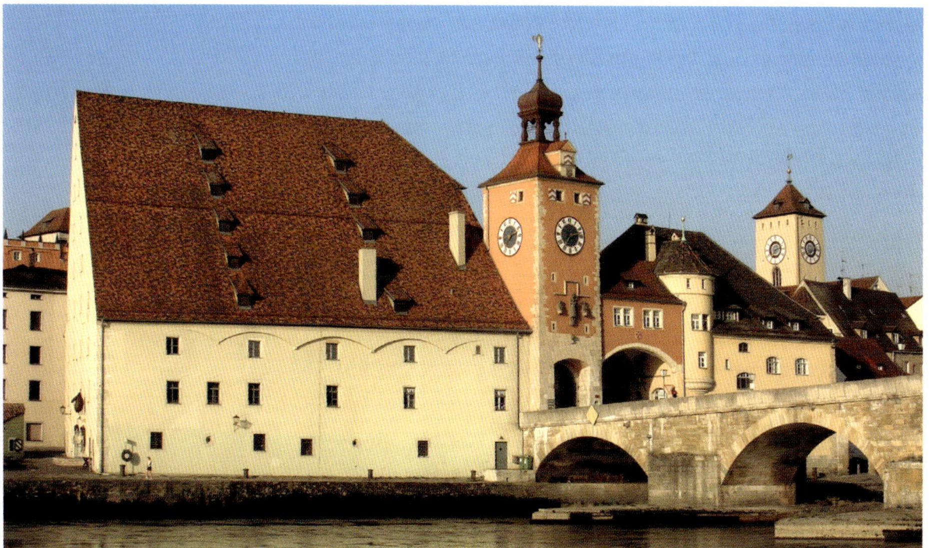

The southern end of the Stone Bridge. Left, the imperial city's salt store (1616–20), beside it the Brücktor (c. 1300) with the arch added in 1910/03; right, the Amberg Salt Store(15th /16th cent.)

room for customers. The former cook-shop did not start to specialise in serving sausages until the 19th century.

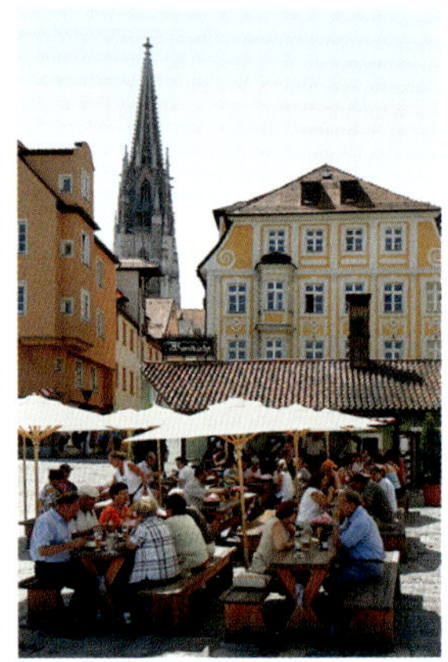

The so-called Sausage Kitchen, built against the city walls on the Danube side in the 17th cent.

On the west side of the bridge is the former **Amberger Salzstadel/Amberg Salt Store (3)**, which was built in 1551 in place of another older warehouse when the mediaeval port canal was filled in. This earlier building, whose layout was still determined by the canal, had been erected by Albrecht IV, the Bavarian duke, during the short period he ruled over Regensburg; it was used to provide a temporary store for the salt destined for Amberg and the Upper Palatinate. The east side of the 1551 building underwent major alterations when the City Architect, Adolf Schmetzer, had two houses that previously adjoined the store demolished in order to widen the bridge-approach in 1902/03. In order to make the vacant site usable as a roadway and, at the same time, to close it optically, Schmetzer designed the arched buttress that spanned his new road onto the bridge.

Before 1903, all the traffic that crossed the bridge passed through the early gothic **Brücktor/Bridge Gate (4, M)**. This is the only one of the three gates on the bridge to have survived. In fact it does not – as it may seem – stand at the beginning of the bridge, but on its first pier. This is because there is another bridge arch which was filled in in 1551 and is no longer visible today; it once spanned the mediaeval port canal. The gate-tower was erected about 1300, and restored in 1648 after suffering damage in the Thirty Years' War. The tower acquired its present-day roof and clock at that time. The heavy iron hinges to which the tower gates were fastened, and also the brackets for the barrier, can still be seen on the outer gate-arch. A tablet recalls the dynamiting (1945) and restoration (completed in 1967) of the bridge's first and tenth piers (new numbering). The north side of the tower is decorated with three portraits of rulers. The sculptures were originally on the tower in the middle of the bridge; when this was demolished in 1784, they were initially transferred to the northern end of the bridge, before being placed in their present position in 1835 (the originals are in the Museum of Regensburg History). The very large middle figure (c. 1280/90) is usually identified as the Emperor Frederick II, to whom the city owed its status as an imperial free city; the figures on thrones at each side (1207?) show King Philipp of Swabia (an inscription identifies him) and, probably, his consort Irene. In 1207, Philipp had granted the city important rights connected with the bridge, and created the legal basis for its later free-city status.

View of the southern end of the Stone Bridge from the Obere Wöhrd. Right – beside the Brücktor (c. 1300) – the Amberg Salt Store (15th/16th cent.)

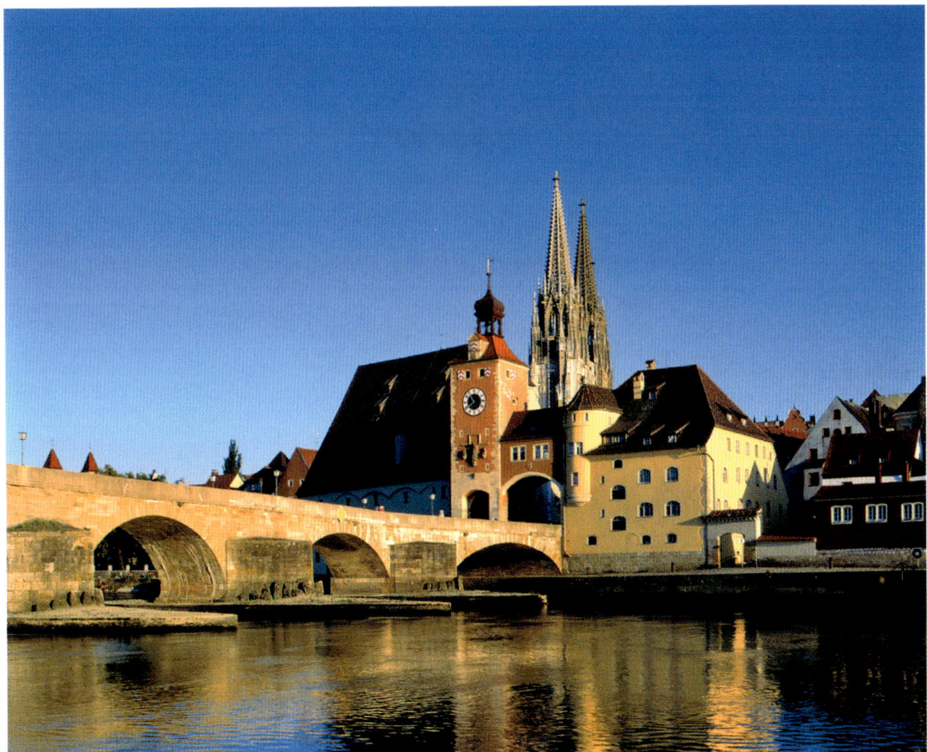

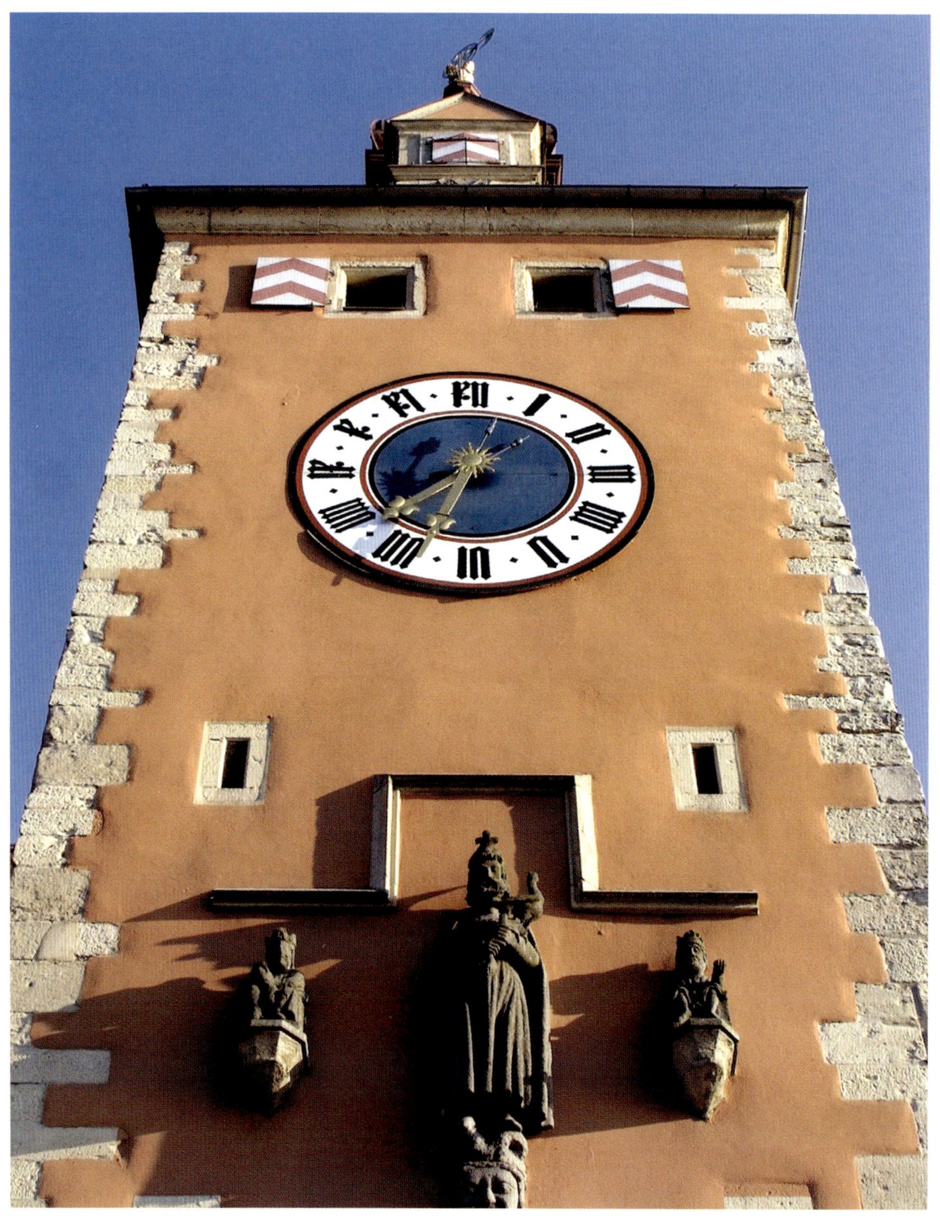

The Brücktor (c. 1300) with the sculptures moved there in 1835: in the middle, Emperor Frederick II (?); beside him, King Philipp of Swabia and his consort Irene

The Stone Bridge

The **Steinerne Brücke/Stone Bridge (5)** ascends gently as far as its central point and then, turning slightly eastwards, goes downhill again towards Stadtamhof. The bridge has had its present width only since 1877/78, when overhanging pavements were constructed. The balustrade was renewed again in 1950.

Looking down from the bridge, one has to be impressed by the piers with their lancet-shaped protective bases, so-called *Beschlächte*. These used to be a bit wider, so that the water was held up by the bridge, causing the currents and eddies that were so dangerous for shipping. On the other hand, the rapid flow of water was advantageous for the numerous mills that were established on the river banks from the 14th century at the latest. These watermills were not only of great importance for the economy in the imperial city; the income they generated was also used for the upkeep of the bridge. The mills were thus carefully maintained until the devastating drifting ice in 1784 destroyed every single one of them.

Despite its purely functional purpose, the bridge has a wealth of decorative sculpture on it. The mostly unclear significance of the figures, some on the balustrade, others on its outer side and scarcely visible, has given rise to stories and legends. This applies not least to the so-called *Bruckmandl*, the little man on the bridge, who sits astride a steep roof, looking into the distance. Today the statue is at the highest point of the bridge. This piece of sculpture goes back to 1854; the mediaeval original dating from 1446 was replaced by another version in 1579, now in the Museum of Regensburg History, which has survived only as a torso; it stood on the roof of a flight of steps that led from the eastern side of the bridge down to a grinding mill, which was once situated on the third pier. The original meaning of the little figure (symbol of sovereignty, pointer towards the south) remains unclear.

Until 1694, a gothic aedicula with a crucifixion group stood approximately where the *Bruckmandl* stands today. From this part of the bridge, one has a good view of the two islands in the Danube, the Upper and Lower Wöhrd, as well as the land between them, which even today shows traces of mediaeval engineering activity – as early as 1304, a weir was constructed on the south bank of the Upper Wöhrd in order to prevent water from overflowing from the southern arm of the Danube into the lower-lying northern arm. This was re-constructed as a stone embankment, the so-called *Hammerbeschlächt*, linking the two islands (see p. 234).

A decision taken by the city council in 1499 led to the construction in 1502 of the ramp-like bridge from the Upper Wöhrd to the Stone Bridge. Sending loads to the flour mill, which had previously been accessible only by ferry from Fischmarkt, became much easier thanks to this bridge, which was originally made of wood and had its own fortified tower. The stonemasons from the imperial city who were responsible for the upkeep of the Stone Bridge also set up their workshop at the foot of this bridge.

Until 1784, the bridge's middle tower stood on the pier just north of the ramp leading down to the Upper Wöhrd. The arms of the city and of the bridge are to be seen on the outside wall of the next arch northwards, on the west side of the bridge. These were legal symbols used in the Middle Ages to indicate the place where, until about 1500, so-called water punishments were administered – for instance, the drowning of adulterers or the ducking of usurers.

Since the demolition of the Black Tower in 1810, it has been possible to look straight ahead, across the former boundary between the imperial city and Bavaria, into the main street of Stadtamhof, while to the left, on the Stadtamhof bank, one sees the buildings and the beer garden belonging to St Katherine's Hospital. During the centuries-long political separation of Regensburg and Stadtamhof, the hospital formed an exclave

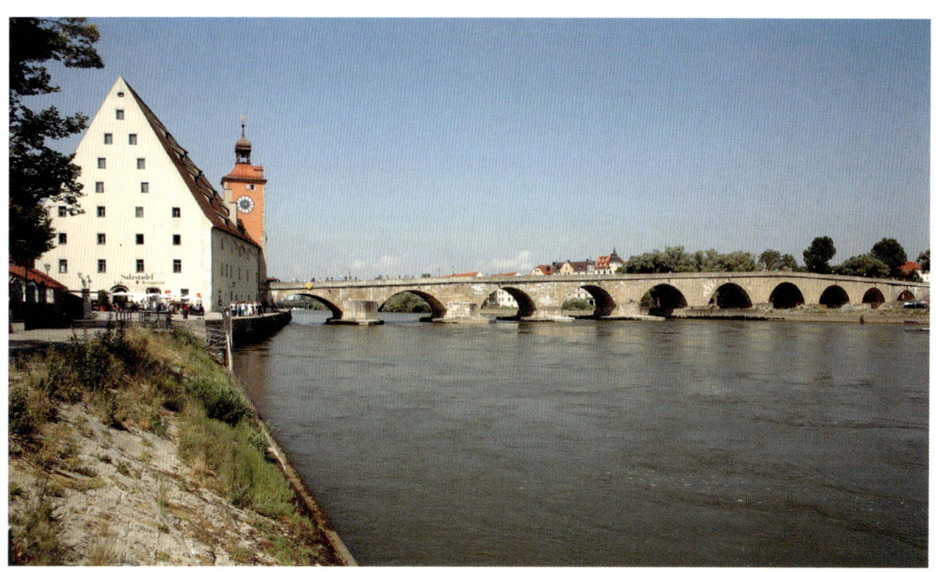

The imperial city's salt store and the Stone Bridge from the east. The huge dimensions of the warehouse become particularly obvious when one looks at the gables

belonging to the city on Bavarian territory; for this reason, it was furnished with its own access road, which forked off right at the end of the bridge, i.e., before the old city boundary. This road has survived, despite the great changes made as a result of rebuilding measures after 1809. From 1353 till 1486, the river-bank below the hospital was the site of the so-called *antwerch*, a winch used to pull boats under the bridge when they were travelling upstream.

St Katherine's Hospital

St. Katharinenspital/St Katherine's Hospital (6) came into being as a result of the amalgamation of the Cathedral Hospital with a city hospital that had already been in existence north of the Stone Bridge since the 12th century. It was the bishop who encouraged the project from about 1210. The new institution, whose infirmary, built about 1220, could accom-

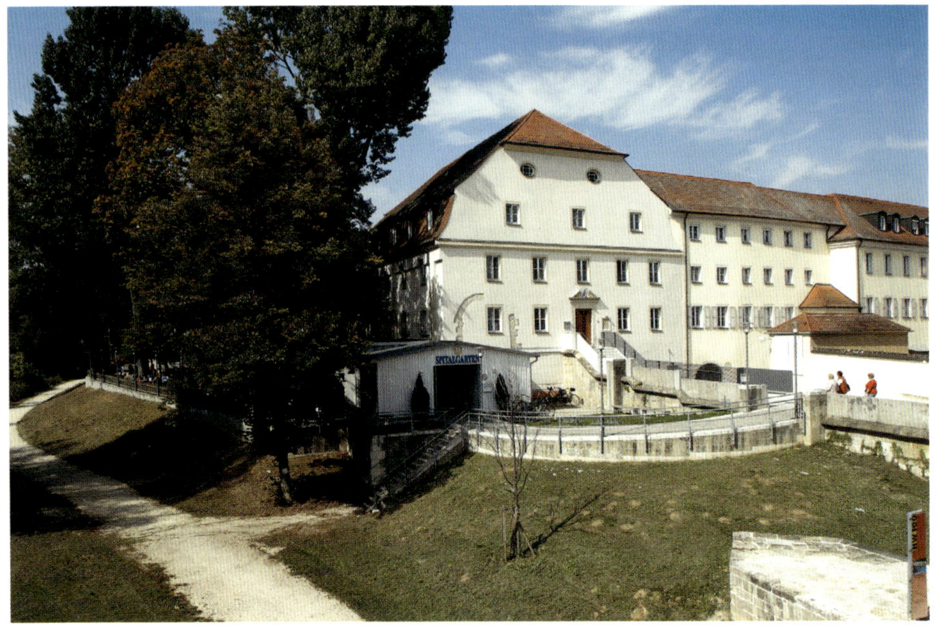

View of St Katherine's Hospital from the Stone Bridge. Left, the open land by the hospital (extended in the 20th cent.); right of the trees, the infirmary, the former grain store and the east wing

modate 100 patients, counted among the largest hospitals of its day. Since 1226, St Katherine's Hospital has been run jointly by representatives of the Cathedral Chapter and of the citizens of Regensburg. As the city hospital, it was Regensburg's central welfare institution until well into the 19th century. The still continuing tradition of beer-brewing at the hospital also dates back to the 13th century.

As they appear today, the hospital buildings nearly all go back to the rebuilding phase in the early 19th century. Fortunately, however, **St Katherine's Hospital Church (7)** – one of Regensburg's most interesting early gothic ecclesiastical buildings – has been preserved. Despite several later extensions, it is still quite easy to see that the original building was a hexagonal, central-plan structure. Heinrich Zant, a Regensburg patrician, had it built by masons from the cathedral as his own burial chapel in 1287 and dedicated it to All Saints.

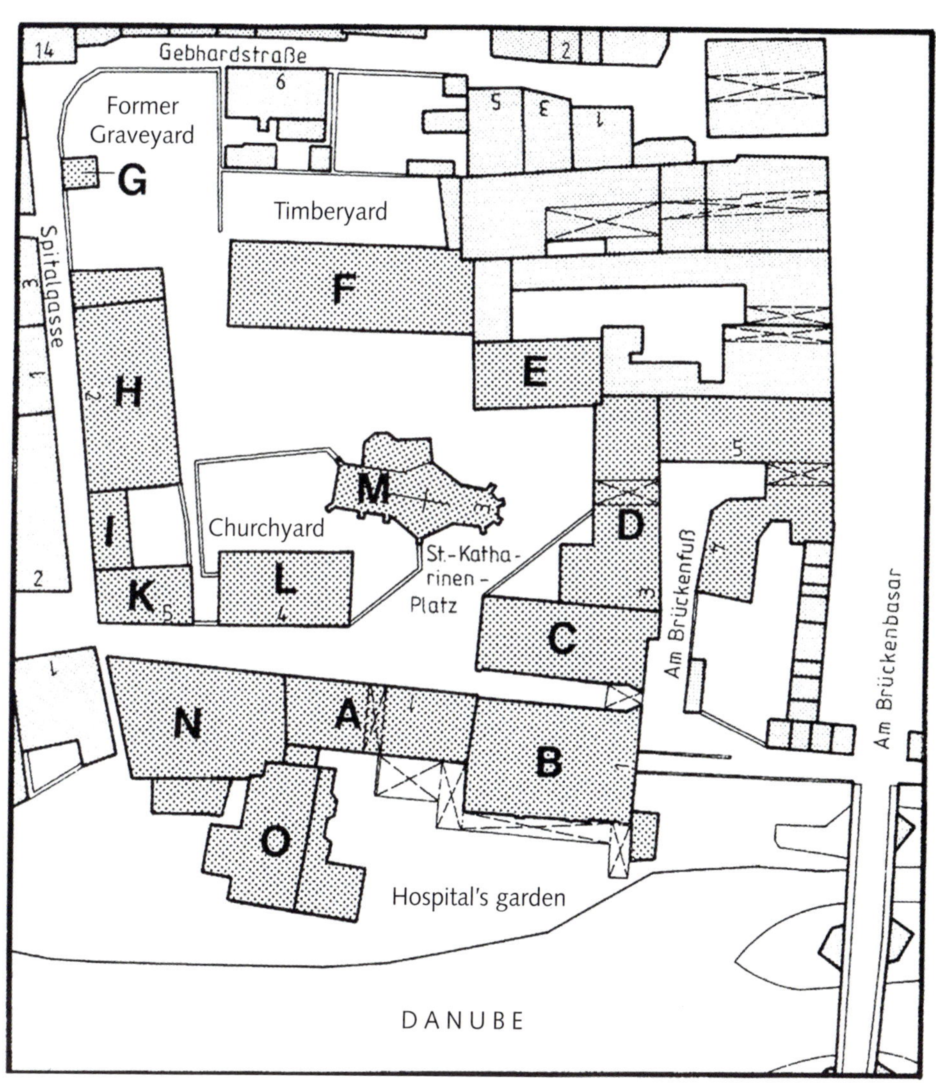

Plan of St Katherine's Hospital – A: central building, B: infirmary, C: grain store, D: east wing, E: north wing, F: coach house, G: former mortuary, H: byre and barn. I: former pigsty, K: clerk's office, L: priest's house, M: parish church, N: brewery, O: public house, until 1809 hospital bath-house (historical map of the City of Regensburg VIII, fig. 28)

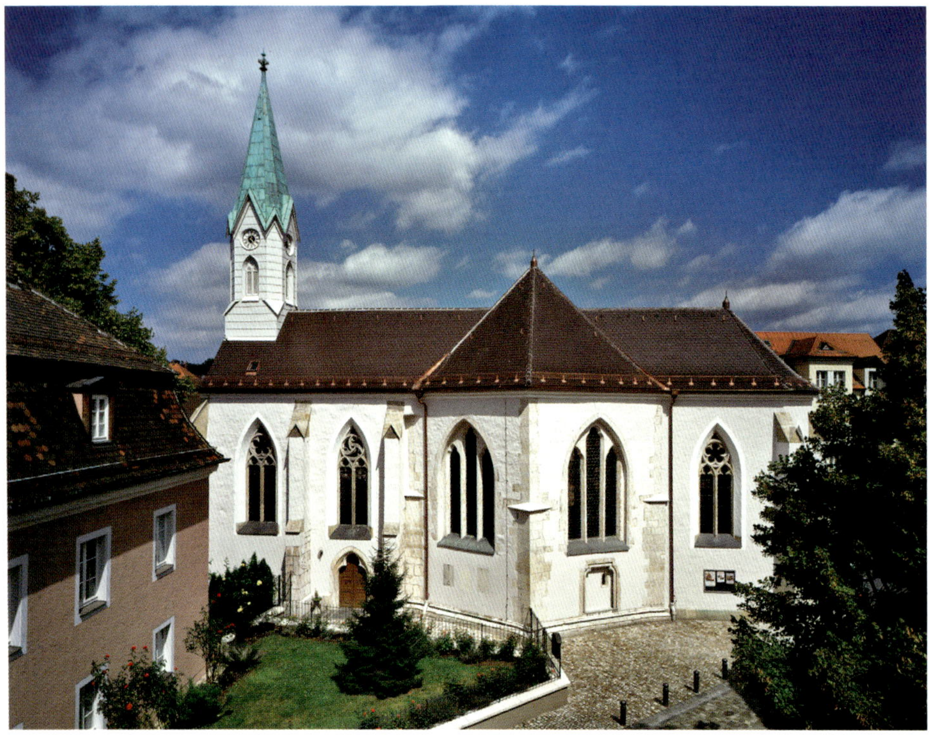

The church at St Katherine's Hospital: originated as a hexagonal mausoleum erected for Heinrich Zant in 1287

It is thus the oldest mausoleum built for a patrician in the German-speaking area. The central building soon had the (originally lower) choir added to it at the east end, and at the same time, or possibly slightly later, the two-bay nave was built to the west. The nave had to be erected before the former mausoleum could become the hospital's parish church. The nave and choir acquired their present-day appearance in the 19th century. The interior has lost virtually all its original furnishings. Nevertheless, the central area, in which the founder's sarcophagus (fragments in the Museum of Regensburg History) probably stood, and the choir possess excellent shaft capitals and vaulting consoles with imaginative foliate ornaments. The two late gothic altars were brought here from

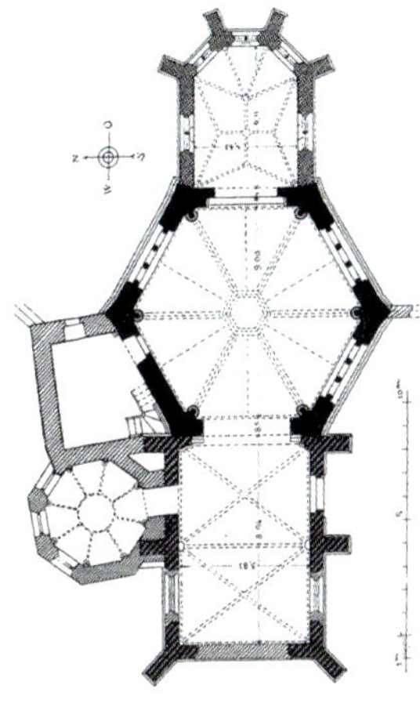

the church in Martinsberg near Hohenfels (Oberpfalz), which was cleared in 1937, when the military training area was established there.

East of the church, one passes through two archways, and thus from the site of the imperial city's hospital into 'Bavarian' Stadtamhof. Looking left, one sees the main street, which was rebuilt in uniform style on the mediaeval building plots after 1809 and leads to a neoclassical gateway (1825) at its northern end. This has a broad, open archway, but now functions only as a kind of aesthetic frame. At the southern end of the main street, too, the site of the defiant Black Tower from the 13th century until 1810, the town-planners decided in favour of a layout that signalled transparency after centuries of political separation. The **Brückenbasar/Bridge Bazaar (8)** has turned its former frontier position into the complete opposite as a result of the commercial (and now also gastronomic) use of its two wings. The gate-tower has been replaced by a panoramic view of Regensburg's mediaeval silhouette.

The Church of St Andrew and St Mang

A little way to the east of the Bridge Bazaar is the church dedicated to **St. Andreas and St. Mang/St Andrew and St Magnus (9)**, formerly an Augustine collegiate foundation. In the mid-11th century, already, St Ulrich of Zell, a monk who had been trained at St Emmeram's and later lived and worked in, among other places, Cluny, had attempted to found a monastery in this area between the Danube and the mouth of the R. Regen. His efforts failed due to the resistance of the Bishop of Regensburg. Finally, in 1138, Gebhard, a Regensburg cleric, succeeded in setting up an Augustinian canonical foundation, with the assistance of Paul, a fellow clergyman. His model was

View of Stadtamhof from the Stone Bridge, showing the tower of the church of St Andrew and St Mang

the canonical foundation of S. Maria in Porto near Ravenna. The contact with that foundation came about through Archbishop Gualtiero of Ravenna, who had ordained Gebhard in 1130. The Augustinian foundation in Stadtamhof thus became the only one of its kind north of the Alps that lived according to the comparatively relaxed regulations of S. Maria in Porto.

Since all the monastery buildings were destroyed in the Thirty Years' War (1634), only the foundation walls remain of the romanesque church on a cruciform base that Gebhard, according to his own record (1146), employed master masons from Como to construct. On the north side, the old foundations indicate that the transept was originally rounded.

The present-day church, usually known simply as St Mang's, was built between 1697 and 1717. Andreas Pichlmaier, who lived in Stadtamhof, is thought to have been the architect. The tower was not given its present-day form until 1875. On the gable facade, which is divided up into sections by means of pilasters, a large niche above the main doorway contains a statue of St Andrew. The interior, impressive due to its height, is a four-bay hall divided up by means of attached piers; it has a transept and a two-bay choir that is much narrower than the nave. The wall and ceiling paintings, probably executed by Otto Gebhard (c. 1750/60), reflect the rococo artist's intention to blur the clear architectural lines of the church. The rich stucco ornamentation demonstrates the stylistic transition from early rococo in the nave to mature rococo in the choir. The nuances in style that feature in late baroque and rococo art can also be studied in the five altars, the remarkable choir-stalls and the other furnishings.

The canonical foundation's buildings were not rebuilt until the 1730s, that is, a century after their destruction. Nowadays the College of Roman Catholic Church Music and Musical Education is housed in the complex.

After walking past the south facade of the church and the end of picturesque Seifensiedergasse, one reaches the **Andreas-**

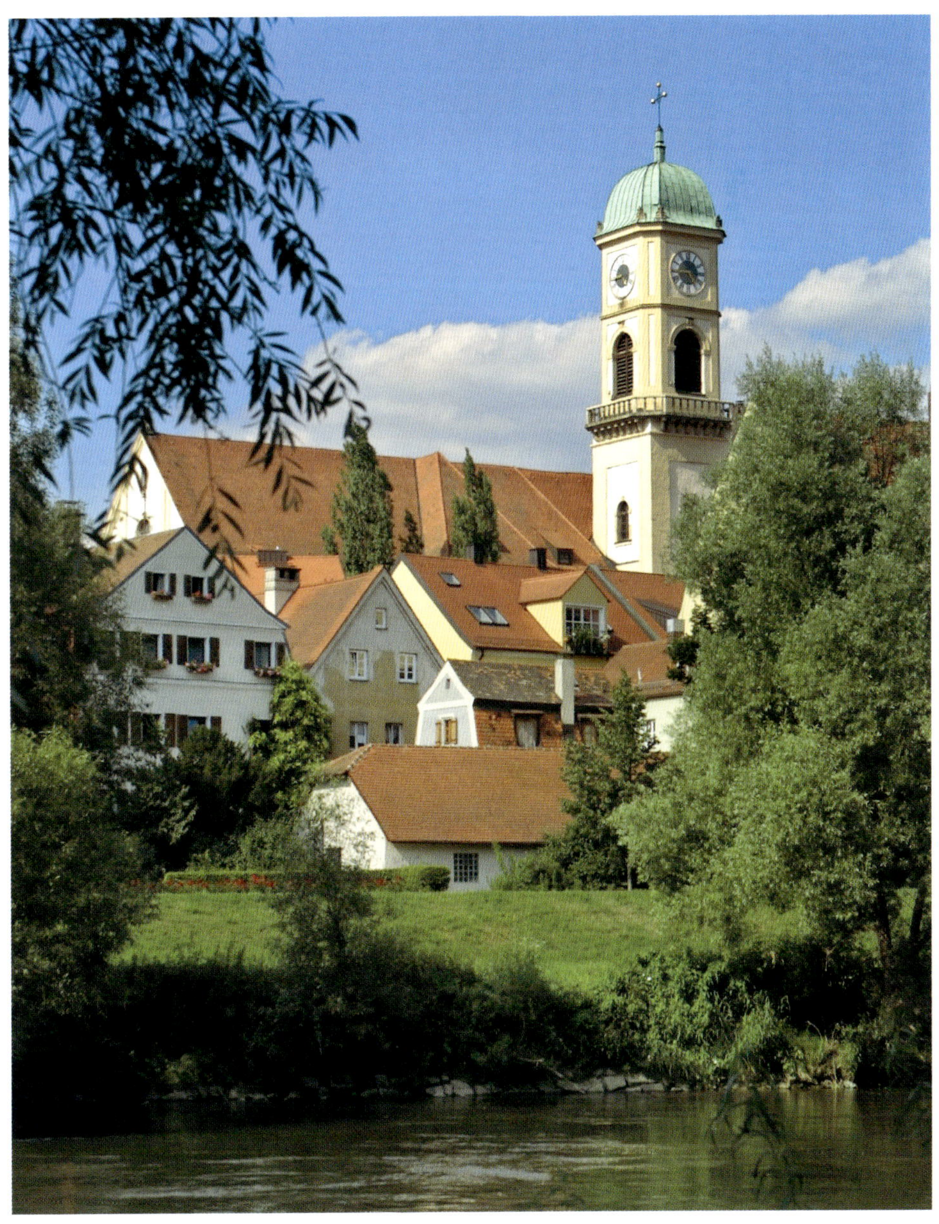

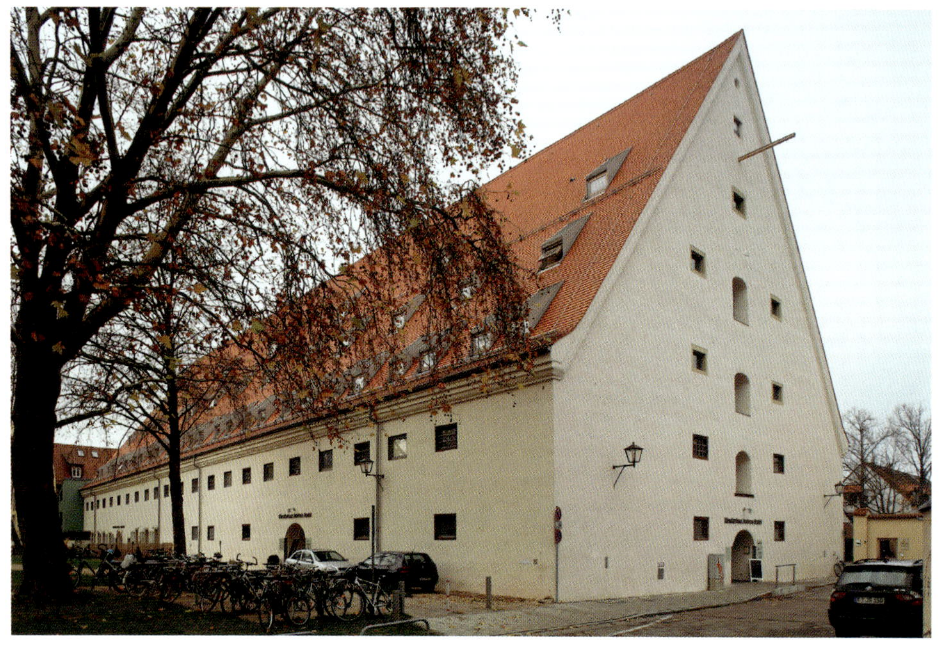

The so-called 'Andreasstadel', erected at the end of the 16th cent. on the banks of the Danube in Stadtamhof as a salt store for the Duke of Bavaria

stadel (10), a large former storehouse that stands between Andreasstrasse and the Danube. The long and massive building was constructed about 1597 as the Bavarian dukes' salt store. After these dukes became imperial electors in 1623, the building was often referred to as the 'Bavarian Electors' Salt Store'. As in the case of the city's salt store on the southern bank of the Danube, its counterpart in imperial Regensburg's trading history, the dimensions are impressive. The building has two complete storeys and a saddle roof with four further storeys under it. Except for its outer walls, the Andreasstadel with its three bays is constructed entirely of wood. When the building was restored before being re-opened as a 'Künstlerhaus' – artists' centre – and hotel in 2004, care was taken to preserve, even if only partially, a sense of the former spaciousness of the storehouse, despite the need to partition the floor-space to form more practical units.

Opposite the eastern gable facade of the salt store, whose loading hatches bear witness to the building's original purpose, is the beginning of the idyllic little street called Am Gries. Its name is derived from the Old High German word *gris* (= sand), which survives in numerous Upper German place-names. In this case, it refers to the sandy, and therefore long uninhabited, spit of land between the Danube and the mouth of the Regen. Not until the 16th century did fishermen and tradesmen settle here, people who profited from living near the two rivers. The oldest houses in the street are on its north side; most still have their typical front gardens.

The Two Islands in the Danube

From the Andreasstadel, the Grieser Steg, a footbridge constructed in 1947, offers a convenient route to the **Unterer Wöhrd/Lower Wöhrd (11)**. In the past, there was no link here between Bavarian Stadtamhof and the island in the Danube that belonged to the imperial city. In the Middle Ages, the only inhabitants of the island were a few tradesmen, nearly all of them raftsmen, shipbuilders or millers, who profited from being near the Danube; others worked in the brick-yards which are known to have been located here from the 15th century. The appearance of the island in the late Middle Ages, however, was characterised especially by various municipal and private sheds or barns. Relics of this use as a place to store goods are the municipal store-houses at Nos 33, 41 and 54 Wöhrdstrasse, which, in their present form, date from the late 16th and 17th centuries. They were linked with the city by a wooden bridge, at whose southern end the city erected a gate-tower with a draw-bridge in the city walls in 1418. This mediaeval Danube crossing was at the point where the Eiserne Brücke (Iron Bridge) stands today. *(From here, it is possible to return directly to the city centre. The following part of this tour is unsuitable for wheelchair-users.)*

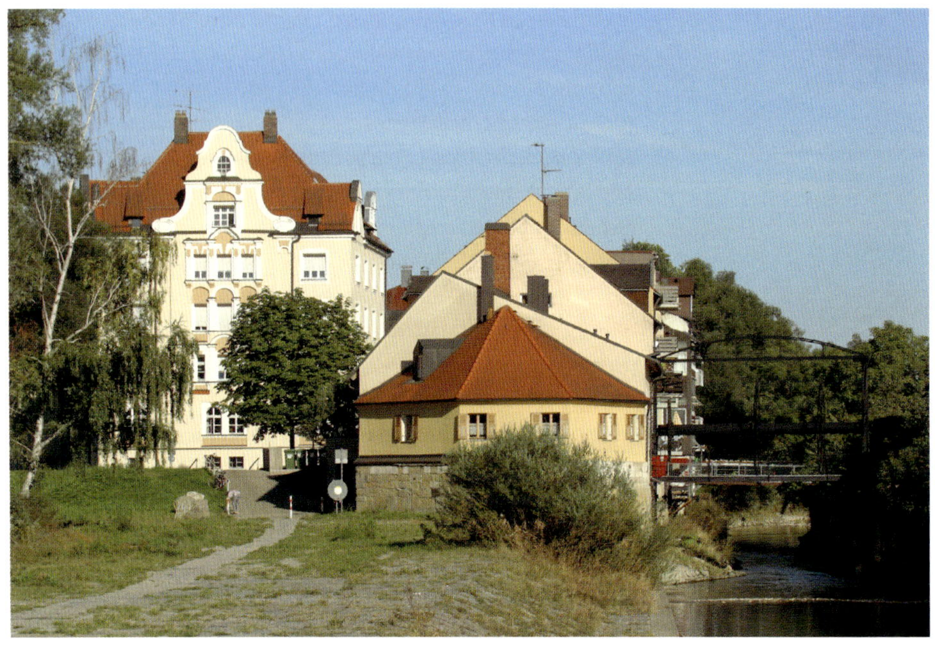

The former Obere Mahlmühle (upper mill) at the western end of the Untere Wöhrd

The route leads along the western Wöhrdstrasse through the former mill district on the Lower Wöhrd, which is now dominated by late 19th-century tenement houses. Beside the 16th -century Obere Mahlmühle (Upper Grinding Mill), at No 2 Wöhrdstrasse, is the beginning of a stone-built embankment, the so-called **Hammerbeschlächt (12)**, which was constructed in 1388 to strengthen the northern bank of the main arm of the Danube. The Hammerbeschlächt runs under the Stone Bridge to the Upper Wöhrd island. On the way, there are magnificent views of the Old Town and, not least, of the bridge itself. It is noteworthy, for example, that the piers of the bridge are larger on the western side and, furthermore, reinforced with foundlings. This was a protective measure against floods, flotsam, and – in particular – the greatly feared pack ice, which could seriously endanger the bridge. On February 24, 1784, for instance, the pressure of the flood of water and the force with which the ice-floes struck the bridge were so great that the middle tower seemed likely to collapse and consequently had to be demolished.

Ever since the Hammerbeschlächt was constructed, a canal has branched off the Danube at the edge of the Upper Wöhrd. Its originally fast-flowing water drove the nearby hammer mills. Although the canal has now been built over in the area of the present-day hotel, the historical waterway is still easily seen.

Until 1502, the Upper Wöhrd was accessible only from the river and was even more sparsely populated than the Lower Wöhrd. Of its two dozen inhabitants in 1471/72, the majority were fishermen and boat-builders. Not until the 16th century did the island acquire its own mill district. The municipal iron mill came into operation in 1529 and the municipal paper mill in 1539.

The present-day buildings here are almost exclusively post-mediaeval, although some properties appear to have been used since the late Middle Ages. This applies, for example, to Nos 2–6 Badstrasse, which one reaches just after crossing the canal bridge at the end of the Hammerbeschlächt. No 2 and No 6 were built by the imperial city in 1590 to replace older housing used by mill-workers, and served henceforth as living quarters for millers and forge employees. No 4 was built on the site of an older house to act as an office for the clerk who supervised the mills.

No 14 Badstrasse, one of the most imposing baroque master boatmen's houses on the Obere Wöhrd

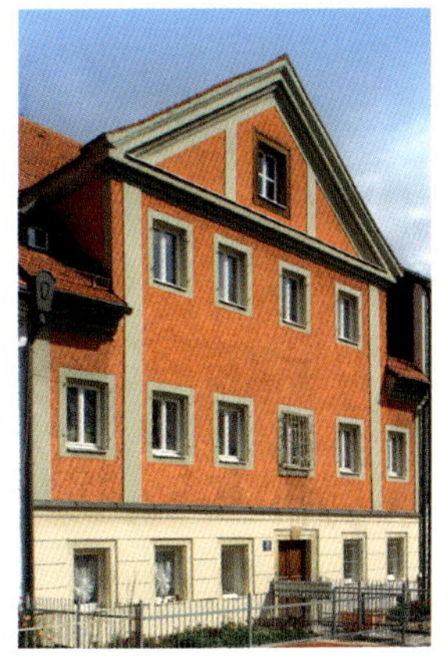

Further along, the majority of houses in Badstrasse are baroque and were owned by master boat-builders. With their front gardens, they form a picturesque ensemble. The row of houses is interrupted by the Gasthaus zur Goldenen Ente, the Golden Duck Inn, part of which – as in the case of No 52 – goes back to the late 15th century. A public house by the mid-17th century at the latest, this inn with its shady beer garden reflects the Upper Wöhrd's traditional popularity as a recreational area for city-dwellers.

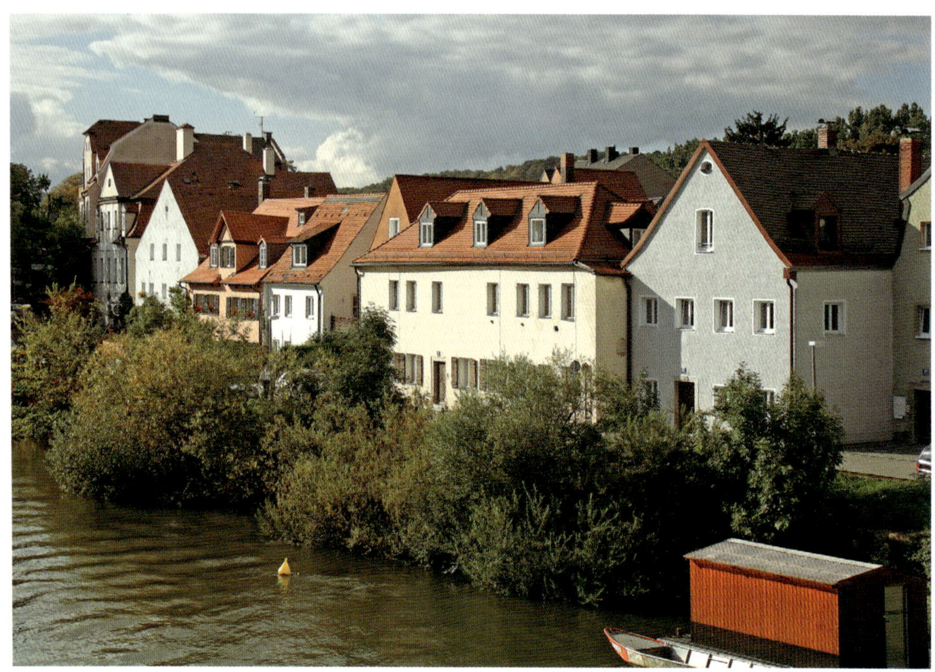

View of the western part of Badstrasse from the footbridge called the Eiserner Steg

The planting of an avenue of trees by the city building authorities in 1654 clearly shows that the population enjoyed going to the Upper Wöhrd in order to escape from the cramped conditions in the mediaeval city and take a walk in the fresh air. Among wealthy Regensburg citizens in the 18th century, it was fashionable to own a summer residence on the island. No 54 Badstrasse was formerly the social club where they met to play billiards or cards. However, the finest architectural survivals of the Upper Wöhrd's function as a popular place for a summer home are to be found in Lieblstrasse on the north side of the island. Nos 13 and 13a date from c. 1730 and bear the signature of Johann Michael Prunner; No 2, on the other hand, a splendid villa with a large garden, reflects the shift to neoclassicism. Georg Friedrich Dittmer, the merchant and banker, had it constructed in 1795 under

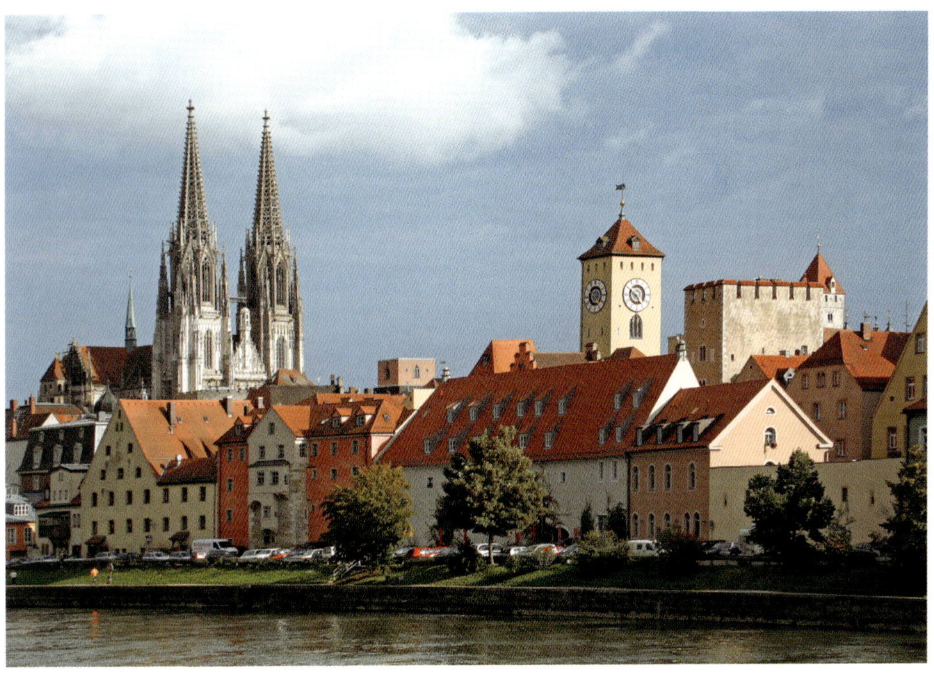

The Old Town seen from the Eiserner Steg footbridge

the supervision of Joseph Sorg, Director of Building to the Prince of Thurn and Taxis.

Opposite the Gasthaus zur Goldenen Ente, a footbridge called the Eiserne Steg, the Iron Footbridge, has permitted pedestrian access to the Old Town since 1902. The bridge, restored in 1946–48, offers magnificent views of the city and of both banks of the river. Half-left is Weinlände, the quay where wine was unloaded in the Middle Ages and half-right, Holzlände, the quay for wood. The site at the end of the bridge, where St Oswald's Church has stood since about 1300, was the most north-westerly point of Arnulf's city fortifications (917–920).

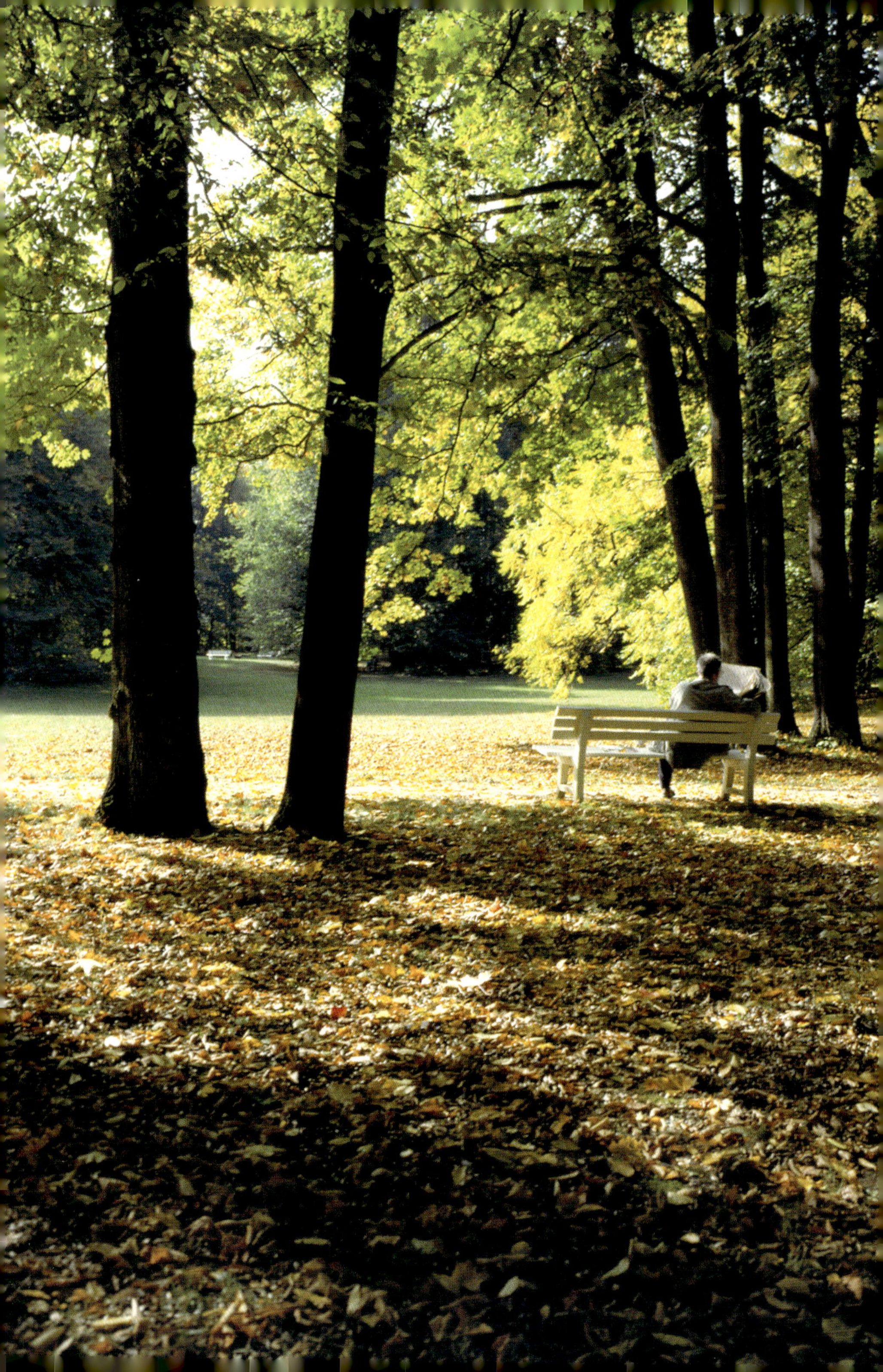

The Tree-Lined Avenue around the Mediaeval City

On April 12, 1779, Prince Carl Anselm of Thurn and Taxis submitted an application to the city authorities. In it, he asked to be allowed to plant an avenue of trees around the city moat 'for the advantage and pleasure of the local residents'. In that same year, 900 trees were planted on either side of a newly levelled path; by 1781, another 600 had been added.

The prince's intention was that the avenue should make the city more beautiful and its citizens healthier – and also that it should serve as a lasting memorial to himself. The noble donor could be sure of the gratitude of Regensburg's population and of the admiration of visitors to the city. The shady promenade, which ran all around the city on the landward side, inspired many poetic descriptions.

As the gift of a prince to ordinary citizens, who were not even his subjects in this case, Regensburg's 'Green Belt' acquired the role of a public garden as early as 1779 – ten years before the opening of the English Garden in Munich, the first public park on the European continent, and 14 years before the Tuileries Gardens in Paris were programmatically re-named the 'Jardin national' (National Gardens). Whilst the Republicans' theory of public education saw the public park as a kind of paradise that would have a positive influence on the individual's character, enlightened princes, for their part, had already taken action in many cases. For the cultural milieu of Prince Carl Anselm, the Emperor's Permanent Representative at the Perpetual Imperial Diet, the point of comparison was in Vienna, where Joseph II had opened the Prater in 1766 and the Augarten in 1775 as recreational areas for the whole population. And in 1781, the year that Regensburg's 'Green Belt' was completed, he had Vienna's ramparts planted with avenues of trees.

The transformation of the fortifications into a promenade meant that, for the first time since the Middle Ages, Regensburg was again the recipient of admiring glances as regards urban development. Compared with similar projects in other cities, two things were new: firstly, the retention of the city walls and, secondly, the creation of an avenue reserved exclusively for pedestrians. The demolition of the city walls would not yet have been justifiable from the military point of view; however, the development of the strip of land outside the walls as pub-

Dörnberg Park, laid out around the house of the same name by 1867

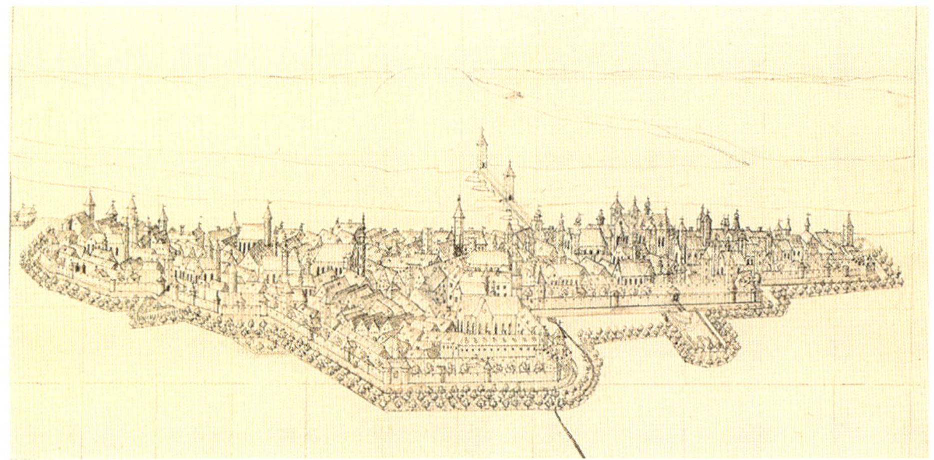

Regensburg seen from the south with the Avenue, completed in 1781; pen-and-ink drawing, before 1784 (Thurn and Taxis Court Library)

lic gardens did put an end – conceptually – to the centuries-old division between city and countryside.

After 1806, Carl von Dalberg, Elector, Arch-Chancellor, Prince-Bishop, and at that time the ruler of Regensburg, had monuments placed in the Avenue, imitating the style of an English landscape garden. Patriotic monuments continued to be set up even after Regensburg had been incorporated into the Kingdom of Bavaria in 1810. It was desired that, when out walking, its citizens should learn about the history of their Fatherland from significant examples of virtue.

Although the 'Green Belt' formed by the avenue was cut through by roads in several places in the 19th and 20th centuries, the overall impression remains of a late mediaeval city with a park-like fringe. Although the walls around the city were gradually removed after 1858, with only few exceptions, the boundaries of the late mediaeval city are thus still clearly to be seen (see fig. p.15).

The starting point for this walk is **Herzogspark/the Ducal Park (1)** just outside the north-western corner of the mediaeval fortifications. What looks like a picturesque landscape garden to-

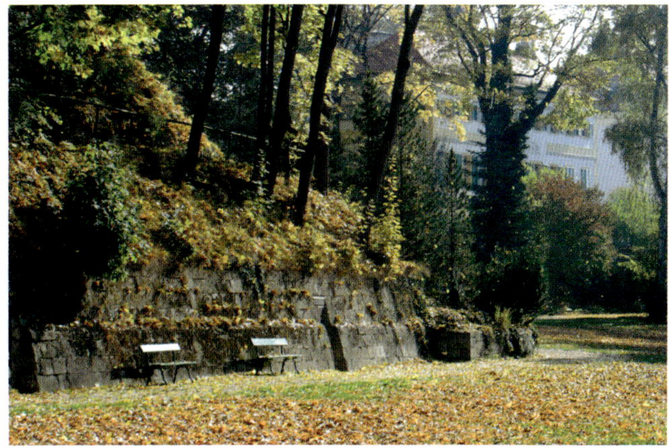

In Herzogspark: this was created from 1804 on, when Regensburg's westernmost bastion was turned into gardens. The Württemberg Mansion is in the background.

day is ultimately the result of large-scale earth-works carried out in order to defend the city. The historical centre of the park is the Prebrunn Gate, erected in 1293. A bastion was constructed in 1552 to protect it from the troops of the Schmalkalden Alliance. Eighty years later, the Thirty Years' War meant a further extension of this fortification, yet this did not prevent the destruction of the mediaeval gate-tower in 1634. When it was rebuilt in 1642, the old inscription dating from 1293 was moved to its present position on the tower's west side. The entrance there actually leads into the first floor because the earth was piled up high on the side away from the river.

The terrain outside the Prebrunn Gate was last used in the city's defence during the War of Spanish Succession in 1706. In 1804, it was purchased by Georg Friedrich von Müller, an official at the Thurn and Taxis court, who built himself a mansion (see p. 173) on the site of a mediaeval tower in the city walls, and had the bastion and moat area turned into a park. The Prebrunn Gate, the revetments of the city moat and other elements of the former fortifications were integrated into the design of the park, very much in the style of a landscape garden.

The Avenue, begun in 1779, runs above the city moat and outside it to the west. Following it southwards, one reaches the

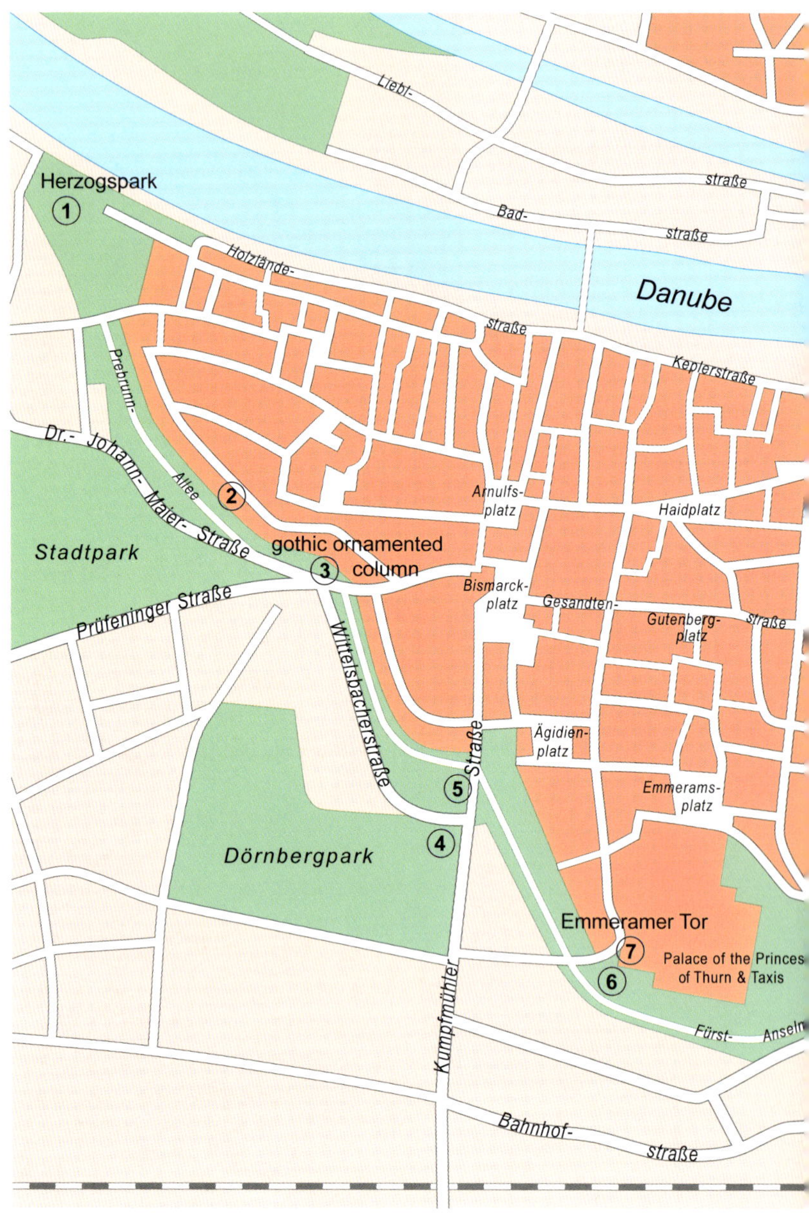
Liebl-
straße
Bad-
straße
Herzogspark
1
Holzlände-
straße
Danube
Keplerstraße
Prebrunn-
Allee
Dr.- Johann- Maier- Straße
2
Arnulfs-
platz
Haidplatz
Stadtpark
gothic ornamented column
3
Prüfeninger Straße
Bismarck-
platz
Gesandten-
straße
Gutenberg-
platz
Wittelsbacherstraße
Ägidien-
platz
Straße
5
Emmerams-
platz
4
Dörnbergpark
Emmeramer Tor
7
Palace of the Princes of Thurn & Taxis
6
Kumpfmühler
Fürst-
Anseln
Bahnhof-
straße

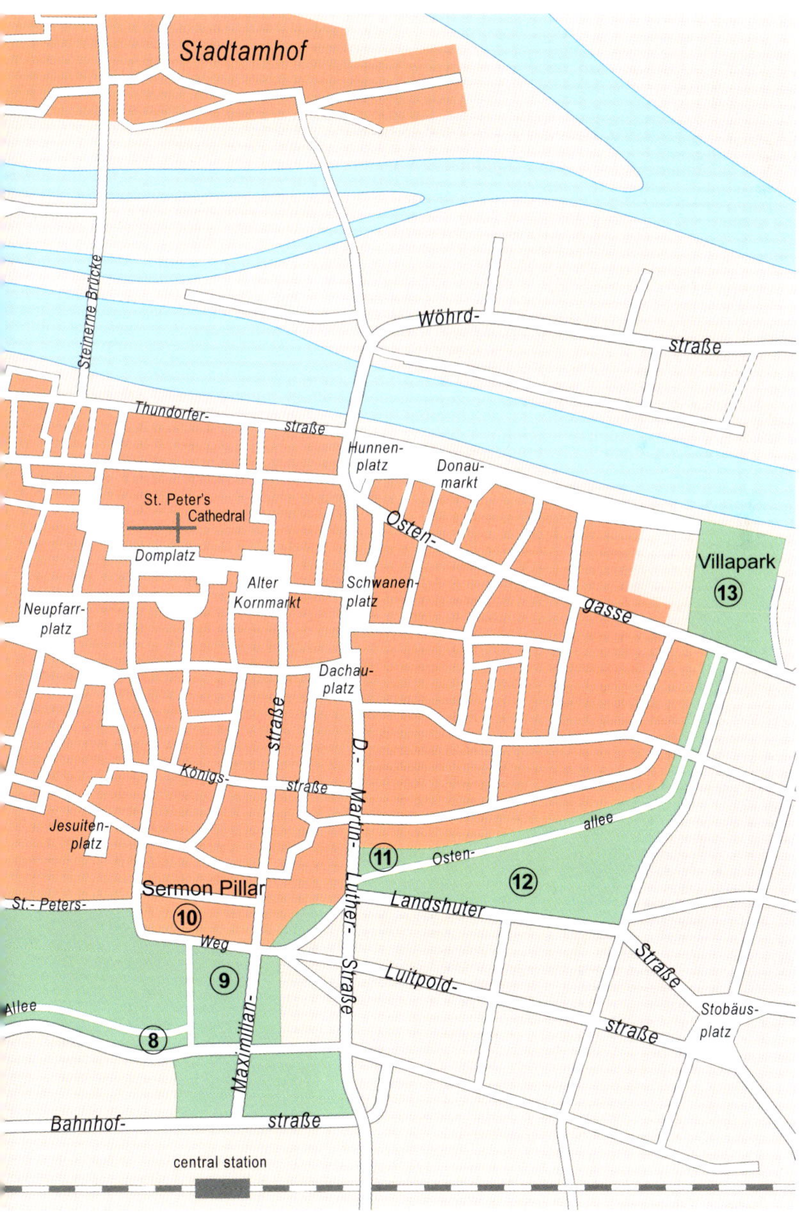
Stadtamhof
Steinerne Brücke
Wöhrd-
straße
Thundorfer-
straße
Hunnen-
platz
Donau-
markt
St. Peter's
Cathedral
Domplatz
Osten-
gasse
Villapark
13
Alter
Kornmarkt
Schwanen-
platz
Neupfarr-
platz
Dachau-
platz
straße
D.-
Martin-
Luther-
Straße
Königs-
straße
Jesuiten-
platz
allee
Osten-
11
12
Sermon Pillar
10
St.-Peters-
Weg
Landshuter
Straße
9
Maximilian-
Luitpold-
straße
Stobäus-
platz
Allee
8
Bahnhof-
straße
central station

Stahlzwinger (2). This section of the fortifications, in which fragments of both the late 13th-century city wall and also of the bailey wall outside it have survived, got its name from crossbow-men (sometimes known as *Stahlschützen).* Their shooting-range was outside the walls until it was destroyed in the Thirty Years' War and then moved within the bailey (= *Zwinger*) in 1640. Parts of the building they used, begun in 1652, have been preserved despite several later conversions (Nos 15/17 Stahlzwingerweg).

Just outside Jakobstor, beside Nos 1/2 Platz der Einheit, one can again see the former moat and a longish section of the bailey wall from the Avenue. This marked the edge of the so-called wood bailey, where the city stored wood for building purposes. On the other side of the Avenue, looking away from the city, one sees a gothic **Bildsäule/ornamented column (3)**, donated in 1459 by Ruger Krugl from Regensburg. Whereas the base and the shaft decorated with figures of the prophets were restored by Ludwig Foltz in 1845, the tabernacle-like top section has both the inscription placed there by the donor and also the original sculptures: around it are Christ and the Twelve Apostles as well as the donor's family; above them there are four reliefs showing, in turn, Christ carrying the cross, his crucifixion, his ascension, as well as Christ appearing as the judge of the living and the dead.

Gothic column carved with images outside Jakobstor (1459, plinth 1845). The monument originally stood a bit further south.

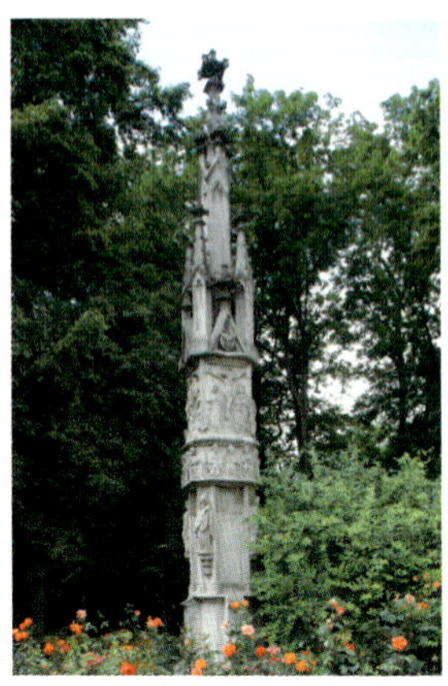

South of what remains of Jakobstor (see p. 183), the Avenue runs parallel to Wiesmeierweg, which once lay directly behind the walls. This street was not constructed until the fortifications were demolished in the second half of the 19th century. Remnants of the mediaeval walls – which here ran along the western and southern boundaries of St James' abbey garden – are still to be found in the houses and in their gardens. To the south, outside the Avenue, Philipp Reichenberger, who was responsible for the Prince of Thurn and Taxis' finances, had a villa built for himself in 1804/05. This neoclassical building, designed by Herigoyen, was extended by Ernst Friedrich, Count Dörnberg, in 1834 and is

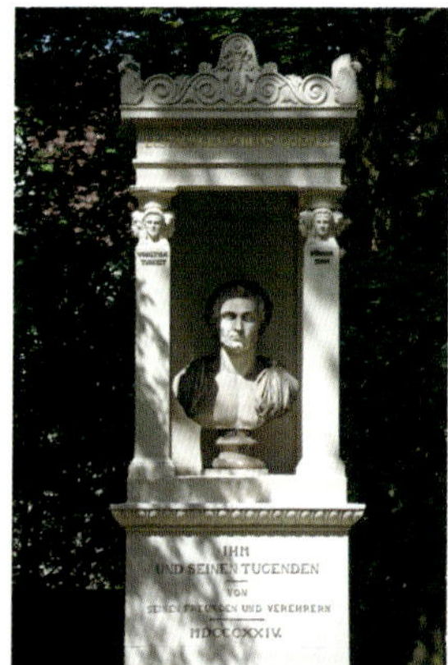

The memorial to Count Eustachius von Schlitz-Görtz designed by Leo von Klenze in 1822

therefore known as **Dörnberg Palais/Dörnberg House (4)**. It was one of the first houses to be built outside the Avenue after about 1800, and thus marked the beginning of the expansion of the modern city beyond the mediaeval city walls.

A neoclassical **memorial to Count Eustachius von Schlitz-Görtz (5)** stands beside Kümpfmühler Strasse in the middle of a small park that lies between the Avenue and Dörnberg Park, the adjoining landscape garden. The monument with its canopy was designed by Leo von Klenze; the inscription on it describes Count von Schlitz, who died in Regensburg, his adopted city, in 1821, as the ideal representative of civic virtues. Formerly the Prussian ambassador to the Imperial Diet, the count had exercised his diplomatic skills on behalf of Regensburg, above all in the difficult days of the French siege. The bust of von Schlitz was executed by Joseph Kirchmayr on the basis of a model by Johann Nepomuk Haller. In terms of art history, the memorial has its roots in the architecture of the French Revolution. Klenze's design was influenced by the projected *Temple à l'Egalité*, a temple dedicated to the equality of all citizens, which the architects Durand and Thibault had announced in Paris in 1794. Thus, in its form, too, the Schlitz-Görtz memorial is in appropriate surroundings; after all, according to the wishes of its princely donor, the Avenue was to be a place of recreation for all Regensburg's inhabitants.

After crossing Kumpfmühler Strasse, the Avenue runs for 150m beside a section of the city walls, which here follow the course of Arnulf's early 10th-century fortifications. Nearby is another of the originally 37 towers built along the walls in the late 13th and early 14th centuries.

After the Helenenbrücke, which crosses the city moat, one comes upon the memorial to **Carl Heinrich Freiherr von Gleichen (6)**. This diplomat, once in the service of the King of Denmark, was a witty member of the community at the Imperial

Diet. He earned his memorial, however, because of his social conscience, from which the poor in the city benefited regardless of their religious denomination. Von Gleichen's nephew erected the monument with a sphinx on it after his death in 1807. The mythical creature is holding a ring with a cross in it. This highly unusual motif refers to the ideas on the nature of matter held by the deceased and remains incomprehensible without a knowledge of his philosophical writings. The sphinx is the work of a Regensburg sculptor, Christoph Ittlsperger.

Behind the monument is **Emmeramstor/Emmeram's Gate (7)**, which stands in the grounds of Thurn and Taxis Palace. Built in the 13th century, it was of secondary importance as a means of access to the city as it was used mainly for bringing supplies to St Emmeram's Abbey, and was opened only when required. At the end of the Middle Ages, it obviously seemed desirable to fortify the gate more strongly since it was reinforced in c. 1500 by constructing a so-called barbican as a further line of defence outside it. When a large number of buildings were erected just outside the gate in the early 20th century, the narrow archway proved unsuitable for modern traffic. This led, in 1907/08, to the construction of Helenentor/Helena's Gate,

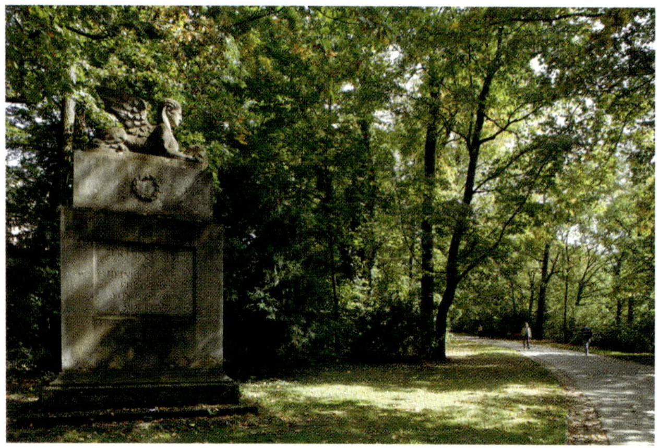

Freiherr von Gleichen's memorial has a sphinx on it (1807).

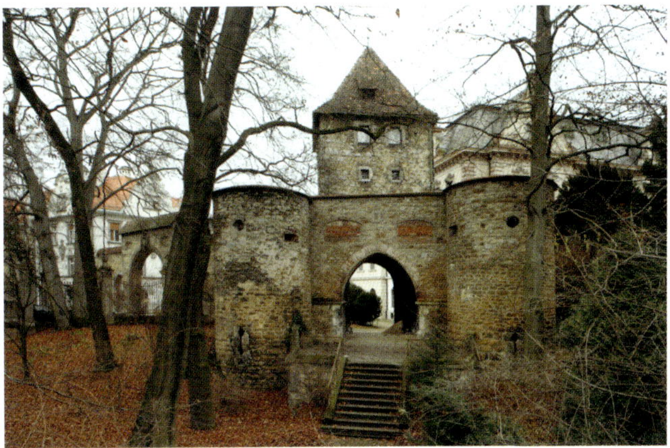

Emmeramer Tor (13th cent.) and the barbican outside it. Left, Helenentor (1907/08) in the background; right, the end of the outer south wing of Thurn and Taxis Palace

which is like a triumphal arch, and nearby Helena's Bridge. Emmeram's Gate was left standing as a specimen of mediaeval architecture (by no means a matter of course at that time) and was, as it were, elevated to the status of a garden monument. Max Schultze, the Thurn and Taxis Director of Buildings, was responsible for this solution, which showed great sensitivity towards the appearance of the city and its ancient monuments. Schultze also oversaw the construction of the 165m-long outer south wing of the palace (see p. 158), which faces the next stretch of the Avenue.

This most southerly section of the city fortifications had been struck by a terrible misfortune on May 8, 1624: the Powder Tower was struck by lightning, leading to an explosion which tore a great hole in the city walls.

Along the boundary between the Avenue and the Palace Park, the terrain still indicates where the city moat lay. No 1 Albertstrasse still stands on the side of the 'Green Belt' that lay beyond the city limits. The eastern half of this building was turned into an inn in 1780. The great popularity enjoyed by this restaurant, generally known as the 'Prince's Garden', is proof of the virtual abandonment at that time of the mediaeval boundary between city and countryside.

Further along the Avenue, the **Obelisk (8)**, erected in honour of the benefactor who created the Avenue, is an eye-catching monument. This memorial was built in 1806, a year after the Prince's death, by Herigoyen, the court architect of Dalberg, who commissioned it. Its form is striking because it has two plinths placed on top of one another. The reason for this uncommonly high base probably lies in the fact that the builders wanted the inscription and the Prince's coat of arms to be visible from afar.

From the Obelisk, one can see another of Herigoyen's works, the **Keplerdenkmal/Kepler Monument (9)**, which initially stood slightly further east. It was originally erected near Kepler's grave in 1807/08, on the initiative of learned Regensburg citizens, to commemorate the astronomer, who had died in Regensburg in 1630. The monument's design, in the form of a Doric *monopteros* (circular temple) with an extremely large bust of Kepler in the middle of it, can probably be traced back to the Leibniz Temple erected in Hanover 20 years earlier. Doell, sculptor at the court in Gotha, executed the bust of Kepler. The relief on the base – showing Kepler's genius unveiling Astronomy – is the work of Dannecker (see p. 161).

Obelisk for Prince Carl Anselm of Thurn and Taxis, who gave the Avenue to the city. It was erected in 1806 to plans drawn up by Emanuel von Herigoyen, Dalberg's court architect.

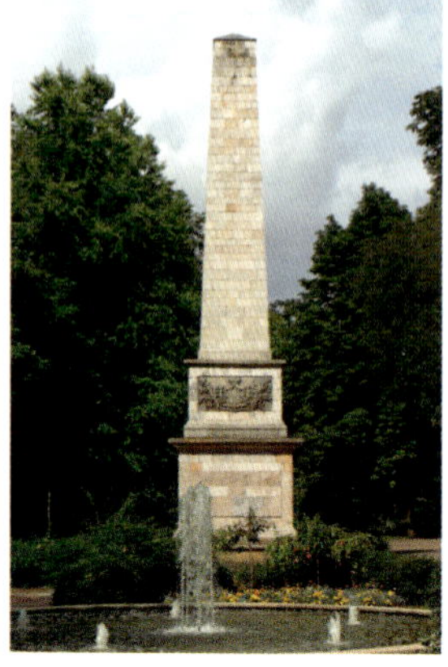

The Avenue now leads northwards. After crossing St. Peters-Weg, one comes to the so-called **Predigtsäule/Sermon Pillar (10)**, erected here in the 14th/15th centuries to commemorate a legendary victory won by Charlemagne over the pagan Huns. The site was regarded as ground hallowed by the blood of the 30,000 Christian soldiers reputed to have died in the battle. The pillar has four sides and six rows of pictures. The two lowest sections show scenes from the Old Testament, some of them hard to interpret, which relate to scenes from the Last Judgement on the next level. The figures of enthroned Apostles are to be seen in the third to fifth sections. The reliefs on the sixth level show Christ on the Day of Judgement. A crucifixion group stands on the top of the pillar. This series of sculptures, which actually has no connection with Charlemagne's victory, suggests that there was another,

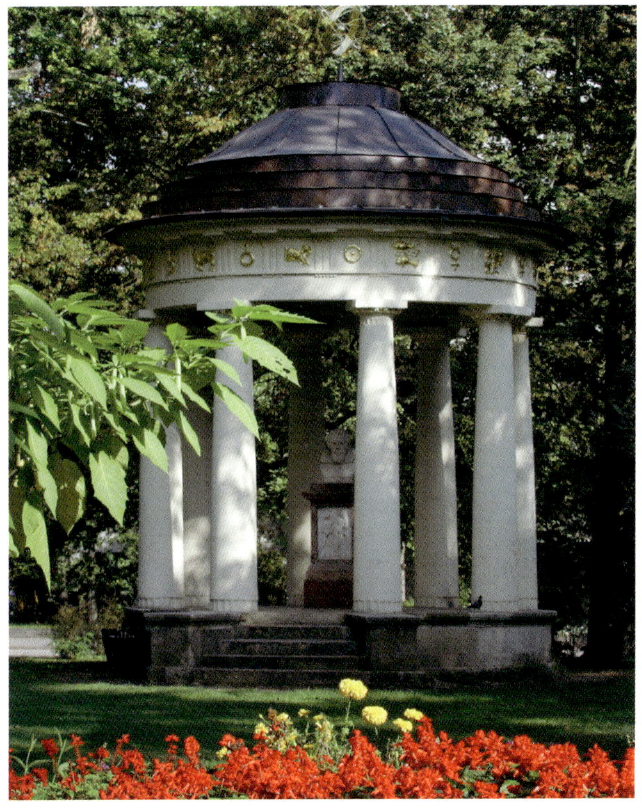

The Monopteros, erected in honour of Kepler in 1807/08. It was designed by Herigoyen; the sculptures were the work of Doell (bust) and Dannecker (relief on the base).

now forgotten, reason for erecting the decorated pillar. Yet, regardless of the difficulty in interpreting this monument, an ornamented mediaeval column was one of the Romantics' favourite props for creating a certain mood in a landscape. In the 19th century, therefore, this pillar – along with the Kepler Monument and the Obelisk – was regarded as an essential element in the Avenue.

Another section of the mediaeval city moat has survived to the north-west of the Sermon Pillar. The bridge that crosses it once led to Peterstor (Peter's Gate). This southern exit from the city, which stood on the site of the Roman camp's *Porta Decu-*

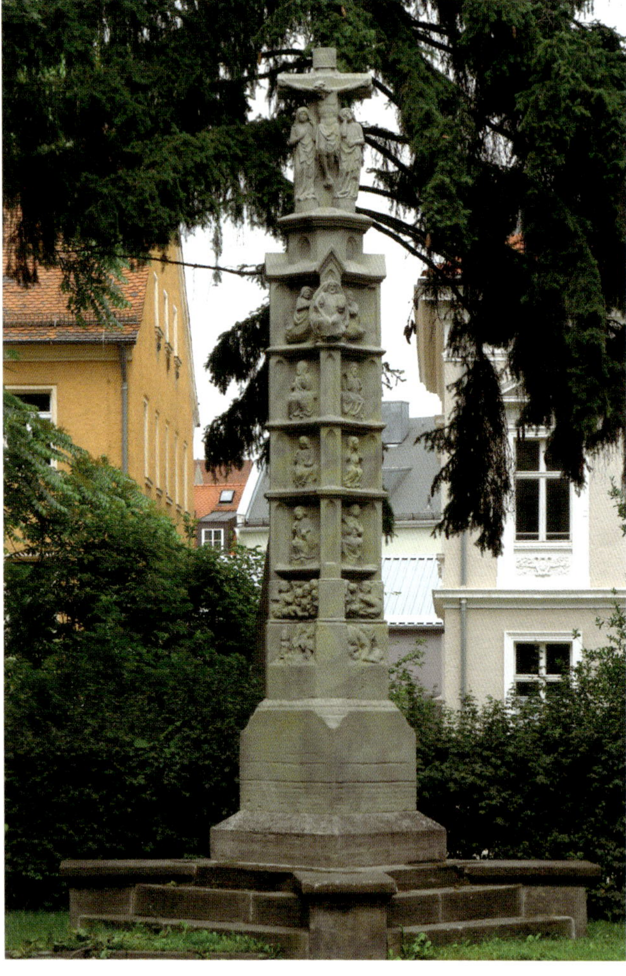

The so-called 'Sermon Pillar', an ornamented gothic column dating from the 14th cent., which stands in the Avenue near St.-Peters-Weg

mana (see p. 34f.), was badly damaged by Napoleonic troops when they stormed Regensburg in 1809, and was demolished altogether in 1875.

The land south of Peterstor was known in the Middle Ages as *Emmeramer Breiten* (Emmeram's Fields). This was where, for example, the plot of land lay that the Jewish community purchased from St Emmeram's in 1210 in order to establish a cemetery, the earlier Jewish burial ground having been much further outside the city. In 1519, when the ghetto and the synagogue were destroyed and the Jewish inhabitants expelled from Regensburg, the cemetery did not escape the devastation, either. Numerous stolen gravestones were used as decorations (trophies, as it were) on 'Christian' houses. There, even today, they bear witness to this dark chapter in the city's history.

Between Maximilianstrasse and D.-Martin-Luther-Strasse, the Avenue largely fell victim to the city's expansion in the 19th and 20th centuries. Nevertheless, the excavation of the south-eastern corner of the Roman walls was a very important side-effect, archaeologically speaking, of the urban development in this area (see p. 33f.). At the same time, parts of the 14th-century city fortifications also came to light, clearly demonstrating that the late mediaeval city walls exactly followed the course of the Roman walls. This is shown both by the tower in the city walls which is also attached to the Roman masonry in the northernmost corner of the excavated site, and also by the course of the bailey wall, which seems to have been built directly outside the Roman walls.

The most easterly section of the 'Green Belt' is the part known as Ostenallee (Eastern Avenue); it has survived as an almost uninterrupted band of green leading to the park by the Royal Villa near Ostentor. Right at the beginning of Ostenallee is the **monument for Police Director Franz Xaver Gruber (11)**. As the 'Father of the Poor', he did a great deal for the ordinary people in the economically difficult years after the destruction in 1809 and the incorporation into Bavaria in 1810. It was thus also citizens of Regensburg who took the initiative to set up the column in 1815, a year after Gruber's death.

The Avenue now runs parallel to Von-der-Tann-Strasse. The house facades overlooking the gardens follow the line of the

14th-century bailey wall, more or less, while the gardens themselves replaced the city moat, which was filled in. The turret-like bay windows of Nos 6 and 18 indicate the position of the former towers in the bailey wall.

A **monument for Friedrich Freiherr** (= Baron) **von Zoller (12)**, Lieutenant-General in the Bavarian Army, was erected in 1821 on the land lying south of the Avenue, roughly opposite No 18. Alluding to the military achievements of the deceased, it shows a trophy and is remarkable, above all, as an early example of a cast-iron monument.

The Avenue ends at the **Villapark (13)**, north of Adolf-Schmetzer-Strasse, the continuation of Ostengasse, beyond the city boundary. From the park, the eastern part of which is open to the public, one has a good view not only of the neogothic villa (see p. 207 ff.), but also of the mediaeval moat and bailey area. Most of the bailey wall was rebuilt in the 19th century and, together with the viewpoints looking out over the bank of the Danube, forms a picturesque architectural background for the small but atmospheric park.

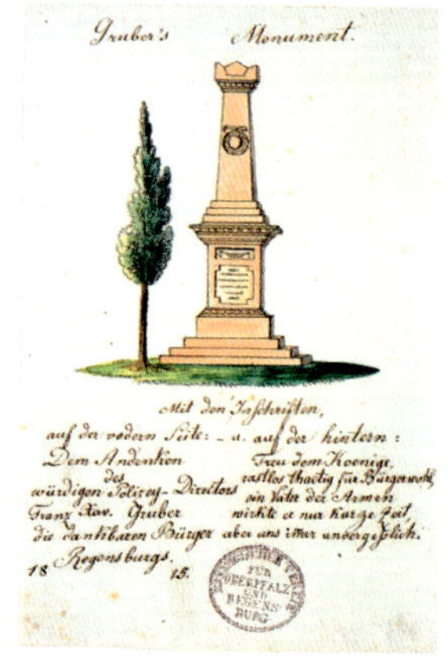

Design for the memorial to Police Director Gruber, 1815 (Museum of Regensburg History)

Museums in Regensburg's Old Town

(Opening times in 2008)

Brückturm-Museum/Bridge Tower Museum
Weisse-Lamm-Gasse 1, 93047 Regensburg,
tel. +49 (0)941 – 507 58 89, www.dsmr.de,
email: kontakt@dsmr.de
Apr–Oct: Tues–Sun 10–5

Diozesanmuseum St. Ulrich/ St Ulrich's Diocesan Museum
Domplatz 2, 93047 Regensburg,
tel. +49 (0)941 – 516 88,
www.bistumsmuseen-regensburg.de
email: museum@bistum-regensburg.de
Apr 1 – Nov 1: Tues–Sun 10–5

***document* Neupfarrplatz**
Information: Museen der Stadt Regensburg,
Dachauplatz 2–4, 93047 Regensburg,
tel. *49 (0)941 – 507 14 42,
www.regensburg.de/museumsportal,
email: museen_der_stadt@regensburg.de
Guided tours only: Fri 2.30, Sat + Sun 11 and 2.30;
additional times for groups by arrangement.
Tickets: Tabak Götz, Neupfarrplatz 3,
93047 Regensburg

***document* Niedermünster**
Due to open in 2009

***document* Schnupftabakfabrik/ Snuff Tobacco Factory**
Information: Museen der Stadt Regensburg,
Dachauplatz 2–4, 93047 Regensburg,
tel. +49 (0)941 – 507 14 42,
www.regensburg.de/museumsportal,
email: museen_der_stadt@regensburg.de
Guided tours only: Fri 2.30, Sat + Sun 11 and 2.30;
additional times for groups by arrangement.
Tickets: Tee- und Schokoladenhaus Hornung,
Gesandtenstr. 5, 93047 Regensburg

Domschatzmuseum/ Cathedral Treasury
Krauterermarkt 3, 93047 Regensburg,
tel. +49 (0)941 – 57645,
www.bistumsmuseen-regensburg.de,
email: museum@bistum-regensburg.de
Apr 1 – Nov 1: Tues–Sat 10–5,
Sun and hols: 12–5
Nov 2–30: closed
Dec 1 – Mar 31: Fri + Sat 10–4, Sun + hols 12–4
Dec 26 – Jan 6: also Tues–Thur 10–4
Dec 24–25, Jan 1: closed

Fürst Thurn und Taxis Museen – Schloss und Kreuzgang St. Emmeram/ Prince of Thurn and Taxis Museums – Palace and St Emmeram's Cloisters
Emmeramsplatz 5, 93047 Regensburg,
tel. +49 (0)941 – 504 82 42,
www.thurnundtaxis.de,
email: uweiss@thurnundtaxis.de
Regular guided tours

Kepler-Gedächtnishaus/ Kepler Memorial Centre
Keplerstrasse 5, 93047 Regensburg,
tel. +49 (0)941 – 507 34 42
www.regensburg.de/museumsportal,
email: museen_der_stadt@regensburg.de

Sat, Sun, hols 10.30–4
Jan 1, Good Fri, May 1, Nov 1, Dec 24–25,
Dec 31: closed

Städtische Galerie „Leerer Beutel"/'Empty Purse' City Art Gallery
Bertoldstr. 9, 93047 Regensburg,
tel. +49 (0)941 – 507 44 49,
www.regensburg.de/museumsportal,
email: museen_der_stadt@regensburg.de
Tues–Sun 10–4, Easter Mon + Whit Mon 10–4
Jan 1, Good Fri, May 1, Nov 1, Dec 24–25,
Dec 31: closed

Historisches Museum Regensburg/ Museum of Regensburg History
Dachauplatz 2–4, 93047 Regensburg,
tel +49 (0)941 – 507 24 48,
www.regensburg.de/museumsportal,
email: museen_der_stadt@regensburg.de
Tues, Wed, Fri, Sat, Sun 10–4
Thur 10–8
Tues–Sun 10–4, Easter Mon, Whit Mon 10–4
Jan 1, Good Fri, May 1, Nov 1, Dec 24–25,
Dec 31: closed

Museum in der Dreieinigkeitskirche
Museum in Holy Trinity Church (tower open!)
Am Ölberg 1, 93047 Regensburg,
tel. +49 (0)941 – 224 44,
www.dreieinigkeitskirche.de,
email: pfarramt@dreieinigkeitskirche.de
May–September: daily 2–6

Naturkundemuseum Ostbayern/East Bavarian Natural History Museum
Am Prebrunntor 4, 93047 Regensburg,
tel. +49 (0)941 – 507 34 43,
www.naturkundemuseum-regensburg.de,
email: fun@naturkundemuseum-regensburg.de
Mo 9–12, Tue–Fr 9–4, Sun 10–5

Reichstagsmuseum und Altes Rathaus/ Imperial Diet Museum and Old Town Hall
Rathausplatz 4, 93047 Regensburg,
tel. +49 (0)941 – 507 44 11,
www.regensburg.de/museumsportal,
email: museen_der_stadt@regensburg.de
Regular guided tours
Apr 1 – Oct 31: English guided tour 3 pm
Nov 1 – Jan 6, Mar 1 – Mai 31: English guided tour 2 pm
Dec 24–25, Jan 1: closed

Further Reading

Thomas Aumüller, Die Porta Praetoria und die Befestigung des Legionslagers in Regensburg. Diss. TU München (2002) [im Druck]

Baualterspläne zur Stadtsanierung, hg. vom Bayerischen Landesamt für Denkmalpflege, Regensburg Bd. 1–10 (1973–1993)

Lutz-Michael Dallmeier, Fundort Regensburg. Archäologische Topographie der Stadt Regensburg (= Regensburger Studien und Quellen zur Kulturgeschichte 10), Regensburg 2000

Denkmäler in Bayern, Bd. III.37: Stadt Regensburg. Ensembles – Baudenkmäler. Archäologische Denkmäler, bearb. von Anke Borgmeyer u. a., Regenburg 1997

Denkmalpflege in Regensburg, hg. von der Stadt Regensburg, Amt für Archiv und Denkmalpflege, Abt. Denkmalpflege, Bd. 1 ff. (1989 ff.)

Artur Dirmeier/Wido Wittenzellner (Hrsg.), Die Spitalkirche zu Regensburg. Mausoleum der Zant, Regensburg 2000

Peter Brielmeier/Uwe Moosburger, Regensburg – Metropole im Mittelalter, Regensburg 2007

Karlheinz Dietz/Thomas Fischer, Die Römer in Regensburg, Regensburg 1996

Christian Forneck, Die Regensburger Einwohnerschaft im 15. Jahrhundert. Studien zur Bevölkerungsstruktur und Sozialtopographie einer deutschen Großstadt des Spätmittelalters (= Regensburger Studien, hg. vom Archiv der Stadt Regensburg, Bd. 3), Regensburg 2000

Friedrich Fuchs, Das Hauptportal des Regensburger Domes. Portal – Vorhalle – Skulptur, München/Zürich 1990

Anneliese Hilz, Die Minderbrüder von St. Salvator in Regensburg 1226–1810 (= Beiträge zur Geschichte des Bistums Regensburg 25), Regensburg 1991

Martin Hoernes, Die Hauskapellen des Regensburger Patriziats. Studien zu Bestand, Überlieferung und Funktion (= Regensburger Studien und Quellen zur Kunstgeschichte, hg. von den Museen und dem Archiv der Stadt Regensburg 8), Regensburg 2000

Achim Hubel/Manfred Schuller, Der Dom zu Regensburg. Vom Bauen und Gestalten einer gotischen Kathedrale, Regensburg 1995

Beatrice Kühl, Die Dominikanerkirche in Regensburg. Studien zur deutschen Bettelordensarchitektur im 13. Jahrhundert, in: Beiträge zur Geschichte des Bistums Regensburg 20 (1986), 75–211

Mittelalter in Regensburg. Bd. 1: Aufsätze, hg. von Martin Angerer und Heinrich Wanderwitz, Regensburg 1995

Peter Morsbach, Kunst in Regensburg, Regensburg 1995

Helmut-Eberhard Paulus, Steinerne Brücke (= Regensburger Taschenbücher 2), Regensburg 1993

Helmut-Eberhard Paulus, Regensburger Brunnen und Plätze. Geschichte, Funktion und Ikonographie (= Großer Kunstführer 203), Regensburg 1998

Helmut-Eberhard Paulus/Hermann Reidel/Paul W. Winkler (Hrsg.), Romanik in Regensburg. Kunst, Geschichte, Denkmalpflege (= Regensburger Herbstsymposion zur Kunstgeschichte und Denkmalpflege 2), Regensburg 1996 (vgl. auch die weiteren Bände dieser Reihe)

Werner Schiedermair (Hrsg.), Die Alte Kapelle in Regensburg, Regensburg 2002

Alois Schmid, Regensburg. Reichsstadt – Fürstbischof – Reichsstifte – Herzogshof (= Historischer Atlas von Bayern, Teil Altbayern, Heft 60), München 1995

Peter Schmid, Regensburg. Stadt der Könige und Herzöge im Mittelalter (= Regensburger historische Forschungen 6), Regensburg 1977

Ders. (Hrsg.), Geschichte der Stadt Regensburg, 2 Bde., Regensburg 2000

Stadtamhof vom Mittelalter zur Neuzeit, hrsg. vom Heimatverein „Statt am Hoff“ und den Museen der Stadt Regensburg, Regensburg 2001

Richard Strobel, Das Bürgerhaus in Regensburg. Mittelalter (= Das deutsche Bürgerhaus XXIII), Tübingen 1976

Ders., Mittelalterliche Bauplastik am Bürgerhaus in Regensburg (= Das deutsche Bürgerhaus XXX), Tübingen 1981

Ders., Zweijochige Rippengewölbe in Regensburg, Hauskapellen der Gotik, in: architectura 35 (2005) H. 2, 113–137

Eugen Trapp, Regensburg und sein Mittelalter. Wege der Wiederentdeckung, Regensburg 1995

Helmut Wolff, Regensburgs Häuserbestand im späten Mittelalter, in: Studien und Quellen zur Geschichte Regensburgs 3 (1985), 91–198